ABORTION
The Catholic Debate
in America

HANS LOTSTRA

IRVINGTON PUBLISHERS, INC.
740 BROADWAY
NEW YORK, N.Y. 10003

Library of Congress Cataloging in Publication Data

Lotstra, Hans.
    Abortion, the Catholic debate in America.

    Bibliography: p.
    Includes index.
    1. Abortion--Religious aspects--Catholic Church.
2. Abortion--United States. I. Title.
HQ767.3.L68 1985   261.8'3666   84-29692
ISBN 0-8290-0728-8

Printed in the United States of America

for
Hemmeterius Lotstra
† 1981

ACKNOWLEDGEMENTS

This book owes a great deal to the encouragement and critique of Professor Seán O'Riordan, C.SS.R., and Professor Augustine Regan, C.SS.R., of the Alphonsian Academy in Rome who very generously put their time and expertise at my disposal. I have other friends in different parts of the world who helped in various ways: Arthur McCormack, John Baur, William Cole, Margaret Moore, Patrick Burns, Tinus Verwijmeren, Joop Bessem, Joan Devane, Norman Myers, James Walls, Leonard Davies, and Alan Macknight. I am especially grateful to Patricia Bennis who, with unfailing patience and unerring accuracy, corrected and typed the manuscript. My thanks are also due to Frank McCarthy and Frank Cowan for their perceptive reading of the proofs.

I gladly acknowledge the financial assistance of my own Missionary Society of Mill Hill, and of two mission aid agencies in my own country of the Netherlands, the *Week voor de Nederlandse Missionaris* and the *Advieskommissie Missionaire Aktiviteiten*.

The interest and support of all these friends entitles them to a large share in whatever credit is due to this book. Its shortcomings are entirely mine.

Hans Lotstra
Mill Hill, London

Contents

ABORTION
The Catholic Debate
in America

Chapter One

The Catholic Church
in the United States
and the Problem of Abortion

Abortion is one of the most urgent moral and legal problems of our day and that on a worldwide scale. In 1967 an American Protestant theologian defined abortion as "the second major moral issue of our society."[1] After the landmark decision of the United States Supreme Court in *Roe* v. *Wade* on January 22, 1973, Luke T. Lee could write:

> Despite continued strong opposition to abortion on various grounds, the general trend points unmistakably towards abortion legalization, so long as the forces working toward it remain unabated. In fact, five of the world's most populous countries comprising a majority of the world's total population—United States, Japan, Soviet Union, India, and China —now have laws which virtually allow abortion on request.[2]

The forces seeking to extend legalization have certainly worked unabatedly. In the period 1967-1976 at least 33 countries have widened the legal grounds for abortion and in 1977 some 18 others were reconsidering their abortion laws.[3] Abortion has become the subject of the most sustained and widespread public debate of any moral issue in modern times. It has shaken European governments and become a major issue in a United States presidential election.

In the United States the first moderately liberalized laws were adopted in 1967. Before then, some 8,000 legal abortions were performed annually. In 1969, the first year for which precise national figures were compiled, 22,670 legal abortions were performed. In 1970 abortion on request became available in several states and the number increased to 193,491, climbing to 485,816 in 1971, and mushrooming to more than 800,000 in 1973 when the Supreme Court established abortion on request as a national policy. In 1975 more than one million legal abortions were performed and it is estimated that in the 1980s the annual abortion rate may reach the two million mark.[4]

There is no need for further statistics to demonstrate the geographical and numerical dimensions of the problem. The global picture must be alarming. The interruption of pregnancy has become one of the most widely practiced methods of birth control in the world.[5]

This sudden and drastic change in legal policies towards abortion has been attributed to the following developments in social and moral attitudes: (1) an increasing awareness of the threat of overpopulation, and of the need to control man's environment through rational planning; (2) a rejection of traditional moral codes, with a new emphasis on the personal liberty of women which should not be hampered by unwanted pregnancies and unwanted children; (3) a rejection of traditional sexual codes, as well as new attitudes to procreation which is no longer considered a divinely ordained aftermath of the act of love; (4) a desire for professional autonomy by medical men who reject extraprofessional criteria and who view abortion as a medical decision reserved to the medically competent; (5) a more pragmatic approach to legislation which takes into consideration that it is difficult to enforce restrictive abortion codes; (6) the feeling that such codes are discriminatory in effect because they are applied more laxly to the affluent than to the poor. Furthermore, in the United States the abortion debate was accelerated by the Sherry Finkbine case and by the newly discovered consequences of rubella.[6] However, I shall return to the sociological analysis of the abortion reform movement at a later stage.

I. Abortion as a Moral and Legal Problem

Complexity
If there is anything that is clear about the issue of abortion, it is that it is multidimensional, complex, and anguishing. The morality and legality of the practice of abortion in the twentieth century is not an easy problem to solve. There is no single causality, and there are no simple solutions.[7]

Threats to pregnancy variously arise from economic want, an unstable family, a broken home, illegitimacy, rape, incest, pressures from the social milieu or the religious tradition, prolonged illness, mental disturbances, contraceptive failure, or apprehensions about the well-being of the future child. In most cases, it is not the pregnancy itself that is the cause of anxiety, but the consequence of the pregnancy: the birth of a baby which has to be accommodated and cared for.

At the level of the individual moral decision, the woman is faced with a problem which has communicational, legal, medical, economic, social, psychological, environmental, ethical, and religious aspects. Included in the existential setting of her predicament are other members of society to whom she might go for consultation or cooperation: her family and friends, physicians, psychiatrists, social workers, lawyers, and clergymen. The expectant mother must consider not only her own complex situation but also the mental attitudes and ethical thinking of those whom she might ask for help.[8]

As a social phenomenon the subject of abortion is a matter of interest and concern to demographers, family planning administrators, physicians, politicians, judges, legislators, psychiatrists, psychologists, sociologists, social workers, anthropologists, economists, historians, feminists, and humanists.[9] Emily C. Moore-Čavar has indicated some of the delicate and highly controversial issues which the various disciplines have to face:

> Some particular issues of interest, for example, are the demographic effects of births averted by abortion (with or without the combined effects of contraception); legal and governmental questions regarding laws designed to protect the pregnant woman or the fetus, the formulation of pro-natalist or anti-natalist policies, and the protection of individual and group rights . . . medical issues regarding mortality and morbidity associated with legal and illegal abortion and children born to women unable to obtain legal abortions; social matters such as the cultural acceptability — promotion or prohibition — of abortion as a means of fertility control, as evidenced indirectly by public opinion polls or directly by incidence of legal and illegal abortion, or differential class access to medically safe abortion facilities and contraceptive services, etc. Thus there is both research interest and argument over controversial aspects for persons of a variety of disciplines.[10]

Emphasizing that abortion is "not readily amenable to one-dimensional thinking," Daniel Callahan has indicated some further aspects of the problem:

> It is a medical problem because the doctor is the person normally called upon to perform an abortion; both his conscience and his medical skills come into play. More broadly, the question is raised of the use of technological developments for the purported improvement of human life. It is a legal problem because it raises the question of the extent to which society should concern itself with unborn life, with motherhood, with family life, with public control of the medical profession. It is a sociological problem because, as Edwin M. Schur has pointed out, it touches on "woman's role in our social system, family organization and disorganization, national demographic policy, and the role of informal and formal sanctions.". . . It is a psychological problem because, in one way or the other, the attitude of human beings toward conception, pregnancy, birth, and child-rearing touches deep-rooted drives, instincts, emotions and taboos.[11]

Abortion, therefore, is not a single issue but involves a whole range of issues, and this complexity persists even after a community has decided to recognize legally the right of women to interrupt pregnancy. Once legality has been secured, the nation has to make a further series of crucial decisions regarding the shape of its public policy on abortion. Some of the questions are: (1) the freedom of conscience of individual doctors and paramedical personnel as well as medical institutions; (2) the rights of the husband whose pregnant wife requests an abortion; (3) the rights of the parents of an unmarried minor who desires an abortion; (4) the rights of the viable fetus which is aborted alive; (5) the legitimate limits of fetal research in connection with abortion; (6) the question of public promotion and public funding of abortions.[12]

Abortion is not just a "simple medical intervention," as some of its proponents naively claim. It lies at the boundaries of a great many disciplines. The woman in distress who feels impelled to seek an abortion is at the center of our thinking about our civilization and its future.[13]

The Moral and Legal Issues

Abortion is a moral problem because it is a human act and the outcome of the agent's free value judgement concerning the nature and control of incipient human life.[14] Any definition of the morality of abortion depends on fundamental insights into the nature of human life, its beginning, and the basic attitude men should adopt towards the lives of others.[15] The crucial moral questions can be formulated as follows: (1) If the fetus is human, and even represents human life, in what sense, if any, can we say that it is a human individual, or a human person? (2) In what ways does the fetus enjoy a claim, or right, to life?[16]

The root issues of the legal question may be framed in the following way: (1) At what point in the early part of man's life cycle should the law acknowledge the existence of a human being and accord him the most basic right recognized and protected by the legal order, the right to survive on a basis of equality with other human beings? (2) Does this right to life result from the civil law, the natural law, the humanity of the fetus, its individuality, or its personhood? (3) In what ways is it permissible or necessary to translate one's philosophical or religious views into public policy and civil law?[17]

At this level of ethical evaluation the abortion problem loses none of its complexity. All parties to the debate are agreed that our attitude about the quality of incipient human life is fundamental to judging the morality and legality of abortion; but there is no school of thought that reduces the ethicist's task to determining, for instance, the moment of ensoulment or to defining the status of the fetus in terms of human life or human personhood.

While there is fundamental agreement that there are other values to be considered in the construction of responsible moral and legal policies, there is wide difference as to how vital these values are in comparison with fetal life.

At this stage the ethicist gets caught in a vicious circle. On the one hand he is told that "facts" are important and that the various disciplines concerned with the abortion phenomenon—social science, medicine, and law —help him to understand it better. Consequently, the moral aspects of abortion should not be treated in isolation from the medical, social, and legal questions: they form a whole.[18] Moreover, like any discussion of a moral problem, this one also "must blend theory and experience, principle and practice, goals and likely consequences.... What is the evidence and how might it be interpreted and used in constructing an abortion ethic?"[19] On the other hand, however, it is admitted that one's evaluation of the evidence will be determined to a considerable extent by one's moral attitude towards abortion and that, in the last analysis, the "factual" information is relevant only in so far as it has been given significance in a prior moral and metaphysical framework.[20]

It is clear, then, that in the abortion debate objectivity is rare and this undoubtedly is one of the reasons for the acrimony which has characterized the discussions.[21] Much of the emotion surrounding the debate arises from women's irritation with nature and society, which have imposed upon them the onerous task of bearing and rearing the child, thus drastically limiting their choice of career and life style. But apart from this, the abortion issue touches basic levels at which people's fundamental beliefs and assumptions about human life, human rights, moral values, and the function of law exist. On the whole these attitudes are held in common but they are maintained in different degrees of relative importance or with different priorities. Challenging someone's view on abortion is the equivalent of suggesting that his whole belief-system stands in need of some fundamental repair.[22] In such a situation, emotionality has a tendency to increase and multiply, and the result is the generation of intense heat rather than clear light.[23]

The debate, therefore, is complicated by the fact that the reformist position, as well as the anti-abortion stand, form part of larger moral and socio-cultural ideologies. The nature and quality of fetal life is not the only issue at stake. Each side has incorporated its particular fetal anthropology into a wider social and moral outlook. There is no need to analyse these ideologies here since the anti-abortion stand will be examined in detail in the following pages, while in Chapter VIII we will pay attention to the rationale of its counterpart. Suffice it to state at this point that other ethical

questions have become part and parcel of the debate on fetal life and that
the discussion has been enriched with all the conflict generated by women's
liberation, genocide, population control, civil rights, health care, crime,
and the quality v. quantity of life debate.[24] Peter A. Facione has stated it
this way:

> The issue immediately became obscured and complicated by "extraneous
> factors," although it is by no means easy to tell what these were. The list of
> candidates included some most unlikely bedfellows: emotionalism, politics,
> intellectualism, ivory-towerism, racism, feminism, religion, irreligion,
> humanism, unhumanism, freedom, rights, separation of church and state,
> utilitarianism, pragmaticism, and the American way.[25]

Nor can the ethicist restrict his analysis to the level of professed
ideologies. He has to take into account that the reformist position as well as
the anti-abortion ethos have been historically and socio-culturally determined and that these cannot just be accepted at face value. Both sides have
to be made aware of this further dimension of their ethical diversity.
Describing the "essential and common religious principles" which are
shared by American Catholics, Protestants, and Jews in regard to the
abortion problem, George H. Williams states that, nevertheless, there are
"significant confessional differences."[26] This diversity stands in need of
historical research.

> Embedded in all traditions are the still emotionally potent and therefore
> morally functioning residues of archaic or superseded genetic,
> embryological and obstetric theories. To bring this submerged biology to
> the surface, a task congenial to the medical or ecclesiastical historian, can
> contribute to the present-day sorting out of the more permanent and the
> merely adventitious elements in the "religious" positions that are being
> currently defended or reconceived.[27]

Williams further explains how "Protestant individualism" and the
"social idealism of postrevivalist Protestantism" helped to shape

> the extreme feminism which has promoted in some religiously Protes-
> tant, not to say merely culturally Protestant, women a self-righteous
> indifference about the destiny of the fetus in their overriding preoccupa-
> tion with "the dignity of woman" as a sovereign individual who should
> not be socially enthralled by motherhood.[28]

At this level the ethicist's task becomes one of historico-cultural analysis
and conscientization:

> (E)ven if the goal of liberal Protestants today and Jews and outright
> secularists in the relaxation of the present abortion laws is identical or

similar, it is useful to distinguish the motivation, especially at the present juncture, when biology and sociology compete with new data and categories in redefining the human person in the context of the abortion issue.[29]

Abortion, then, is one of today's most urgent moral problems. It is so at the individual level. More women than ever before are now in a position to have a legal abortion if they demand one, and they will be under increasing social pressure to do so. It is so at the legislative level, for civil authority realizes that rights once granted cannot be easily revoked and that it has to make a decision without a clear picture of the long-term effects in a variety of fields. It is so for the ethicist who feels he has to guide the choice of the individual as well as that of the community; who has to honor the principle of the sanctity of life without closing his eyes to the limitations of many human situations; and who has to uphold the moral ideal without losing sight of the fact that in a morally pluralistic and secular society the actual social and political possibilities are restricted. Richard A. McCormick states it as follows:

> Abortion is a matter that is morally problematic, pastorally delicate, legislatively thorny, constitutionally insecure, ecumenically divisive, medically normless, humanly anguishing, racially provocative, journalistically abused, personally biased, and widely performed. It demands a most extraordinary discipline of moral thought, one that is penetrating without being impenetrable, humanly compassionate without being morally compromising, legally realistic without being legally positivistic, instructed by cognate disciplines without being determined by them, informed by tradition without being enslaved by it. . . . [30]

Not in Isolation

The abortion problem requires of the ethicist maximum commitment and maximum responsibility. It does so not only because of its statistical and geographical proportions and its complexity, especially in the face of conflicting ideologies, but also because abortion is a deeply human problem. In a large majority of cases the decision for or against abortion is still considered and experienced — with varying degrees of intensity — as a decision for or against life. In the abortion debate there is no room for leisurely and sophisticated armchair speculation: decisions have to be taken here and now, and whichever way the decision goes it will have consequences for the individual and for society at large.

Questions like abortion act as catalysts in the development of ethical thinking. An established theory finds itself suddenly and dramatically opposed by a growing ethos which is supported by an explicit ideology. Ethicists are thus forced to reexamine their traditional positions and, in this way, the abortion debate blazes a trail. It is a feature of the moral life that to reconsider one moral question in depth is to reconsider all moral questions. New ethical approaches and attitudes towards abortion will sooner or later be reflected in other fields of ethical interest, and trends in the abortion debate may well be indicative of future trends in ethics as a whole. Moreover, the abortion question is only ''the curtain raiser for a long series of problems which medical and biological advances are going to raise about our control over human life.''[31] In this context James J. Diamond has reminded us that we live

> in a day when ova are being fertilized by nonspermatic material, when unfertilized ova are brought to term-births of organisms, when human sperm can be made to fertilize nonovarian cells and indeed fertilize mature cells from species other than man with the production of embryonic gene material.... [32]

The evolution of ethical thinking is a complex process. The many issues that are at stake in the abortion debate are not exclusive to it nor are they the exclusive concern of ethical science. However, they did mature in the abortion controversy and significantly so. Other areas of ethical concern will be affected by it. In the words of Richard McCormick:

> Abortion... is a severe testing ground for moral reflection. It is transparent of the rigor, fulness, and balance (or lack thereof) that one brings to moral problems and is therefore probably a paradigm of the way we will face other human problems in the future.[33]

II. The Catholic Church in the United States and the Abortion Issue

The United States
In the contemporary abortion debate, ethical thinking in the United States on this problem deserves special attention since American attitudes in this field will inevitably have repercussions elsewhere in the world. This is so because the political and socio-cultural influence of the United States is worldwide and, more specifically, because this country plays a significant role in family planning organizations and population programs.

Over the past twenty years the United States has been occupied on a world level with the rapid rates of population growth, playing a leading part in population studies and population action by providing information, education, and means with regard to family planning. This has been done through private organizations such as the International Planned Parenthood

Federation whose Western Hemisphere headquarters are in New York. An affiliate of the IPPF, the Family Planning International Association, funds population projects in the Third World. Furthermore, the United States has many excellent faculties of demography in renowned universities such as Princeton, Yale, the University of California at Berkeley, and other centers for population studies which have trained a good number of demographers for developing countries. At governmental level, the first AID budget, with population and family planning items equal to $1.1 million, was approved in 1966 and by 1975 the United States had given approximately $500 million for population activities.[34] Since abortion is at least a potential means of population control, it goes without saying that American attitudes on this issue are important since these could conceivably be reflected in population programs all over the world.[35]

From the point of view of the ethical debate, the religious and political traditions of the United States provide an almost ideal climate for the abortion issue to mature, especially in its legal aspects. Traditionally, the United States is a Christian country. Its mores and its laws have been shaped by the Reformed Churches of the Nonconformist, Puritan, and Presbyterian traditions. As a state, however, it is strictly secular: the separation of Church and State was articulated in the First Amendment to the Constitution. Its citizens pride themselves on their democratic tradition, and they treasure their constitutional rights of liberty and equality as guaranteed in the Fifth and Fourteenth Amendments. The Fifth Amendment reads: ''...nor shall any person...be deprived of life, liberty, or property without due process of law.... '' The Fourteenth reads: ''...nor shall any State deprive any person of life, liberty or property without due process of law, nor deny to any person within its jurisdiction the equal protection of the laws.''

As in many other countries, in the United States a new secular and pragmatic ethos has challenged the traditional religious and legal attitudes towards abortion. Abortion is an issue on which many Americans had strong religious and ethical feelings. At the same time they had to argue their case in a climate which was pluralist, democratic, and strictly secular, and which traditionally emphasized the importance of constitutional rights. It was to be expected that the ensuing debate would have much to offer on issues like the relationship between morality and law, the legal status of the unborn child, and the rights of the mother in contradistinction to the rights of the fetus.

It must also be noted that in the United States the abortion debate was bound to be more intensive than in any other country of the world. In this country abortion is a matter for penal legislation at state level. Each state has this legislative power, as has Congress for the District of Columbia. Consequently, the country has at any one time fifty-two different sets of statutes pertaining to abortion. Even after the Supreme Court decision in 1973, the individual states still had to enact their own legislation. It is clear that this situation has intensified the debate to a considerable extent. Fifty-two jurisdictions has meant fifty-two legislative debates.

The Catholic Church

The Catholic Church in the United States has played a significant part in the abortion controversy. Catholics are numerous and well-organized and Catholic opposition to abortion has been clear and vocal.[36] However, its opponents have often overemphasized its role by reducing the anti-abortion stand to Catholic ethical principles and Catholic organization.[37] This is a twofold oversimplification. In the first place, the anti-abortion stand has drawn support from a wide variety of Christian and non-Christian denominations.[38] Secondly, while the Catholic Church as a whole has certainly adopted the anti-abortion position in the strictest sense of the word, it is also true that this does not apply to all individual Catholics[39] and especially not to all Catholic theologians, as will become clear in the following pages. The abortion problem cuts across lines of religious and denominational affiliation. However, while opinions are naturally divided as to the quality of the Catholic contribution, there is general agreement that the quantity has been significant.[40]

In this book I propose to present an inventory, an analysis, and an evaluation of this contribution, because I believe that American Catholic thinking on abortion is relevant to the current worldwide debate. It is so for two reasons. First, it is generally recognized that since World War II American Catholic theology has come into its own and that its contributions have become increasingly important. It therefore deserves a hearing, especially on a serious and complex moral question which it has been able to study in a socially, politically, and legally unique setting. Furthermore, while the abortion reform movement in the United States has often seemed unaware of the variety of Catholic arguments regarding abortion and of the divergency of views within the Catholic tradition, it has done even less justice to what are generally called the Church's ''ulterior motives.'' At the International Conference on Abortion, held in Hot Springs, Virginia, in November 1968, the Christian anti-abortion stand was variously interpreted as protection of the family institution as the core of social life, pro-natalist ideology, antisexual prejudice, antihedonistic bias, and reluctance to surrender power on the part of the male.[41] Statements like these present a further incentive to analyse at least one segment of the Christian anti-abortion stand—the position of the Catholic Church in the United States—and verify any of them or none. Such an analysis should contribute towards a better appreciation of the rationale of the Christian position generally.

III. Methodology

Discerning the Issues

As I indicated earlier, the abortion problem has a twofold dimension: the morality of the individual abortive act and the moral implications of state legislation regarding abortion. This distinction is fundamental for any moral problem which has legal repercussions.

It is of the utmost importance that the individual and social moral dimensions be studied separately because the basic moral questions are fundamentally different. The abortive act must first be studied from the point of view of private morality and considered at the level of the individual's private moral decision. A subsequent analysis will concern itself with the social aspects of this decision and will look at it from the point of view of public morality or law. The failure to separate rigidly the two issues—and to do first things first—has resulted in a lot of muddled thinking, unnecessarily complicating the abortion debate. I will, therefore, consider the two aspects separately. I will examine the development of Catholic ethical thinking on each question, and I will try to discern the rationale of the traditional stand as well as that of the new trends and approaches which have subsequently developed within the Catholic camp.

John Connery has recently warned that the time is not yet ripe to attempt a final assessment of the various views on abortion: "Thought needs the test of time to assess its validity, and not enough time has elapsed as yet to provide this test of current opinions."[42] It is true that the debate has by no means come to an end, and therefore my conclusions will be descriptive and provisional rather than hortatory and conclusive.

Determining the Sources

The American Catholic literature on abortion is so vast that only part of it could be dealt with. I have concentrated on the more professional efforts, thus discarding a vast amount of writing at the popular level. This is not meant to imply that this literature is without significance or relevance but rather that it would merit a study in its own right. Only those publications have been examined that are the result of Catholic reflection on abortion and abortion laws. Thus I have included the contributions of Catholics

towards "mixed" or "neutral" symposia, while those of Protestant or
non-Christian thinkers to Catholic symposia or periodicals have not been
directly considered. Naturally, this selection reflects in no way on the value
of the latter, nor do I wish to imply that there is an exclusively Catholic
argument on abortion.

Only those Catholic publications have been examined that treat a particular aspect of the abortion problem with a direct or indirect reference to
the moral issues at stake, even if the authors write from a nonsectarian point
of view or discuss the legal, medical, or social aspects of the question.
Furthermore, I have restricted myself to that literature which was published
originally in the United States, whether or not the authors are United States
citizens. This excluded the Amerian editions and translations of foreign
publications, as well as writings of Americans only published abroad.

Terminology

In the debate on the morality of the interruption of pregnancy, "abortion" generally means "induced abortion" and this, in a wider sense,
refers to any procedure which purposely destroys the fetus. It includes both
the expulsion of a nonviable fetus and attacks on the unborn at a later stage
of development. However, Catholic authors do not include in their definition the use of medicine or surgery which indirectly and unintentionally
results in the death of the fetus (e.g., the removal of a cancerous pregnant
uterus). They refer to such treatments and procedures as "indirect abortion." The term "fetus" generally applies to the product of human sexual
intercourse from the moment of fertilization until birth.[43] The term "indication" must be understood as a general category of reasons suggestive of
the need for, or the desirability of, abortion. There is no agreement as to
how these categories should be distinguished or defined.[44]

From a legal point of view, abortion is a direct or indirect concern of
various types of law: constitutional law, criminal law, administrative law
(licensing), and civil or common law (malpractice). Moral authors usually
do not make distinctions here, generally using the term "state law" or
"law." In this context it is useful to keep in mind that, roughly speaking,
there are three different schemes of legal regulation of abortion which
could be characterized as follows: (1) The restrictive legal code regards the
fetus as a human being and demands unconditional respect for its human
rights. It prohibits the interruption of pregnancy and it treats abortion as
murder, except in cases where the life of the mother is at stake. (2) The
moderate legal code respects the rights of the fetus but not absolutely so. It
recognizes that in certain situations the rights of the woman may prevail, as
in cases where her physical or mental health is threatened. It therefore

permits abortions when these are authorized by official personnel and under defined but wider categories of medical, psychological, or quasi-medical conditions. (3) The permissive or liberal legal code emphasizes freedom. It is based on the conviction that at least during the first months of pregnancy the fetus is not a human being. It allows the woman to decide for herself whether she will continue her pregnancy, and it only prohibits abortions performed by persons who are unqualified from a medical point of view ("abortion on request").[45]

Catholic authors as well as others frequently refer to "the Church's position on abortion." It has to be kept in mind, as Daniel Callahan has pointed out, that it has become in many areas increasingly problematic to speak of "the Church's position" on anything.[46] Callahan explains this as follows:

> Broadly taken, "the Church" includes all those who belong to the Roman Catholic community; this is increasingly the sense in which the term is being used within that community. More narrowly, "the Church" has meant the teaching authority of the Church, which has traditionally been located in the office of the Pope and the Bishops. To talk, then, of the "Church's position" or "Church teaching" is ambiguous: it can mean either the convictions of the entire Roman Catholic community or the formal teachings of the Popes and Bishops. It is not always the case that they coincide.[47]

In the case of abortion it has become problematic to speak of "the Church's position" as the teaching of the Pope and the bishops has not gone unquestioned by their flock. Consequently, Callahan defines "the Church's position" as far as abortion is concerned as "the position taken by the Popes, by the Second Vatican Council and by those theologians attempting to make their own writings consistent with the position of hierarchical authority."[48]

IV. A Short History of Abortion Legislation in the United States

In order to appreciate fully the development of the Catholic contribution towards the American abortion debate, it is important to have some understanding of the history of the abortion reform movement, the evolution of popular attitudes and professional insights, the changing views of religious and nonreligious denominations, and especially the developments in abortion legislation. The purpose of this book does not require an exhaustive analysis of this background; I will merely extract the salient items which have a direct and significant bearing on the formation of the Catholic argument.

The Original Laws and the Beginnings of the Reform Movement: 1926-1945

Prior to 1967, practically all the states prohibited abortion except when performed to protect the life of the pregnant woman. The laws of Alabama (1951) and the District of Columbia (1901) allowed the intervention not just to preserve life but also for reasons of "health." Mississippi (1966) recognized pregnancy resulting from felonious intercourse as a valid reason for abortion.[49]

Opinions are divided as to the original intent of American traditional restrictive statutes. Anti-abortionists generally hold that these embody the Judeo-Christian prohibition against the destruction of innocent human life and that they were enacted to protect the fetus.[50] Reformists usually argue that they were designed to protect the woman from the medical risks of abortion which in the past was a dangerous and often fatal procedure. Another view holds that the conscious or unconscious intent of these statutes was to confirm and maintain the woman's role as childbearer and childrearer and thus to perpetuate male control over women.[51] In practice there has been little effort at enforcing these laws. Most cases arose only after a reported maternal death or injury caused by an illegal abortion, and generally prosecution was initiated only against those who were believed to perform illegal abortions as a regular practice.[52]

The beginning of the abortion reform movement in the United States was marked by the founding in 1926 of the National Commitee on Maternal Health by Dr. Robert Latou Dickinson. This committee, "a private group which organized the more venturesome wing of the American birth control movement," sponsored a study on abortion by Dr. Frederick J. Taussig, which was published in 1936 and which was to exert considerable influence on the later reformists.[53] In particular, Taussig's figures regarding the incidence of illegal abortion and concomitant maternal injury and death rates were magical figures until well into the 1960s.[54]

In 1942 the committee sponsored a two-day conference on abortion at the New York Academy of Medicine which Dr. Taussig attended. For Dr. Taussig, "the purpose of this meeting should be primarily directed to drafting a model abortion law which could well be accepted by all the states in this country."[55] The conference, however, eventually got no further than passing two mild resolutions. The first called for "free and open public discussion of human reproduction and the problems of abortion." The other called for another meeting in the future.[56] These two resolutions are indicative of the lack of impetus of the abortion liberation movement before the end of World War II. Germain G. Grisez suggests that this was partly due to the lack of support from the American Birth Control League which retained an ambivalent attitude towards abortion, possibly because it did not want to antagonize public opinion or divert public attention from its primary objective: contraception.[57]

The Drive for a Moderate Code and the Reform Laws: 1950-1970

It was only in the early 1950s that the movement gained momentum. In 1954 Dr. Harold Rosen, a psychiatrist at Johns Hopkins Hospital, edited a symposium volume which considered the abortion issue from the various angles of the disciplines involved. His was a serious and conscientious effort and the overall tendency of the book was undoubtedly to investigate the possibilities of a less restrictive legal code.[58] Also in 1954, Joseph Fletcher, an Episcopalian minister and professor of Christian Ethics at the Episcopal Theological School in Cambridge, Massachusetts, became the first theologian to declare the reform movement ethically acceptable to the Christian ideology, finding grounds for the justification of abortion as well as euthanasia.[59]

In 1957 Glanville Williams, a British professor of law, published *The Sanctity of Life and the Criminal Law,* the outcome of a series of guest lectures at Columbia University School of Law. The main contention of this book was that while laws against murder are justified by pragmatic and utilitarian considerations, there is no such justification for laws against contraception, sterilization, artificial insemination, abortion, infanticide, euthanasia, and suicide. What Taussig's book was for the statisticians, Williams' book became for the liberation ideologists, because it contained practically the full range of arguments which were later to be employed by the reform movement.[60] Grisez summarizes Williams' arguments as follows:

> Thus he argues that existing laws cause doubts among physicians, that they work special hardship on the poor, that they are widely violated with a huge toll of maternal deaths, that their enforcement is impossible, that their repeal would not have serious medical consequences, that repeal of these laws made by males is favored by women, that a half-conscious reason for maintaining these laws is a desire to punish incontinence, that anti-abortion laws try to "legislate morality," and that the laws themselves lead to great social evils. All these arguments are set in a context of argument which falsely treats Roman Catholicism as the sole serious obstacle to humane reform. . . . [61]

In 1958 Mary Steichen Calderone published *Abortion in the United States,* the result of a 1955 conference sponsored by the Planned Parenthood Federation of America. The trend of this conference was a plea for relaxation of the laws against abortion, as was evident from the post-conference statement that carried significant support and which was included in the volume. This document presented illegal abortion as a problem which could not be solved in the context of existing legislation. It strongly recommended less restrictive laws and suggested, among other things, that legal commissions, including the American Law Institute, "should study the abortion laws in the various states and frame a model law that could, perhaps jointly, be presented to the states for their consideration to replace existing statutes."[62] This model law might include provisions permitting physicians to induce abortion legally on psychiatric, humanitarian, and eugenic indications.[63]

The year 1959 became a milestone for the liberalization movement because in that year the prestigious American Law Institute published a tentative draft of a revised statute on abortion to be included in the institute's *Model Penal Code.* The proposed statute was finally approved by the ALI membership in 1962 with relatively minor changes.[64] The ALI proposed to introduce into the law a positive declaration of the justifiability of abortion in specified categories of cases. These were defined in fairly general and elastic terms, e.g., *grave* impairment of *physical or mental health* on the part of the mother, *grave* physical or mental *defect* on the part of the fetus, and, in the context, *rape.* Unlike the existing legislation in about half the states, the ALI proposal did not require that the indication be factually present. The relevant criterion was the physician's belief in its presence. The ALI proposal further recommended that the abortion be performed in a licensed hospital after certification by two physicians, one of whom might be the operating physician. It excluded from the category of abortion abortifacient methods of contraception.[65]

The reform movement was greatly aided by the thalidomide tragedy of the early 1960s, by the rubella epidemic of 1964-1965, and by a change in attitude on the part of the birth control movement.[66] During the middle 1960s the liberationists concentrated on popularizing the findings of the conferences and studies of the previous decade,[67] and they succeeded in generating support for relaxation of the abortion laws along the lines of the limited ALI proposals. This support was evidenced both by public opinion polls[68] and by the resolutions of important professional or religious groups which declared themselves in favor of some degree of liberalization, as did the General Board of the National Council of Churches of Christ, the Church Council of the American Lutheran Church, the Iowa Council of

Churches, the Protestant Council of the City of New York, the National Association of Evangelicals, and the American National Crime Commission.[69] Perhaps the greatest impetus given to the reform movement came from the American Medical Association (June 1967) and the American College of Obstetricians and Gynecologists (May 1968), both of which passed policy statements on therapeutic abortion that were fairly close to the ALI proposal.[70]

Colorado, on April 25, 1967, became the first state to enact an abortion law modelled after the ALI proposal. By 1970, thirteen states had these laws but some had significant variations from the model.[71] In 1972 Florida became the fourteenth state, after the Florida Supreme Court had declared that the Florida statute was unconstitutionally vague, indefinite, and uncertain.[72]

The Drive for Abortion on Demand and the Repeal Laws: 1965-1976

Soon after the publication of the ALI proposal it became clear that a significant section of the liberationist movement was not going to be satisfied with relaxation along these restrictive lines and that they considered this, at best, as a means towards an end, a necessary step on the road to complete liberalization.[73] This has been the policy of the *Society for Humane Abortion, Inc.*, founded in 1965 by Patricia M. Maginnis, and of another organization, *Legalize Abortion*.[74]

Mrs. Alice Rossi took the position that abortion should be performed at the woman's request and that the medical procedure should be regulated only to the extent to which other surgery is regulated by medical practice laws. Mrs. Harriet Pilpel considered abortion in the same terms as any other surgery and advocated a legal strategy aimed at liberalization of the existing legislation by medical practice and judicial interpretation, thus bypassing the long and arduous road of innovative legislative action.[75] This pragmatic policy was supported by Mrs. Judith Blake who, as late as 1971, had to confess that 80 percent of the country's white population disapproved of complete liberalization.[76] She saw a Supreme Court ruling concerning the constitutionality of existing state restrictions as the only road to rapid change in the legal grounds for abortion.[77]

Lawrence Lader's *Abortion*, published in 1966, explained at a popular level the mass of abortion reform material that had been collected by doctors, psychiatrists, and lawyers in the previous fifteen years. Lader declared that the right of every woman to legalized abortion was the final freedom implied by feminism and the birth control movement.[78] The year 1968 was another milestone in the history of the reform movement because in the course of that year some influential, nationwide organizations

declared themselves in favor of abortion on demand. The American Civil
Liberties Union stated that restrictive laws violate constitutional rights and
asserted that the woman and any licensed physician have a right to decide
for abortion until the time the fetus becomes viable. Therefore, all laws
prohibiting abortions by licensed physicians should be repealed.[79] That
same year the American Baptist Convention, the Unitarian Universalist
Association, Planned Parenthood-World Population, and the American
Public Health Association adopted a similar position; they were followed
by the American Ethical Union in 1969. In 1970 the Moravian Church in
America and the American Friends Service Committee also fell into line
with the ACLU position.[80]

At the end of the 1960s several large conferences on abortion were held
at which the proponents of abortion on demand were represented. In February 1969 a conference was held in Chicago to launch a new National
Association for Repeal of Abortion Laws. Approximately forty organizations sent over three hundred delegates to this meeting. The conference
resolved that "to compel a woman to bear a child against her will violates
her basic human rights" and recommended that abortion should receive the
same amount of legal attention as any other medical procedure.[81]

In the course of 1970, Alaska, Hawaii, New York, and Washington
repealed all criminal penalties for abortion and enacted statutes which
made the intervention a part of regular medical practice. The decision was
left to the woman and her physician provided that the abortion was performed early in pregnancy (although New York permitted it up to twenty-
four weeks).[82]

Between 1969 and 1971 many restrictive laws were challenged in court,
including ALI-type reform laws. Charles Alan and Alexander Susan char-
acterize these judicial activities as follows:

> These court challenges met with much early success, and only a few
> setbacks. Successful arguments were that Victorian era abortion laws,
> which made criminal all abortions except those "necessary to preserve"
> the woman's life, were void for vagueness, and that restrictions on abor-
> tion per se (whether narrow or broad) violated a woman's right to per-
> sonal, sexual and marital privacy without justification in a compelling
> countervailing state interest. The equal protection argument was occa-
> sionally, but not strongly, asserted.[83]

Norma G. Zarky has defined the legal issues involved in these court
challenges as follows: (1) Restrictive statutes violate a fundamental right of
women to determine the number of offspring they will bear (the "right of
privacy"). (2) These statutes invade the right of physicians to give medical
advice and treatment in accordance with their professional knowledge. (3)

No sufficient state interest requires such restriction of the fundamental rights of women and physicians. (4) Most of the state statutes are vague and indefinite and therefore invalid. (5) Restrictive abortion statutes may violate the requirements of the equal protection clause by discriminating, without justification, against certain classes of women.[84]

In April 1971 the United States Supreme Court decided for the first time on the constitutionality of an abortion law. In *U.S.* v. *Vuitch,* the Court upheld the traditional restrictive statute of the District of Columbia which was under attack for vagueness, declaring that the clause "necessary for the preservation of the mother's life or health" was not unconstitutionally vague. At the same time the Court explicitly interpreted the term "health" to include mental health.[85]

In 1972 the Presidential Commission on Population Growth and the American Future published the report on its findings and recommendations. The majority of its members believed that women should be free to determine their fertility and that the abortion decision should be left to the conscience of the mother in consultation with her physician. Consequently, "states should be encouraged to enact affirmative statutes creating a clear and positive framework for the practice of abortion on request."[86]

The Supreme Court settled the issues of right of privacy and equal protection of the law in landmark decisions in *Roe* v. *Wade* and *Doe* v. *Bolton* on January 22, 1973. *Roe* v. *Wade* involved the constitutionality of the old-style Texas statute which prohibited all abortions except "an abortion procured or attempted by medical advice for the purpose of saving the life of the mother." On the date of the decision, thirty-one states had similar statutes. *Doe* v. *Bolton* involved the constitutionality of the procedural restrictions of the Georgia ALI-style law which required (1) that the patient be a resident of the state; (2) that the abortion be performed in a hospital accredited by the Joint Commission on Accreditation of Hospitals; (3) that the performing physician's judgement be approved by a hospital staff abortion committee; (4) that the performing physician's judgement be confirmed by two other physicians. At the date of the decision, fifteen states had somewhat similar statutes.[87]

In *Roe* v. *Wade* the Court accepted the due process clause of the Fourteenth Amendment as the legal basis for the abolition of state control over abortion. This clause protects the citizen's personal liberty by restricting state intervention: "...nor shall any State deprive any person of life, liberty or property without due process of law...." The Court decided that "the word 'person,' as used in the Fourteenth Amendment, does not include the unborn" but that the word "liberty" does include a woman's right to an abortion.[88] The legal argument of the Court could be summarized as follows: (1) The woman has a Fourteenth Amendment right to privacy which includes a qualified right to terminate her pregnancy. (2) This right is qualified by the state's interest in protecting the woman's health and in protecting potential human life. (3) Each of these interests may become "a compelling state interest" at some point during the pregnancy.[89]

The state interest in maternal health may become compelling only at the end of the first trimester because an abortion performed before that time is considered by medical authorities to be safer than carrying a child to term. Prior to approximately the end of the first trimester, the abortion decision and its execution must be left to the medical judgement of the physician. For the last six months of pregnancy, the state may regulate the abortion procedure to the extent that the regulations reasonably relate to protection of maternal health.[90] The state interest in potential life may become dominant at the beginning of viability when the fetus, in the words of the Court, "presumably has the capability of meaningful life outside the mother's womb." After viability the state may, if it chooses, regulate and even prohibit abortion except where it is judged medically necessary for the preservation of the life or health of the mother.[91] With respect to the procedural requirements of a liberalized abortion law, the Court held further, in Doe v. Bolton, that legal restrictions based on residence, accreditation of hospitals, abortion committees, and confirmation by other physicians were all violative of the Fourteenth Amendment.[92]

The Roe and Doe decisions reduced legislative control of abortion to a minimum. Even if laws are passed to regulate the very narrow area of permissible prohibition, they are practically unenforceable since the decision is firmly in the hands of the woman's physician while the preservation of the woman's health, in the wide sense of the word, is an acceptable indication. Moreover, after the U.S. v. Vuitch decision, in a criminal action involving alleged violation of the abortion statute the prosecution has to prove that the indication was nonexistent. It also must establish the viability of the fetus. In practice the United States Supreme Court initiated a policy of abortion on demand.[93] Roe and Doe invalidated thirty-one strict statutes. Fifteen moderate codes had to be thoroughly rewritten and four liberal statutes could be slightly broadened.[94]

The Supreme Court confirmed its 1973 position on July 1, 1976, when it rendered judgement in Planned Parenthood of Central Missouri v. Danforth and in two associated decisions. The Court struck down three sections of Missouri's 1974 statute and held that a woman who wants an abortion does not need the consent of her husband; that a girl under 18 years of age who wishes to have an abortion does not need the permission of her parents;

and that when an abortion is desired, the physician is not obliged to preserve the life of the fetus, even though it might be viable.[95] The reform movement had achieved its aim: a century of restrictive abortion legislation had come to an end.[96]

NOTES

[1] George H. Williams, "The No. 2 Moral Issue of Today," *America* 116 (1967), p. 452.

[2] Luke T. Lee, "International Status of Abortion Legalization," in Howard J. Osofsky and Joy D. Osofsky (eds.), *The Abortion Experience: Psychological and Medical Impact* (Hagerstown, Maryland: Medical Department Harper and Row, 1973), p. 356.

[3] "Ten Years of Change in Abortion Law 1967-76," *Risk* (Geneva: World Council of Churches) 13 (1977), No. 1, pp. 46-48.

[4] Bishops' Committee for Pro-Life Activities, National Conference of Catholic Bishops, *Respect Life! The 1976 Respect Life Handbook* (Washington, D.C.: Respect Life Committee NCCB, 1976), p. 17. See also: National Conference of Catholic Bishops, United States Catholic Conference, *Documentation on the Right to Life and Abortion* (Washington, D.C.: Publications Office USCC, 1974), pp. 35-36. For a survey of the current legal status of abortion in various countries and recent United States statistics, see: Christopher Tietze, *Induced Abortion: A World Review, 1981* (New York: Population Council, 1981), pp. 7-22.

[5] Kenneth Vaux, "The Giving and Taking of Life: New Power at Life's Thresholds," *Christian Century* 92 (1975), pp. 386-387.

[6] John T. Noonan, Jr., "Introduction," in *id.* (ed.), *The Morality of Abortion: Legal and Historical Perspectives* (Cambridge, Mass.: Harvard University Press, 1970), pp. xii-xvii; Elizabeth N. Moore, "Moral Sentiment in Judicial Opinions on Abortion," *Santa Clara Lawyer* 15 (1975), pp. 592-593. Mrs. Finkbine, fearing that she was carrying a thalidomide-deformed fetus, failed to obtain an abortion in the United States and had to travel to Sweden for this purpose. The aborted fetus was in fact deformed. See: Lawrence Lader, *Abortion* (Indianapolis: Bobbs-Merrill, 1966), pp. 10-16; *Newsweek*, August 13, 1962, p. 54.

[7] Richard A. McCormick, S.J., "Notes on Moral Theology: The Abortion Dossier," *Theological Studies* 35 (1974), p. 354; Robert L. Perkins, "Introduction," in *id.* (ed.), *Abortion: Pro and Con* (Cambridge, Mass.: Schenkman, 1974), pp. 7-12.

[8] John F. Monagle, "The Ethics of Abortion," *Social Justice Review* 65 (1972), p. 112.

[9] Emily C. Moore-Čavar, *International Inventory of Information on Induced Abortion* (New York: International Institute for the Study of Human Reproduction—Columbia University, 1974), p. 1.

[10] *Ibid.*, p. 1.

[11] Daniel Callahan, *Abortion: Law, Choice and Morality* (New York: Macmillan, 1970), pp. 1-2.

[12] Joseph P. Witherspoon, "Impact of the Abortion Decisions upon the Father's Role," *Jurist* 35 (1975), pp. 47-49; Editorial, "The Bishops' Plan for Pro-Life Activities," *America* 133 (1975), p. 454.

[13] "A New Catholic Strategy on Abortion," *Month* 234 (1973), p. 163.

22   The Morality of Abortion

14 Callahan, *op. cit.*, p. 2; *id.*, "Abortion: Some Ethical Issues," in David F. Walbert and J. Douglas Butler (eds.), *Abortion, Society, and the Law* (Cleveland: Press of Case Western Reserve University, 1973), pp. 96-97.

15 Stanley Hauerwas, "Abortion and Normative Ethics: A Critical Appraisal of Callahan and Grisez," *Cross Currents* 21 (1971), p. 400.

16 Peter A. Facione, "The Abortion Non-Debate," *Cross Currents* 23 (1973), p. 352.

17 *Ibid.*, p. 352; Donald A. Giannella, "The Difficult Quest for a Truly Humane Abortion Law," *Villanova Law Review* 13 (1968), p. 257.

18 Callahan, *Abortion: Law, Choice and Morality, op. cit.*, p. 12.

19 *Ibid.*, p. 12.

20 *Ibid.*, pp. 26, 69, 83-84, 115, 116, 305, 484.

21 *Ibid.*, pp. 3-6, 16.

22 Facione, *op. cit.*, p. 350; Thomas A. Wassmer, S.J., *Christian Ethics for Today* (Milwaukee: Bruce, 1969), pp. 194, 196; B. James George, Jr., "The Evolving Law of Abortion," in Walbert and Butler (eds.), *op. cit.*, p. 3; Callahan, "Abortion: Some Ethical Issues," *op. cit.*, p. 89.

23 Wassmer, *op. cit.*, p. 194.

24 Betty Sarvis and Hyman Rodman, *The Abortion Controversy* (New York: Columbia University Press, 1973), pp. 1-4.

25 Facione, *op. cit.*, p. 350. See also: Bishops of Texas, "Open Letter on Abortion — April, 1971," in Daughters of St. Paul (eds.), *Yes to Life* (Boston: St. Paul Editions, 1977), pp. 237-239.

26 George H. Williams, "Religious Residues and Presuppositions in the American Debate on Abortion," *Theological Studies* 31 (1970), p. 12.

27 *Ibid.*, p. 13.

28 *Ibid.*, p. 50.

29 *Ibid.*, p. 52.

30 McCormick, *op. cit.*, p. 313.

31 Editorial, "The Abortion Debate," *Commonweal* 92 (1970), p. 132.

32 James J. Diamond, "Abortion, Animation, and Biological Hominization," *Theological Studies* 36 (1975), p. 324.

33 McCormick, *op. cit.*, p. 313.

34 Personal communication, Arthur McCormack, Director of the Population and Development Office in Rome, July 1, 1980.

35 Robert F. Drinan, S.J., "The Jurisprudential Options on Abortion," *Theological Studies* 31 (q970), pn 153; "U.S. Bishops Protest Program Against 'Right to Life'," in Daughters of St. Paul (eds.), *op. cit.*, pp. 219-221. Donald P. Warwick has recently investigated how much aid is given by governmental and private agencies in the United States for abortion programs abroad. He estimates that foreign aid for this purpose amounts to less than a quarter of one percent of the total spent on population assistance; "Foreign Aid for Abortion: Politics, Ethics, and Practice," in James T. Burtchaell, C.S.C. (ed.), *Abortion Parley: Papers Delivered at the National Conference on Abortion Held at the University of Notre Dame in October 1979* (Kansas City: Andrews and McMeel, 1980), pp. 301-322.

36 Robert E. Hall, "Foreword," in Walbert and Butler (eds.), *op. cit.*, p. x; Joseph P. Kennedy *et al.*, "Church-State: A Legal Survey: 1966-1968," *Notre Dame Lawyer* 43 (1968), pp. 701-702; Dennis J. Doherty, "The Morality of Abortion," *American Ecclesiastical Review* 169 (1975), pp. 37-38.

[37] In 1966 Mrs. Harriet F. Pilpel, a leading advocate of abortion liberalization, stated before a New York State Assembly committee that the idea of the fetal right to life has its roots in Catholic theology. See: Germain G. Grisez, *Abortion: The Myths, the Realities, and the Arguments* (New York: Corpus Books, 1970), p. 451.

[38] The majority of the anti-abortion groups in the United States are nonsectarian in ideology and organization. See: Constance Balides *et al.*, "The Abortion Issue: Major Groups, Organizations, and Funding Sources," in Osofsky and Osofsky (eds.), *op. cit.*, pp. 509-518. See also Kennedy *et al.*, *op. cit.*, p. 701; Grisez, *op. cit.*, pp. 348-351.

[39] Judith Blake, "Elective Abortion and Our Reluctant Citizenry: Research on Public Opinion in the United States," in Osofsky and Osofsky (eds.), *op. cit.*, pp. 449-455, 465; Kennedy *et al.*, *op. cit.*, p. 701.

[40] See, for instance, the activities of the United States Catholic Conference Family Life Bureau as summarized by Balides *et al.*, *op. cit.*, pp. 516-517.

[41] Robert E. Hall (ed.), *Abortion in a Changing World: The Proceedings of an International Conference Convened in Hot Springs, Virginia, November 17-20, 1968, by the Association for the Study of Abortion* (vols. I-II; New York: Columbia University Press, 1970); vol. I, pp. 51, 52; vol. II, pp. 110-111, 112, 210-211. I presume that "anti-heathenistic" (vol. II, p. 112) is a wrong transcription from the tapes.

[42] John Connery, S.J., *Abortion: The Development of the Roman Catholic Perspective* (Chicago: Loyola University Press, 1977), p. 5.

[43] Grisez, *op. cit.*, pp. 5-9.

[44] Callahan, *Abortion: Law, Choice and Morality, op. cit.*, pp. 25-26; Grisez, *op. cit.*, p. 8.

[45] John M. Finnis, "Three Schemes of Regulation," in Noonan (ed.), *op. cit.*, pp. 173-203.

[46] Callahan, *Abortion: Law, Choice and Morality, op. cit.*, p. 441, footnote 17.

[47] *Ibid.*, pp. 441-442, footnote 17.

[48] *Ibid.*, p. 442, footnote 17.

[49] Joseph A. Lampe, "The World in Perspective," in Thomas W. Hilgers and Dennis J. Horan (eds.), *Abortion and Social Justice* (New York: Sheed and Ward, 1972), pp. 94-95; George, *op. cit.*, pp. 7-17.

[50] Grisez, *op. cit.*, pp. 190-193; David W. Louisell and John T. Noonan, Jr., "Constitutional Balance," in Noonan (ed.), *op. cit.*, pp. 223-226; Robert F. Drinan, S.J., "The Inviolability of the Right to be Born," in Walbert and Butler (eds.), *op. cit.*, pp. 136-137.

[51] Sarvis and Rodman, *op. cit.*, pp. 16-21. A recent contribution to this debate is James C. Mohr, *Abortion in America: The Origins and Evolution of National Policy, 1800-1900* (New York: Oxford University Press, 1978).

[52] Robert E. Cooke *et al.* (eds.), *The Terrible Choice: The Abortion Dilemma. Based on the Proceedings of the International Conference on Abortion Sponsored by the Harvard Divinity School and the Joseph P. Kennedy Jr. Foundation* (New York: Bantam Books, 1968), p. 49.

[53] Grisez, *op. cit.*, p. 226.

[54] Frederick J. Taussig, *Abortion, Spontaneous and Induced: Medical and Social Aspects* (St. Louis: C.V. Mosby, 1936); Grisez, *op. cit.*, pp. 58, 226-227.

[55] Grisez, *op. cit.*, p. 227.

[56] *Ibid.*, p. 229.

[57] *Ibid.*, p. 229.

[58] Harold Rosen (ed.), *Therapeutic Abortion: Medical, Psychiatric, Legal, Anthropological and Religious Considerations* (New York: Julian Press, 1954); Grisez, *op. cit.*, p. 231.

[59] Joseph Fletcher, *Morals and Medicine* (Boston: Beacon Press, 1960); Grisez, *op. cit.*, p. 232.

[60] Glanville Williams, *The Sanctity of Life and the Criminal Law* (New York: Knopf, 1957); Grisez, *op. cit.*, pp. 232-235.

[61] Grisez, *op. cit.*, pp. 234-235.

[62] Mary Steichen Calderone (ed.), *Abortion in the United States: A Conference Sponsored by the Planned Parenthood Federation of America, Inc.* (New York: Hoeber-Harper, 1958), p. 183; Grisez, *op. cit.*, pp. 235-236.

[63] Calderone, *op. cit.*, p. 183; Grisez, *op. cit.*, p. 236.

[64] American Law Institute, *Model Penal Code: Proposed Official Draft* (Philadelphia: American Law Institute, 1962), Section 230, pp. 187-193; Grisez, *op. cit.*, pp. 236-237.

[65] Grisez, *op. cit.*, pp. 237-238; Giannella, *op. cit.*, pp. 257-261; Charles P. Kindregan, *Abortion, The Law, and Defective Children* (Washington: Corpus Books, 1969), pp. 13-14.

[66] Grisez, *op. cit.*, p. 239; Herbert Ratner, "A Doctor Talks about Abortion," *Catholic Mind* 64, May 1966, p. 48; Kindregan, *op. cit.*, pp. 16-17.

[67] Grisez, *op. cit.*, pp. 239-240.

[68] *Ibid.*, pp. 241-242; Callahan, *Abortion: Law, Choice and Morality, op. cit.*, p. 10; Edward J. Ryle, "Some Sociological and Psychological Reflections on the Abortion Decisions," *Jurist* 33 (1973), pp. 218-220; Kindregan, *op. cit.*, pp. 14-17.

[69] Callahan, *Abortion: Law, Choice and Morality, op. cit.*, pp. 10-11; Moore-Čavar, *op. cit.*, pp. 19-21.

[70] Grisez, *op. cit.*, pp. 242-244.

[71] Lampe, *op. cit.*, p. 96; George, *op. cit.*, pp. 23-28.

[72] Ruth Roemer, "Legalization of Abortion in the United States," in Osofsky and Osofsky (eds.), *op. cit.*, p. 285.

[73] Grisez, *op. cit.*, p. 257.

[74] *Ibid.*, pp. 257-258.

[75] *Ibid.*, pp. 258-259. Mrs. Rossi has also been a leading proponent of the liberationist cause.

[76] Judith Blake, "Abortion and Public Opinion: The 1960-1970 Decade," *Science* 171 (1971), p. 548. In a later study she came to the conclusion that in 1972 abortion on demand was unacceptable to approximately two-thirds of American adults. See: Blake, "Elective Abortion and Our Reluctant Citizenry: Research on Public Opinion in the United States," *op. cit.*, p. 465. In 1974 the National Committee for a Human Life Amendment, Inc., an organization established and funded by the United States Catholic bishops, commissioned an extensive public opinion poll on abortion. According to this survey, 70 percent of the population supported legal action to reverse the 1973 Supreme Court decisions and impose some legal restrictions on abortion. See: Bishops' Committee for Pro-Life Activities, National Conference of Catholic Bishops, *Abortion, Attitudes, and the Law* (Washington, D.C.: Bishops' Committee for Pro-Life Activities, no date), pp. 1-6.

[77] Blake, "Abortion and Public Opinion: The 1960-1970 Decade," *op. cit.*, p. 548.

[78] Lawrence Lader, *Abortion* (Indianapolis: Bobbs-Merrill, 1966), pp. 167-175, 204-205; Grisez, *op. cit.*, p. 240.

[79] Grisez, *op. cit.*, p. 259.

[80] *Ibid.*, p. 259; Moore-Cavar, *op. cit.*, pp. 21-22.

[81] Grisez, *op. cit.*, pp. 259-261.

[82] Roemer, *op. cit.*, p. 286. In 1972 the New York State legislature voted to repeal its liberal statute which was only saved by Governor Rockefeller's veto of the attempted repeal. See: Moore, *op. cit.*, p. 593.

[83] Charles Alan and Alexander Susan, "Abortions for Poor and Nonwhite Women: A Denial of Equal Protection?" *Hastings Law Journal* 23 (1971), p. 148.

[84] Norma G. Zarky, "Grounds for Legal Challenge," in The California Commitee on Therapeutic Abortion (Carl Reiterman, ed.), *Abortion and the Unwanted Child* (New York: Springer, 1971), p. 27. See also: George, *op. cit.*, pp. 28-30.

[85] Roemer, *op. cit.*, p. 288.

[86] Presidential Commission on Population Growth and the American Future, *U.S. Population Growth and the American Future* (The Rockefeller Report), (Washington, D.C.: U.S. Government Printing Office, 1972), pp. 103-104.

[87] David Granfield, "The Legal Impact of the *Roe* and *Doe* Decisions," *Jurist* 33 (1973), pp. 113, 115-116; Roemer, *op. cit.*, pp. 280-281, 283.

[88] Granfield, *op. cit.*, p. 114; Roemer, *op. cit.*, p. 282.

[89] Granfield, *op. cit.*, p. 114; Roemer, *op. cit.*, pp. 282-283.

[90] Granfield, *op. cit.*, pp. 114-115; Roemer, *op. cit.*, pp. 280, 282-283.

[91] Granfield, *op. cit.*, pp. 114-115; Roemer, *op. cit.*, pp. 280, 283.

[92] Granfield, *op. cit.*, pp. 115-116; Roemer, *op. cit.*, pp. 280-281, 283.

[93] Granfield, *op. cit.*, pp. 116-119; Roemer, *op. cit.*, pp. 281, 288.

[94] Granfield, *op. cit.*, p. 116.

[95] George E. Reed, "Supreme Court Rejects Spousal and Parental Rights in Abortion Decision," *Hospital Progress* 57, August 1976, p. 18; Bishops' Committee for Pro-Life Activities, *Respect Life! The 1976 Respect Life Handbook, op. cit.*, pp. 15-16.

[96] For a more extensive survey of the history of abortion liberalization in the United States, see: Malcolm Potts *et al.*, *Abortion* (Cambridge: Cambridge University Press, 1977), pp. 332-373. Since 1976 the discussions have concentrated on the public funding of abortions and on nullification of the 1973 Supreme Court decisions by a constitutional amendment. See: Tietze, *op. cit.*, p. 9.

SECTION I

ABORTION AS A PERSONAL OPTION

The Inheritance from the Past: Abortion in the Traditional Manuals of Catholic Ethics

An analysis of contemporary Catholic thinking on any moral issue appropriately takes as its point of departure the traditional manuals of Catholic philosophical and theological ethics. Until the 1960s these handbooks were widely used in the professional formation of candidates for the ministry and were frequently consulted by pastors on a great variety of moral and pastoral problems. Since they were invariably published with the approval of hierarchical authority, they were considered to present a reliable summary of the Church's moral doctrine. These handbooks not only established the fundamental principles of Catholic morality but also applied them specifically and in detail to a great variety of concrete cases. In this chapter, then, I will examine the position of the American Catholic manuals on the subject of abortion.

I. Human Life: A Right of Justice

Following St. Thomas Aquinas,[1] the American manuals of Catholic ethics treat crimes against human life in the context of the moral virtue of justice, which "regulates human actions and renders to others their due"[2] and, more specifically, under the heading of commutative justice which "is exercised by all who practise fair dealing with their equals, that is, by states with states, families with families, societies with like societies, individuals with individuals..."[3] The manuals either explicitly or implicitly classify crimes against the human person (homicide, mutilation and imprisonment) as "vices against commutative justice,"[4] with a further definition as "deeds against the person,"[5] "committed in involuntary commutations."[6]

Killing is defined as a human act or a human omission, which is the efficacious cause of the death of a human being, and it is morally lawful in only two cases: capital punishment and individual or communal self-defense against an unjust aggressor.[7] The killing of the innocent, that is, of those who are neither criminals nor unjust aggressors worthy of death, if it is done directly and intentionally, is always immoral, whether the agent is a private individual or society. If, however, the killing is indirect and unintentional, it is not immoral when there is a serious reason for performing the act from which death results; for it is lawful to perform a morally good or a morally indifferent act which has an evil effect, as well as a good effect, if the good effect is intended and the evil effect only permitted, and if there is a sufficiently grave reason for performing the act (the principle of double effect).[8] Similarly, there are circumstances in which a person has a right to do things which entail risk to life and even the *indirect* loss of life.[9] However, direct killing of the innocent is gravely immoral. It is a violation of the virtue of justice because it is an injury to the rights of God, to the rights of the individual, and to the rights of society.[10]

The Rights of God

The American manuals describe unlawful killing primarily as "an obvious usurpation of the exclusively divine prerogative of absolute dominion over human life."[11] The destruction of human life represents an exercise of ownership over such life and this is lawful only to him who owns it. Human life is God's exclusive property. Therefore exercising dominion over life is lawful to God alone and one who destroys life violates God's right by doing what only God may lawfully do.[12] Human life is something over which man can have, at most, useful dominion. Absolute dominion over this life is a divine prerogative.[13]

God, therefore, has a right to human life because he owns it and this right is absolute and exclusive because his ownership is absolute and exclusive. The manuals establish such ownership from the following premises:

1. The divine law forbids the killing of the innocent in the Fifth Commandment of the Decalogue: "You shall not kill." To judges the special command was given: "Do not slay the innocent and righteous." Sacred Scripture further states that the manslayer destroys the image of God, a crime so detestable that God declares that he will revenge the blood of man, even if it is shed by a beast.[14]

2. By natural law God bestows certain rights on man but in virtue of the same law he has to withhold other rights which by their very nature are exclusively his. One of these divine prerogatives is the direct or absolute dominion over the human person which is exercised by killing. God grants to man an indirect or useful dominion over himself and concedes to him the use and stewardship of his person, but God cannot relinquish his direct dominion over it. By his eternal law he decrees that all his creatures attain the end for which he has created them and rational man can attain this end only by doing morally good acts. Now God has allotted to each man a

certain span of life for doing them and it is for God, and not for man, to decide that this life may come to a close and that the acts performed are of sufficient quantity and quality to entitle their agent to his last end. Therefore suicide and murder invade God's exclusive domain: they make further works impossible and they are the equivalent of telling him that he will have to be satisfied with the acts performed so far because there are simply going to be no more. The creature thus usurps an essentially divine prerogative which God cannot cede to him without ceasing to be God. [15]

3. God has created human life in a special way and he therefore owns it in a special way. Every living thing has within itself some force of life, an animating principle which makes it live. In a human being this principle of life is the soul and since the soul is spiritual and immortal, it must come directly from God. It follows then that no man is his own master in the full sense of the word: God is the master and man is only the steward of his life, of his bodily members, and of his spiritual and corporeal functions which he is allowed to direct by his free will. [16]

The manuals have no difficulty in reconciling God's absolute dominion over human life with the justifiability under limited circumstances of capital punishment. They explain that the state may take the life of duly convicted criminals if the application of this penalty is deemed necessary for the common good. The state has a duty to maintain social order and to protect the rights of its citizens to life and property. It must be allowed to use all the means that are necessary to procure this end because God, the author of human society, could not wish public authority to exist without conferring on it the right to employ such measures as are necessary for its proper functioning. If the state were not in a position to apply the maximum penalty to the most serious crimes, the rights of its citizens would be in constant jeopardy. Consequently, the state has that right. This is evident from reason as well as from divine law. [17]

The Rights of Man and of Society

Unlawful killing also violates the rights of the individual. The manuals establish these rights in the following manner:

1. Life is man's chief natural good and his primary natural right. The source of this right to life is the natural law which ordains that man use all his capacities, particularly his rational powers, to attain perfection and, ultimately, his last end. If man could lawfully be deprived of the use of these faculties by others, these powers and the end towards which they are directed would have no meaning. Natural law, however, bestows upon each person the right to exercise his rational powers and this requires in the first place that his life be respected. [18]

2. Reason tells us that when God, our creator, placed us in this world, he

evidently intended that we conserve the life which he gave us. It is obvious, then, that we have the duty to protect our body against any forces that would interfere with the divine gift of life and health. Consequently, we have the right to preserve our life and not to be unjustly deprived of it by others.[19]

In this context the manuals also justify the lawfulness of killing in certain cases of unjust aggression. They state that man's right to life implies the right to protect his life by the use of force, even a deathblow, against an unjust aggressor if this is the only way of protecting himself. This constitutes no violation of the rights of the other because the assailant's right to life may be considered suspended during his unjust attack. Moreover, he can easily regain his right to life by desisting from the assault.[20]

Finally, the manuals consider the morality of killing in a wider social perspective. They describe direct killing of the innocent as an outrage against society because it unduly deprives the community of one of its members and the relatives and friends of the murdered person of his love and service. It causes grave scandal and is bound to disturb the peace and security of society. Hence, the law has always inflicted the severest punishment on slayers of the innocent.[21]

II. The Fetus: An Innocent Human Person

There are indications that the traditional American manuals were not particularly preoccupied with the fundamentals of the abortion question and that in its essentials they considered the problem a relatively simple one. Charles J. McFadden is of the opinion that the issue does not warrant a lengthy and laborious discussion,[22] and Thomas J. O'Donnell writes:

> Presupposing a thorough understanding of the principles regarding the inviolability of human life, a medico-moral discussion need not be concerned at great length with the morality of abortion, as that word is commonly understood, since it represents such an obvious usurpation of the exclusively divine prerogative of absolute dominion over human life.[23]

As far as the morality of abortion is concerned there is a basic unanimity among the authors. Abortion constitutes an act of direct killing because the fetus is expelled before it is viable and thus removed from the only environment in which it can live. Naturally, the manuals reject the argument that in an abortion the child dies from natural causes after it has been born, and they point out that all killing consists in interfering with nature in such a way that a person dies of it. Austin Fagothey presents the example of a man who has been kept without food and who could be said to have died from the natural effects of starvation. Yet this is also murder.[24] There is equal unanimity as to the basic premise of the assertion that abortion is unlawful killing. The authors agree that the object of the intervention is an innocent human person. However, they come to this conclusion with varying degrees of certainty and for a variety of reasons. These deserve a closer examination.

The Fetus: Definitely a Human Person

Some authors have no doubt at all about the personhood of the fetus and declare unequivocally that it is a human being from the moment of fertilization onwards. John Marshall arrives at this certainty by considering the need of ensoulment. He explains that the physical structure of the body owes its existence to the activity of biological forces which the constant influence of God's power has kept operative since the beginning of time, and, more specifically, to the interaction of molecules contained in the genes of sperm and ovum which impart to the zygote the property of self-reproduction. However, something more is needed to establish a new human being and this additional requirement is the soul which results from the direct creative act of God. Unlike the body, the soul has no chain of preceding determinants but rises *de novo* each time a sperm and ovum unite.[25] The zygote has something more than what is contributed to the union by its physical components and therefore it merits special ethical consideration which differs essentially from our attitude towards sperm or ovum. The zygote is man and although it can be destroyed through injury, disease, or human intervention, its soul continues to live and will be reunited with its body at the Resurrection.[26] Marshall finds support for the immediate ensoulment view in embryology, arguing that also on biological grounds we must conclude that the fetus becomes man at the time of fertilization because it has from the beginning a degree of autonomy with regard to the mode of its development which is not controlled by its mother. In the early stages of its life it needs maternal nutrition to sustain growth but, long before it is born, it is viable and capable of an independent existence. It is therefore a human being from the very outset.[27]

Joseph B. McAllister offers a philosophical combination of Marshall's theological and biological arguments and presents fertilization as the point of departure for an orderly process of growth which reaches its physical climax in the early adult years of the human being. Throughout this period of development and transformation the human organism manifests a fundamental unity which must be attributed to the organizing activity of one and the same living principle. It is this principle which is responsible for the growth and development of the fetus and which later manifests itself in the intelligence and free will of the adult. The fetus, therefore, is fundamentally capable of intelligence, and this capacity makes it a person and gives it the inalienable rights of a person.[28]

Edwin F. Healy derives his certainty about the quality of fetal life from the baptismal practice of the Church. He argues that if the divine promise to preserve the Church from errors in matters pertaining to its life and work is to be fulfilled, the Church should know to whom it may administer its sacraments. In canon 747 the law of the Church states that all living aborted fetuses, irrespective of their age, should be baptized, and this not conditionally but unconditionally. Since the Church does not baptize any being that is not human, we must conclude that the human fetus is a human person.[29]

McAllister further points to the attitude which all reputable physicians adopt towards direct abortion. He states that they condemn the intervention as immoral, illegal, and simply murder, and concludes that the fetus must be a person with the rights of a person.[30]

The Fetus: Probably a Human Person

There are more authors who affirm that the fetus is a human person but, while they do so on essentially the same grounds as the previous group, they state their views in a manner which is considerably less categorical. Healy, whose certainty regarding fetal personhood derives from the pastoral practice of the Church, indicates that the theological and biological evidence is less than perfectly conclusive. Arguing in the manner of Marshall from the need of ensoulment, he considers the total process of prenatal and post-natal development and points out that during all this period the body does not receive a single organ which it did not have in an undeveloped state from the beginning. If the Creator made the fertilized ovum so complete that it will develop into a mature adult without any additions from outside, "*it is not unreasonable to assume* that He infuses into the ovum at the instant when it is to become a living being the soul without which it would be a mere animal and not a man."[31]

Thomas J. Higgins presents much the same argument as McAllister and defines the human person as a distinct organism which is fundamentally capable of intelligence. The fetus represents the first stage in the development of the human individual and therefore "the likeliest opinion" is that the infusion of the rational soul occurs when, at fertilization, a distinctly new living being is formed.[32] John P. Kenny states it this way:

The opinion that the fetus is not animated until the period of quickening, when fetal movement is felt, is unscientific. In former times there was a theory, based on the teaching of Aristotle, that the rational soul is not infused until the body is sufficiently developed. According to this theory, the rational soul vivified the male embryo after forty days, and entered the female embryo after eighty days. This theory is rejected by moralists; the common opinion is that *fetal life begins at the moment of conception.* The rational soul is present as soon as the ovum is fertilized by the male germ cell. If the fetus were not animated by a rational soul from the first moment of conception, it would not develop into a human being.[33]

Healy also places a question mark behind mediate animation theories and points out that, if one postpones the infusion of the soul to a later stage of pregnancy, one might with equal logic postpone it to the time of delivery or to the point where the infant becomes able to reason. Therefore the immediate ensoulment view must at least be given the benefit of the doubt and the burden of proof rests on those who take a different position.[34]

The Fetus: Possibly a Human Person

Gerald Kelly is the most articulate representative of those authors who confess themselves undecided as to the precise moment of ensoulment. He explains that in the Catholic tradition there are two theories on this issue and that each of these is supported by respected Catholic philosophers and theologians. St. Thomas Aquinas, for instance, presented a theory of mediate animation according to which the rational soul is not infused into the body until the fetus has reached a certain stage of development. This opinion was commonly held for a long time; then it was more or less abandoned. However, in Kelly's reading of contemporary ethical thought, many philosophers and theologians propose once again the mediate animation theory as the more acceptable explanation of the beginning of human life. At the same time, the immediate ensoulment view has a good number of sponsors. Catholics are free to speculate on this issue because divine revelation is silent on this point, and there have been no official pronouncements which have clearly committed the Church to either theory. Theoretically both opinions may be considered tenable.[35]

The Morally Safer Course

At a speculative level, then, there is considerably less than perfect agreement among the manuals as to the quality of fetal life. It must be emphasized, however, that their theoretical differences are not in any way reflected in their practical moral approach towards the abortion decision. They are unanimous in their conclusion that abortion is immoral, and this is the view even of those authors who are unwilling to rule out the possibility of mediate animation.

Healy states that even if the fetus at some initial stage of its development does not possess a human soul, God still intends to give it its soul in the course of time and make it a human being. Therefore, even if an abortive act does not actually kill a human person, the beginnings at least of a person are destroyed which is quite different from killing a mere animal.[36] The same author classifies the immediate animation theory as the one which is "more commonly favored" by moralists. It is therefore probable, though not certain, that the object of the abortion procedure is a human being. Under these circumstances the attacker is guilty of murder in his heart, whether or not the fetus is in fact a person.[37]

With a slightly different emphasis Kelly, Fagothey, and others argue along the same line. Theoretically they consider both animation theories tenable but they point out that there remains a doubt and that this doubt revolves around a fact, the fact of animation. In such cases Catholic morality obliges us to follow the safer line of action and, therefore, we must always treat a living fertilized ovum, whatever the stage of its development, as a human person with all the rights of a person, even if it is the result of rape.[38]

III. The Principle of Double Effect

It must be emphasized that in their discussions on the morality of abortion, the American manuals are not preeminently concerned with the nature of fetal life or the fetal right to life. They devote far more attention to the medical complications of pregnancy and childbirth, and they subject these problems and the various therapeutic procedures to a medical and moral examination in the light of the principle of double effect.

Indirect and unintentional killing, or rather permission of death, is considered morally lawful in cases where there is a proportionately grave reason, such as the preservation of the life of the mother. The manuals affirm the permissibility of administering to the pregnant woman the remedies which are necessary to cure a mortal disease, such as medicinal drugs or injections, or operations on the uterus, even if these result in the abortion of the fetus.[39] Similarly, the manuals explain that in tubal pregnancies the tube itself is in a pathological condition long before it ruptures; it can be removed as a diseased organ of the human body.[40]

The manuals are at pains to remove from the lay mind the most common misconception on this subject, namely, that a Catholic doctor in a difficult obstetrical situation is obliged to save the child at the expense of the mother's life. Pointing out that an act which is intrinsically wrong is never justified and that moral evil may not be willed in order that something good may be obtained, the authors stress that there can be no direct attack either on the life of the mother or on the life of the child. Healy makes this point very strongly. The true choice, he says, lies between the following: (1) directly killing either the mother or the fetus who are both innocent human beings and (2) permitting (not causing) the death of both. He continues:

> The first, a moral evil, is immeasurably worse than the second, a merely physical evil. Hence, even considering the physician's action as a choice between two evils, it must be condemned. It is never permissible to commit a sin, a moral evil, in order to prevent any other evil, physical or moral. It is preferable by far that a million mothers and fetuses perish than that a physician stain his soul with murder.[41]

The manuals also emphasize that in cases where a difficult pregnancy endangers maternal life the fetus as the cause of this condition does not become an unjust aggressor who thereby forfeits the right to life. A fetus cannot possibly be considered as an aggressor, neither formally, because it is incapable of volition, nor materially, because its existence is not the result of its own free decision but of the voluntary act of others.[42] Nor can one claim that since the mother's life is endangered by childbearing, her right to life is prior to that of the child. Neither the mother nor the fetus has prior rights to life. They are human beings equally and they have equal rights to life. Any action which is intentionally directed against the life of either is murder.[43]

As the manuals review the possible complications of pregnancy and childbirth, they invariably arrive at the same conclusion: if in such a situation a particular therapeutic procedure cannot be justified by the principle of double effect, then there is usually an alternative solution which remedies or alleviates the problem, which is in no way opposed to ethical principles. Consequently, genuine "medical indications" for abortion are extremely rare, if there are any at all, and "therapeutic abortion" has to be rejected not only from an ethical point of view but also on medical grounds.[44] O'Donnell writes:

> Many of the standard authors in obstetrics put down various medical indications for therapeutic abortion. These are dealt with, in some detail, in the following pages.
> There is, however, an abundance of testimony of competent and well-known obstetricians attesting to the fact that even among those whose

lack of moral consciousness leads them to an unrealistic attitude toward human life, there is today practically no medical indication for therapeutic abortion which is recognized as valid.[45]

IV. The Argument of the Manuals and the Subsequent Debate

Having analysed the position of the American manuals of Catholic ethics on the morality of abortion, I must now attempt an evaluation of the constituent elements of their arguments. I will be guided by two considerations. In the first place, the traditional stand presented by these handbooks has been reviewed in the course of the subsequent Catholic debate on abortion. Naturally, this critique must be registered. Secondly, it is not sufficient to consider the traditional position merely from the point of view of Catholic theology or Catholic ethics. There is another criterion: how acceptable is this argument in a pluralistic society? Abortion is an issue which far exceeds the confines of an individual's private conscience or the moral discipline of a religious group. Anti-abortionists as well as liberationists agree that the interruption of pregnancy is a concern of society at large. Daniel Callahan has made this point as follows:

> If abortion is actually the murder of a human being (as many would argue), then it is not sufficient to convince only oneself or one's group that this is so; the practice of other individuals and other groups must be of concern also—because murder has to be the concern of all groups. But if, at the other extreme, the permission for abortion is actually an act of necessary compassion toward women in distress or a matter of justice toward their needs and rights, then any attempt by opponents of abortion to deny women such basic rights should be a moral question for everyone. Similarly, if a highly restrictive legal system tends to multiply dangerous illegal abortions, then those who help sustain such restrictions bear some responsibility for this at times murderous consequence. Those who would bring a permissive system into public acceptance would, for their part, bear some responsibility for the abortions which would then take place. One way or the other, then, what is of concern to one faction should be of concern to other factions.[46]

Any group which wants to make a genuine contribution to the solution of the abortion problem should not restrict itself to a further elaboration of its own moral insights and then proceed to enforce these in some way or other on society as a whole. If it wants to make a lasting impact to any extent at all, it will avoid as much as possible the use of parochial assumptions, and it will express its moral convictions in the largest possible number of commonly accepted values, employing a moral language which is likely to gain the widest comprehension. In the instance of abortion, purely intramural solutions are not very helpful, however valid they may be, because their appeal is limited to those who acknowledge the same value system.[47]

Theism and Teleology

Unlike most of their Catholic contemporaries, the American manuals, in the wake of St. Thomas Aquinas, make a serious attempt to describe the full dimensions of the malice of murder. Many traditional handbooks adopt an almost Nominalistic approach towards the crimes against human life and treat of these exclusively in the context of the Fifth Commandment of the Decalogue. They base the moral illicitness mainly on the divine prohibition and give insufficient prominence to other ethical dimensions of homicidal acts.[48] The American manuals, however, classify crimes against life as sins against justice which violate fundamental rights of God and man, and they stress the dignity of man who is more than a mere animal and destined to a last end. This constitutes a positive contribution to contemporary Catholic thinking on the sanctity of human life.

At the same time, the American manuals express the value of human life primarily in theistic terms. They base man's worth principally on his being owned by God, an ownership which the Creator has retained to himself. Life, therefore, is not really presented as inviolable in itself, because it is *human life*, but because the rights of God, its owner, are inviolable. Admittedly, the manuals invoke natural law to emphasize the value of human life but, again, they use the natural law argument primarily to establish God's ownership of man. It is also true that some do adduce natural law as the foundation of man's own right to life, but the concept of natural law which they employ is based on a theistic and teleological anthropology rather than on a secular and existential understanding of man.[49] It is against this background that McFadden could write:

> There is, of course, no possibility of profitably discussing the morality of direct abortion, particularly therapeutic abortion, with one who has a materialistic concept of life. The moral truth herein involved is based upon very fundamental principles of Natural Law. It follows from an accepance of the spiritual nature of man, the spiritual and eternal objective of human existence, the intrinsic morality of human actions, and the supreme dominion of God over all creatures. One who does not accept these truths cannot possibly have the same scale of values as one who does.[50]

At a later stage in the Catholic debate, Callahan would indicate the advantages of the theistic approach to the value of human life:

> The main advantage is that the foundation is laid for a theory of human life which locates man's dignity outside the evaluation of other human beings; our ultimate worth is conferred by God, not by men. Thus, in principle, the value of human life is guaranteed beyond the judgment that an erratic human evaluation might accord it, whether in the form of human laws or mores. Another advantage is that the sanctity of human life is given an ultimate grounding: in God, the creator of everything which exists. Man is not forced to create his own worth; God has, from the outset, given him value.[51]

The disadvantages, however, are equally prominent:

> One is that a considerable portion of humanity is not Christian and does not accept this foundation for the sanctity of human life. Hence, it does not readily provide a consensual norm to which all men can have recourse. Another disadvantage is that it leaves unclear the extent of man's intrinsic dignity. It seems to presuppose that, apart from God's conferral of dignity, man in his own right would be something less than valuable.[52]

A theistico-teleological anthropology describes man's dignity primarily as coming "from above" and presents man as the object of God's providence and care rather than as the architect of his own destiny. Callahan has further pointed out that a one-sided theistic approach to the inviolability of the human person can have alienating effects by "obscuring the necessity that human beings define terms, make decisions and take responsibility for the direct care of human life."[53] Naturally, such passivity is unacceptable to exponents of the secular and existential school of thought, as is the emphasis on the spiritual and eternal dimensions of man's existence on earth.

Ensoulment and the Safer Course

As we have seen, there is no unanimity among the authors with regard to the quality of fetal life, but they are generally agreed that human personhood is brought about by ensoulment which they present as a direct and additional intervention from God. Marshall has underlined the importance of the ensoulment argument for the Catholic view on abortion:

> (T)his united sperm and ovum have something more than what is contributed to the union by each. This is the soul, which is the direct creation of God at the time of conception, and which has an eternal destiny. . . .
> This view of the embryo cannot be too strongly emphasized, for the whole of Catholic ethics with regard to pregnancy depends upon it.[54]

As I have indicated, most authors do not put the case for immediate ensoulment as strongly as Marshall does. There are those who adopt a less theological approach and establish immediate hominization from biological and philosophical evidence, but it is generally felt that these arguments too are less than conclusive. Celestine N. Bittle states:

> The *exact moment* when the soul enters the fetus and makes it a human person, is obviously an important factor. Philosophically and medically, the time is unknown. It is disputed whether the rational soul enters the body at the moment of conception or at a later period.[55]

This emphasis on ensoulment is a further manifestation of the theistic and teleological character of the traditional arguments. The personhood of the fetus is based on its having a God-given spiritual soul with an eternal destiny. Again, man's dignity is expressed in extrinsic rather than intrinsic terms. Furthermore, most manuals establish a less than perfect link between the quality of fetal life and the morality of abortion. Since they have no absolute certainty that the fetus is a human person from the moment of fertilization onwards, they cannot propose the quality of fetal life as the direct determinant of the morality of the abortive act. They are forced to present the prohibition of abortion in terms of an obligation to follow the morally safer course: we do not know at which point ensoulment takes place and thus "for all practical purposes"[56] we must consider the moment of conception as the first instant of new life. Higgins has admitted quite bluntly that the traditional prohibition is basically a pragmatic one: "The morality of the problem has no relation to the dispute as to the time when the rational soul is infused into the embryo."[57]

It was to be expected that, as an argument, this combination of ensoulment and the safer course would fail to impress ethicists of a more secular and existential school of thought. One of these, Burton M. Leiser, would later charge that the traditional Catholic position is based on assumptions: it assumes that there is a rational soul and it assumes that this soul enters the embryo through a miraculous act of God. Such assumptions are unprovable by any empirical test, and many embryologists and physiologists do not believe in animation in the Catholic sense of the word.[58] Leiser also questions the argument of the morally safer course and points out that in the Catholic view

> protection of the right to life turns out to be an absolute ban on abortion, right from the moment of conception, because of our lack of certainty about the moment of animation. Even though we do not *know* when the fetus is animated, we must *act as if* it were animated at conception in order to protect what *we will assume* is human life, though we cannot be sure that it is. How does this compare to those cases in which the mother's

life is in danger? . . . (I)t would be reasonable to assume that the fetus is only a *possible* human being, whereas the mother is *certainly* a human being. Permitting the mother and the fetus to die by doing nothing may not be murder, technically speaking, but for the mother and her family the end result is the same. The refusal to save the life of a living human being, who is loved and needed by others, on such technical grounds, strikes me as being indefensible.[59]

Reasonable Limits and Exceptions

The American manuals affirm in unequivocal terms the rights of God regarding human life and man's own right to life, and in this context they often use the qualification "absolute." At the same time they admit that there are circumstances in which we may conclude that God has surrendered his rights or that man has lost his. Kenny has said it this way:

> (T)he right to life is *inviolable*. This does not mean that it can never, under any circumstances, be forfeited. Such a right would not be in harmony with the wisdom of God. On the contrary, it implies that the right to life is inviolable *within certain reasonable limits*. Within these limitations the right is sacred; otherwise it is no right at all. Beyond these limits, the inviolability in some instances ceases to exist. Man may not take the life of another person, nor may his own right to life be violated, except in those cases where it is lawfully conceded by God.[60]

By their recognition of certain "reasonable" limits, the manuals admit the rational factor into the life or death decision. God's dominion over life may not be touched but this applies only to *innocent* human life. An innocent man has an absolute right to life; no one may ever kill him *directly*. Indeed, the rights of God and man are absolute but they are interpreted by reason. It is mainly a judgement of reason which tells us that God has renounced his rights over guilty human life and that indirect killing under certain circumstances is permissible. The principle of double effect is a construction of human logic, a product of man's rational faculties, and it is for man to ascertain whether the conditions for its application are verified in a particular situation. The determination of what constitutes "a proportionally grave reason" and the distinction between "guilty" and "innocent," and between "just aggression" and "unjust aggression" must necessarily be the outcome of a rational judgement on the part of the individual or the community. Apparently it is up to man to decide whether in a particular set of circumstances God has surrendered his rights and the individual has forfeited his. In any case, the absoluteness allows for exceptions and, as far as innocent human life is concerned, the principle of double effect indicates the "reasonable" limits of human intervention.[61]

The subsequent American debate has questioned the reasonableness of the limits set by this principle. Secular ethicists have characterized the traditional distinction between direct and indirect abortion as ''specious'' and have opted for an approach which takes into consideration ''the total spectrum of goods and evils that are involved in the concrete case.''[62] Arguing from a Catholic perspective Bernard J. Ransil has discovered a justification for this new moral methodology in the principle of double effect itself. He appreciates this principle because of its realism: it is based on a recognition that there are multi-valued moral situations, i.e., complex situations which involve more than one moral value or norm. Furthermore, the principle ''sets a very useful precedent'' because it represents a serious speculative attempt to cope with such cases: ''it offers one solution—not necessarily the best one—for handling them.''[63] The principle opens the door for a new Catholic moral approach.[64]

The Secularization of the Catholic Position

The arguments which have been listed and analysed in the foregoing pages represent the ethical thinking of the American Catholic Church on abortion until the early 1960s when the American Law Institute published its *Model Penal Code*. An examination of the Catholic literature which was produced in the course of the ensuing nationwide debate reveals that the presentation of the Catholic stand underwent a drastic change. The position itself, at least initially, remained the same and its new formulation was not an outcome of new ethical attitudes or insights. The Church became aware that the abortion issue could no longer be argued in terms of ''parochial assumptions'' and ''intramural solutions and value systems,''[65] with little relevance to the secular mind.

The theistic and teleological approach towards the value of human life and the quality of fetal life was gradually abandoned and only survived, as was right, in the individual and joint statements issued by the American bishops in the context of the national debate. The bishops said in their official pronouncement on the 1973 Supreme Court decision:

> The basic human rights guaranteed by our American laws are . . . unalien-able because their source is not man-made legislation but the Creator of all mankind, Almighty God. No right is more fundamental than the right to life itself and no innocent human life already begun can be deliberately terminated without offense to the Author of all life. Thus, there can be no moral acceptance of the recent United States Supreme Court decision which professes to legalize abortion.[66]

But even the official pronouncements of the hierarchical authorities did not restrict themselves to considerations of Catholic theology and employed a variety of other arguments of a more secular nature, as I will show in the following chapter. Catholic theologians, as was to be expected, abandoned the criterion of ensoulment and gave less prominence to the pragmatic policy procedure of the morally safer course. The latter was perpetuated in the *New Catholic Encyclopedia:*

> After a certain stage of intrauterine development it is perfectly evident that fetal life is fully human. Although some might speculate as to when that stage is reached, there is no way of arriving at this knowledge by any known criterion; and as long as it is probable that embryonic life is human from the first moment of its existence, the purposeful termination of any pregnancy contains the moral malice of the violation of man's most fundamental human right—the right to life itself.[67]

In the course of the nationwide political debate which followed the ALI proposals, Catholic theology searched for a new argument, an argument attuned to the requirements of the political arena. The manuals had concentrated on God. The new argument turned to man.

NOTES

[1] *Summa Theologica*, II-II, qq. 64-65.
[2] John A. McHugh, O.P., and Charles J. Callan, O.P., *Moral Theology: A Complete Course. Based on St. Thomas Aquinas and the Best Modern Authorities;* revised and enlarged edition by Edward P. Farrell, O.P. (vols. I-II; New York City: Joseph F. Wagner, 1958); vol. II, p. 30.
[3] *Ibid.*, p. 63.
[4] *Ibid.*, p. 98.
[5] *Ibid.*, p. 98.
[6] *Ibid.*, p. 98.
[7] *Ibid.*, pp. 99-100; Edwin F. Healy, S.J., *Moral Guidance: A Textbook in Principles of Conduct for Colleges and Universities* (Chicago: Loyola University Press, 1942), pp. 167-170, 175-177.
[8] McHugh and Callan, *op. cit.*, p. 112; John P. Kenny, O.P., *Principles of Medical Ethics* (2nd ed.; Westminster, Maryland: Newman Press, 1962), pp. 5-6.
[9] Gerald Kelly, S.J., *Medico-Moral Problems* (St. Louis: The Catholic Hospital Association of the United States and Canada, 1958), p. 5.
[10] McHugh and Callan, *op. cit.*, pp. 112-113; Edwin F. Healy, S.J., *Medical Ethics* (Chicago: Loyola University Press, 1956), p. 10; Kenny, *op. cit.*, p. 129.
[11] Thomas J. O'Donnell, S.J., *Morals in Medicine* (2nd ed.; Westminster, Maryland: Newman Press, 1959), p. 155. See also: McHugh and Callan, *op. cit.*, p. 112; Thomas J. Higgins, S.J., *Man as Man: The Science and Art of Ethics* (Milwaukee: Bruce, 1949), p. 252.
[12] Kenny, *op. cit.*, p. 128; Charles J. McFadden, O.S.A., *Medical Ethics* (3rd ed.; Philadelphia: Davis, 1953), p. 172; Healy, *Moral Guidance, op. cit.*, p. 155.

[13] Kenny, *op. cit.*, p. 115; O'Donnell, *op. cit.*, p. 55. Therefore God could command the death of an innocent person, as he did when he bade Abraham to sacrifice his son (Gen. 22. 2). See: McHugh and Callan, *op. cit.*, p. 112.

[14] Ex. 20. 13; 23. 7; Gen. 9. 5-6; McHugh and Callan, *op. cit.*, pp. 112-113; Healy, *Moral Guidance, op. cit.*, pp. 170-171.

[15] Austin Fagothey, S.J., *Right and Reason: Ethics in Theory and Practice* (3rd ed.; Saint Louis: C.V. Mosby, 1963), pp. 237, 239-240; Augustine J. Osgniach, O.S.B., *The Christian State* (Milwaukee: Bruce, 1943), pp. 209-210. The relationship between eternal law and natural law will be explained in Chapter VI.

[16] Celestine N. Bittle, O.F.M.Cap., *Man and Morals: Ethics* (Milwaukee: Bruce, 1950), pp. 368, 374; Kelly, *op. cit.*, p. 5.

[17] Lev. 24. 17; Healy, *Moral Guidance, op. cit.*, p. 167; Osgniach, *op. cit.*, p. 214; Fagothey, *op. cit.*, pp. 348-349.

[18] McHugh and Callan, *op. cit.*, p. 113; Joseph B. McAllister, *Ethics: With Special Application to the Medical and Nursing Professions* (2nd ed.; Philadelphia: W.B. Saunders, 1955), p. 216; Kenny, *op. cit.*, pp. 114, 129.

[19] Healy, *Moral Guidance, op. cit.*, p. 154.

[20] *Ibid.*, p. 168; Fagothey, *op. cit.*, pp. 244-249. Opinions are divided as to whether the killing of an unjust aggressor is direct or indirect; Fagothey, *op. cit.*, pp. 246-247.

[21] McHugh and Callan, *op. cit.*, p. 113; Kenny, *op. cit.*, p. 129; Healy, *Medical Ethics, op. cit.*, p. 10.

[22] McFadden, *op. cit.*, p. 167.

[23] O'Donnell, *op. cit.*, p. 155.

[24] Fagothey, *op. cit.*, p. 241; Higgins, *op. cit.*, pp. 253-254; Healy, *Moral Guidance, op. cit.*, p. 173.

[25] John Marshall, *Medicine and Morals;* Twentieth Century Encyclopedia of Catholicism, vol. 129 (New York: Hawthorn Books, 1960), pp. 29-30.

[26] *Ibid.*, p. 78. McFadden simply states that the science of ethics regards the fetus as a human person from the very outset of pregnancy; *op cit.*, p. 167.

[27] Marshall, *op. cit.*, p. 79. McFadden agrees that biology regards the fetus as a human being from conception but he does not support this statement with any explanations; *op. cit.*, p. 167.

[28] McAllister, *op. cit.*, p. 223.

[29] Healy, *Medical Ethics, op. cit.*, pp. 193-194. McFadden simply says that church law as well as civil law considers the fetus a person from the moment of conception; *op. cit.*, p. 167.

[30] McAllister, *op. cit.*, p. 223.

[31] Healy, *Medical Ethics, op. cit.*, pp. 191-192; emphasis supplied.

[32] Higgins, *op. cit.*, p. 254. See also: O'Donnell, *op. cit.*, pp. 7, 308.

[33] Kenny, *op. cit.*, p. 185; see also p. 195.

[34] Healy, *Medical Ethics, op. cit.*, p. 192.

[35] Kelly, *op. cit.*, p. 66. See also: McHugh and Callan, *op. cit.*, pp. 115-116; Fagothey, *op. cit.*, pp. 241-242; Bittle, *op. cit.*, p. 327. Kelly grants, however, that the contemporary teaching of the Church favors immediate animation; *op. cit.*, p. 67.

[36] Healy, *Medical Ethics, op. cit.*, p. 192.

[37] *Ibid.*, p. 193.

[38] Kelly, *op. cit.*, pp. 66-67; McHugh and Callan, *op. cit.*, pp. 115-116; Fagothey, *op. cit.*, pp. 241-242; Bittle, *op. cit.*, p. 372. The authors consider that in this case there is no "dubium iuris" or doubt about the existence of the law: one is not allowed to kill an

innocent human being. The doubt extends only to the fact of animation or personhood ("dubium facti"). Probabilism and the other traditional moral systems (i.e., methods of arriving at moral certainty from a state of practical doubt) can only be applied in cases of "dubium iuris." If the doubt concerns a fact, the morally safer course must be followed. See: H. Noldin, S.J., and A. Schmitt, S.J., *Summa Theologiae Moralis;* 33rd edition by Godefridus Heinzel, S.J. (vols. I-III; Innsbruck: Felizian Rauch, 1961); vol. I, pp. 219-220.

[39] O'Donnell, *op. cit.*, pp. 153-154, 226-227; Healy, *Moral Guidance, op. cit.*, pp. 173-174; *id.*, *Medical Ethics, op. cit.*, pp. 184-185; McFadden, *op. cit.*, pp. 168, 217-218; Higgins, *op. cit.*, p. 255.

[40] McHugh and Callan, *op. cit.*, p. 116; Francis J. Connell, C.SS.R., *Morals in Politics and Professions: A Guide for Catholics in Public Life* (Westminster, Maryland: Newman Press, 1955), p. 118.

[41] Healy, *Medical Ethics, op. cit.*, p. 196. See also: McFadden, *op. cit.*, p. 168; Higgins, *op. cit.*, p. 255.

[42] Higgins, *op. cit.*, pp. 254-255; Fagothey, *op. cit.*, p. 244. This definition of material aggression is unsatisfactory. I will discuss "aggression" by the fetus in Chapter X.

[43] Higgins, *op. cit.*, p. 255; Fagothey, *op. cit.*, pp. 243-244; Frederick L. Good and Otis F. Kelly, *Marriage, Morals and Medical Ethics* (New York: P. J. Kenedy, 1951), pp. 22-26.

[44] O'Donnell, *op. cit.*, pp. 153-235; Healy, *Medical Ethics, op. cit.*, pp. 185-285; Kelly, *op. cit.*, pp. 84-114; McFadden, *op. cit.*, pp. 184-249.

[45] O'Donnell, *op. cit.*, p. 159. See also: *ibid.*, pp. 219-226; McFadden, *op. cit.*, pp. 169-171; Kelly, *op. cit.*, pp. 75-83; Healy, *Medical Ethics, op. cit.*, pp. 196-203. Healy also rejects social indications and refers to the dangers inherent in the abortion procedure; *ibid.*, pp. 202-204. McFadden rejects socio-economic indications; *op. cit.*, p. 168.

[46] Daniel Callahan, *Abortion: Law, Choice and Morality* (New York: Macmillan, 1970), pp. 14-15.

[47] *Ibid.*, p. 15; Francis Simons, "The Catholic Church and the New Morality," *Cross Currents* 16 (1966), p. 429.

[48] See, for instance, Noldin and Schmitt, *op. cit.*, vol. II, pp. 290-325.

[49] I will elaborate this in Chapter VI.

[50] McFadden, *op. cit.*, pp. 164-165.

[51] Callahan, *op. cit.*, pp. 312-313. See also: *ibid.*, pp. 315, 316; Claude U. Broach (ed.), *Seminar on Abortion: The Proceedings of a Dialogue Between Catholics and Baptists* (Charlotte, N.C.: The Ecumenical Institute, 1975), p. 23.

[52] Callahan, *op. cit.*, p. 313. See also: Amitai Etzioni, *Genetic Fix* (New York: Macmillan, 1973), pp. 40-41. Writing from a Methodist perspective, Stanley Hauerwas affirms the relevance of a specifically Christian discourse on abortion and argues that Christians should not accept too easily the level of discussion offered by society; "Abortion: Why the Arguments Fail," in James T. Burtchaell, C.S.C. (ed.), *Abortion Parley: Papers Delivered at the National Conference on Abortion Held at the University of Notre Dame in October 1979* (Kansas City: Andrews and McMeel, 1980), pp. 325-352.

[53] Callahan, *op. cit.*, p. 417. See also: *ibid.*, pp. 311-312; Robert H. Springer, S.J., "Notes on Moral Theology," *Theological Studies* 32 (1971), p. 486. Marvin Kohl, an American secular ethicist, makes virtually the same observation; *The Morality of Killing: Sanctity of Life, Abortion and Euthanasia* (London: Peter Owen, 1974), pp. 4-6.

[54] Marshall, *op. cit.*, p. 78.

[55] Bittle, *op. cit.*, p. 372.

[56] Fagothey, *op. cit.*, p. 242.

[57] Higgins, *op. cit.*, p. 254. See also: Connell, *op. cit.*, p. 118.

[58] Burton M. Leiser, *Liberty, Justice and Morals: Contemporary Value Conflicts* (New York: Macmillan, 1973), p. 103. See also: Garth L. Hallett, S.J., "The Plain Meaning of Abortion," *America* 124 (1971), pp. 632-633; Gary M. Atkinson, "The Morality of Abortion," *International Philosophical Quarterly* 14 (1974), p. 348.

[59] Leiser, *op. cit.*, pp. 103-104.

[60] Kenny, *op. cit.*, pp. 115-116; second emphasis supplied. See also: Fagothey, *op. cit.*, p. 211.

[61] Robert H. Springer, S.J., "Notes on Moral Theology," *Theological Studies* 31 (1970), pp. 492-493. The principle of double effect does not always lead to unanimous conclusions. Both O'Donnell and McFadden discuss puncture of the fetal sac in hydramnios; McFadden holds that this is a forbidden direct attack on the fetus, O'Donnell concludes that it is indirect and therefore permitted; O'Donnell, *op. cit.*, pp. 183-190; McFadden, *op. cit.*, pp. 172-176.

[62] Harry W. Rudel *et al.*, *Birth Control: Contraception and Abortion* (New York: Macmillan, 1973), p. 295.

[63] Bernard J. Ransil, *Abortion* (Paramus, N.J.: Paulist Press Deus Books, 1969), p. 60.

[64] Callahan, *op. cit.*, pp. 422-424, 426.

[65] *Ibid.*, p. 15.

[66] "Pastoral Message of the Administrative Committee, National Conference of Catholic Bishops," in Daughters of St. Paul (eds.), *Yes to Life* (Boston: St. Paul Editions, 1977), p. 262. See also: "Collective Pastoral Letter: Human Life in Our Day—November 15, 1968," *ibid.*, p. 201; Joseph T. Mangan, S.J., "The Wonder of Myself: Ethical-Theological Aspects of Direct Abortion," *Theological Studies* 31 (1970), pp. 125-127, 134-140; Kevin D. O'Rourke, O.P., "Because the Lord Loved You," *Hospital Progress* 54, August 1973, pp. 73-77.

[67] Thomas J. O'Donnell, S.J., "Abortion, II (Moral Aspect)," in *New Catholic Encyclopedia* (New York: McGraw-Hill, 1967); vol. 1, p. 29. See also: *id.*, "A Traditional Catholic's View," in Robert E. Hall (ed.), *Abortion in a Changing World: The Proceedings of an International Conference Convened in Hot Springs, Virginia, November 17-20, 1968, by the Associaton for the Study of Abortion* (vols. I-II; New York: Columbia University Press, 1970); vol. I, pp. 37-38; Richard A. McCormick, S.J., "Abortion," *America* 112 (1965), pp. 877, 879; Paul V. Harrington, "Abortion," *Linacre Quarterly* 33 (1966), pp. 166-167; 35 (1968), p. 133; 37 (1970), p. 272. Several authors have questioned the validity of the ensoulment criterion. See: Ransil, *op cit.*, pp. 65-70; Leonard F.X. Mayhew, "Abortion: Two Sides and Some Complaints," *Ecumenist* 5, July-August 1967, pp. 75-76; Albert R. di Ianni, S.M., "Is the Fetus a Person?" *American Ecclesiastical Review* 168 (1974), pp. 323-324, footnote 6. The 1974 *Declaration on Procured Abortion* by the Vatican's Sacred Congregation for the Doctrine of the Faith argues that ensoulment is not a morally decisive factor in the abortion decision and this for two reasons: "(1) supposing a belated animation, there is still nothing less than a *human* life, preparing for and calling for a soul in which the nature received from parents is completed; (2) on the other hand, it suffices that this presence of the soul be probable (and one can never prove the contrary) in order that the taking of life involve accepting the risk of killing a man, not only waiting for, but already in possession of his soul." See: Daughters of St. Paul, *op cit.*, p. 81, footnote 19.

Chapter Three

The Empirical Argument:
The Evidence of Embryology,
Genetics, and Medicine

The ideologists of the abortion reform movement often accuse the Catholic Church and other opponents of trying to impose a sectarian morality on society at large.[1] Having analysed the traditional Catholic assessment of the value of the human person and the nature of unborn human life, we cannot but agree that this charge is justified as far as the Church's original proposition is concerned, which indeed relied on intramural concepts and values. In this chapter I will present the efforts of American Catholic ethical thinking to construct a nonsectarian argument on the quality of fetal life and to formulate its traditional moral attitude in less parochial terms to meet the requirements of the secular political debate.

After the publication of the ALI *Model Penal Code,* the Catholic contribution to the abortion debate underwent a significant change. The approach of the manuals was abandoned, and the arguments no longer concentrated on God's ownership of the human person and the ensoulment of the fetus. Instead, the Church turned towards the empirical life sciences. It is from these that it derived support for its continued opposition to direct abortion. This new emphasis is clearly reflected in hierarchical pronouncements. The bishops of Maryland stated in 1968:

> Direct voluntary abortion of a non-viable human fetus is a grave evil. Modern microbiology has shown that there is no qualitative or essential difference between the fetus at the time of conception and the adult human person. To fix a point after conception for attributing the dignity of humanity to a human fetus is both arbitrary and without scientific foundation. Voluntary abortion is, therefore, an assault upon the life of an innocent human person that is not essentially different from any other willful destruction of an innocent human life.[2]

A year later the bishops of Illinois expressed their opposition to abortion and to liberal abortion laws in a similar fashion:

> (T)he Church affirms that human life begins at the time of conception, and that from that time the fetus has the rights of a human person and that

48

its basic right to life may never be superseded by the rights of another. . . .

Science proclaims that human life begins at the time of conception. An authoritative statement of this fact may be found in the published report of the International Conference on Abortion sponsored by the Harvard Divinity School and the Kennedy Foundation in late 1967. At this conference it was agreed that the medical, genetic and microbiological evidence all points to the presence of the human person from the time of conception.[3]

A similar trend is clearly discernible in non-hierarchical writings. Catholic periodicals and reviews of the late 1960s and early 1970s abound with articles by members of the medical profession who point out that the recent findings of the various bio-medical disciplines leave no option regarding the evaluation of fetal life. An active proponent of the new empirical argument is Eugene F. Diamond who wrote in 1967:

Recent genetic advances certainly do not support the notion that the embryo lacks any essential quality of human life. From conception, the zygote has a genetic code in the DNA structure which is unique, determinative and complete. There is no scientific support for the notion that the fetus passes through a sub-human stage before qualifying for humanity. If a fetus is not a human being, what is it?[4]

Not only genotypically but also phenotypically the scientic evidence points to the fetus as being a person. Diamond writes in a later publication:

To consider the fetus not to be a separate person but merely a part of the mother has not been tenable since the sixteenth century when Arantius showed that the maternal and fetal circulations were separate—neither continuous nor contiguous. . . Once implanted, [the separate human embryo] requires only time and nutrition. Only two possible futures are open to it. It can become a live human being or a dead human fetus.[5]

Admittedly, the empirical approach was not completely new: we discovered the hesitant beginnings of it in the manuals of John Marshall, Charles J. McFadden, Joseph B. McAllister, Edwin F. Healy, and Thomas J. Higgins. These authors, however, presented the biological evidence as helpful but less than conclusive, and they employed it primarily to support the immediate animation view. At the present stage of the debate the empirical argument is proposed with much greater emphasis, and many authors consider the bio-medical evidence conclusive with regard to the personality of the fetus. At the same time they no longer relate the scientific data to fetal ensoulment.

I. The Empirical Analysis of Fetal Development

There is no need to list in detail the multitudinous bio-medical assertions that Catholic authors have made regarding the genesis of a human individual; many merely state the obvious or beg the question. Thus it is observed that fetal life is life,[6] that it is life belonging to the human species,[7] that if left to its own devices it will develop into a mature adult,[8] and that from a very early stage it has distinctively human features which include sensory and motoric characteristics.[9] The more relevant thrust of the argument is directed towards ascertaining the *individuality* of fetal life, and this is affirmed in terms of functional independence, genetic self-determination, and biological continuity from the moment of conception.

Embryology and the Phenotype

Considering the fetus phenotypically, Catholic authors indicate the process of fertilization as constitutive of fetal individuality. At fertilization, or conception, the individuality of the progeny is established in relation to the parents. While the sperm and ovum may be considered part of those in whom they originate, it is clear that parental ownership is terminated at the zygote stage. The unicellular organism which is the result of the unification of the mature parental sex cells manifests life of a new order which can no longer be identified with either of its components. The sperm and ovum have a unique but limited function which is reproduction. If this function is not exercised, they inevitably and rapidly die. The zygote, on the other hand, is geared towards cellular cleavage, sequential differentiation, and growth.[10] It has an inner anthropo-teleological orientation which reveals itself in a strikingly coherent organization at every step along the way to adult maturity. Every later event is dependent upon earlier events.[11]

The phenotype's structural development is impressive in its size and complexity. The one-celled zygote extends by cleavage into an organism with trillions of cells weighing approximately six billion times more than the fertilized ovum. By differentiation these innumerable cells specialize as muscle, nerve, bone, digestive, respiratory, excretory, circulatory, and sex cells. The cells will form tissues and the tissues will develop into organs and organ systems, vital parts of the living organism.[12] The goal-oriented inner mechanism of the fetus organizes this extensive, complex, and rapid development which follows a strict timetable regulating the progress of each organ in accordance with the requirements of the overall growth process.[13]

On these premises, Catholic authors argue that from the moment of conception there is a gradual, continuous, and consistent development which derives from the fetus itself and which is directed towards the mature adult person. From the very outset of pregnancy, the zygote and each subsequent cell of the growing organism are geared to, and contribute towards, the ultimate thinking, willing, feeling, mature creature that we call adult man. This is a continuous process in which one phase merges into another without any real point of demarcation. Implantation and viability are important stages in fetal development but they are no more than that; they cannot be adopted as criteria of personhood.[14]

In the context of such phenotypical observations, Catholic authors usually disprove some popular misconceptions:

1. The fetus may be dependent on the mother but it is not part of the mother. While nutrition is administered through the infant's placenta which constitutes the vital point of contact between fetal and maternal life, it is evident from the very structure of this organ that the child's biological status is one of "essential independence of the mother in the context of a temporary dependence."[15] The placenta which derives from both mother and embryo is functionally a blood pool in which a biochemical exchange takes place between the mother's bloodstream and that of the child to cater for fetal nutrition, respiration, excretion, and various forms of protection. The permeability of the membranes which divide mother and fetus allows their bloodstreams to interact but keeps them apart so that there is no direct contact or intermingling of blood.[16] The phenotype is an independently functioning unit with its separate principle of growth and development, its own nervous system, blood circulation, skeleton, musculature, brain, heart, and vital organs. All it needs is shelter, nutrition, and time.[17] Furthermore, if the fetus is merely a "part" of the mother's body it is certainly a very unusual part, for no other part of her body becomes a human being in its own right.[18]

2. The fetus cannot be considered a parasite of the maternal organism. From a scientific point of view this comparison is unsound because a true parasite differs in species from the host organism which it harmfully invades. In its early stages the fetus does not have its own system of organs, and it necessarily relies on the maternal system which it uses indirectly. But it is not a parasite because there is no question of a harmful presence and the fetus, while being individually distinct from the mother, belongs to the same human species. Their relationship is symbiotic, not parasitic.[19]

3. Equally objectionable are comparisons which equate the fetus with an acorn and merely grant it some dormant potential. Such statements are "biologically fallacious"[20] because—as is the case with most seeds—the acorn represents an inactive phase in the reproduction process of the mother plant. Human procreation admits of no such stage.[21]

4. To take quickening as the stage at which the fetus achieves personhood is subjective and archaic since this phenomenon is related to the
woman's physiological and psychological sensitivity to the activity of the
baby in her womb. The child is actually stirring long before the mother
becomes aware of its movements.[22]

5. Nor is viability acceptable as the standard of personhood:

(a) Viability is not an exact criterion. There is considerable elasticity in
the range of viability which depends on the degree of anatomical and
functional development rather than on age. The pace of this development is not the same in all fetuses. Moreover, viability differs with
race. If viability would be the norm, the standard for humanity and
for abortion would vary with color and with other individual characteristics.[23]

(b) Viability does not terminate the fetus' dependence on the mother.
Even after normal parturition, an infant is incapable of survival
without the assistance of a mother who undertakes the responsibility
of feeding, clothing, and protecting it. Uncared for, the viable fetus
and the young infant will die as surely as the nonviable fetus which is
detached from its mother.[24]

(c) In view of recent technological advances, the twenty-week surviv-
ability limit is about as sacred as the four-minute mile. With the
development of an effective artificial placenta even the twelve-week
fetus may survive to become a mature adult.[25]

6. Birth is a dramatic moment in the life of man but, in fact, it is no more
than a bridge between intrauterine and extrauterine existence. It is not a
fixed event because the child is viable for a number of weeks before it is
born and, during this period, it can survive premature birth or surgical
removal from the womb. Birth, therefore, has as little factual relevance to
the personhood of the fetus as has viability. It reflects a geographic rather
than a developmental change.[26]

Genetic Physiology and the Genotype

Under this heading the Catholic empirical argument establishes once
again the individuality of the fetus in relation to its parents. Genetically, the
zygote disconnects itself from its parents as soon as it is formed. It is
unified in its own character and distinct from theirs since it derives half its
genetic inheritance from each. Its combination of genes is not possessed by
either parent alone.[27]

Cleavage is the first function of the zygote, which it achieves rapidly and
repeatedly. Each daughter cell, although smaller, reduplicates the gene
structure of the original cell. When the mature body has been formed, all its

cells possess that same structure.[28] The unicellular zygote contains the complete genetic code of the future adult, and this includes not only sex but the whole spectrum of human traits, both external and internal, organic and functional: physique, intellectual capacity, temperament, the color of the eyes, skin and hair, and so on.[29] Recent discoveries of biology have designated deoxyribonucleic acid (DNA), which is found exclusively in the chromosomes, as the genetic material, the plasma of life. Its giant molecules contain the full spectrum of encoded instructions for the formation of the phenotype and by cell division these instructions are reduplicated. Thus we can assert that the complexity of the mature adult body is substantially present in the zygote and that the zygote accommodates the individual's definite hereditary endowment.[30] Fertilization, therefore, marks the point of departure of an ineluctably forward-moving continuity which lasts until death. This continuity is basically self-sufficient: no essential human element is added from outside.[31]

The authors emphasize that even the early embryo cannot be considered a mere piece of maternal tissue. From the very beginning the fetus has an entirely different potential. Moreover, there is a genetic incompatibility between the tissue of the mother and that of her offspring, and the child would be rejected by the mother's body if it were not enclosed in the amniotic sac.[32] Nor can the value of the zygote be equated with that of a set of blueprints for a particular structure. Unlike the blueprints of a house, the zygote is alive and autodynamic. It is in continuous and vital contact with the end product, the mature individual, while blueprints are merely an external point of reference for the builders, disposable when the house is finished.[33] On the whole, then, the Catholic argument would readily subscribe to Daniel Callahan's reading of the morphological and genetic data:

> Throughout the process of development, the conceptus is an entity which, while dependent upon the woman for nourishment, is independent as discrete being. It possesses its own genetic dynamism of development and growth, its own organs, circulatory system and metabolic processes. Its genotype and phenotype are distinct from those of the woman. It is its own source of unity, organic coherence and genetically programmed development.[34]

II. The Philosophical Interpretation

The Fetus: Definitely a Human Person

When they come to their philosophical interpretation of these data and to their assessment of the status of the unborn child, most Catholic authors express themselves in favor of a "straight-forward acceptance of biological realities."[35] Thus they base their evaluation of fetal life on the empirical observation that, at conception, a living and human continuity arises which is terminated only by death. This human organism is characterized by wholeness and purposefulness, by structural perfection and regulatory mechanisms.[36] If the growth and development of the human conceptus follows such a constant and consistent sequential pattern, then one must conclude that there is no particular moment in that process which marks the transformation of a nonhuman entity into a human being.[37] Certain signs can be observed in the continuous transition from zygote to adult but none of these constitutes a point in development where the biological form and function of the human individual are suddenly added.[38]

The criterion of personhood, therefore, is an objective one. It is derived from biology and it is verified at conception: from the very beginning the fetus is individual human life, a human being, a human person. John T. Noonan, Jr., formulates this position as follows:

> The positive argument for conception as the decisive moment of humanization is that at conception the new being receives the genetic code. It is this genetic information which determines his characteristics, which is the biological carrier of the possibility of human wisdom, which makes him a self-evolving being. A being with a human genetic code is man.[39]

Emphasizing the need of an objective evaluation of unborn human life, many authors refer to other, "subjective" standards of personhood and point out that such criteria are illogical and have dangerous implications:

1. *Consciousness and experience.* Some proponents of liberalization claim that the fetus represents "unformed humanity" because it lacks consciousness, rationality, and self-determination, or because it has not accumulated experience: it has not lived and suffered and it has no memories.[40] But such statements are only partly correct and, in any case, consciousness and "formative experience" are not valid standards of personhood:

(a) Even at the zygote stage the fetus is alive and responds to its environment. It reacts to touch after eight weeks and at least at that point is experiencing at a sensory level.[41]

(b) If consciousness or certain central experiences such as learning or loving are necessary for one to qualify as man, then human beings who are unconscious or who have failed to love or to learn should logically be excluded from humanity: the older fetus, the younger child, the gravely retarded, the insane, the patient in coma. Likewise, the experiential criterion becomes problematic in the event that amnesia has erased adult memory: has it also erased humanity?[42]

(c) The criterion of consciousness reflects an outdated Cartesian dualism which classifies body and mind as separate entities and identifies man's nature exclusively with rationality. Moreover, the refusal to recognize the fetus' claim to human nature on the ground that it lacks self-determination betrays the influence of Sartrean existentialism which equates humanity with freedom.[43]

2. *Social perception.* Admittedly, the human conceptus is not an individual with whom an adult readily identifies himself, especially in the early stages of its development. Parental grief over a miscarriage is limited. The child's presence is not really perceived until quickening occurs in the fourth month of pregnancy and it remains an anonymous "it" until birth. We find it much easier to sympathize with a woman who begs for an abortion or who has been injured in a clandestine abortion than with an unseen fetus.[44] Yet there is no justification for making the quality of unborn human life contingent on the sensory perception or the emotional response of parents or of society at large:

(a) Human sentiment is a notoriously unreliable index of the dignity of others. Many communities have experienced difficulties in feeling that persons of a different color, creed, language, or sex were truly human.[45]

(b) We mourn the death of an adolescent more than the loss of his baby brother or of his old grandfather but this does not point to any substantial difference in the humanity of baby, boy, and octogenarian.[46]

(c) Sight is even more untrustworthy than feeling in determining humanity. By sight, color became an acceptable criterion for saying who was man. Minorities of various kinds exist today who are "invisible," such as those in prisons and mental institutions who are out of sight. These minorities are often not recognized as fellow-humans by the society with which they have "lost touch."[47]

(d) Perception of the fetus requires no greater effort than that which is needed to penetrate physical and psychological barriers in recognition of other human beings. The main problem is that this perception demands a follow-up in the form of personal response and personal attention. Society therefore seeks to limit to a minimum the number of those who are entitled to its protection and care, and this lack of generosity restricts the scope of its perception to a convenient group.[48]

(e) The reluctance to perceive the fetus as man reflects the influence of empiricism which does not recognize the existence of reality and truth beyond the finite range of sense observation. A similar bias has affected the entire field of medicine. Historically, the medicine of adults preceded the medicine of the infant, the neonate, and the fetus. This created a tendency in the medical profession to take adult life as the point of departure and then work backwards. Thus the fetus and the newborn are treated as underdeveloped adults rather than as well-developed babies.[49]

3. *Social acceptance.* Some exponents of the abortion reform movement are reluctant to accept a definition of man on the basis of individualistic biological phenomena alone. They stress the importance of human relationships and suggest a more "personalistic" criterion for the beginning of human life in the form of the relation of recognition and acceptance by the parents and by society:[50]

(a) Although the existence of society answers a natural human need, it has no substantial being because it owes its origin to agreement or convention. Man does have substantial being. He precedes society in actual existence and society exists for his benefit. Definitions of human life which concentrate on acceptance by the community lack a substantial basis in reality. Acceptance by society follows a real event in the objective order—conception by a man and a woman—no matter how imperfect and halting the recognition.[51]

(b) If one employs a relational criterion to determine the quality of life, there seems to be little logic in applying this only to life before birth. After birth the relationship between the child and its parents could so deteriorate that one could judge that the baby did not enjoy enough acceptance to qualify as a truly human being.[52]

(c) The relational criterion which is proposed has an inherent inconsistency. Truly human relations are mutual and thus it should be argued that the child has to be able to recognize and acknowledge the acceptance of the parents before there is a genuinely human relationship present.[53]

(d) Criteria which are suggested for determining the beginning of human life must be in conformity with the standards acceptable for establishing the end of human life, the time of death. At present all definitions of death and tests for the presence of death are based on an individualistic understanding of man and concentrate on physical or biological phenomena. There would seem to be great problems in introducing a criterion which declares that death has ocurred when the patient is outside the range of human relationships.[54]

(e) Admittedly, relationality is important to man, and the fetus obviously does not represent human life in its fullest actuality. At the same time the fetus does fulfil the minimum conditions which are required for human existence. It is an individual human being and it enters into relationships with others in the course of its growth and development.[55]

(f) If humanity depends on social recognition, individuals or whole groups may be dehumanized by being denied any status in society. This has actually happened to many men in many societies: slaves, prisoners, the alien, the heterodox.[56]

4. *Social functioning*. This criterion describes personhood in terms of social involvement and social value. In order to qualify as a human being one must do something or be capable of doing something that will enhance the welfare of society. Humanity is an achievement, not an endowment, and the fetus only becomes human when it begins to function in the human socialization process:[57]

(a) Humanization is not brought about by an extrinsic agent, assembling already existing components or injecting social personality into sub-human raw material. Man realizes his potential by self-actuation and in a process of give-and-take with society. This process begins when the embryo causes the mother to miss her menstrual period and learn of her new status. Man develops with the help of society, not by the power of society.[58]

(b) The fetus becomes socially active and socially involved immediately after conception because it develops by interaction with the maternal organism. These early biological communications mark the beginning of the individual's social functioning.[59]

(c) Human life is an unfolding process rather than a finished product. A human being has a variety of abilities, some of which are lost as he grows older; the "social functioning" of the earlier stages gives way to a different mode of socialization in later life. The earliest years of our lives are not necessarily the best ones but we should not embellish the "functional humanity" of the adult to such an extent that we deprive his infancy and his life before birth of all human quality.[60]

(d) This criterion reduces the unborn to mere objects whose meaning and value depend on what their parents think of them. It opens the door not only to abortion but also to infanticide, and it implies that those who regard themselves as humanized and socialized would be justified in doing away with any group they did not consider "functionally human."[61]

5. *Independence*. This criterion questions the humanity of the fetus on the ground that it depends on the mother for survival:[62]

(a) Strictly speaking, the unborn child is not dependent on the mother. The viable fetus is independent to the same extent that a newborn child is . After the development of an artificial placenta, even the early conceptus will be potentially independent at any stage and could be saved at any time should the mother die.[63]

(b) The appeal to the fetus' dependence in order to justify abortion is a massive *non sequitur*. The commonly accepted principle reads just the reverse: greater dependence requires greater, not lesser, responsibility. It is more wrong to mistreat one's child when it is two than when it is fifteen, precisely because the two-year-old is more dependent and therefore more vulnerable to harm.[64]

(c) If dependence on the mother justifies abortion, it also justifies infanticide and the removal of those unfortunate cripples and chronic patients who depend on a mother or nurse for survival.[65]

6. *Potentiality*. Some liberationists hold that the fetus is a potential human being whereas the pregnant woman is an actual human being:[66]

(a) Such statements rest on a metaphysical distortion. The unborn child definitely exists and this existence is itself an actuality. Pure potency does not exist because potency needs an actualized substance.[67]

(b) The unborn child undoubtedly has potentiality: it will live outside the womb as an infant, an adolescent, and an adult. All these stages represent future and unfulfilled potential but already at the embryo stage fetal life is real, actually existing, human life. Later developments will only be further steps in a process of qualitative continuity which began at conception, and they are not the result of any essential changes in the status of the individual. Even at birth the being with human life is not a perfect and mature person, but complete maturity cannot be the criterion by which the presence of humanity is to be judged. The conceptus is not "inferior" any more than an infant in its mother's arms or a child in grade school. If the unborn child is "immature," "rudimentary," or "inchoate," so are all infants, children, and adolescents who need food, care, and protection to reach adulthood. The fetus is a human individual in the process of living and developing. It is a human being with potential, not a potential human being.[68]

(c) We cannot understand the meaning of a being unless we give it a chance to unfold its value before us in time. One only understands the nature of fetal life if one considers the total biography of the unborn child from conception to natural death. We should not reduce its lifetime to a few weeks and thus foreclose its future. It is not, in reality, simply a fetus. It is also a future adult.[69]

The main thrust of these arguments is clear. The authors employ a simple and comprehensive criterion for humanity, namely, conception by human parents, and they refuse to discriminate among human beings on the basis of their varying achievements. In the words of the bishops of Texas:

> The value and sanctity of human life rests ultimately on the singular value God has placed on it. It does not rest on the goodness, age or social importance of the individual, or whether he is normal or wanted, or whether he is a burden or an asset to others. It is not a characteristic that is acquired, developed or earned, and thus we hold that it is present at the very instant of generation, at that precise moment when it begins to be.[70]

Logically, in this perspective, abortion constitutes an assault upon the life of an innocent human person that is not essentially different from any other intentional destruction of innocent human life. Abortion is murder.[71]

The Fetus: Probably a Human Person

Not all Catholic authors, however, were convinced that the biological data warranted definite philosophical conclusions and straightforward moral imperatives. As late as 1967 Thomas J. O'Donnell was remarkably restrained in his interpretation of the empirical evidence:

> The philosophical-physiological-theological speculations as to when the products of human conception are human (i.e., endowed with an individual soul or independent human life, albeit still within the womb and physically dependent on the mother) has never been, and perhaps never will be, definitively settled...
>
> While the moment of new human life still evades any known investigative process, it is interesting to note that the same scientific method of investigation, aided today by modern microscopy, indicates chromosomal patterns in the nuclei of the earliest stages of cell division as specifically human and indeed already personally individualized, thus seeming to support the probability that, even from this moment, the embryo is not only specifically human, but likewise specifically George.[72]

That same year Father James T. McHugh, director of the Family Life Bureau of the National Catholic Welfare Conference, made a similar point at a conference of diocesan lawyers in Washington. He stated that on the issue of conception and ensoulment there were questions to which as yet there were no final answers. He emphasized the need for more adequate scientific data and cautioned against overstating the biological case.[73] Again in 1967 Edward J. Lauth, Jr., proposed that a distinction be maintained between the empirical question and the philosophical question.

Science can ascertain the *biological presence* of *human life* but it is for philosophy to determine when a *human being* comes into existence.[74]

Germain G. Grisez accepts this distinction and rejects an automatic translation of factual or biological data into philosophical conclusions and moral prohibitions. The factual question is: At what point in the reproductive process does the human individual originate? This is answered by biology which states that the fetus is a living human individual from the time of conception. Grisez then points out that the philosophical or moral problem is quite different: Should we treat all living human individuals as persons, or should we adopt a concept of personhood that will exclude some living human individuals because they do not meet certain additional requirements which we have previously incorporated in the idea of "person?" There is no amount of empirical facts that will settle this question. Yet we have some reason to believe that the fetus is a person, namely, the fact that it is a living human individual, as well as the inconclusiveness of the arguments that try to withhold personhood from the unborn child.[75] It is clear, therefore, that there are no compelling reasons to exclude the fetus from this category: "we must admit, at the very least, that the embryo can as well be considered a person as not."[76] For Grisez, then, to deny personality to the unborn is nothing more than a rationalization of a reluctance to allow them to live.[77]

Rudolph J. Gerber reduces the debate on the quality of fetal life to one fundamental question: Is humanity *given* to *all* or is it *achieved* only by *some?* He admits that the problem is a complex one but suggests that personhood be extended to all, not just because the fetus should at least be given the benefit of the doubt, as Grisez states, but because a community which truly values human life will opt for a comprehensive criterion of humanity rather than for a narrow one:[78]

> (T)he narrow and precise definitions of humanity in terms of certain functions are more restrictive, more inhumane than broad and permissive categories. Humanity, like the creativity it engenders, is more enhanced the less it is defined and prescribed. Hermit-like Robinson Crusoe is but the other face of a humanity which is Falstaff; by the same token, a fetus is but the beginning of an old age, each a differing face of the same human spirit which deserves to be liberated rather than discarded.[79]

Therefore, for a practical moral rule, some authors revert to the morally safer course. Grisez writes:

> In being willing to kill the embryo, we accept responsibility for killing what we must admit *may* be a person...
> *To be willing to kill what for all we know could be a person is to be*

willing to kill it if it is a person. And since we cannot absolutely settle if it is a person except by metaphysical postulate, for all practical purposes we must hold that to be willing to kill the embryo is to be willing to kill a person.[80]

The Meaning of Abortion

Even if the empirical-philosophical arguments did not lead to unanimous conclusions on the quality of unborn human life, the authors clearly had little doubt about the practical moral imperative and condemned abortion as fundamentally incompatible with the value of human life. On the whole, American Catholic theology has made no significant effort to elaborate this rationale and present the destruction of the fetus in a wider moral perspective. This would have intensified the appeal of its basic argument but, while many authors were at pains to establish that the conceptus represents individual human life or personal life, they apparently regarded the value of such life as self-evident and not in need of further rationalization, and were satified with the classical definitions of abortion, such as "murder of the innocent." Only two authors have attempted to describe the evil of abortion in a broader moral context and their efforts must now be registered.[81]

David Granfield presents "a new scientific and philosophic dimension" of the interruption of pregnancy and defines it in terms of "anticipated entropy."[82] He notes that there are two different tendencies operating in the cosmos. One is a positive evolutionary trend which manifests itself in nature's progress towards more and more highly ordered enclaves. But another force is at work in an opposite direction, towards a state of utter disorder. This is entropy, the tendency of things to a random state of statistical uniformity of energy and temperature. The overall trend in the universe is entropic: the cosmos moves irreversibly in a downhill direction to the most probable state of stable equilibrium. Yet the world teems with evolutionary or antientropic processes, since each of the many varieties of life represents a victory over the general entropic decline and a thrust towards individual progress and perfection, towards amazing peaks of organized achievement. All living organisms have this antientropic tendency rooted in their basic functions and man has it in its most perfect form. At the same time life is precarious because all living beings inevitably age and thus manifest their own entropic decline. This very limitation should make us respect and safeguard human life all the more and, in this light, abortion becomes a deliberate infliction of entropy.[83] Granfield concludes:

(A)bortion is anticipated entropy whereby the human organism with its precious inheritance of energy and potential is purposely and freely degraded. Its intricate beauty and functional dynamism are reduced to a

rubble of lifeless disorder. To understand abortion in its cosmic proportions it is necessary to see it as an entropic contribution to chaos, as a
devastating attack on that improbable perfection which is human life.[84]

Donald DeMarco points to the interdependence of all things and to the
myriad relationships which join beings to one another. Everything belongs
to the universe and nothing stands in isolation because the cosmos unfolds
through material interaction and at every level of reality there is relationship. The unborn child owes its existence to the sexual union of its parents,
and it enjoys an intimate partnership with its mother who in turn is in
relationship with her husband. The parents in turn are in relationship with
their family, with society, and with the universe. Society will make progress only when its members, through their understanding of these interrela-
tionships, discover the wholeness of reality and begin to appreciate their
world as an integrated and organic totality, rather than as a haphazard
collection of independent fragments. The fetus therefore is not an isolated
entity but belongs to the world. When the unborn is degraded so that he can
be deprived of the protection to which he was entitled, then sexuality,
marriage, the family, and society will also be devalued. If sexual intercourse, at best, can only produce creatures of such limited dignity that they
do not deserve to be treated with justice, then the act of love depreciates,
and human love and human life likewise depreciate.[85] For DeMarco, then,
abortion shakes the universe: "For the want of a shoe a kingdom was lost.
For the want of a proper regard for the human unborn, a civilization may be
lost."[86]

Apart from Granfield and DeMarco there have been no other philosophical elaborations on the evil of the interruption of pregnancy. At the 1968
convention of the Catholic Theological Society of America, partly devoted
to the abortion problem, Leo O. Farley presented a paper, "The meaning of
Life and Divine Transcendence," but apart from the fact that he confessed
himself to be "somewhat at sea in the formal presentation," he intended
"neither to define the meaning of life nor to demonstrate the reality of
divine transcendence."[87] In the March 1970 issue of *Theological Studies,*
entirely devoted to the abortion question, Joseph T. Mangan affirmed the
validity of the traditional view on abortion. While he employed the empirical approach as far as the quality of fetal life is concerned, he used scrip-
tural and theological arguments to justify the Catholic emphasis on the
value of man.[88] His observations are undoubtedly valid within the
framework of Catholic theology but they are intramural and therefore
exercise a limited appeal.

Direct and Indirect Abortion

In my analysis of the traditional treatises on abortion we have seen that the distinction between direct and indirect killing as expressed in the principle of double effect indicates the limits of the Church's willingness to interfere with innocent human life.At a later stage of the debate many Catholic authors have questioned this criterion and their views will be presented in Chapter V. Others have remained within the confines of the Church's declared teaching; the observations of those who have explicitly confirmed the validity of this position must be registered here.

Noonan explains that the principle of double effect is not a doctrine fallen from heaven but a rule formulated by theologians, which adjudicates in an equitable manner where different interests or values present conflicting claims, as do the rights of the fetus and other human rights in the case of a problematic pregnancy. The principle recognizes the fully human status of the fetus, and it affords the unborn the protection they are entitled as persons. It therefore establishes a general rule of inviolability for fetal life and, in cases of conflict, it draws a line so tightly fixed in favor of the child that abortion is rarely justified, indeed only in the very unusual events of an ectopic pregnancy and a cancerous uterus. In each of these cases the fetus itself has little chance of survival even if the pregnancy is not terminated. Underlying the decision to exempt only two uncommon situations is the realization that all but the most special exceptions will be pushed further and extended. The principle of double effect forestalls a multiplication of these exceptions and thus prevents an erosion of the protection which the conceptus deservedly enjoys.[89] Noonan emphasizes that for the Christian community the formulation and implementation of this rule is not a mere rational calculation or a purely abstract exercise, but an expression of its obedience to the injunction of Scripture — to love your neighbor as yourself — and a token of its willingness to accept the unborn child as a neighbor whose life has equal value to one's own.[90]

Noonan, therefore, presents the principle of double effect as a prudential and pragmatic policy geared towards the protection of the unborn child. Germain Grisez, David Granfield, and Thomas M. Garrett give this rule a different and deeper moral grounding, and they stress that it has been formulated on the basis of an appropriate analysis of the intention of the agent and the causality of his act. The requirement of indirect efficient causality incorporated in the principle of double effect actually limits fetal destruction to very few instances, but it would be incorrect to interpret the distinction between direct and indirect abortion in terms of a rule which generally protects unborn life but allows for exceptions in difficult cases. The principle does permit an indirect abortion but this permission does not correspond to an exception to the general rule nor does it contradict in any other way the law of the inviolability of innocent human life. In an indirect abortion the death of the fetus is not willed either as an end or as a means but occurs as an unintended and unavoidable side effect of some intervention designed to protect the life of the mother. An indirect abortion does not treat the fetus as a means, as a thing which has no right to life, nor does it assume that anyone has direct and complete control over the life of an innocent human being. In this procedure the will remains intent on the protection of life since the death of the child is an unwanted and incidental side effect of a directly life-saving act. The principle of double effect realistically acknowledges the fact that many of our acts, however well-intentioned, result in a combination of good and bad effects, and it helps us solve conflict situations that arise.[91] In the words of Granfield:

> Moralists faced with the actuality of double effects have worked out a principle of double effects to enable us to live reasonably, responsibly, and lovingly in a world of double effects. The principle helps us achieve a delicate balance: We are not totally incapacitated by a moral impasse, nor are we irresponsibly dispensed from moral choice. We are still bound by our basic insights into the reality of human dignity. We must always value the inalienable right to life. We cannot intentionally destroy this life directly or indirectly. Nevertheless, if the object of our intention and our action is good and reasonable, if the grounds for seeking it are compelling and proportionately grave, we are morally free to pursue our goal even if unfortunate and unintended effects result. The principle of double effect is by no means a casuistical trick to enable us to do indirectly what we cannot do directly. Its sole function is to enable us to do good things directly when the total situation justifies that direct action, despite the presence of bad effects as an unintended and indirect by-product of that good action.[92]

III. The Nonvalidity of Abortion Indications

Throughout the debate on abortion and abortion laws, Catholic authors have paid a great deal of attention to the so-called "indications for abortion" which proponents of liberalization put forward as a major argument in favor of more lenient moral attitudes and less restrictive legal codes. In this section I want to summarize the observations which the Catholic argument has made in this regard and I will do so under four headings: (1) *Physio-medical indications* are physio-pathological conditions in expectant mothers which are caused or aggravated by their pregnancy and which endanger their life or physical health. (2) *Psycho-medical indications* are psycho-pathological situations which are caused or precipitated by pregnancy and which pose a threat to the mother's mental health. A termination of pregnancy on a physio-medical or psycho-medical indication is often called a "therapeutic" abortion.[93] (3) *Humanitarian indications* comprise pregnancies resulting from rape, incest, and extramarital relations and refer primarily to the severe mental stress that surrounds such pregnancies. (4) *Eugenic or fetal indications* are physical or mental defects in the unborn and include genetic malformations as well as imperfections due to outside interference, such as by viruses, drugs, or radiation. In a eugenic abortion it is assumed that the child's handicap would make its postnatal life cruelly painful or meaningless.[94]

Physio-medical Indications: The Physical Health of the Mother

Catholic opinion on these indications can be summarized as follows:

1. Medicine has now arrived at a point where, when pregnancy and disease coexist, the pregnancy has no longterm effects upon the disease if good medical supervision is obtained. Consequently, the former "either-or situation" (either the mother's life or the child's) no longer exists. Medical science has perfected the technique of Cesarean delivery and can cope adequately with multiple maternal afflictions (such as pernicious anemia, serious diabetes, uncontrollable vomiting, and pulmonary tuberculosis) without recourse to direct abortion. In cases of irremediable afflictions (such as renal deficiency and cardiopathic conditions) there is no clinical certainty that a therapeutic abortion will save the mother's life. In any case, the harmful effects of an abortion might be more damaging than the effects of a pregnancy brought to term.[95]

2. Anyone, therefore, who performs a therapeutic abortion is either ignorant of modern medical methods of treating the complications of pregnancy and childbirth or is unwilling to use them. The answer to these problems is good medical care for the mother and not the destruction of her child.[96]

3. As far as maternal survival rates are concerned, hospitals with a "no abortion" policy compare favorably to those which permit therapeutic abortion.[97]

Psycho-medical Indications: The Mental Health of the Mother

The evaluation by Catholic authors of the psycho-medical indications for abortion corresponds to their assessment of the physio-medical reasons and is expressed in the following observations:

1. "Mental health" and "mental disease" are very vague standards which are a perpetual subject of debate within the medical profession itself.

Psychiatrists often refer to the 1961 World Health Organization definition which describes health as a state of complete physical, mental, and social well-being, and not a mere absence of disease. They then justify termination of pregnancy on grounds of mental health but their definitions of the specific indications for such abortions remain nebulous. Moreover, both the diagnosis and prognosis of mental disturbances during pregnancy are uncertain. It is practically impossible for a psychiatrist to predict that an abortion will be less detrimental to mental health than bringing the baby to term.[98]

2. The decision to abort on psychiatric grounds is usually taken not by a specialist but by an ordinary physician who has little more competence in the field of psychiatry than a lawyer or a dentist.[99]

3. Many psychiatrists tend to align themselves with so-called progressive social change and this affects the objectivity of their medical judgement.[100]

4. Psychiatric situations lend themselves easily to the management of symptoms. These can be exaggerated without too much difficulty, either by the psychiatrist or the patient, to meet various legal requirements.[101]

5. Reputable psychiatrists testify that psycho-medical indications have become practically nonexistent. Pregnancy does not cause psychoses or psychoneuroses. When psychiatric patients become pregnant, the risk of exacerbation or precipitation of their mental condition is small and unpredictable, and suicide is extremely rare. Moreover, the termination of pregnancy, either by delivery at term or abortion, will not significantly alter the duration and longterm pattern of such disturbances.[102]

6. Psychotherapeutic techniques for treating the mental condition are frequently available during pregnancy and after delivery.[103]

7. The effects of abortion on mental patients are unpredictable because therapeutic abortion has its own psychological sequelae. The more serious the mental affliction, the more likely a psychiatric complication will develop as a result of guilt feelings and self-reproach.[104]

8. Very often the woman's problem is not really a psychiatric one at all and is not caused by the pregnancy as such. Social and economic factors have become the prime reason for the termination of pregnancy. These are converted into "indications for therapeutic abortion," with the plea that what is not good for the patient is bound to make her sick sooner or later.[105]

9. Indications for abortion on the ground of damage to maternal mental health are flimsy disguises to cloak a situation which allows abortion on request and are intended to soothe the guilt feelings over abortion of both mother and society. The psychiatric indication is as hypocritical as the other medical indications are.[106]

Humanitarian Indications: Rape, Incest, and Illegitimacy

The observations of Catholic authors on this category of indications are less technical and more ethical in character than their evaluation of the medical reasons for abortion. Their arguments refer primarily to pregnancies resulting from rape and incest but some of their assertions are equally applicable to the condition of the unwed pregnant woman. Their position can be summarized as follows:

1. "Humanitarian indication" is a misnomer since there is no humanitarianism in destroying children. [107]

2. Rape is easy to allege and difficult to prove. Cases of genuine rape are relatively rare. Many pregnancies purported to be the outcome of a single act of rape are really the result of a prolonged cohabitation. Moreover, while there may be scattered statistics concerning alleged rape and incest, it is doubtful whether a significant number of pregnancies are caused thereby. [108]

3. Any woman who has been raped should have the benefit of good medical care immediately. In this case the Church permits contraceptive measures on the ground that the rapist is an unjust aggressor: the victim of this aggression is allowed to prevent the conception which might result from such conduct. [109]

4. Undoubtedly, pregnancies resulting from rape and incest cause severe mental strain and thus would conceivably qualify for a "psychiatric indication." Nevertheless, the life that has been conceived is human life, and it must be accorded the rights and protection associated with the life which results from normal sexual relations and legitimate conceptions. [110]

5. Rape arouses deep emotions and a desire for revenge. The woman will be strongly inclined to view the child as an extension of her aggressor and his brutal deed; but if she decides to strike at the life within her she responds to the violence done to her with violence to another, to an innocent human being who also has sprung—although unwittingly—from herself. Abortion is a submission to evil rather than a triumph over it. It implies hatred and aggression and an admission that evil is stronger than forgiveness, goodness, generosity, and love. [111]

6. If pregnancy were to result from rape it is questionable whether the psychological trauma would be remedied or intensified by adding to the woman's sense of shame the possible sense of guilt of abortion. The woman's basic problem is one of self-acceptance, of realizing that she is not inherently damaged or tainted by her unfortunate experience. The unborn child is partly hers, and she must accept it if she is really to accept herself and overcome her sense of self-rejection. To abort the child is to evade the issue. This evasion may bring temporary relief but it may also prove a permanent obstacle to achieving inner peace. [112]

7. Even in cases of statutory rape the relevance of abortion is questionable. Teenage girls who become pregnant are often alienated from their parents and socially isolated. They welcome their child as a compensation for their loneliness and they are reluctant to present themselves for an abortion. [113]

8. Incestuous pregnancies are often not identified as such because the interested parties (daughter or mother) are unwilling to face the social and financial consequences involved in the conviction of a father, brother, husband, or son. In cases where the true nature of the woman's condition does become apparent, the pregnancy is usually not recognized or admitted until it has become physically evident and gone beyond the time when an abortion would be feasible. [114]

9. Instead of condoning abortion, society must do all it can to assist in cases of incestuous or forceful assault pregnancy. Many have emphasized the need for adequate social legislation regarding the care of children thus conceived. [115]

Eugenic or Fetal Indications

Catholic authors have also addressed themselves to arguments which would exclude fetal life from society's moral and legal protection because of physical or mental handicaps. Their objections to such propositions are partly medical and partly ethical in character and center around the following points:

1. If it is morally in order to kill an unborn child which is abnormal, one is also allowed to kill newborn babies which are abnormal and adults who have contracted serious physical or mental disabilities. [116]

2. The handicapped can lead a meaningful life if they are surrounded with loving care. They have a human spirit which might well manifest a superior intelligence and nobility and render great service to mankind. [117]

3. A handicapped child can bring out the best in us in terms of love and service. Caring for such unfortunates is beneficial also to the community because this emphasis on the value of man will enhance the respect for life and the quality of life in that society. [118]

4. There is no such thing as a fetal indication: no fetus survives the abortion. It is clear that the indication is really a social one and reflects parental concern over the birth of an unwanted child. There is no evidence that the fetus does not want to live, and it cannot be consulted on the issue. We have no proof that those with physical or mental abnormalities would rather not have lived. Such evidence would exist if suicide rates in this group were higher than in other groups but this is not the case. [119]

5. In cases of German measles, only one in six of the children borne by

mothers who contracted this disease during the first trimester of pregnancy are defective in some way. Furthermore, many of these defects are minor and can be corrected. Aborting all fetuses of such mothers would be equivalent to sacrificing the vast majority of healthy children in order to save a small minority from a difficult life.[120]

6. In serious instances of Rh-factor, the child is either stillborn, dies in the first hours of life, or survives. When it survives, a good prognosis can be given for normalcy if, when indicated, blood transfusions are carried out.[121]

7. Most thalidomide-damaged children manifest normal mental and emotional maturation, and many of them have potential for higher education. With specialized orthopedic, social, and educational assistance their capacities can be developed to such an extent that they still value life despite their great handicaps.[122]

8. Recent medical techniques provide for early detection and treatment of an increasing number of fetal defects.[123]

9. Parents with a significant transmissible defect will profit in the future from the rapidly expanding knowledge of genetics which will make the abnormal gene subject to modification.[124]

IV. The Official Teaching of the Catholic Church

It is clear that in the 1960s American Catholic ethics developed a new approach to the abortion issue. Its moral position remained in keeping with the manuals but it no longer expressed its belief in the inviolability of unborn human life in terms of "parochial assumptions" and "intramural value systems."[125] It found a new formulation and presented an empirical, and therefore nonsectarian, argument which undoubtedly proved more relevant to the political debate.

Our examination of the manuals on the issue of fetal life revealed an inherent weakness in the traditional Catholic stand on abortion. The majority of the handbooks were reluctant to establish a definite causal connection between the quality of unborn life and the immorality of abortion and would only accept the immediate animation view as "tenable" or "possible." We have seen that the new empirical argument has generated much greater certainty. For most authors the biological data are clear and conclusive, and the moral imperative is self-evident. They see no qualitative difference between the prenatal and the postnatal person and therefore they grant the fetus the same moral protection which it will enjoy as an adult. They question the validity of nonbiological definitions of personhood, and they do so on philosophical grounds by pointing out that such subjective criteria are never employed for assessing the human status of adults. Consequently, these standards cannot logically be applied to the unborn.

But even at this stage of the debate the Catholic position is less than perfectly unanimous. Some authors are reluctant to equate philosophy with biology; in their view the judgement of personhood is not a mere empirical observation but presupposes a "metaphysical postulate" (Grisez). They admit that in a society which truly values life this postulate will logically take the form of a broad and permissive definition of humanity (Gerber); and that by its biological individuality and continuity the fetus does present a respectable claim to membership in the brotherhood of man (Grisez). But at the same time they maintain that the empirical data cannot be philosophically conclusive: all we can say is that the unborn child is *very likely* a human person and that it should *at least* be given the benefit of the doubt (Grisez). Nevertheless, even if there is no absolute unanimity on the quality of fetal life, we do find a general consensus that the biological data are highly significant, that nonbiological criteria of personhood are questionable, and that abortion is murder—except under circumstances for which the principle of double effect provides.

There is another issue on which Catholic authors find themselves in fairly firm agreement. They point out that medical science can now cope adequately with practically all physical and psychological complications of pregnancy and childbirth and that therefore, from a purely medical point of view, abortion rarely is the only solution to such problems, if it is a solution at all. We have seen that they also question the validity of humanitarian and eugenic indications. Their arguments on these two categories are a combination of medicine, morals, and a good deal of common sense which leads them to conclude that the distress surrounding such pregnancies can and should be alleviated by means other than the destruction of the unborn child.

There can be little doubt that the Catholic position on the medical indications for abortion is valid because it reflects a substantial consensus among medical professionals who now generally recognize that very few true indications remain. Medicine has reached a state where abortion has become a non-necessity; even in the most severe diseases a pregnancy can now be successfully brought to term without serious harm to the mother.[126] Daniel Callahan who, as we will see, argues in favor of less restrictive moral and legal codes not only concedes this point[127] but is even skeptical about the therapeutic value of terminating a pregnancy. Discussing the propriety of the term "therapeutic abortion" he draws attention to the fact that "abortion is not notably therapeutic for the fetus."[128] He continues:

Perhaps, then, abortion is therapeutic for the woman who receives it. That it is beneficial to her in some ways seems undeniable; she is relieved of an unwanted social, economic, or psychological burden. But is it proper to employ language which has a very concrete meaning in medicine—the correction or amelioration of a physical or psychological defect—in a case where there is usually no physical pathology at all? Except in the now-rare instances of a direct threat to a woman's life, an abortion cures no known disease and relieves no medically classifiable illness. [129]

Much less is the term "therapeutic abortion" applicable in cases of humanitarian or eugenic indications. A termination of such pregnancies could only be justified on the ground of human compassion because there is absolutely no question here of a "medical necessity" in the sense of a threat to the life of the mother. [130] Abortion, therefore, is rarely a "medical necessity." With very few exceptions the abortion dilemma consists in the mother's dilemma—whether or not the life interest of the fetus will prevail over some less-than-life interest of her own. The Catholic answer to this question is clear. It is equally clear that the abortion decision is a moral decision, not a medical one. [131]

The argument that has been outlined in this chapter was the common American Catholic view on the morality of abortion throughout the 1960s. It can be presented as the "official" or "orthodox" Catholic position because it reflects the teaching of the American bishops until today. In the following two chapters I will describe the divergencies which have emerged within the Catholic camp and which led to a degree of dissent on each of the major contentions of the orthodox Catholic stand. A good number of Catholic moralists will question not only the official interpretation of the biological phenomena but the very validity of purely empirical criteria of personhood. They will reconsider the classical emphasis on the direct efficient causality of the act as well as the rationale and the formulation of the principle of double effect. In sum, the Church's traditional stand on the morality of abortion will be seriously reexamined. Unanimity will be maintained on only one issue, namely, that abortion is a moral and not a medical problem.

NOTES

1 Thus churches are charged with making "a mockery of the provisions set forth in the First Amendment"; Byron N. Fujita *et al.,* "Referendum 20—Abortion Reform in Washington State," in Howard J. Osofsky and Joy D. Osofsky (eds.), *The Abortion Experience: Psychological and Medical Impact* (Hagerstown, Maryland: Medical Department Harper and Row, 1973), p. 257. This issue will be discussed in Chapter VIII.

2 Bishops of Maryland, "Statement on Abortion," *Catholic Mind* 66, March 1968, p. 2.

3 Bishops of Illinois, "Statement on Abortion—March 20, 1969," in Daughters of St. Paul (eds.), *Yes to Life* (Boston: St. Paul Editions, 1977), pp. 203-204. See also: Bishops of Missouri, "Statement on Abortion—December, 1970," *ibid.,* pp. 225-226; Bishops of Massachusetts, "Declaration on Abortion—March, 1971," *ibid.,* p. 234. The Harvard-Kennedy Conference statement reflected a biological observation rather than a philosophical insight. The Conference did not come to unanimous conclusions with regard to the morality of abortion or the personhood of the unborn. See: Robert E. Cooke *et al.* (eds.), *The Terrible Choice: The Abortion Dilemma. Based on the Proceedings of the International Conference on Abortion Sponsored by the Harvard Divinity School and the Joseph P. Kennedy Jr. Foundation* (New York: Bantam Books, 1968), pp. 39, 81-89.

4 Eugene F. Diamond, "The Physician and the Rights of the Unborn," *Linacre Quarterly* 34 (1967), p. 178.

5 Eugene F. Diamond, "Who Speaks for the Fetus?" *Linacre Quarterly* 36 (1969), p. 58.

6 *Ibid.,* p. 58; Paul V. Harrington, "Human Life and Abortion," *Catholic Lawyer* 17 (1971), p. 34; Bishops of Missouri, *op. cit.,* p. 225.

7 Diamond, "Who Speaks for the Fetus?" *op. cit.,* p. 58; Harrington, *op. cit.,* p. 34; Bishops of Missouri, *op. cit.,* p. 225. See the comment of Roland M. Nardone, "The Nexus of Biology and the Abortion Issue," *Jurist* 33 (1973), p. 154.

8 Richard P. Vaughan, S.J., "Abortion and the Law," *Homiletic and Pastoral Review* 66 (1966), p. 649; Rudolph J. Gerber, "Abortion: Two Opposing Legal Philosophies," *American Journal of Jurisprudence* 15 (1970), p. 22.

9 Paul V. Harrington, "Abortion: Part XV," *Linacre Quarterly* 37 (1970), p. 126; Richard R. Romanowski, "Abortion—A Fetal Viewpoint," *Linacre Quarterly* 34 (1967), p. 276; Bishops of Massachusetts, "Joint Statement on Abortion—February, 1972," in Daughters of St. Paul, *op. cit.,* pp. 252-253.

10 Germain G. Grisez, *Abortion: The Myths, the Realities, and the Arguments* (New York: Corpus Books, 1970), pp. 13, 274; Joseph T. Mangan, S.J., "The Wonder of Myself: Ethical-Theological Aspects of Direct Abortion," *Theological Studies* 31 (1970), p. 128. John T. Noonan, Jr., points out that at fertilization there is a sharp shift in biological probabilities. Prior to conception an individual spermatozoon or ovum has only a tiny statistical probability of development but once the conceptus has been formed there is an immense increase in potentialities beause the chance that a child will result is then four out of five; "An Almost Absolute Value in History," in John T. Noonan, Jr. (ed.), *The Morality of Abortion: Legal and Historical Perspectives* (Cambridge, Mass.: Harvard University Press, 1970), pp. 55-57. See the comments of John O'Connor, "On Humanity and Abortion," *Natural Law Forum* 12 (1968), pp. 129-130; Daniel Callahan, *Abortion: Law, Choice and Morality* (New York: Macmillan, 1970), pp. 381-382.

[11] Grisez, *op. cit.*, pp. 13-23; David Granfield, *The Abortion Decision* (revised edition; Garden City, N.Y.: Doubleday Image Books, 1971), pp. 16-23.

[12] Granfield, *op. cit.*, pp. 23-24; Grisez, *op. cit.*, pp. 14-21.

[13] Granfield, *op. cit.*, p. 24.

[14] Diamond, 'The Physician and the Rights of the Unborn," *op. cit.*, p. 178; Grisez, *op. cit.*, pp. 32-33; Harrington, "Abortion: Part XV," *op. cit.*, p. 126; Bishops of Missouri, *op. cit.*, pp. 225-226.

[15] Granfield, *op. cit.*, p. 22.

[16] *Ibid.*, p. 23; Grisez, *op cit.*, p. 18; Diamond, "Who Speaks for the Fetus?" *op. cit.*, p. 58. See also: Nardone, *op. cit.*, p. 155.

[17] Granfield, *op. cit.*, p. 23; Diamond, "Who Speaks for the Fetus?" *op. cit.*, p. 58; Harrington, "Abortion: Part XV," *op. cit.*, p. 125. See also: Nardone, *op. cit.*, pp. 156-157; Daniel Callahan, "Abortion: Some Ethical Issues," in David F. Walbert and J. Douglas Butler (eds.), *Abortion, Society, and the Law* (Cleveland: Press of Case Western Reserve University, 1973), p. 99.

[18] Gerber, *op. cit.*, pp. 6-7.

[19] Grisez, *op. cit.*, pp. 16, 275.

[20] *Ibid.*, p. 16.

[21] *Ibid.*, pp. 16-17.

[22] Robert M. Byrn, "Abortion-on-Demand: Whose Morality?" *Notre Dame Lawyer* 46 (1970), pp. 9-12; Harrington, "Human Life and Abortion," *op. cit.*, p. 39; Norman St. John-Stevas, "Abortion, Catholics, and the Law," *Catholic World* 206 (1968), p. 150.

[23] Gerber, *op. cit.*, pp. 7-8; Grisez, *op. cit.*, pp. 32-33; Noonan, *op. cit.*, p. 52.

[24] Gerber, *op. cit.*, pp. 7-8, 22; Noonan, *op, cit.*, p. 52; Robert M. Byrn, "Abortion: A Legal View," *Commonweal* 85 (1967), p. 680.

[25] Noonan, *op. cit.*, p. 52; Harrington, "Human Life and Abortion," *op. cit.*, p. 39; Denis Cavanagh, "Legalized Abortion: The Conscience Clause and Coercion," *Hospital Progress* 52, August 1971, p. 88. In *Roe* v. *Wade* the U.S. Supreme Court declared that at the beginning of viability the fetus "presumably has the capability of meaningful life outside the mother's womb." On viability see further: Byrn, "Abortion-on-Demand: Whose Morality?" *op. cit.*, pp. 12-14.

[26] Byrn, "Abortion-on-Demand: Whose Morality?" *op. cit.*, p. 15; Harrington, "Human Life and Abortion," *op. cit.*, p. 34; Gary M. Atkinson, "The Morality of Abortion," *International Philosophical Quarterly* 14 (1974), pp. 351-353; Richard Stith, "The World as Reality, as Resource, and as Pretense," *American Journal of Jurisprudence* 20 (1975), pp. 142-145.

[27] Grisez, *op. cit.*, pp. 13-14, 274; Mangan, *op. cit.*, pp. 127-128. Catholic authors frequently refer to the "uniqueness" of the zygote's genetic package. Strictly speaking this term should only be used to indicate the genetic discontinuity between parents and offspring. It is not applicable to the genetic endowment as such, since monozygotic twins are genetically identical individuals. See: Grisez, *op. cit*, p. 274. On genetic and phenotypic "uniqueness" see further: Grisez, *op. cit.*, p. 274; Granfield, *op. cit.*, p. 35; James J. Diamond, "Abortion, Animation, and Biological Hominization," *Theological Studies* 36 (1975), pp. 313-314.

[28] Granfield, *op. cit.*, pp. 17, 28.

[29] Harrington, "Abortion: Part XV," *op. cit.*, p. 122; Walter R. Trinkaus *et al.*, "Abortion Legislation and the Establishment Clause," *Catholic Lawyer* 15 (1969), p. 112;

Mangan, *op. cit.* p. 128; Bishops of New Jersey, "Pastoral Letter on Abortion—March, 1970," in Daughters of St. Paul, *op. cit.*, p. 212; Indiana Catholic Conference, "Declaration on Abortion—December, 1972," *ibid.*, pp. 257-258.

[30] Granfield, *op. cit.*, pp. 27-28; Diamond, "The Physician and the Rights of the Unborn," *op. cit.*, p. 178. Stith points out that not *everything* we ever become is genetically determined because some aspects of what we become are shaped environmentally rather than genetically, especially after our birth. He therefore warns against overstating the "conceptionist" case; *op. cit.*, p. 143.

[31] Trinkaus *et al.*, *op. cit.*, p. 112. Louis Dupré admits that fetal development is strictly continuous but he is reluctant to grant the early embryo full personal status; "A New Approach to the Abortion Problem," *Theological Studies* 34 (1973), pp. 481-488. Dupré's position will be presented in Chapter V.

[32] Grisez, *op. cit.*, pp. 17, 275; Bishops of New Jersey, *op. cit.*, p. 212. See also: Callahan, "Abortion: Some Ethical Issues," *op. cit.*, p. 95.

[33] Grisez, *op. cit.*, pp. 275-276; Mangan, *op cit.*, pp. 128-129. See also: Callahan, "Abortion: Some Ethical Issues," *op. cit.*, p. 95.

[34] Callahan, *Abortion: Law, Choice and Morality*, *op. cit.*, p. 377. However, Callahan's view on the quality of fetal life and the morality of abortion differs from the official Catholic position; see Chapter V.

[35] Granfield, *op. cit.*, p. 28. See also: *ibid.*, pp. 38-39; William T. O'Connell, "The Silent Life: An Embryological Review," *Linacre Quarterly* 35 (1968), pp. 180, 186; Mangan, *op. cit.*, p. 133; Harrington, "Abortion: Part XV," *op. cit.*, p. 126; Bishops of Illinois, *op. cit.*, pp. 203-204, 207; *id.*, "Statement on Abortion—February 3, 1971," in Daughters of St. Paul, *op. cit.*, p. 232; Bishops of Massachusetts, "Declaration on Abortion—March, 1971," *op. cit.*, p. 234. In an earlier publication Harrington considered the empirical data less conclusive; "Abortion: Part IX," *Linacre Quarterly* 35 (1968), pp. 133-134.

[36] Granfield, *op. cit.*, pp. 28-29.

[37] O'Connell, *op. cit.*, p. 184; Bishops of Missouri, "Statement on Abortion—December, 1970," *op. cit.*, pp. 225-226; "Pastoral Message of the Administrative Committee, National Conference of Catholic Bishops—February 13, 1973," in Daughters of St. Paul *op. cit.*, p. 261.

[38] Diamond, "The Physician and the Rights of the Unborn," *op. cit.*, p. 178; William J. Kenealy, S.J., "Law and Morals," *Catholic Lawyer* 9 (1963), pp. 205-206; Harrington, "Abortion: Part XV," *op. cit.*, p. 122.

[39] Noonan, *op. cit.*, p. 57. See also: Carol A. Berger and Patrick F. Berger, "The Edelin Decision," *Commonweal* 102 (1975), p. 77. See the comments of O'Connor, *op. cit.*, pp. 127, 129-131. Other Catholic authors, e.g., Daniel Callahan, question this "genetic" or "conceptionist" criterion on the ground that genetic individuality alone is too narrow a standard to establish that one is truly a human being. Their position will be discussed in Chapter V.

[40] Donald DeMarco, *Abortion in Perspective: The Rose Palace or the Fiery Dragon?* (Cincinnati: Hiltz & Hayes, 1974), pp. 11-12, 13-14; Noonan, *op. cit.*, p. 52.

[41] Noonan, *op. cit.*, p. 53; Harrington, "Abortion: Part XV," *op. cit.*, pp. 125-126; Gerber, *op. cit.*, p. 8. For a more elaborate discussion of "fetal consciousness," see Grisez, *op. cit.*, pp. 21-23, 281-282.

[42] Noonan, *op. cit.*, p. 53; Berger and Berger, *op. cit.*, p. 77; Harrington, "Abortion: Part XV," *op. cit.*, pp. 125-126; Grisez, *op. cit.*, pp. 280-281; Gerber, *op. cit.*, p. 8. See the comment of O'Connor, *op. cit.*, p. 128.

[43] DeMarco, *op. cit.*, pp. 12, 14-15; Grisez, *op. cit.*, pp. 280-282; Albert R. Di Ianni, S.M., "Is the Fetus a Person?" *American Ecclesiastical Review* 168 (1974), pp. 318-320.

[44] Noonan, *op. cit.*, p. 53; DeMarco, *op. cit.*, pp. 15-16.

[45] Noonan, *op. cit.*, p. 53.

[46] *Ibid.*, p. 53.

[47] *Ibid.*, pp. 53-54; *id.*, "Responding to Persons: Methods of Moral Argument in Debate over Abortion," *Theology Digest* 21 (1973), pp. 301-302; Berger and Berger, *op. cit.*, p. 77.

[48] Noonan, "Responding to Persons," *op. cit.*, p. 302. See the comment of O'Connor, *op. cit.*, p. 128.

[49] DeMarco, *op. cit.*, pp. 16-17.

[50] Noonan, "An Almost Absolute Value in History," *op. cit.*, p. 54; DeMarco, *op. cit.*, pp. 17-19; Charles E. Curran, "Abortion: Law and Morality in Contemporary Catholic Theology," *Jurist* 33 (1973), p. 175.

[51] DeMarco, *op. cit.*, pp. 19-20; Noonan, "An Almost Absolute Value in History," *op. cit.*, p. 54.

[52] Curran, *op. cit.*, pp. 176-177.

[53] *Ibid.*, p. 177.

[54] *Ibid.*, p. 177.

[55] *Ibid.*, p. 177. Strictly speaking, however, Curran is not a "conceptionist"; see Chapter V.

[56] Noonan, "An Almost Absolute Value in History," *op. cit.*, pp. 54-55. See the comment of O'Connor, *op. cit.*, p. 128.

[57] DeMarco, *op. cit.*, pp. 17-19; Grisez, *op. cit.*, pp. 277-278; William E. May, "Abortion as Indicative of Personal and Social Identity," *Jurist* 33 (1973), p. 210.

[58] DeMarco, *op. cit.*, pp. 19-20; Grisez, *op. cit.*, p. 279.

[59] Grisez, *op. cit.*, p. 278.

[60] *Ibid.*, pp. 278-279.

[61] *Ibid.*, pp. 278, 279-280; Atkinson, *op. cit.*, p. 350; Gerber, *op. cit.*, pp. 23-24. Daniel Callahan also has serious objections to the "social consequences school," since it fails to take account of the very significant genetic evidence, and also because its moral policy rests on a vague and potentially dangerous moral principle: define as you wish; *Abortion: Law, Choice and Morality, op. cit.*, pp. 390-401.

[62] Atkinson, *op. cit.*, p. 351; Di Ianni, *op. cit.*, p. 313; Noonan, "An Almost Absolute Value in History," *op. cit.*, pp. 51-52.

[63] Atkinson, *op. cit.*, pp. 351-352; Di Ianni, *op. cit.*, pp. 313-314; Noonan, "An Almost Absolute Value in History," *op. cit.*, p. 52. See the comment of O'Connor, *op. cit.*, pp. 127-128.

[64] Atkinson, *op. cit.*, p. 353.

[65] Gerber, *op. cit.*, pp. 21-22.

[66] DeMarco, *op. cit.*, p. 164; Grisez, *op. cit.*, pp. 250, 283-286, 303, 423.

[67] DeMarco, *op. cit.*, p. 164. See further: *ibid.*, pp. 14-15, 59-63.

[68] Harrington, "Abortion: Part XV," *op. cit.*, pp. 123-124, 126; Gerber, *op. cit.*, pp. 8-9, 21-22; Mangan, *op. cit.*, pp. 128-129; Peter A. Facione, "The Abortion Non-Debate," *Cross Currents* 23 (1973), p. 352; Bishops of Texas, "Open Letter on Abortion—April, 1971," in Daughters of St. Paul, *op. cit.*, p. 242; U.S. Bishops, "Pastoral Letter on Moral Values—November, 1976," *ibid.*, pp. 292-293.

[69] Grisez, *op. cit.*, p. 286; DeMarco, *op. cit.*, pp. 89-91; Bishops of Texas, *op. cit.*, p.

242. Stith distinguishes between "self-developing potentiality-capabilities" and "externally-to-be-determined possibilities"; cfr. *supra*, note 30. Di Ianni tentatively suggests that at the earliest stages of fetal development we are dealing with "the potentiality for a human body" rather than with an actual human body or "achieved corporeity"; *op. cit.*, p. 325. Callahan opts for the position of the "developmental school." This school is sufficiently sensitive to the biological data to ascribe human life even to the zygote but requires a certain degree of development before allowing one to speak of a "person." Thus this school leaves room for flexibility when hard choices must be made. See: *Abortion: Law, Choice and Morality, op. cit.*, pp. 384-390, 394-401. The views of Di Ianni and Callahan will be presented more extensively in Chapter V. For further reflections on the significance of fetal potentiality, see: Stanley M. Harrison, "The Unwilling Dead," *Proceedings of the American Catholic Philosophical Association* 46 (1972), pp. 199-208; Harry A. Nielsen, "Toward a Socratic View of Abortion," *American Journal of Jurisprudence* 18 (1973), pp. 105-113; Francis C. Wade, S.J., "Potentiality in the Abortion Discussion," *Review of Metaphysics* 29 (1975), pp. 239-255.

70 Bishops of Texas, *op. cit.*, pp. 242-243. See also: Noonan, "An Almost Absolute Value in History," *op. cit.*, p. 51; Gerber, *op. cit.*, p. 8.

71 Bishops of Maryland, *op. cit.*, p. 2; *id.*, "Statement on Abortion—January 27, 1971," in Daughters of St. Paul, *op. cit.*, p. 231.

72 Thomas J. O'Donnell, S.J., "Current Medical-Moral Comment," *Linacre Quarterly* 34 (1967), pp. 364-365.

73 Thomas A. Wassmer, S.J., *Christian Ethics for Today* (Milwaukee: Bruce, 1969), pp. 195-196. A year later the bishops of Maryland declared the scientific evidence to be conclusive; "Statement on Abortion," *Catholic Mind* 66, March 1968, p. 2.

74 Edward J. Lauth, Jr., "Liberal Abortion Laws: The Antithesis of the Practice of Medicine," *Linacre Quarterly* 34 (1967), p. 372. See also: Vaughan, *op. cit.*, p. 649; Thomas M. Garrett, S.J., *Problems and Perspectives in Ethics* (New York: Sheed and Ward, 1968), pp. 211-212.

75 Grisez, *op. cit.*, pp. 273-274, 306. A similar position is adopted by Di Ianni, *op. cit.*, pp. 310-312; Atkinson, *op. cit.*, pp. 350, 356-358; Noonan, "Responding to Persons," *op. cit.*, pp. 298-299; O'Connor, *op. cit.*, pp. 130-133; James M. Humber, "The Case Against Abortion," *Thomist* 39 (1975), pp. 70-71. At a later stage of the debate Noonan modified his original emphasis on the decisiveness of biological criteria. See also his *A Private Choice: Abortion in America in the Seventies* (New York: Free Press, 1979), pp. 2-3.

76 Grisez, *op. cit.*, p. 306.

77 *ibid.*, p. 306.

78 Rudolph J. Gerber, "Abortion: Parameters for Decision," *International Philosophical Quarterly* 11 (1971), p. 584.

79 *Ibid.*, p. 584. See also: Di Ianni, *op. cit.*, p. 321; May, *op. cit.*, pp. 210-211; Stith, *op. cit.*, pp. 146-147.

80 Grisez, *op. cit.*, p. 306. See also: Lauth, *op. cit.*, p. 372; O'Donnell, *op. cit.*, p. 365; Humber, *op. cit.*, p. 71; Statement of Fr. McHugh in Wassmer, *op. cit.*, p. 196. Humber later adjusted his position and accepted conception as the decisive criterion of personhood. See his "Abortion: The Avoidable Moral Dilemma," in James M. Humber and Robert E. Almeder (eds.), *Biomedical Ethics and the Law* (New York: Pflaum Press, 1976), pp. 71-91.

81 Callahan feels that it is almost impossible to furnish the principle of the sanctity of

human life with a metaphysical foundation which can be reconciled with divergent world views and thus be made acceptable to large segments of an increasingly pluralistic society; *Abortion: Law, Choice and Morality, op. cit.*, pp. 319-320.

[82] Granfield, *op. cit.*, p. 36.

[83] *Ibid.*, pp. 36-37.

[84] *Ibid.*, p. 37.

[85] De Marco, *op. cit.*, pp. 4-5.

[86] *Ibid.*, p. 5. *See also: ibid.*, pp. 8-10, 67-71, 72-75; Granfield, *op. cit.*, pp. 137-138. Archbishop Humberto S. Medeiros, "A Consistent Ethic of Life and the Law," *Catholic Mind* 70, May 1972, pp. 35-42; Mary F. Rousseau, "Abortion and Intimacy," *America* 140 (1979), pp. 429-432.

[87] Leo O. Farley, "The Meaning of Life and Divine Transcendence," *The Catholic Theological Society of America: Proceedings of the Twenty-Third Annual Convention, Washington, D.C., June 17-20, 1968* 23 (1968), p. 109.

[88] Mangan, *op. cit.*, pp. 125-148.

[89] Noonan, "An Almost Absolute Value in History," *op. cit.*, pp. 50, 57-58.

[90] *Ibid.*, pp. 58-59. See also: Granfield, *op. cit.*, p. 132; Gerber, "Abortion: Two Opposing Legal Philosophies," *op. cit.*, p. 4. See the critique of Callahan, *Abortion: Law, Choice and Morality, op. cit.*, pp. 424-426; and the reply of Noonan, "Responding to Persons," *op. cit.*, pp. 298-301. For a historical analysis of the distinction between direct and indirect abortion, see: Noonan, "An Almost Absolute Value in History," *op. cit.*, pp. 36-50; John Connery, S.J., *Abortion: The Development of the Roman Catholic Perspective* (Chicago: Loyola University Press, 1977), pp. 225-303.

[91] Germain G. Grisez, "Abortion and the Catholic Faith," *American Ecclesiastical Review* 159 (1968), p. 112; Granfield, *op. cit.*, pp. 132-133, 138; Garrett, *op. cit.*, p. 214. See also: William E. May, "Abortion and Man's Moral Being," in Robert L. Perkins (ed.), *Abortion: Pro and Con* (Cambridge, Massachusetts: Schenkman, 1974), pp. 27-29. Grisez will later propose a redefinition of the principle of double effect; see Chapter V.

[92] Granfield, *op. cit.*, p. 138. See also: John Finnis, "The Rights and Wrongs of Abortion: A Reply to Judith Thomson," *Philosophy and Public Affairs* 2 (1973), pp. 132-137.

[93] Callahan questions the validity of the term "therapeutic abortion." See: "Abortion: Some Ethical Issues," *op. cit.*, pp. 96-97; cfr. *infra*, notes 128 and 129.

[94] Humanitarian indications are also referred to as ethical, legal, and criminal; Granfield, *op. cit.*, p. 104. The socio-economic indications will be considered in Chapter VIII, as will the medical sequelae of abortion.

[95] Diamond, "The Physician and the Rights of the Unborn," *op. cit.*, p. 177; Granfield, *op. cit.*, p. 98; Harrington, "Human Life and Abortion," *op. cit.*, pp. 30-31; William J. Tobin, "Ethical and Moral Considerations Concerning Abortion," *Homiletic and Pastoral Review* 68 (1967), pp. 51-52; Bishops of Illinois, "Statement on Abortion— March 20, 1969," *op. cit.*, p. 208. Grisez admits as genuine indications heart and kidney diseases which are complicated by progressively failing heart and/or kidney functions, especially during the first trimester; *Abortion: The Myths, the Realities, and the Arguments, op. cit.*, p. 73. However, he considers that an "adjustment" of the principle of double effect would provide for such situations; see Chapter V.

[96] Tobin, *op. cit.*, p. 51; Alfred C. Murphy, O.P., "Abortion, Sterilization, Birth Control: A Medico-Moral Viewpoint," *Dominicana* 47 (1962), pp. 254-255; Harrington, "Human Life and Abortion," *op. cit.*, pp. 30-31; Bishops of Illinois, "Statement on Abortion—March 20, 1969," *op. cit.*, p. 208.

97 Joseph P. Lavelle, "Is Abortion Good Medicine?" *Linacre Quarterly* 35 (1968), pp. 16-17; Diamond, "The Physician and the Rights of the Unborn," *op. cit.*, p. 177; Harrington, "Human Life and Abortion," *op. cit.*, pp. 30-31.

98 Tobin, *op. cit.*, p. 52; Granfield, *op. cit.*, p. 102; Harrington, "Human Life and Abortion," *op. cit.*, pp. 32-33; Grisez, *Abortion: The Myths, the Realities, and the Arguments, op. cit.*, pp. 81-82.

99 Granfield, *op. cit.*, p. 103. Even the psychiatrist's competence is limited and does not extend to the social and economic factors that play a role in many "psychiatric indications"; Harrington, "Human Life and Abortion," *op. cit.*, p. 33.

100 Tobin, *op. cit.*, p. 53; Lavelle, *op. cit.*, p. 18.

101 Tobin, *op. cit.*, p. 53; Frank J. Ayd, Jr., "Liberal Abortion Laws: A Psychiatrist's View," *American Ecclesiastical Review* 158 (1968), pp. 85-86; Granfield, *op. cit.*, p. 103; Harrington, "Human Life and Abortion," *op. cit.*, pp. 32-33.

102 Lavelle, *op. cit.*, pp. 17-18; Ayd, *op. cit.*, pp. 74, 85; Diamond, "The Physician and the Rights of the Unborn," *op. cit.*, pp. 177-178; Grisez, *Abortion: The Myths, the Realities, and the Arguments, op. cit.*, pp. 77-87, especially pp. 80-81; Harrington, "Human Life and Abortion," *op. cit.*, pp. 31-32.

103 Tobin, *op. cit.*, p. 53; Ayd, *op. cit.*, pp. 74-75; Harrington, "Human Life and Abortion," *op. cit.*, p. 32.

104 Tobin, *op. cit.*, p. 52; Grisez, *Abortion: The Myths, the Realities, and the Arguments, op. cit.*, pp. 82-87; Granfield, *op. cit.*, pp. 102-103; DeMarco, *op. cit.*, pp. 48-49. Noonan questions the validity of this argument; "Responding to Persons," *op. cit.*, p. 304.

105 Tobin, *op. cit.*, pp. 53-54; Ayd, *op. cit.*, pp. 74, 76-77, 87-88; Grisez, *Abortion: The Myths, the Realities, and the Arguments, op. cit.*, p. 82; Harrington, "Human Life and Abortion," *op. cit.*, pp. 32-33.

106 St. John-Stevas, *op. cit.*, p. 152; Thomas L. Shaffer, "Abortion, the Law and Human Life," *Valparaiso University Law Review* 2 (1967), p. 97.

107 Granfield, *op. cit.*, p. 104.

108 Norman St. John-Stevas, "Abortion Laws," *Commonweal* 85 (1966), p. 165; Diamond, "The Physician and the Rights of the Unborn," *op. cit.*, p. 177; Tobin, *op. cit.*, p. 55; Granfield, *op. cit.*, pp. 106-108.

109 Lauth, *op. cit.*, p. 371; Noonan, "Responding to Persons," *op. cit.*, p. 294; Grisez, *Abortion: The Myths, the Realities, and the Arguments, op. cit.*, pp. 431, 464; Robert F. Drinan, S.J., "The Inviolability of the Right to be Born," in Walbert and Butler (eds.), *op. cit.*, pp. 125-126.

110 Tobin, *op. cit.*, p. 55; Lavelle, *op. cit.*, pp. 22-23; Gordon C. Zahn, "A Religious Pacifist Looks at Abortion," *Commonweal* 94 (1971), p. 282; Grisez, *Abortion: The Myths, the Realities, and the Arguments, op. cit.*, pp. 343-344.

111 DeMarco, *op. cit.*, pp. 86-88; Grisez, *Abortion: The Myths, the Realities, and the Arguments, op. cit.*, pp. 295-296, 343; Noonan, "Responding to Persons," *op. cit.*, pp. 294-295; Di Ianni, *op. cit.*, p. 321.

112 Diamond, "The Physician and the Rights of the Unborn," *op. cit.*, p. 177; *id.*, "Who Speaks for the Fetus?" *op. cit.*, p. 60; Drinan, *op. cit.*, pp. 134-135; Grisez, *Abortion: The Myths, the Realities, and the Arguments, op. cit.*, pp. 343-344.

113 Diamond, "Who Speaks for the Fetus?" *op. cit.*, p. 60.

114 *Ibid.*, p. 60. Grisez fails to see why, in discussions on abortion, incest is often coupled with rape, except for the fact that both arouse in most people an emotion of revulsion which proponents of abortion seek to divert from parties who are guilty to individuals

who are innocent—the unborn; *Abortion: The Myths, the Realities, and the Arguments, op. cit.,* pp. 343-344.

[115] Tobin, *op. cit.,* pp. 55-56; Lauth, *op. cit.,* p. 370; Zahn, *op. cit.,* p. 282; Grisez, *Abortion: The Myths, the Realities, and the Arguments, op. cit.,* p. 464.

[116] Lauth, *op. cit.,* pp. 371-372; Romanowski, *op. cit.,* p. 280; Drinan, *op. cit.,* pp. 129-131.

[117] Romanowski, *op. cit.,* pp. 276-277; Di Ianni, *op. cit.,* p. 321; Grisez, *Abortion: The Myths, the Realities, and the Arguments, op. cit.,* p. 342; Bishops of Illinois, "Statement on Abortion—March 20, 1969," *op. cit.,* p. 207.

[118] Norman St. John-Stevas, "The Tragic Results of Abortion in England," *Linacre Quarterly* 39 (1972), p. 37; Di Ianni, *op. cit.,* p. 321; Charles P. Kindregan, *Abortion, the Law, and Defective Children* (Washington: Corpus Books, 1969), p. 40.

[119] Grisez, *Abortion: The Myths, the Realities, and the Arguments, op. cit.,* pp. 75, 87; Diamond, "Who Speaks for the Fetus?" *op. cit.,* pp. 58-59; St. John-Stevas, "Abortion, Catholics, and the Law," *op. cit.,* p. 152; Noonan, "Responding to Persons," *op. cit.,* p. 294. See also: Andre E. Hellegers, "Law and the Common Good," *Commonweal* 86 (1967), p. 420.

[120] Tobin, *op. cit.,* p. 54; Romanowski, *op. cit.,* p. 277; Diamond, "Who Speaks for the Fetus?" *op. cit.,* pp. 58-59; *id.,* "The Physician and the Rights of the Unborn," *op. cit.,* pp. 175-176; Bishops of Illinois, "Statement on Abortion—March 20, 1969," *op. cit.,* p. 207. See also: Hellegers, *op. cit.,* p. 420.

[121] Lavelle, *op. cit.,* p. 21; Granfield, *op. cit.,* p. 112; Grisez, *Abortion: The Myths, the Realities, and the Arguments, op. cit.,* pp. 90-91. See also: Hellegers, *op. cit.,* p. 420.

[122] Diamond, "The Physician and the Rights of the Unborn," *op. cit.,* pp. 176-177; *id.,* "Who Speaks for the Fetus?" *op. cit.,* p. 59; Grisez, *Abortion: The Myths, the Realities, and the Arguments, op. cit.,* pp. 91-92. For a more extensive discussion of the risk factor inherent in the various "fetal indications" (viral infections, Rh-factor, drug and radiation damage, genetic defects), see: Grisez, *ibid.,* pp. 87-96; Granfield, *op. cit.,* pp. 108-112; DeMarco, *op. cit.,* p. 133.

[123] Tobin, *op. cit.,* p. 55; Lavelle, *op. cit.,* p. 21; James A. Fitzgerald, "Abortion on Demand," *Linacre Quarterly* 37 (1970), pp. 185-186; Bishops of Illinois, "Statement on Abortion—March 20, 1969," *op. cit.,* p. 207. See also: Hellegers, *op. cit.,* p. 420; Kindregan, *op. cit.,* pp. 17-20, 39-40.

[124] Fitzgerald, *op. cit.,* p. 186. Such parents can also "elect not to conceive by judicious use of contraceptives or by sterilization"; *ibid.,* p. 186. See also: Kindregan, *op. cit.,* p. 40.

[125] Callahan, *Abortion: Law, Choice and Morality, op. cit.,* p. 15.

[126] Harry W. Rudel *et al., Birth Control: Contraception and Abortion* (New York: Macmillan, 1973), pp. 228-232; Betty Sarvis and Hyman Rodman, *The Abortion Controversy* (New York: Columbia University Press, 1973), pp. 71-83.

[127] Callahan, *Abortion: Law, Choice and Morality, op. cit.,* pp. 496-497. He arrives at this conclusion after an extensive review of the medical literature; *ibid.,* pp. 27-120.

[128] Callahan, "Abortion: Some Ethical Issues," *op. cit.,* p. 96.

[129] *Ibid.,* p. 96.

[130] Rudel *et al., op. cit.,* p. 232.

[131] Callahan, "Abortion: Some Ethical Issues," *op. cit.,* pp. 96-97; *id., Abortion: Law, Choice and Morality, op. cit.,* pp. 496-497.

Chapter Four

The Empirical Argument Questioned

In the previous chapter I described how, in the course of the debate on the abortion statute proposed by the *Model Penal Code,* American Catholic ethics developed a new argument on the quality of fetal life. We saw that many Catholic authors attached the greatest significance to the "recent discoveries" of embryology and genetics and that these findings led them to define human life as an autodynamic and autodeterminant biological continuity from conception until death. In their view, man's ontogenetic process does not manifest any biological leaps, and this rules out the possibility of ontological mutations. Man's life is individual and personal at any stage of its development, and the zygote must be held just as inviolable as the mature adult.

At the same time we observed that not all authors were prepared to accept the biological facts as philosophically conclusive. We will see in this chapter that at a later stage of the debate others went a step further and seriously questioned the direct translation of empirical findings into philosophical concepts, and of philosophical concepts into moral imperatives. In addition, they presented data drawn from the positive life sciences which, in their opinion, were irreconcilable with the Church's declared stand on the incipience of personal human life.

I. The Limitations of Biology

The first Catholic author who expresses misgivings about the empirical-ethical argument is Thomas L. Hayes in 1967. In his view, biological qualities alone do not establish a "human person": biology is but one of the available criteria and its importance should not be exaggerated. Therefore the concept of personhood falls outside the scope and competence of the positive sciences and, if these are left to their own resources, they will never be able to tell if the fetus at a particular stage of its development has fulfilled all the conditions. It is the task of the speculative disciplines, philosophy and theology, to determine what constitutes a human person and these standards should transcend the empirical observations and verifications of scientists.[1] Hayes stresses that when the criteria of personhood are formulated a wider range of human qualities must be taken into consideration:

> Science can only contribute in a secondary way to the solution of the question of the origin of the human individual. The criteria that define just what constitutes a human person must come from the disciplines of philosophy and theology, and these criteria should include human qualities known through all of our cognitive processes—not just the impersonal observations and logic of science. If the definition of a human person, as postulated by the theologians, does happen to contain some scientific criteria, then the scientist can make observations to ascertain if these qualities are present in a particular living system. However, science cannot lead theology, and for the theologian to limit such a definition of the human person to scientific qualities alone is to ignore the important personal and experienced modes of knowing reality.[2]

Hayes, therefore, is the first Catholic author who pleads for a multidimensional and multidisciplinary assessment of unborn human life. He further points out that biological data are hardly a factor when life or death decisions are actually made. Some human persons are deprived of their right to life because they are convicted murderers, dangerous assailants, or enemy soldiers, but the justification of such verdicts does not depend on the "certain knowledge of science": it is philosophy and theology that provide the moral foundation for this course of action. The empirical evidence alone does not, and cannot, establish that a human person is morally entitled to life under all circumstances. The life or death decision is essentially a moral one.[3]

At the 1968 convention of the Catholic Theological Society of America Leo O. Farley discussed the question "Is prenatal life a person or a thing?" and expressed the opinion that science cannot answer this:

> Perhaps one is prepared to confirm pre-natal life either as a person or a thing. If so we suggest it can only be dogmatically asserted either through an appeal to a higher wisdom—what I am now inclined to regard as a god of the gaps—or by pressing science beyond its own limits thereby forcing it to say what it does not mean to say. In neither case is the response mediated by human wisdom.[4]

Like Hayes, Farley emphasizes the limitations of science as far as the verification of fetal personhood is concerned. He presents prenatal life as an empirically observable phenomenon which, through the eyes of science, we are able to understand, and to understand well. We identify the fetus as a highly sophisticated form of animal life, classifiable as human, and remarkably individuated within this species "since no two appearances are ever exactly the same."[5] Scientists have not yet discovered all the secrets of the unborn, but it is only a matter of time before they will see and measure what is now hidden. When all the data are in, however, nothing will be known beyond what it is given to the senses to know. The answer to the "person or thing question" is not dogmatically dictated by the empirical evidence, and the predicate of personhood is not awarded by the positive sciences. Farley is prepared to leave the decision entirely in the hands of the moral agent, who has to exercise his freedom and his responsibility when formulating a personal response to prenatal life.[6]

Two years later Andre E. Hellegers made the same point when he observed that the personhood of the fetus, in the sense of its human dignity or its human inviolability, cannot be established by empirical analysis. These qualities do not pertain to any positive science but are attributed to the conceptus by a "societal judgement."[7] Science cannot verify their presence; it can only describe the organic development of the unborn child and predict its biological future.[8] Hellegers also draws attention to the fact, as did Hayes, that the "person or thing" question is only one of the aspects of the abortion issue. Even if a definitive statement could be made about the nature of fetal life, the moral problem would not have been settled because our certainty about the presence of personal life does not prevent us from taking such life if we feel justified in doing so.[9]

Again in 1970, Daniel Callahan defended a similar position. He pointed out that biological data do not carry with them self-evident interpretations, no matter how great the detail and the subtlety of the scientific investigation. Neither God nor nature attaches clear labels to zygotes, embryos, or fetuses, which enable us to identify them directly as persons or as things.[10] Callahan is convinced that "personhood" is outside the range of empirical research:

> There are few scientific arguments about the broad outline of what is going on at different stages of embryological or fetal development. For all that, men who can agree on the biological facts can and do differ when it comes to saying that certain embryological facts *prove* the presence of a "human being." It is neither plausible nor reasonable to (a) assume that one group of scientists, theologians or philosophers understands the "facts" better than another (for the "facts" are not all that obscure, open only to "correct" interpretations by a gifted handful); or (b) assume that some future scientific discoveries will decisively answer the question about when human life begins; or (c) expect that, with enough scientific

"objectivity," a consensus on the "meaning" of the facts could be established for the purpose of ethical discourse on abortion or any other moral problem. To ask people simply to "stick to the facts" is naïve. The "facts" must be used and interpreted, and science provides no fixed rules for the interpretation of facts in moral reasoning.[11]

It is not immediately evident, therefore, how the biological data of prenatal life can help us to evaluate the human status of the unborn child.[12] Callahan then underscores a point made by Hayes and Hellegers; there is a second problem to be solved. We need to know whether the conclusion that the person begins to exist at a given time entails that his life should be protected from that time onwards, and we have to determine the degree to which his life should be protected: absolutely or relatively? It is clear that the empirical data are hardly relevant to this second question, which is patently a moral issue.[13]

For Joseph F. Donceel the question of the incipience of personhood is fraught with difficulties. It can be answered neither by the scientist alone nor by the philosopher alone. What is needed is a dialogue between science and philosophy; the philosopher must consult his colleagues in the laboratory, and the scientist will have to listen to his colleagues in philosophy.[14] But the discussions are bound to be laborious, and Donceel seems doubtful about the results:

Unfortunately, philosophers and scientists do not speak the same language, and efforts of either to hold forth about the other's field are bound to sound naïve, untechnical, often ill-informed. There is not much a mere philosopher can do about this, except to hope that the scientists will be tolerant when they hear him mention, in his own crude language, some facts he has gathered from science and see him trying to interpret these facts philosophically.[15]

It would not be correct to conclude that these authors reject the very substance of the Church's official teaching on the human dignity of the unborn child. We will see that on this issue they do not *fundamentally* disagree with the "orthodox" view which I have presented in the previous chapter. But while they grant the value of fetal life, they do question the premises which led to a strictly empirical definition of personhood and a categorical prohibition of abortion. Primarily, they challenge the contention that in the abortion decision our only option is a "straight-forward acceptance of biological realities." In their view the orthodox argument practically reduces the abortion problem to empirical verification.[16] They consider this kind of moral reasoning an oversimplification from a philosophical as well as a moral point of view. They believe that the biological

facts of prenatal life are not philosophically self-explanatory and that
biological individuality cannot simply be equated with human personhood.
Furthermore, they draw attention to the fact that there are situations in
which the taking of "personal life" seems morally jusitifed. If, then, the
adult person does not have an absolute right to life, the fetal person cannot
have an absolute right to life. The direct translation of human personhood
into human inviolability is therefore a short cut in moral reasoning, and a
second and separate argument is needed which balances the rights of the
fetus against the rights and interests of others. In sum, our authors hold that
science by itself provides no matrix of values; it can ascertain biological
individuality but it cannot establish personal inviolability. "Person" is a
philosophical concept; "inviolability" is a moral conclusion. [17]

II. The Objections from Biology

Science, as Hayes observed, cannot lead theology but if theology
decides to recognize an organism as a human person because this entity
satisfies a number of empirically verifiable criteria, the scientist is entitled
to ascertain if these qualities are really present in the subject under consideration. [18] This is precisely what some Catholic authors have done regarding the personhood the Church ascribes to fetal life. They have reexamined
the biological foundations of the official bioethical thesis that asserts that
the life of the individualized homo begins at fertilization and that, therefore, the homicidal act extends to all efforts to terminate the natural reproductive process from that time onwards. Their biological observations and
their corresponding bio-moral conclusions must now be registered.

1. *The chain of life*. It is not correct to say that fertilization represents the
beginning of human life because life does not arise continually from strictly
nonliving matter. Like all living systems, the fetal organism forms a link in
a chain of life which extends backward into the past and which will presumably extend forward into the future. Human life is present after conception
but it cannot be said to originate in that process because the zygote receives
the quality of life from two *living* cells, the sperm and the ovum. Human
life does not *begin;* it is merely *handed on*. [19]

2. *Gradual individualization*. Biology cannot determine at which point
the fetus becomes a human person. Individualization is a gradual process,
and it could well be argued that this process is initiated *before* conception
occurs. The instructions which regulate the development of the offspring
have been deposited in the nuclei of the sperm and the ovum which have
each received, at random, one half of the genetic material of their parents'

body cells. Since it is extremely unlikely that one sperm (or one ovum) would have received exactly the same genes as another, we may say that each sex cell represents a unique selection of parental genetic material. When sperm and ovum fuse to form the first genetically complete cell of the individual, they hand over their endowment in equal amounts to this organism. There can be little doubt, therefore, that the zygote is unique in terms of its genetic make-up but, in a sense, it is also true that its development commences with the selection of the genes for the gametes from the parental genetic pools. Moreover, the zygote is not a tiny human body that only needs to grow in size to become a standard human person. At the single cell stage the organism does not yet possess many of the attributes of form and function that are associated with the human individual. The transition from single cell to complete human individuality is gradual and continuous, and biology is unable to designate the point at which the biological form and function of the human individual are suddenly achieved. In fact, such a point does not exist.[20]

3. *Genotype and phenotype.* The zygote does contain the individual's complete genetic endowment but a homo, the phenotype, is not simply an enlarged or a grown-up genotype. Although all body cells derive by division from the first embryonic cell and therefore have the same genetic composition, they acquire their specialized form and function through the process of differentiation (a liver cell is quite different from a nerve cell). The genetic code alone, then, does not determine the form and function of a cell. The expression of this form and function depends on the interaction of the genes and their environment in the cell, tissue, and organism. Even the genetic material itself may change in form and function. It is clear, therefore, that genetic individuality alone is too narrow a criterion to establish that one is truly a human being.[21]

4. *The undifferentiated embryo.* Biologists have made a number of discoveries which indicate that the human embryo in the first days of its life cannot be considered an "individual":

(a) Experimental embryologists have succeeded in splitting the early cell mass of lower organisms and bringing the individual parts to complete adult maturity. This is the twinning process which also occurs naturally, as it does in man. It is well established scientifically that at the earliest stages of human embryonic development the sphere of cells may divide into identical parts to form identical twins. This may happen as late as the fourteenth day when conjoined twins can still be produced.[22]

(b) If such separated cell masses are allowed to grow individually but are rejoined before differentiation sets in, only one adult form will eventuate. If an early cell mass separates incompletely and the two parts remain attached in one area, the end product will be Siamese twins.[23]

(c) Experiments carried out on mice have shown that it is even possible to combine the early embryos taken from two pregnant females. The resultant genetic mosaic manifests characteristics of both sets of parents. Recently this phenomenon has also been observed in human reproduction where nonidentical twins may combine into one individual (chimera).[24]

(d) If, prior to differentiation, cells from one area of the morula are grafted into a different area of the morula, the eventual form of the individual is not affected. However, if a similar transplant is performed after differentiation, the result will be a monster.[25]

(e) The initial cell divisions of the zygote are brought about by the maternal genetic material without the assistance of the father's genetic contribution. The zygote has its own DNA which it has derived equally from its father and its mother, but until implantation has been completed all the activities of the embryo are directed by the RNA (ribonucleic acid, the messengers of the DNA) that has been developed by the ovum alone before fertilization. The zygote's own RNA is not yet active and, although the organism is alive and functions, it will come under its own genetic direction only later. At the earliest stages of embryogeny the fuels and tools are maternal, not embryonic.[26]

It remains true that at fertilization a new genetic package is established within the confines of one cell but these discoveries do show that not all the genetic material is decisively activated at this point and that final irreversible individuality is yet to be achieved. Before differentiation each cell of the embryo is pluripotent and is potentially a brain cell, bone cell, etc. Its definite form and function are not determined until some time after fertilization.[27]

5. *Parthenogenesis.* Experimentally induced parthenogenesis has succeeded in a number of lower animal organisms, and there is a distinct possibility that it will succeed in humans. In that event, if the power of becoming a person makes an organism into a person, we shall have to say that even an unfecundated human ovum possesses personhood because each such ovum would be potentially, virtually, a human person.[28]

6. *Cloning.* There is increasing evidence that almost any cell of an organism is capable of producing another complete, genetically identical organism. It is already possible to produce complete new plants from single cells of many plant species, and it seems only a matter of time before the same can be achieved with animal and human cells. If the totipotency of a

major portion of human body cells is accepted, the zygote loses its claim to uniqueness. One then has to treat each body cell as potentially, and therefore essentially, a human person (and thus forgo all surgery), or one has to reject the concept that a fertilized ovum is a human person.[29]

7. *Pathological growths.* Even though the incidence of hydatidiform moles is slight, one could say that the zygote has the potentiality of becoming a hydatidiform mole. This would be a further indication that there is no question of irreversible human individuality at the very early stages of embryonic life.[30]

8. *Natural fetal loss.* It is now generally recognized that a considerable percentage of all fertilized ova do not achieve implantation or differentiation to any significant degree and are spontaneously aborted in the first few weeks of pregnancy when women are not even aware of the loss of embryonic life. Due to natural deficiencies in either the sperm, the ovum, or the zygote itself, some zygotes fail to cleave, cleave only a few times, or cleave incompletely, fail to differentiate, or differentiate only rudimentally, or differentiate incompletely. It appears, therefore, that many zygotes lack the capacity to form a subsequent homo and cannot even be considered *potential* human beings. The phenomenon of natural fetal loss seems to argue against immediate hominization.[31]

9. *Ancestral recapitulation.* There is a distinct possibility that the development of fetal life reflects the evolutionary phases which have characterized the genesis of the human race, and that human ontogeny is a recapitulation of human phylogeny. The evolution of man from lower animals took place in a strain of primates whose brain, specifically the cerebral cortex, developed in size and complexity until consciousnes or self-awareness became possible. The brain of modern man has, of course, advanced far beyond this breakthrough level, but it seems reasonable to propose that each human fetus progresses through a continuous series of developmental stages and ultimately arrives at the level of complexity where it achieves self-awareness. This then would be the point at which the fetus changes from a potential into an actual human person, and embryological studies on the developing cerebral cortex suggest that this degree of complexity is probably not realized until several months have elapsed.[32]

The point of these observations is not to deny the significance of the zygote's genetic package but rather to question any direct equation of the human genotype with human individuality and human personhood. These biological discoveries show, first of all, that not all the genetic material becomes active at fertilization.[33] Moreover, it is clear that the early embryo exhibits a disturbing indetermination which is especially evident in cases of identical twinning.[34] The authors therefore conclude that the possession of the human genetic code does not at all guarantee that eventually *one* homo will materialize.[35] Nor is the zygote's virtuality or power of developing into an adult person a definite proof that the organism *is* already a human person. If that would be true, every single cell of the morula or blastula — indeed, most cells of the adult body —would be a human person because at the earliest stages of embryogeny each cell possesses such power and virtuality: each cell may, if separated early enough from the others, develop into a human being.[36]

The general feeling among these authors is that these biological discoveries considerably weaken the official thesis on the beginning of individual and personal human life.[37] James J. Diamond adequately expresses their consensus when he observes that there are enough serious and only partly answered questions surrounding the earliest days of reproduction to warrant the thoughtful attention of those moralists who recognize the necessity for a constant reexamination of the biological substratum to bioethical issues.[38]

III. The Objections from Philosophy

Not only empirical arguments were put forward against the Church's emphasis on the significance of conception. In 1967 and 1968 Joseph F. Donceel reconsidered the official position from a philosophical angle, and he expressed serious metaphysical reservations about ontogenetic theories which locate the beginning of personal human life at fertilization. His writings on this subject drew a great deal of attention in the late 1960s and early 1970s.[39]

Donceel takes as his point of departure the teaching of St. Thomas Aquinas who believed in mediate animation or delayed hominization. St. Thomas held that the human embryo is organized out of the menstrual blood of the mother which has been activated by the semen. The organism is then animated successively by a vegetative soul, an animal soul, and finally a human or rational soul, and it is at this point that the fetus joins humanity. This process of successive ensoulment takes forty days for males and eighty days for females, and the implication is that the human fetus must have realized a certain degree of organization before it can become the seat of a rational principle.[40]

Donceel admits that this argument contains some erroneous biological information, but he claims that this does not invalidate the substance of its anthropological conclusion. Even if Thomas' empirical observations reflect an outdated medieval biology, his basic scientific insight was sound.

It consisted simply in the undeniable fact that at the beginning of pregnancy there is no question yet of a fully organized human body:[41] "Whatever is growing in the mother's womb is potentially, virtually, a human body. It cannot, if everything goes well, turn into any other kind of body. Yet, at the start, there is not at once a highly organized body, a body with sense organs and a brain."[42]

Moreover, St. Thomas applied to this valid biological premise a sound philosophical principle, namely, his hylomorphic conception of man, a conception which in Donceel's view continues to make sense even today, at least to one who understands it. Hylomorphism presents the soul as the substantial form of man and holds that a substantial form can exist only in matter which is capable of receiving it. In the case of man this means that his soul can exist only in a human body which is *suitably formed or organized*. St. Thomas could not accept that an *actual* human soul could be united with an unformed or *virtual* human body. This was irreconcilable with his hylomorphic view on man, and that, combined with his common-sense biological insight, was enough to establish firmly his position of delayed hominization.[43]

Donceel emphasizes that immediate hominization cannot be squared with the Thomistic understanding of man because hylomorphism considers matter and form, body and soul, as strictly complementary. The body which receives the soul and which is determined by it must prepare itself for this reception and determination. Man's higher, spiritual faculties are immaterial and intrinsically independent from matter. Thus they have no organs of their own and need for their functioning the assistance of the highest sense powers, the imagination, the memory, the "cogitative power" of the Scholastics; these faculties cannot operate until the brain is fully developed. Therefore the embryo is first animated by a vegetative soul and then by a sensitive soul. As it continues to develop it reaches higher levels of organization and complexity, and when the cortex is ready another ontological leap takes place. The fetal organism is now sufficiently organized to receive a new substantial form: the spiritual, immortal soul. Only at this stage may we speak of personal human life.[44] Donceel is convinced that hylomorphism postulates delayed hominization: "If form and matter are strictly complementary, as hylomorphism holds, there can be an actual human soul only in a body endowed with the organs required for the spiritual activities of man. We know that the brain, and especially the cortex, are the main organs of those highest sense activities without which no spiritual activity is possible."[45]

Donceel further points out that in the Church the delayed animation view has always enjoyed significant support, and he states that those who turned to immediate ensoulment did so on two questionable premises, a scientific one and a philosophical one. The scientific premise was provided by the erroneous biological theory of preformation, which held that the first cell of the embryo contains every part of the individual in miniature and that fetal development merely consists in an increase in size. This thesis naturally favored immediate animation. The philosophical influence came from Cartesianism which professed a dualistic concept of man and defined the soul as the efficient cause of the human body. Again, this position required ensoulment at fertilization.[46] However, the preformation theory has had to yield to the theory of epigenesis which presents embryogeny as a long process of maturation, differentiation, and organization. Moreover, contemporary philosophy is strongly antidualistic and, as a result, Catholic philosophers and theologians are more clearly aware of the real import of hylomorphism. Donceel therefore foresees that the tide will turn again in favor of the Thomistic understanding of man's ontogeny, a view which he considers much more congenial to the Catholic tradition than immediate animation.[47]

Finally Donceel suggests that the philosophical criterion of human personhood is human activity, and that the most typically human activity consists in "reflection, self-awareness, the power of saying 'I'." Before applying the predicate "person" to a human organism we are entitled to require the presence of a rational soul, and this presence depends on the availability of the organs needed for rational activity: the senses, the nervous system, the brain, and especially the cortex. These are not ready at the early stages of pregnancy; therefore it seems certain that the fetus is not a human person before it is several weeks old.[48]

IV. The Impulse from Ecumenism

Parallel to the growing conviction that the human conceptus achieves personhood only at a later stage of pregnancy, we witness in the American Catholic abortion literature of the late 1960s an increasing awareness and appreciation of Protestant thinking on the value of fetal life. An analysis of the Protestant position on this subject lies beyond the scope of this book, and it is neither feasible nor necessary to register and verify the multitudinous observations which Catholic authors have made regarding Protestant attitudes towards abortion and abortion laws. Yet there can be no doubt that Protestant thought on these issues has had some influence on the Catholic debate and the main thrust of this impetus must be indicated.

The Third International Symposium of the National Commission on

Human Life, Reproduction, and Rhythm, which was held in New York in November 1967, was devoted to a "probing consideration of both abortion and periodic continence."[49] In a report on this symposium John J. Lynch refers to the papers on abortion read by exponents of the Anglican, Lutheran, Catholic, and Jewish positions and observes that "despite the diversity of their religious commitments, the four theologians were in strikingly substantial agreement on the moral issue at stake."[50] He continues:

> In the interests of totally honest reporting it should be stated that on this question of the morality of therapeutic abortion Lutheran, Anglican, and Jew differ agreeably in at least one notable respect from Roman Catholic. Where Fr. Corcoran said, "Never," to the procedure, Pastor Neuhaus, Fr. Carroll, and Rabbi Jakobovits apparently restricted themselves ... to a "hardly-ever" position. (The exception which the latter had in mind was the instance — more theoretical than practical in medical opinion that is virtually unanimous — in which therapeutic abortion would be necessary to save the life of the mother.)[51]

Again at the end of 1967, Robert F. Drinan reviewed contemporary Protestant thinking on abortion as manifested in the statements of various Churches and in the writings of individual theologians. He warned Catholics not to underestimate the commitment of Protestants to unborn life even if they propound their views less vigorously than Catholics:

> The relative absence in Protestant thought of a highly articulated moral attitude toward abortion, a phenomenon regretted by a significant number of contemporary Protestant theologians, should not give rise to the inference that silence means consent. At the same time, the clearly articulated Catholic moral position regarding abortion should not lead Catholics to the conclusion that unless Protestants adopt the entire body of Catholic thinking on abortion, Protestants are in effect following a policy of allowing abortion for trivial reasons.[52]

At the 1968 convention of the Catholic Theological Society of America, Richard A. McCormick analysed the writings on abortion of Paul Ramsey and James M. Gustafson. Describing Ramsey's view as an attempt "to narrow the category of direct killing"[53] and Gustafson's proposition as a probing "into all factors of the moral judgement to discover values which create the possibility of an exception to the traditional norm,"[54] McCormick suggests that Catholic moralists engage themselves in similar efforts. He points out that the contemporary formulation of the Church's teaching on abortion hinges on two concepts, *direct* and *innocent,* and he observes that these were formed and determined in the course of the centuries. Therefore their development "was controlled by the categories of thought and scientific information available at the time.''[55] Thus it is possible that the Catholic position stands in need of a ''sharpening and delimiting of the category of abortion.''[56] McCormick concludes:

> Our constant theological effort is to isolate and formulate the malice of forbidden theft, forbidden lying, forbidden sterilization and so on. We must do the same for abortion; otherwise we are in no position to understand what ''direct killing of the innocent'' really means. It would seem that no reading of Church teaching can be accepted which eliminates on principle this necessary theological task. And for this reason our constantly expanding understanding of reality and the reworking of our categories in light of this growth cannot be read as an attempt to change Church teaching. It is an attempt only to purify it, even if this attempt is clumsy and perhaps leads us to an honest mistake.[57]

Leonard F.X. Mayhew has been the first Catholic author to draw attention to the ''positive aspects'' of the Protestant approach to the abortion problem. He explains that their moral methodology takes an existential rather than a theoretical view of the woman's dilemma. It will not dictate a solution on the basis of abstract theories but pays attention to the observable facts of the personal and social circumstances: the physical and psychological health of the mother, the origin of the pregnancy (rape, incest, etc.), and the prospects of the child (wanted or unwanted, the likelihood of deformity). It also takes into consideration the evidence of physicians, psychologists, and social workers whose direct contact with the actual conditions gives their opinion a ''concreteness that recommends it against speculative theorizing.''[58] Behind this concreteness, ''there is the implicit conviction that moral decisions can be systematized only with great difficulty, if at all.''[59] In Mayhew's view the Protestant approach has a twofold advantage. It realistically acknowledges the limitations of many human situations, and it leaves room for personal decision-making:

> (I)t allows the discussion to be placed squarely on the level of morality, i.e., clearly in terms of the elements by which free decisions can and must be made, rather than on dogmatic grounds. The psychological and social implications of sexuality, marriage and child-bearing form an area of enormous moral concern for modern society. The complications involved in determining personal freedom in these areas are a commonplace of post-Freudian civilization. Moral theories that leave room for them are prima facie more acceptable to contemporary thinking than those which ignore them. These complications affect the discussion of abortion in numerous ways, a fact which the Catholic position does not seem to recognize.[60]

At a later stage of the debate Gregory Baum also draws attention to the "liberal" position of some Protestant Churches on abortion which, like Mayhew, he attributes to their traditional emphasis on man's personal moral decision-making. While the Catholic Church teaches that man enters into his destiny by conforming to the given order of nature, the Protestant view proposes that man reaches his final end by assuming responsibility for himself and his environment, by creating his own future. The Protestant tradition sees God's providence not as coming from above but as "a gracious action within human life, freeing and enabling people ever to expand the area of their responsibility."[61] Thus contraception is not considered as a grave and undue interference with an order of nature which reflects God's providence. God's providence "is believed to be operative through the grace-sustained free choice of mother and father," and this conviction leaves the decision on the number of children in the hands of the parents.[62] It is this world view of man's ever-increasing responsibility for his future, for the number of children born, and for the kind of life these children will have that has led some Protestant Churches and Protestant theologians to acknowledge abortion as a legitimate moral choice in extreme cases. In this perspective abortion remains a drastic intervention into the life process but under certain circumstances it seems justified.[63] Baum then calls for a change in attitude on the part of the Catholic Church which must engage itself in an ecumenical dialogue on the abortion issue:

> Since no one claims that the traditional position is revealed by God, Catholics should not adopt a tone of voice as if their position is beyond challenge. Catholics may hold that, from their point of view, a liberal position on abortion is immoral, possibly due to false consciousness induced by the social conditions of industrial society, but they have no right whatever to suggest that the thinkers who differ from them are immoral, that their position reflects a lack of virtue and that the theologians and the theologically-oriented among them have refused to search the gospel to find God's will in regard to this contemporary problem.
>
> The ecumenical ecclesiology, found in the Decree on Ecumenism, which has been commonly adopted by Catholic theologians in North America, demands that we regard the abortion issue as a complex one. While Catholics may repudiate certain extreme positions on abortion with vehemence and passion, I do not see how they can do this to the more nuanced and careful positions of Christian thinkers and their churches. The idea that Catholics can solve the moral and pastoral problems of the present age simply by themselves, without relying on ecumenical dialogue and cooperation and without hoping that wisdom and insight will be exchanged among various Christian communities, living as they do in such varied circumstances, seems to me contrary to the ecclesial foundation of the Christian faith.[64]

The statements which have been presented and analysed in this chapter clearly indicate that in the late 1960s a number of Catholic authors began to develop reservations about the empirical-ethical argument on abortion which had recently emerged in American Catholic thinking. Their basic contention was that biology is no substitute for ethics. Biology can only give an empirical description of the origin and growth of the human organism and predict its biological future. Whether and at which point and to what extent this entity constitutes a morally inviolable human person is not for the positive sciences to decide but must be determined by proper ethical reasoning. They further held that, from a biological point of view, the individualization of fetal life cannot be said to take place at conception, so that philosophically it is incorrect to designate this point as the beginning of human personhood. Thus some Catholic authors began to feel the need of reexamining systematically the principles underlying the traditional Catholic verdict on abortion. This feeling was reinforced by their growing awareness that the more liberal positions of Protestant churches and theologians were the result of serious attempts to present ethical formulations of an attitude that was genuinely pro-life and genuinely Christian. This does not mean to say, however, that they would eventually come to consider "pre-personal life" as less than very valuable and worthy of protection.[65] Nor would there be question of a wholesale acceptance of Protestant thought on the abortion issue.[66]

The empirical-ethical argument was one-dimensional in its emphasis on the biological characteristics of fetal life and its right of survival under almost any circumstances. The new approach will attempt a wider definition of personhood while its moral methodology will try to take into consideration the multiplicity of values that are at stake in the abortion decision. The new argument will be multidimensional. Describing it will be the task of my next chapter.

NOTES

[1] Thomas L. Hayes, "Abortion: A Biological View," *Commonweal* 85 (1967), p. 676.
[2] *Ibid.*, p. 676. See also: Leonard F.X. Mayhew, "Abortion: Two Sides and Some Complaints," *Ecumenist* 5 (1967), p. 76.
[3] Hayes, *op. cit.*, p. 676.
[4] Leo O. Farley, "The Meaning of Life and Divine Transcendence," *The Catholic Theological Society of America: Proceedings of the Twenty-Third Annual Convention, Washington, D.C., June 17-20, 1968* 23 (1968), p. 114.
[5] *Ibid.*, pp. 114-115.
[6] *Ibid.*, pp. 115-117.

[7] Andre E. Hellegers, "Fetal Development," *Theological Studies* 31 (1970), p. 9.

[8] *Ibid.*, p. 9.

[9] *Ibid.*, p. 3.

[10] Daniel Callahan, *Abortion: Law, Choice and Morality* (New York: Macmillan, 1970), pp. 351-352.

[11] *Ibid.*, pp. 352-353.

[12] *Ibid.*, p. 378. See also: *id.*, "Abortion: Some Ethical Issues," in David F. Walbert and J. Douglas Butler (eds.), *Abortion, Society, and the Law* (Cleveland: Case Western Reserve University, 1973), p. 94; Bernard J. Ransil, *Abortion* (Paramus, N.J.: Paulist Press Deus Books, 1969), pp. 66-67; Garth L. Hallett, S.J., "The Plain Meaning of Abortion," *America* 124 (1971), p. 632.

[13] Callahan, *Abortion: Law, Choice and Morality, op. cit.*, p. 378.

[14] Joseph F. Donceel, S.J., "Immediate Animation and Delayed Hominization," *Theological Studies* 31 (1970), p. 97.

[15] *Ibid.*, p. 97.

[16] This is the substance of Daniel Callahan's criticism of the traditional Catholic position or the "genetic school"; *Abortion: Law, Choice and Morality, op. cit.*, pp. 396, 399, 400, 419-420.

[17] Similar observations were made at the 1967 International Conference on Abortion. See: Robert E. Cooke *et al.* (eds.), *The Terrible Choice: The Abortion Dilemma. Based on the Proceedings of the International Conference on Abortion Sponsored by the Harvard Divinity School and the Joseph P. Kennedy Jr. Foundation* (New York: Bantam Books, 1968), pp. 81-89. See also: Albert R. di Ianni, S.M., "Is the Fetus a Person?" *American Ecclesiastical Review* 168 (1974), pp. 310-317.

[18] Hayes, *op. cit.*, p. 676.

[19] *Ibid.*, p. 677; Callahan, *Abortion: Law, Choice and Morality, op. cit.*, p. 382; James J. Diamond, "Abortion, Animation, and Biological Hominization," *Theological Studies* 36 (1975), pp. 308, 309-310.

[20] Hayes, *op. cit.*, pp. 677-678; Ransil, *op. cit.*, p. 69; Callahan, *Abortion: Law, Choice and Morality, op. cit.*, pp. 382-383, 384. Callahan identifies Hayes as an exponent of the "developmental school"; *ibid.*, p. 384. Nor does an analysis of the fetus' potentiality lead to a single point in time when the new individual comes into existence. Hayes points out that human potential is not a property which is found exclusively in the zygote. It extends back to the individual sperm and ovum cells, even in part to the cells of the testes and ovaries of the parents. From this early stage onwards the living system exchanges potential for realized form and function in a continuous way. The sperm and ovum each have a wide potential and can develop into many kinds of individuals. When fusion takes place, some of the potential is realized but at the same time the possibilities are narrowed and some of the potential is lost; *op. cit.*, p. 678. Richard Stith objects to this argument: to see no difference between an unfertilized and a fertilized egg is to fail to distinguish *probability* from *potentiality*: "A Secular Case Against Abortion on Demand," *Commonweal* 95 (1971), p. 152.

[21] Hayes, *op. cit.*, p. 677; Callahan, *Abortion: Law, Choice and Morality, op. cit.*, pp. 374-375, 382; Diamond, *op. cit.*, pp. 313-314; John F. Dedek, "Abortion: A Theological Judgment," *Chicago Studies* 10 (1971), p. 318.

[22] Joseph F. Donceel, S.J., "Abortion: Mediate V. Immediate Animation," *Continuum* 5 (1967), p. 171; *id.*, "Immediate Animation and Delayed Hominization," *op. cit.*, pp. 98-99; Diamond, *op. cit.*, p. 312; Bernard Häring, "A Theological Evaluation," in

John T. Noonan, Jr. (ed.), *The Morality of Abortion: Legal and Historical Perspectives* (Cambridge, Massachusetts: Harvard University Press, 1970), p. 130; Hellegers, *op. cit.*, p. 4; Hayes, *op. cit.*, p. 678. David Granfield attempts to reconcile immediate animation with twinning and proposes as the more reasonable explanation that at the moment of radical cleavage an additional spiritual soul is infused just as one was infused at conception. In both instances a prepared human organism receives its principle of life, unity, and spirituality at the very beginning of its independent existence; *The Abortion Decision* (revised ed.; Garden City, N.Y.: Doubleday Image Books, 1971), p. 31. See also: Joseph T. Mangan, S.J., "The Wonder of Myself: Ethical-Theological Aspects of Direct Abortion," *Theological Studies* 31 (1970), p. 132; Gary M. Atkinson, "The Morality of Abortion," *International Philosophical Quarterly* 14 (1974), p. 349; James M. Humber, "The Case Against Abortion," *Thomist* 39 (1975), p. 69. Germain G. Grisez points out that before cleavage identical twins certainly do not lack individuality when considered in comparison with others, even though their individuality in relation to each other may be qualified and puzzling. However, if anyone wishes to argue that identical twins cannot be individuals until they are distinct from each other, he shall have to hold that conjoined identical twins, especially those sharing some organs, are not human individuals at all; *Abortion: The Myths, the Realities, and the Arguments* (New York: Corpus Books, 1970), p. 26.

[23] Diamond, *op. cit.*, p. 312.

[24] Hellegers, *op. cit.*, pp. 4-5; Dedek, *op. cit.*, p. 318. Granfield considers the fate of the supernumerary soul and states that after recombination the composite of the two bodies is animated by one vital principle, perhaps by that of the twin which had a stronger hold on its own material substance. For the other twin this separation is a kind of death, which the separation of body and soul essentially implies; *op. cit*, p. 31. Grisez says in reference to mosaics that the two morulae are distinct individuals until they are combined. They they cease to exist as such and form a new individual; *op. cit.*, p. 27. See also: Granfield, *op. cit.*, p. 35. Thomas W. Hilgers admits that cell fusion and recombination of early zygotic material can be accomplished under carefully controlled laboratory conditions. However, there is no evidence whatsoever that recombination occurs "naturally" in man; "Human Reproduction: Three Issues for the Moral Theologian," *Theological Studies* 38 (1977), pp. 149-151.

[25] Diamond, *op. cit.*, p. 312.

[26] *Ibid.*, p. 310; Hellegers, *op. cit.*, p. 5; Bernard Häring, "New Dimensions of Responsible Parenthood," *Theological Studies* 37 (1976), p. 126.

[27] Hellegers, *op. cit.*, p. 5; Diamond, *op. cit.*, pp. 311-312; Häring, "New Dimensions of Responsible Parenthood," *op. cit.*, p. 126; Donceel, "Immediate Animation and Delayed Hominization," *op. cit.*, p. 98. Hilgers states that these highly specialized experiments have no essential relation to the normal, natural process of embryogeny. In human reproduction such occurrences are extremely rare and are merely the result of abnormal, diseased development. These accidents of nature should not form the basis of moral decision-making; *op. cit.*, pp. 149-151.

[28] Donceel, "Immediate Animation and Delayed Hominization," *op. cit.*, p. 99. Grisez is of the opinion that, even if all ova of all species could be stimulated into parthenogenetic development, this would by no means prove the equivalence of the zygote and the unstimulated ovum. It would rather demonstrate the opposite, for the stimulation leading to such extraordinary development is precisely what the fertilized ovum does not have to undergo; *op. cit.*, p. 24. Humber discusses the status of the "natural" parthenogenetic conceptus; *op. cit.*, pp. 67-69.

[29] Roy U. Schenk, "Let's Think About Abortion," *Catholic World* 207, April 1968, p. 16. Granfield fails to refute this argument when he explains that the fetus' uniqueness does not consist in its genetic structure which may be reduplicated but in its phenotypical identity which is established by the interaction of the genetic heritage with its specific environment; *op. cit.*, p. 35. Donceel refers to the *in vitro* fertilization of human ova with human spermatozoa and wonders about the status of these microscopic organisms; "Abortion: Mediate V. Immediate Animation," *op. cit.*, p. 171. See also: Diamond, *op. cit.*, pp. 323-324.

[30] Rudolph Ehrensing, "The I.U.D.: How It Works: Is It Moral?" *National Catholic Reporter*, April 20-27, 1966, p. 6; Callahan, *Abortion: Law, Choice and Morality, op. cit.*, pp. 381-382. Granfield thinks that pathological growths are due to nonensoulment: the conceptus never received the vital, organizing principle of unity; *op. cit.*, p. 35. Grisez discusses various "monsters" and comes to the conclusion that not everything coming from the womb should be considered a human being; *op. cit.*, pp. 27-30. It is not clear from the medical literature whether a hydatidiform mole is a defective ovum or a defective placenta. See: Callahan, *ibid.*, pp. 402-403 (note 36).

[31] Diamond, *op. cit.*, pp. 312-313; Häring, "A Theological Evaluation," *op. cit.*, p. 130; Callahan, *Abortion: Law, Choice and Morality, op. cit.*, pp. 381-382; Donceel, "Immediate Animation and Delayed Hominization," *op. cit.*, pp. 99-100. Hilgers admits that there is some early embryonic loss but stresses that it is very small and that its cause is still unknown. Moreover, he does not attach any moral significance to this phenomenon: abnormalities of growth, development, and function which occur before birth should be viewed in the same fashion as those that occur after birth; *op. cit*, pp. 147-149, 151. See also: Grisez, *op. cit.*, pp. 30-32.

[32] Schenk, *op. cit.*, p. 16; Häring, "A Theological Evaluation," *op. cit.*, p. 130; Donceel, "Immediate Animation and Delayed Hominization," *op. cit.*, pp. 100-101. See also: Ehrensing, *op. cit.*, p. 6. Donceel maintains that the immediate animation view is a remnant of the traditional Catholic aversion to the "hypothesis" of evolution; *ibid.*, p. 100. Granfield admits a kind of general parallelism but not an exact historical recapitulation of the stages of evolution. The zygote can in no way be compared with the hypothetical unicellular organism which marked the beginning of phylogeny. Moreover, ontogeny cannot run through an ancestral series because the embryo of the higher animal form is never identical with a lower animal form. The members of the various phylogenetic series are independent living forms and their embryonal stages are mere developmental stages. A human organism remains human from zygote to corpse but at various stages of its development it reflects its forbears. It does not become them but represents the ancestral features that have survived, if only as useless vestiges; *op. cit.*, pp. 32-33. See also: Grisez, *op. cit.*, pp. 19-20; Rudolph J. Gerber, "Abortion: Parameters for Decision," *International Philosophical Quarterly* 11 (1971), p. 569.

[33] Hellegers, *op. cit.*, p. 5.

[34] Dedek, *op. cit.*, p. 318.

[35] Hayes, *op. cit.*, p. 678.

[36] Donceel, "Immediate Animation and Delayed Hominization," *op. cit.*, p. 98.

[37] Dedek, *op. cit.*, p. 318.

[38] Diamond, *op. cit.*, p. 307. Some authors reflect on the implications which these biological discoveries have for the immediate ensoulment theory. See: Hellegers, *op. cit.*, p. 5; Donceel, "Immediate Animation and Delayed Hominization," *op. cit.*, p. 99; Thomas A. Wassmer, S.J., *Christian Ethics for Today* (Milwaukee: Bruce, 1969), p. 199. The American bishops state in 1974 that the scientific data on twinning, recombination, and

the early activity of the zygote's genetic material are still fragmentary with the result that interpretations are necessarily quite speculative. In the meantime the "known norm" that individual human life originates at fertilization should be the basis of law; "Testimony of United States Catholic Conference on Constitutional Amendment Protecting Unborn Human Life before the Sub-Committee on Constitutional Amendments of the Senate Committee on the Judiciary—March 7, 1974," in National Conference of Catholic Bishops, United States Catholic Conference, *Documentation on the Right to Life and Abortion* (Washington, D.C.: Publications Office U.S.C.C., 1974), p. 32, note 18.

[39] Cfr. his articles cited in notes 14 and 22, *supra*. Donceel expounded his position at the 1968 International Conference on Abortion; "A Liberal Catholic's View," in Robert E. Hall (ed.), *Abortion in a Changing World: The Proceedings of an International Conference on Abortion Convened in Hot Springs, Virginia, November 17-20, 1968, by the Association for the Study of Abortion* (vols. I-II; New York: Columbia University Press, 1970); vol. I, pp. 39-45. A good number of Catholic authors took a positive view of Donceel's delayed hominization theory: Wassmer, *op. cit.*, pp. 197-200; Robert H. Springer, S.J., "Notes on Moral Theology," *Theological Studies* 31 (1970), pp. 500-501; Callahan, *Abortion: Law, Choice and Morality, op. cit.*, pp. 432-433. See also: Mayhew, *op. cit.*, p. 76; Richard A. McCormick, S.J., "Abortion," *America* 112 (1965), p. 879; Robert F. Drinan, S.J., "The Jurisprudential Options on Abortion," *Theological Studies* 31 (1970), p. 151. For less emphatic endorsements see: Atkinson, *op. cit.*, p. 349; Louis Dupré, "A New Approach to the Abortion Problem," *Theological Studies* 34 (1973), p. 483.

[40] *In Libros IV Sententiarum* II, d. 18, q. 2, a. 3; *Questiones Disputatae de Potentia* III, q. 9; *Summa Contra Gentiles* II, 87-89; *Summa Theologica* I, q. 118, a. 2. Cfr. Donceel, "Immediate Animation and Delayed Hominization," *op. cit.*, pp. 78-79.

[41] Donceel, "Immediate Animation and Delayed Hominization," *op. cit.*, pp. 79-80.

[42] *Ibid.*, p. 80.

[43] *Ibid.*, pp. 79-82, 83.

[44] *Ibid.*, pp. 82-83. However, Donceel does not attribute animation to a categorical intervention of God into the processes of nature; *ibid.*, p. 83, note 25; pp. 84-85. Ransil thinks that the Church's insistence on fertilization as the moment of animation is based on pragmatic considerations—since fertilization is the only event capable of precise temporal definition; *op. cit.*, pp. 66-68. Mayhew imputes the immediate animation view to the casuistry of theologians who were anxious to protect the "dogmatic abstraction of the immediate divine creation of the individual soul"; *op. cit.*, p. 76. Some authors consider ensoulment arguments ethereal and unreal. See: Di Ianni, *op. cit.*, pp. 323-324, note 6; Hallett, *op. cit.*, pp. 632-633; Atkinson, *op. cit.*, pp. 347-350; Ransil, *op. cit.*, pp. 66-68.

[45] Donceel, "Immediate Animation and Delayed Hominization," *op. cit.*, p. 83. See also: Häring, "A Theological Evaluation," *op. cit.*, p. 130. Diamond does not see much future in pursuits of the time of animation, which are based on explorations of a formal cause before 14-22 days; *op. cit.*, p. 317. See also: Roland M. Nardone, "The Nexus of Biology and the Abortion Issue," *Jurist* 33 (1973), pp. 157-158.

[46] Donceel, "Immediate Animation and Delayed Hominization," *op. cit.*, pp. 85-96.

[47] *Ibid.*, pp. 88-92, 93, 96, 102-104.

[48] *Ibid.*, p. 101. Granfield maintains that the Thomistic ensoulment theory is inconsistent. It defines the vegetative and animal souls as "formal causes" and at the same time affirms

that these souls prepare fetal life for the reception of the rational soul. If the first two souls can work architecturally in spite of being formal causes, the rational soul can do the same. According to Thomistic philosophy, the rational soul has the powers of the lesser principles of life. At the moment of fertilization, then, a rational soul is infused which has the powers of three (vegetative, animal, and rational). This soul constitutes the "vital principle" or "life force" of the fetus from the very beginning; *op. cit.*, pp. 29-31. See also: Vitale H. Paganelli, "A Review of the March, 1970, *Theological Studies;* Abortion Issue," *Linacre Quarterly* 37 (1970), p. 209. Gerber considers Donceel's approach an "anachronistic escape"; *op. cit.*, p. 565. Grisez holds that St. Thomas' biological errors invalidate his anthropological conclusions. If St. Thomas had known about the specific and individual genetic uniqueness of the zygote which makes it biologically a living organism of the human species, he would have supported immediate animation. Moreover, Donceel's view disregards the fact that fetal development is a continuous process. Thus he does not explain why the fetus, which in his opinion cannot be a human body at the zygote stage, can be one after a few weeks; *op. cit.*, p. 283. See also: Mangan, *op. cit.*, pp. 129-131. Donceel is aware of these objections but he insists that immediate animation smacks of Platonic or Cartesian dualism. He admits that fetal development is continuous but in his opinion this does not exclude ontological shifts; *ibid.*, pp. 82-83, 100-101.

[49] John J. Lynch, S.J., "Legalized Abortion: Commission Hears Ecumenical Discussion," *Linacre Quarterly* 35 (1968), p. 38.

[50] *Ibid.*, p. 54.

[51] *Ibid.*, pp. 39-40.

[52] Robert F. Drinan, S.J., "Abortion: Contemporary Protestant Thinking," *America* 117 (1967), p. 715. Note that Drinan's observations reflect the situation as it was in 1967 and that Protestant attitudes towards the *legality* of abortion have been considerably more liberal than their positions on the *moral* issue. See also: Catholic Bishops of Texas, "An Open Letter on Abortion—April, 1971," in Daughters of St. Paul (eds.), *Yes to Life* (Boston: St. Paul Editions, 1977), p. 237; Editorial, "Abortion and U.S. Protestants," *America* 128 (1973), pp. 156-157.

[53] Richard A. McCormick, S.J., "Past Church Teaching on Abortion," *The Catholic Theological Society of America: Proceedings, op. cit.*, p. 149.

[54] *Ibid.*, p. 149.

[55] *Ibid.*, p. 150.

[56] *Ibid.*, p. 150.

[57] *Ibid.*, p. 150.

[58] Mayhew, *op. cit.*, pp. 76-77.

[59] *Ibid.*, p. 77.

[60] *Ibid.*, p. 77. See also: Donceel, "Immediate Animation and Delayed Hominization," *op. cit.*, pp. 104-105. In Grisez's view, Protestant ethics is situationist and unsatisfactory from a philosophical point of view. However, it calls attention to an issue that must be faced by any ethical system: the problem of conflict situations and the possibility of admitting exceptions to the general rule in extreme cases of conflict; *op. cit.*, p. 303.

[61] Gregory Baum, "Abortion: An Ecumenical Dilemma," *Commonweal* 99 (1973), p. 233.

[62] *Ibid.*, p. 233.

[63] *Ibid.*, pp. 233-234.

[64] *Ibid.*, p. 232. Baum refers to the *Decree on Ecumenism* of Vatican II, *"Unitatis Redintegratio."* See also: Wassmer, *op. cit.*, pp. 201-202. For good examples of ecumenical

dialogue on abortion, see: Noonan, *The Morality of Abortion: Legal and Historical Perspectives, op. cit.;* Charles E. Curran, *Politics, Medicine, and Christian Ethics: A Dialogue with Paul Ramsey* (Philadelphia: Fortress Press, 1973), pp. 110-131; Paul Ramsey, "Abortion: A Review Article," *Thomist* 37 (1973), pp. 174-226; Claude U. Broach (ed.), *Seminar on Abortion: The Proceedings of a Dialogue Between Catholics and Baptists* (Charlotte, N.C.: The Ecumenical Institute, 1975).

[65] Hallett, *op. cit.,* p. 633; Häring, "A Theological Evaluation," *op. cit.,* p. 131; Donceel, "Immediate Animation and Delayed Hominization," *op. cit.,* p. 105.

[66] In Mayhew's view, the chief problem in the Protestant position is that it fails to provide a criterion of adequate or proportionate cause to justify abortion; *op. cit.,* p. 77.

Chapter Five

Delayed Hominization, Proportionate Reason, and Personal Responsibility

We have seen that the late 1960s and early 1970s witnessed considerable uneasiness among American Catholic authors with the biological emphasis in the formulation of the official Catholic teaching on abortion. At the same time there was growing appreciation of the Protestant view which seemed to recognize more adequately the personal moral responsibility of man and the existential complications of many pregnancies. In this chapter, which will conclude our analysis of the debate on the moral aspects of the abortion issue, I will describe how a significant number of American Catholic authors have tried, not only to establish a new criterion of personhood, but also to construct a wider basis from which an abortion decision should be taken.

My approach will again be a thematic one. Rather than listing the various authors and their opinions, I will attempt to identify the areas where their views converge. It stands to reason that this method does less than full justice to the personal positions of the authors. However, by concentrating on totality and trends rather than on individual efforts, I hope to present a clear and comprehensive survey of the further evolution of the Catholic debate.

I. Biological and Behavioral Observations

In the previous chapter we saw that some authors questioned, from an empirico-biological point of view, the validity of propositions which identify hominization or personalization with fertilization. James J. Diamond and Bernard J. Ransil have pursued this line of investigation and have presented further insights which would seem to challenge the Catholic contention that personhood is coextensive with human life and that, therefore, at any stage of its development, the fetus is a human being in the same degree as its mother. Ransil emphasizes that an adequate grasp of the biological facts is an essential prerequisite for a moral judgement on abortion.[1] His observations can be summarized as follows:

1. *The biological status of the unborn child.* From a biological point of view it is incorrect to state that mother and fetus have equal functional status throughout the prenatal period. Mother and fetus constitute a symbiotic system but there is no question of functional equality; we are dealing with an independent host organism (the mother) which harbors and nourishes a dependent organism (the conceptus). The fetus is so dependent that it requires the maternal circulatory system for its very survival. The mother provides for all physical needs of the conceptus while the child takes all and gives nothing in return.[2]

2. *The fetus as a parasite.* Normally the symbiotic relationship between the mother and her fetus is a benign one; it primarily benefits the child and has very few or no adverse effects on the health of the mother. Sometimes, however, this relationship assumes a different character and becomes antagonistic, as is the case in toxemia of pregnancy. In such conditions the benign functional balance beween mother and fetus is disturbed, and the fetus becomes a parasite in the sense that its continued presence threatens the welfare of the host organism.[3]

3. *The fetus as a tumorous growth.* From a functional point of view the fetus could also be described as a cancerous growth. In fact a tumor may first be mistaken for a pregnancy. In the vast majority of cases pregnancy is benign and from a histological and structural point of view there is no resemblance between the conceptus and a tumor. But sometimes the fetus functions somewhat like a malignant growth because it develops at the expense of the maternal host organism.[4]

Ransil's biological insights lead him to assert that in pregnancy there is no question of two equivalent individuals in the sense of two independent beings of equivalent morphology and function.[5] Diamond presents a different argument. Like Ransil, he offers empirical data in order to "provide input to the moralist who recognizes that when the facts of a moral situation change, the moral considerations appropriate to the situation also change."[6] In Diamond's view, the following embryological facts have moral significance:

1. *The vital activity of the early fetus.* A "free" sperm, which has detached itself from the circulatory-respiratory system of the male parent, and a "free" ovum, which has broken free from the ovary, are both self-supporting in their nutritional and respiratory needs. This applies also to the zygote, the morula, and the blastula which internally generate the fuel supplies necessary for continued physico-chemical functioning. These entities live off themselves but this self-cannibalism depletes their internal

resources. Unless the fertilizatum succeeds in establishing, within a given period of time, an alternative and fully functional source of nutrition, it will die. Its self-consumptive mode of sustenance comes to an end from the fourteenth day after fertilization to seven to ten days later, depending on individual circumstances. It is during this period that its internal supplies are exhausted and it makes a functional entry into the maternal circulatory system which then takes over. At this point the embryo begins to grow. The heart starts to beat and human death mechanisms can now be distinguished for the first time. There is, therefore, a radical difference between the vital activity of the unimplanted entity and that of the implanted blastocyst.[7]

2. *The hominal organizer.* In the cell mass of the morula and blastula there is potential for differentiation which is oriented towards the future coherent emergence of the various parts of the adult body. The individual cells retain this differentiability until the end of the second week when the hominal or primary organizer begins to operate in the blastocyst. This primary organizer appears on the posterior lip of the blastopore, and it orders the pluripotent cells to differentiate into specific organ systems so that a homo will form. If it does not appear or if it is removed, no such differentiation will take place. Furthermore, once the organizer is operative in the cell mass, the unity of the individual has been irrevocably established because beyond this point twinning and recombination are no longer possible.[8]

Diamond believes that the biological events which occur between the fourteenth and the twenty-second day should weigh extremely heavily in the calculation of the beginning of personal life.[9] He reduces the significance of conception: at fertilization are laid down *only* the genotypical and phenotypical characteristics of the subsequently hominizable entity or entities. But individualization and hominization do not take place until the later part of the second or the early part of the third week:[10]

> In all scientific candor, I suggest that the overwhelming weight of biological data tilts the objective scientist toward that inexactly definable time period of 2 to 3 weeks after fertilization as the time or point in process when biological hominization occurs.[11]

Diamond and Andre E. Hellegers have offered some parallel observations of a nonempirical nature. Diamond admits that these propositions carry no intrinsic metaphysical or moral weight but he believes that they have some relevance and that, like the biological data, they postulate delayed personalization:[12]

1. *The biological sign of motherhood.* The earliest point at which a woman can become aware of her pregnancy is approximately fourteen days

after ovulation and fertilization, when she misses her period. Before this time she is physically unable to consider herself a "mother." On the fourteenth day the primary organizer has begun its activities. At this stage twinning is no longer possible and the brain and the heart have differentiated. Hominization has just occurred.[13]

2. *The medical diagnosis of pregnancy.* Before implantation to diagnose the woman's condition is impossible even for a doctor applying a pregnancy test.[14]

3. *Medical practice.* Gynecological operations such as curettage are frequently performed during the second half of the menstrual cycle, i.e., after ovulation but before the woman is due to have her period. This is common medical practice in spite of the fact that at this time a fertilized ovum could well be present. Curettage frustrates the implantation of the blastocyst because this operation removes the lining of the uterus, but there has never been a medical tradition to restrict such interventions to the time immediately following menstruation when no fertilized egg can be present. Nor are women instructed, before a curettage, not to have sexual intercourse in order to avoid possible interference with a zygote.[15]

4. *Popular opinion.* The act of abortion has been understood for centuries as an attack upon the conceptus *in the womb.* No one has ever considered the prevention of implantation as abortion, not even after the use of anti-implantational agents became common. Couples and doctors who would never consent to an abortion take a different view of the prevention of implantation, regarded as contraception: not the destruction of nascent life but the prevention of the nascence of life and therefore nonhomicidal in character.[16]

5. *Abortion laws.* States which firmly legislated against abortion never included the prevention of implantation in this prohibition.[17]

6. *The practice of the Church.* While the Church has emphasized that innocent human life must be protected from the very first moment of its existence, it has never enunciated criteria by which it must be established that this existence has begun. Moreover, the Church has never defined the prevention of implantation as homicidal, and its excommunication attached to the crime of abortion does not extend to anti-implantational acts. This justifies a distinction between "expulsion from the womb" and "prevention of impulsion into the womb."[18]

Hellegers seems reluctant to identify hominization with fertilization.[19] Diamond is much more definite. The object of a homicidal act must be a homo and since anti-implantational acts are not antihominal they cannot be classified as homicidal.[20] A similar view of the significance of implantation is adopted by Gabriel Pastrana, Richard A. McCormick, and Philip S.

Keane, while Michael V. Viola and Denis Cavanagh incline towards Diamond's position.[21]

II. Philosophies of Personhood

The authors have not restricted their observations on the quality of unborn human life to biological and behavioral propositions. In fact, most of the arguments presented on the question of fetal personhood are of a more philosophical nature, even if they avail themselves of insights from biology and other empirical disciplines. It is these reflections that we must consider now.

The Fundamental Question

A few authors have expressed reservations about formulating the basic problem in terms of "person or nonperson." Some feel that this question cannot be answered, while others maintain that it should not be asked at all. They make the following points:

1. *A dangerous question.* "Is the fetus a person?" is potentially a dangerous question because it might create the impression that personhood is the decisive ethical factor in the abortion decision, to the extent that the unborn child has no claim to respect if it is not a person.[22] (Daniel C. Maguire)

2. *A question of semantics.* In considering the problem of fetal personhood we must separate the factual question, concerned with biological phenomena and animation, from the conceptual question which regards the value of the unborn child. Reducing the conceptual issue to proving or disproving that the fetus is a human person is fighting a purely verbal battle won by the side that is better in semantics. The most important fact about abortion is that it eliminates a human existence. Unless the child is removed from its mother's womb it will grow up and live an adult human life. In this respect it differs little from a baby. Whether or not at the moment of its death the fetus should be called a human person is merely a question of terminology.[23] (Garth L. Hallett)

3. *The continuity of human life.* Preoccupation with the problem of fetal personhood leads to concentration on the momentary status of the conceptus and thus restricts attention to a limited segment of life and a narrow range of facts. This approach neglects an essential characteristic of human life, viz., the continuity of its development which constitutes the strongest argument in favor of the official Catholic position on abortion. It is ironic that pragmatists like James and Dewey emphasize precisely this aspect of

life while the later work of Wittgenstein is interested in the totality of life rather than in isolated sections.[24] (Hallett)

4. *Formal cause and human form of the early fetus.* If we examine the status of a very early fetus in the light of the metaphysical principle that the formal cause of an entity —in this case the soul —does not come into existence until the entity has acquired form —in this case the human form — we are faced with the problem of how to define fetal human form. It seems inappropriate to compare the form of a zygote, morula, or blastula with that of an adult. The fetus at a particular stage of its development must be compared with other human fetuses of the same age. In the case of the very early conceptus this means resorting to the microscope, but here the microscopic evidence is not satisfactory. At the present level of man's ability to measure, a mutual comparison of undifferentiated cell masses presents considerable difficulties. It is, therefore, not really possible to ascertain that human form does exist prior to differentiation.[25] (Diamond)

5. *Inconclusive evidence.* The question regarding the beginning of human personhood cannot be answered with absolute certainty. In some sense of the term human life undoubtedly exists from the moment of fertilization but, as far as personhood is concerned, the only honest conclusion one can draw from the biological and philosophical data is that these are less than absolutely conclusive.[26] (John F. Dedek; James M. Humber)

It is in this perspective of uncertainty that the statements of several authors must be read. Diamond and Hellegers "do not see much future for pursuits of the time of animation which are based on explorations of a formal cause before 14-22 days."[27] Hellegers further points out that the definition of personhood does not pertain to the science of biology but is rather a "societal judgement."[28] Thomas L. Hayes, a biologist, indicates how this societal judgement might take shape. He recognizes the significance of fertilization and admits that the zygote contains most, if not all, of the information necessary for the development of the complete human person. At the same time, few elements of this information, if any, are actually expressed in the form and function of the cell itself. Hayes is prepared to leave it to philosophy and theology to determine whether this unexpressed potential confers on the zygote the nearly absolute right of survival which is associated with the developed individual. Philosophers and theologians might decide to designate an arbitrary point early in pregnancy at which time the fetus is declared a person and endowed with the right of existence. Biology could provide some ideas as to how this point could be reasonably located.[29]

Hallett concedes that conception is "the least arbitrary moment" at which to draw the line but questions the wisdom of making definite demarcations. A definite "line" of personhood would imply that after this time abortion could never be justified under any circumstances. In Hallett's view, such an absolute position would be incompatible with the nature of moral judgement, which must take a variety of factors into account depending on the individual case.[30] Hellegers and Dedek propose that the fundamental problem be rephrased. The theoretical question cannot be solved since the biological and philosophical data are inconclusive. We must therefore ask ourselves what practical ethical policy we should adopt in this situation of theoretical uncertainty.[31]

Individualization

Other authors have not been so hesitant about asking and answering the fundamental question. They consider the empirical and metaphysical data to be sufficiently clear, and they are reluctant to leave room for societal judgements to draw arbitrary lines. One of these is Charles E. Curran who believes that the fundamental question can be answered on the basis of biological insights. Discussing the approach of the "relational" or "social consequences" school, he accepts the importance of relationality in man's existence but points out that at the very beginning of human life we are obviously not dealing with man at his highest level of development. At this very early stage we should ascertain whether the bare minimum required for human existence is present.[32] In Curran's analysis, this minimum is constituted by biological individuality and this criterion implies delayed hominization:

> My own particular opinion is that human life is not present until individuality is established. In this context we are talking about individual human life, but irreversible and differentiated individuality is not present from the time of fecundation. The single fertilized cell undergoes cell division, but in the process twinning may occur until the fourteenth day. This indicates that individual human life is not definitely established before this time. Likewise in man there is also some evidence for recombination —one human being is formed from the product of more than one fertilization. Thus I would argue that individuated human life is not present before this time. Corroborating evidence is the fact that a great number of fecundated ova are expelled from the uterus before they could ever reach this stage of the fourteenth day.[33]

Bernard Häring shares this view. Like Curran, he refers to the phenomenon of twinning and observes that since Boëthius (480-524) the human person has been defined as "an individual substance of a rational nature." Definite individuality is only achieved fourteen days after fertilization; this

means that the morula is not an individual substance. It cannot be a person
or an individual with the dignity and the rights of a full member of the
human species, although it may be granted respect and protection for
different reasons.[34] McCormick adopts the same position and recognizes
individualization as the crucial developmental stage.[35] Robert H. Springer
looks at the issue from the point of view of animation and declares that he is
unable to reconcile immediate hominization with twinning. He finds it
difficult to hold that a person is present from the very beginning and then
somehow divides into two "souls."[36]

The Brain

Some authors feel that the fetus does not meet all the requirements for
personhood even at individualization, and they propose the functioning of
the brain as the criterion of hominization. I mentioned in the previous
chapter that Joseph F. Donceel is one of these. He draws attention to the
rational nature of man and to the fact that the biological substratum of
man's rational activity is not available until later in pregnancy, when the
fetus is "several weeks" old:

> Philosophically speaking, we can be certain that an organism is a human
> person only from its activities. The most typically human activity is
> reflection, self-awareness, the power of saying "I.". . . The least we may
> ask before admitting the presence of a human soul is the availability of
> these organs: the senses, the nervous system, the brain, and especially the
> cortex. Since these organs are not ready during early pregnancy, I feel
> certain that there is no human person until several weeks have elapsed.[37]

Roland M. Nardone is also of the opinion that the question of hominization cannot be settled without reference to the development of the fetal
brain. He asserts that the minimum requirement for personhood is "conscious apprehension" and that this activity requires a biological foundation
in the form of the specialized sensory cells and organs associated with the
nervous system. On the 26th day some sensory tissues, especially those of
the eyes, begin to develop but the earliest reflexes appear only on the 42nd
day, while the first brain waves become discernible a day later. These brain
waves are the first concrete indication that sensory communication in a
primitive form may now be possible. However, it is only in the third month
that the fetus begins to manifest a variety of purposeful body movements
and individualized behavior. Nardone therefore concludes that a three-
months-old fetus is "a sentient moving being, whose psychosomatic self is
well under way."[38]

Roy U. Schenk supports the view that fetal ontogeny is a recapitulation
of ancestral phylogeny. He notes that in the process of phylogenic evolu-

tion a strain of primates achieved hominization by a biologial breakthrough in the cortex which made self-awareness or consciousness possible. He observes a parallel phenomenon in fetal growth: the conceptus becomes a person when its developing cerebral cortex reaches the level of complexity at which consciousness is realized. Schenk suggests that this level is not achieved before the sixth month of pregnancy.[39]

Rudolph H. Ehrensing refers to the fact that the cessation of brain activity is progressively accepted as a valid indication of death. This means that the beginning of brain activity is the crucial factor in hominization: personhood is established by the existence of a living human brain. Ehrensing maintains that it is not the *potential* for the development of a human brain that constitutes a human person, but the *actual accomplishment* —the actual brain structure. Unlike Schenk he does not indicate at what point in pregnancy, by use of the brain criterion, personhood is actually attained.[40] Bernard Häring is willing to consider theories which relate hominization to the development of the cortex, and he believes that these have some tenability, deserve serious consideration and discussion, but at the present stage of the debate it is safer to adopt the criterion of individualization.[41]

The Significance of Potentiality

Several authors have examined the value of fetal life from the point of view of its potentiality and have discussed the logic of Tertullian's maxim, "He is a man who is about to be one." Arguing from a biological point of view, Daniel Callahan and Louis Dupré are doubtful if the very early fetus can be defined as a "homo in potentia." Callahan admits that *statistically* a particular zygote may have a better than even chance of developing into an adult but this does not mean that it will *in fact* realize its biological objective.[42] Its development may well be frustrated by internal or external conditions:

> Because of genetic or other abnormalities, a particular fertilized egg may be destined for spontaneous abortion or to become a hydatidiform mole. The zygote can develop or fail to develop in a number of directions. Under favorable circumstances, it will develop into a human being; but this is not biologically (or statistically) inexorable. The potentiality of a zygote to become a human being need not *necessarily* be fulfilled; that possibility will in any specific case depend upon many other conditions to bring this potentiality to actuality.[43]

Callahan stresses that only time will tell if a particular zygote is potentially capable of human acts. It is then uncertain whether abortion of a very early conceptus is homicidal. One can decide to take no risks and adopt a moral policy which protects all zygotes *as if* they will all develop into human persons. Such a choice would not be incompatible with the biological data but it is not directly necessitated by these data.[44]

Ransil questions the equation of becoming with being on philosophical grounds, and he questions it emphatically. The principle that "what is about to be, is" leads to logical inconsistencies and practical absurdities, and it is not acceptable in any other human situation. Ransil illustrates this with an example from evolution. The evolution of man from lower forms of animal life took millennia, and we may presume that similar processes are continuing around us at their own imperceptible pace. Certain humanoid animals may well be the generic precursors to an advanced form of human life which will emerge in the far distant future. This prospect, however, does not deter us from killing such animals now. The zygote, embryo, and five-months-old fetus are "precursive forms to the viable human infant," and there is no reason to make an exception in their case and classify their becoming as being.[45]

Diamond presents an argument which manifests clear parallels with the biological observations of Callahan and the philosophical exposé of Ransil. Diamond will not even accept the conclusion that, since at least *some* zygotes will in time become hominal organisms, at least *these* zygotes are *homines in potentia*. He admits that some zygotes do have the intrinsic capacity of developing into a human adult but adds that they will only realize this objective if the right extrinsic events occur, and if the wrong extrinsic events are prevented from happening. But, says Diamond, the very same applies to the ovum; the ovum also has the potentiality for becoming a homo if the right event, fertilization, takes place. He therefore feels that in the biological order the concept of potentiality should not be employed[46] and, like Ransil, he finds support for this position in evolution:

> I am not comfortable with divisions of a continuum into subcontinua, and the biodynamic continuum leading to you and me is 3 billion years old and contains a virtual infinity of subcontinua and potentiations for acquiring subsequent potencies.[47]

The statement of Albert R. Di Ianni is less categorical. He is not fully convinced that the potentiality of the early fetus somehow incorporates its future actuality and that the judgement on the quality of the embryo must in some measure give credit to what the conceptus will become.[48]

Developing Personhood

Some authors have adopted a more radical approach to the question of the status of the unborn child and have gone beyond mere attempts to postpone the time of hominization. This has resulted in a more thorough reassessment of the quality of nascent human life and in a new concept: developing personhood.

Ransil again underlines the relevance of the empirical data. When man confronts the various developmental stages of fetal life he has only one instrument at his disposal to understand and classify these biological phenomena: his senses. The verdict of the senses is simple. No one looking at the zygote and its immediate successive forms will equate them with a human being, just as he will not call a fertilized hen's egg a chicken. The evidence of the senses is confirmed by empirical science. On anatomical, physiological, biochemical, and behavioral grounds science can say with certainty that the zygote, the embryo, and the five-months-old conceptus are just that, and as such are "precursive forms" to the viable human infant. Ransil has no doubts about the quality of fetal life. The zygote is not a human being, and the later fetus is not a human being in the same degree as its mother. [49]

Maguire has tried to refine this view. He defines fetal development as a "trajectory to personhood" and draws atention to the importance of the time element in this process. [50] There is a significant difference between the minute zygote and a fetus approaching viability:

> A newly fertilized ovum is a microscopic speck. Of course, it already contains its own genetic code and thus has its genetic individuality and its own innate potentiality. Nevertheless, it is at this point largely potentiality. It has not yet been able to interact with its environment and become more of what it can be. When, by around the fortieth day, it has developed the basic structure of a typically human cerebral cortex, it obviously *is* something significantly more. And when it has developed all of its organs and systems and is near viability..., it is something else again. At a certain point in a pregnancy, abortion becomes very like infanticide. [51]

Di Ianni qualifies fetal growth as a gradual and nonsaltatory continuum, and he inclines towards Maguire's position. He does not want to exclude the possibility that there may be a significant difference in *kind* between the conceptus at the beginning of its development and the "same" entity towards the end of that process. Di Ianni further considers that a true human body is a "necessary and sufficient feature in our concept of personhood"; he points out that the very early fetus is not a homunculus but a rather nondescript mass of protoplasm, even if it is fully programmed genetically and highly complex scientifically. [52] He then proposes to distinguish between the conceptus that is radically incomplete as to human form and function, and the being with achieved corporeity: [53]

> Could it not be suggested that at the earliest stages we are dealing with not the presence of a human body but with the *formation* of a human body?

Could it not be that the physiological basis of personhood is adequately formed only at some point after conception? Could we not suggest that theologians and philosophers might after diligent study of the biological facts draw a safe line at some point well before the end of the sixth week when all the organs are rudimentarily formed? They would thus be marking the end of the formation period and the beginning of the period of the actual presence of the human body and its more proper development. They would be marking the point at which it might be said that the ground plan of the body is completed and its implementation is beginning.[54]

Di Ianni suggests that a line could safely be drawn at the end of the third or fourth week. At this early stage the fetus would not be a person because of its lack of a true human body, and the possibility to allow abortions during this period might be considered for extremely serious reasons.[55]

Callahan underlines the significance of the biological substratum in the evolution of fetal life and refuses to entertain any definition of personhood which fails to do justice to the fact that human development has a biological and genetic basis.[56] Yet he does not assess the status of the unborn child by this criterion alone; he observes that the modern life sciences —zoology, anthropology, psychology, and even theology —will not accept a one-dimensional or monotypistic description of man because they consider that an exclusive emphasis on one single quality does not reflect the full existential complexity of the human person. An adequate definition of the human will be multidimensional and teleological in the sense that it will pay attention to the wide variety of biological, psychological, and cultural factors whose progressive interaction eventually constitutes a human adult.[57] At the same time, any attempt to define personhood must give due recognition to the presence of potentialities or capacities. It may not confine itself to actualized human characteristics or achieved human qualities because, at any given moment in life, a human being may be giving little evidence of actualized human potential (a baby; a person who is drugged or asleep). Obviously this would not be a sufficient reason to cancel his membership of the brotherhood of man.[58]

Callahan, therefore, adopts a holistic and multidimensional criterion of personhood and employs "a rich, biologically based definition, giving ample room to the importance of teleological direction and unactualized potentiality."[59] He rules out the treatment, even of the early conceptus, as a mere piece of "tissue" having no human significance or value, and he asserts that the taking of such life constitutes a moral problem even if one looks upon the unborn child as a *potential* person, in the process of actualizing his potential through growth and development.[60] He further concedes that abortion is an act of killing, and he hopes that this fact will not be glossed over by euphemism and circumlocution. However, it is not the destruction of a human person because, while fertilization does lay the genetic foundation for personhood, some degree of development is required before this quality is actually realized.[61] A zygote does have the genetic potential to become a person but actualized personhood presupposes "actualized rationality, interaction with others, affectivity, culture making."[62] Callahan will not identify human person with human life and concludes that "at no stage of its development does the conceptus fulfill the definition of a person, which implies a developed capacity for reasoning, willing, desiring and relating to others." In this perspective abortion becomes "the destruction of an important and valuable form of human life."[63]

Louis Dupré employs a different terminology and offers a different argument. He makes a distinction between the structural and the functional, between the biological and the behavioral, and states that the "fully human" transcends the purely biological. This means that the determination of personhood cannot be entrusted to physiology and that we have to turn to the behavioral sciences, psychology and sociology, which deal with the "functions" of persons. But these disciplines fail to present a univocal definition which would enable us to identify "nonpersons": none of them will determine the beginning of personhood or indicate what the minimum requirements are for this qualification. This is because the descriptions of personhood adopted by these sciences vary according to the issues under consideration and are, therefore, pragmatic and partial. Moreover, says Dupré, these pragmatic and partial definitions are also maximalistic because they indicate the characteristics of *mature* humanity. They contribute towards our understanding of the "fully human" in terms of behavior, but they are clearly not applicable to those whose "functioning" leaves much to be desired, such as the newborn, the senile, the insane, and the unconscious. Yet we claim at least some degree of personhood for all these. It is clear that the presence of personhood does not completely depend on the presence of its *functions*. Human life may lack some of the attributes of mature personhood but this does not necessarily imply that it has ceased to be personal.[64]

Dupré is convinced that the existence of personhood precedes the possession of the predicates which we usually attribute to it. Personhood is an "underived" and "original" reality in the sense that it is not acquired. This means that its beginning must coincide with that of human life and that the personal is *coextensive* with the human. However, it does not follow that we can equate personhood and humanity. Early human life lacks most, if not all, of the qualities of mature personhood; it cannot be personal in the same way in which it will be personal in the future. Human life has no gradations: life is either human or it is not. Personhood, on the other hand, is a dynamic quality and allows gradations or "degrees of actuality." The various stages of human development are not personal in an equal degree, and personhood is only minimally present at the very beginning of life.[65]

Ransil observes that this new evaluation of fetal life has implications for Catholic ethical methodology. The official position on abortion grants equivalent personal status to mother and child and takes a static view of their relationship. The new proposition defines fetal personhood as a dynamic process and this requires the elaboration of an "ethics of development" which will determine values and establish priorities in accordance with the nature of the biological entities involved and their relative stages of human development. Ransil states that this is untouched territory in Catholic moral science. The present system of ethics is applicable to static situations but fails to cater for alterations introduced into entities and conditions by growth, development, and differentiation.[66]

III. Abortion as a Human Act

The analysis in Chapters II and III of the official Catholic view on abortion revealed that this position is based on two principles. The first refers to the status of the unborn child which is considered to embody personal human life. The second proposition regards the termination of the fetal life process by human hand. Here the Church affirms its distinction between the direct and the indirect effects of a human act, between direct and indirect killing, and permits an indirect and uninentional abortion if there is a proportionately grave reason such as the necessity of the mother undergoing medical treatment (the principle of double effect). Direct interventions, however, are absolutely prohibited. In this chapter we have so far concerned ourselves with the developments in American Catholic thought on the quality of fetal life. We must now examine the critique formulated by a good many authors of the method or technique which the Catholic moral tradition employs in its analysis and evaluation of the human act, in this case the act of abortion.

The Prevention of Implantation

We have seen that some authors will not equate hominization with fertilization because they hold that the fetus can only be considered a person once its individuality has been established or its implantation achieved. This view has affected their moral evaluation of the use of "abortifacient contraceptives" such as intrauterine devices and the "morning-after" pill. In their analysis, these appliances interfere with the life of the prepersonal fetus and are, therefore, nonhomicidal in character. As Diamond observed, the patient of a homicidal act must be a homo. Consequently, the prevention of implantation cannot be described as "abortive" or "abortifacient" but must be defined as contraceptive.[67]

Diamond and Häring have made explicit statements to this effect. Diamond wants to help the theologian to reassess the moral evil of anti-implantational interventions. His understanding of the biological data (which we have considered) makes him conclude that there is an essential difference between the prevention of a fertilizatum's implantation and the abortion of a differentiated and implanted conceptus. He suggests that conception be identified with implantation and that then a distinction be introduced between (a) antifertilizational measures, (b) anticonceptive (i.e., anti-implantational) interventions, and (c) abortions, i.e., the destruction of biologically hominized entities.[68] Häring supports this proposal. He admits that there is a qualitative difference between the prevention of fertilization and the interruption of the life process between fertilization and implantation but he is reluctant to classify anti-implantational devices as "abortifacient":[69]

> Between the fertilization which can occur up to at least ten days (*sic*) after intercourse (and which takes several hours) and implantation and final individualization of the embryo there is a gray area. To disturb or to interrupt the life process during this phase is, in my eyes, not an indifferent matter. But it seems to me that it does not have the same gravity or malice as the abortion of an individualized embryo, that is, of the embryo after successful implantation or specifically at a time when twinning is no longer possible.[70]

The Less Safe Course

We have seen that some participants in the debate are undecided about the moment of hominization because they feel that the relevant biological and philosophical data are not conclusive. These authors, therefore, have had to work out a practical moral policy which responsibly accommodates this uncertainty about the status of the unborn. Traditional Catholic moral theology defines such dilemmas as cases of a practical doubt of fact. In these situations the use of probability as permitted by probabilism is not applicable because this provision extends only to doubts of law. In cases of doubt of fact involving considerations of human life the morally safer course must be followed.[71] It will be remembered from Chapter II that the manuals which regarded the theory of immediate animation as doubtful or even as tenable adopted precisely this policy.

Dedek and Thomas A. Wassmer have pointed out that Catholic moralists have not applied this principle consistently and have, in some cases of a doubt of fact concerning human life, authorized the adoption of the less safe course if other life values were at stake. Dedek and Wassmer make the following observations:

1. Catholic moralists allow a woman who has been raped a vaginal douche; this as late as ten hours after the assault. At this time conception could have occurred.[72]

2. In cases of terminal illness they permit the omission or discontinuation of extraordinary therapeutic procedures if in all likelihood the patient will not recover.[73]

3. Reputable European moralists assert that when there is substantial doubt about the conceptus being alive one does not always have to follow the safer course, but may in some cases favor the certain rights of the mother rather than the uncertain rights of the fetus. For instance, if it is doubtful whether a particular growth is a tumor or a fetus, and if there is danger to the life of the mother, the growth may be treated as a tumor. Similarly, these moralists permit a craniotomy to save the life of the mother if the fetus is probably, but not certainly, dead. The theory of mediate hominization probably being valid, there is no substantial difference between a probably dead fetus and a probably nonanimated fetus. If the former can be aborted to save the life of the mother, so can the latter.[74]

4. The doubt of fact concerning the quality of unborn human life gives rise to a doubt of law because it raises a doubt about the physician's personal moral obligation towards the unborn child. In the language of probabilism, such a dubious obligation is not binding and therefore the prohibition of abortion is not absolute as long as the presence of personal life in the conceptus remains uncertain.[75]

5. Respect for human life implies that human life is not deliberately attacked or needlessly endangered. Man is under a general obligation not to run the risk of killing a human being, but the Catholic moral tradition does allow one to take such a risk if there is a proportionate reason. We should not lightly take chances with human life but this does not mean that we can never take any chances at all.[76]

Wassmer concludes that the Catholic moral tradition does not absolutize human life to such an extent that where there is doubt about its presence the safer course is always obligatory and other values can never warrant its forfeiture. He notes that sometimes other values do get the benefit of the doubt, and it is for this reason that he formulates a tentative proposition of his own: if the theory of delayed hominization is philosophically, theologically, and scientifically respectable, could it be utilized in situations where there are other important values at stake? Wassmer suggests that this approach might possibly provide for an early abortion in the rare cases of rape, incest, or a predictably defective infant.[77]

Dedek adopts a similar position and affirms that one may run the risk of killing a human being if there is a reason proportionate to the risk. Therefore he holds that when there is a conflict between the life of the "doubtfully ensouled conceptus" and the life of the mother, the certain rights of the mother must prevail over the uncertain rights of the child.[78] Regarding the moment of hominization Dedek considers that "there is at least a prudent doubt until the twelfth week and perhaps even until the fetus is technically viable."[79] This means that the early stages of pregnancy require less serious indications for performing an abortion:

> Here the reason need not be proportionate to the disvalue of homicide but to the degree of probability that one's action at a certain stage of gestation is in fact homicidal. To be concrete, I would think that circumstances like rape or perhaps even grave socio-economic reasons could justify an abortion before the beginning of the third week while the zygote is still not even irreversibly an individual.[80]

But as the pregnancy continues, the likelihood increases that the fetus is in fact a human person. Dedek then demands a more substantial indication, such as grave danger to the physical or mental health of the mother or some very serious physical or mental deformity of the child.[81] Unlike Dedek, Schenk does not distinguish explicitly between early and later pregnancy but states generally that one must weigh the *possibility* of the fetus being a person against the *probabilities,* not only of the mental anguish of the mother bearing an unwanted fetus, but also of the misery of the unwanted child. The more certain evil must be given greater weight.[82]

Natural Law and Human Acts

Catholic moral theology discerns three "sources of morality" or factors which determine the moral content of an act. Traditional moral evaluation focuses its attention first and foremost on the *finis operis,* the physical or structural content of the act or the end to which the act by its very nature primarily and necessarily directs itself—in the case of abortion, the killing of a fetus. Then there are two subsidiary factors: the circumstances of the act and its subjective end (the *finis operantis* or the intention of the agent). These can modify and even change the moral significance of the physical act but never to such an extent that an evil act becomes morally good. The end, therefore, does not justify the means.[83] This strong emphasis on the intrinsic structure of the human act, of the act of abortion, has been questioned by a good many authors. They have argued that the traditional criterion is abstract and narrow, as there are cases in which it fails to do justice to the existential motive of the agent (the *finis operantis*) or to the situational meaning of the act (the "circumstances").

Bishop Francis Simons maintains that at least some abortions must be viewed in a wider perspective, and he defends this position in the context of a plea for a more dynamic approach to natural law. Simons accepts the validity of the natural law concept and agrees that on a number of important moral issues mankind has arrived at a substantially correct view of the implications of this law. The human condition, however, is subject to change, and recent developments, such as the latest advances in medical science and the population explosion, present new problems which cannot be solved by an application of the traditional principles. Consequently, there is need for further investigation of what the natural law demands. Perhaps this will lead to new rules or to an adjustment in the application of the old rules.[84]

Simons observes that in its formulation of a "body ethic" Catholic moral theology has employed a notion of natural law derived from an analysis of the nature and purpose of the organs involved and the acts performed. But he believes that the real basis of the natural moral law is the welfare of mankind: the goal of all natural law is the good of man. He proposes that Catholic moral analysis incorporate into its natural law concept, as a fundamental criterion, the demands made by the welfare of man, in society, and individually. The Church's moral methodology must therefore adopt a more consequentialist approach to the human act and weigh the various results of a line of action, which may be good or harmful in different ways and at different levels in the near or in the distant future, to a single individual, or a community, or a nation, or to the whole of mankind. Attention must be paid not only to the individual act and its implications but also to the consequences that would follow if the act would become generally permissible.[85]

Simons recognizes as a general rule the validity of the prohibition, "Thou shalt not kill," and affirms that reverence for human life serves the good of mankind. This means that we should close the door to any erosion of society's respect for human life and permit no killing, not even of immature human life. However, killing can be allowed for very serious reasons, "when the greater good of mankind really demands or permits it" or when the act is "demanded and compensated for by the need and right to preserve existing human life from serious harm."[86] Once we admit that the welfare of man constitutes the rationale of the various natural moral rules, we have to accept that this same welfare will indicate the limits of these rules and determine the point at which they are no longer applicable. They are not to be taken as absolute and as admitting of no exceptions because they are meant to promote the good of man; they cease to bind if they no longer serve this purpose.[87] Thus Simons would permit an abortion if this would be the only way of preventing the death of both mother and child.[88] Similarly, the licitness of an abortion performed for the sake of the health of the mother is at least arguable:

> A therapeutic abortion would seem licit...at a stage when danger of death or serious injury to the health of the mother is imminent; or, in case it is foreseen that later no competent medical help will be available, even at an earlier stage, but only if the danger foreseen is both serious and very probable.[89]

Ransil agrees with Simons that the Catholic moral tradition takes too narrow a view of at least some terminations of pregnancy, and he proposes a more consequentialist interpretation of abortions which are performed on a eugenic indication. Referring to spontaneous abortions or miscarriages he explains that medical science now tends to attribute this phenomenon to the selective activity of a natural and built-in mechanism by which the maternal organism rejects defective fetuses. Ransil accepts this theory as a reasonable hypothesis which deserves continued testing. This natural mechanism may slip up or break down because of the presence of a drug or because of irregular hormonal balances. It is the task of medicine to help the body to correct its disorders and restore its defective functions. Viewed from this perspective, a eugenic abortion could be judged on other merits — "as a potential means of correcting the failure of a defective natural body mechanism, and therefore as a technique which could assist nature in fulfilling itself."[90] In that case there would be no moral objection to a therapeutic abortion on a fetal indication:

> (S)urgical removal of a defective product of conception [would then be] tantamount to assisting nature in performing a function which the body, left to itself, is unable to accomplish because of some defect in the natural abortion mechanism. In this case the rationale for use of therapeutic abortion would be based on the assumption that (1) the product of conception is known to be defective, and (2) the mechanism for spontaneous abortion is known to be defective.[91]

Julian R. Pleasants is equally of the opinion that the act of abortion deserves a different exegesis and a more positive evaluation. He refers to experiments with an artificial placenta being developed in order to save the lives of premature babies whose lungs fail to function after birth. This placenta will be the first step towards the creation of an artificial womb to accommodate spontaneously or artificially aborted fetuses whose respiratory and digestive systems cannot cope with extrauterine existence and who at present are bound to die. In the future, abortion will no longer terminate the life of the fetus; thus there is no necessary connection between abortion and death. Pleasants maintains that "the death of the baby is not due to the abortion; it is due to our failure to have or to use the technology needed to keep the baby alive."[92] He further observes that abortion during the second trimester is performed in approximately the same manner as the induction of birth after viability, viz., by inducing premature labor or by a Caesarian operation. This type of intervention has saved the lives of countless babies whose mothers developed toxemia or severe diabetes in the later stages of pregnancy. It follows then that artificial expulsion from the womb is not bad in itself.[93]

The Traditional Exceptions

Curran and McCormick have also pleaded for a more consequentialist assessment of the act of abortion, and they have argued that this would not really constitute a drastic innovation in the Catholic moral tradition because the teaching of the Church provides for this approach, albeit implicitly and restrictively. They refer to the exceptions generally admitted to the "absolute" rule of the inviolability of human life, listed earlier as capital punishment, and individual and communal self-defense against an unjust aggressor. Curran proposes to apply the traditional concept of self-defense to certain pregnancy situations. His argument can be summarized as follows:

1. The Catholic moral tradition has always recognized that the commandment, "Thou shalt not kill," does not apply in cases of legitimate self-defense. However, Catholic moralists have offered diverse explanations to justify this exception to the rule. Some have qualified the killing of an unjust aggressor as indirect because the agent's direct intention and action are oriented towards the incapacitation of the assailant and the protection of his own life. Others hold that the agent directly intends to kill his aggressor as a means of defending himself and, since in this case they cannot permit the homicidal self-defense on the basis of the principle of double effect, they introduce a different justification such as the killing being a legitimate method of safeguarding one's inalienable right to life.[94]

2. It is clear, therefore, that in the case of unjust aggression moralists either accept a distinction between direct and indirect killing which does not depend on the physical causality of the act or apply a norm other than

the principle of double effect to solve the problem. It is equally manifest that in cases of conflict between developed human lives Catholic morality has adopted a policy which is different from its position on dilemmas involving immature human life and abortion, where it concentrates exclusively on the physical structure of the operative act.[95]

3. It is also part of the Catholic moral tradition that other values, such as material and spiritual goods of great importance, may be defended even by killing the aggressor. It is evident that Catholic morality equates other values with physical human life itself.[96]

4. We may therefore conclude that tradition has developed a pattern for the solution of conflicts when human life is at stake. This model is not exclusively determined by a rigid distinction between direct and indirect killing based on the physical structure of the act, and it recognizes other values as commensurate with human life. It should be extended to abortion situations where it will justify an intervention for the sake of the life of the mother or for other important reasons commensurate with that life.[97]

Curran admits that official Catholic teaching does not permit the application of the unjust aggressor model to the abortion dilemma because the Church does not consider the fetus, which is not subjectively guilty, to be a formal aggressor. Nor does tradition qualify the conceptus as a material aggressor because the child is not doing anything else than what it should be doing, and this cannot be termed aggression.[98] It is on this last point that Curran disagrees: he thinks it is justifiable to allow in a pregnancy that is seriously problematic the same possibility of defense against aggression that is admitted outside the womb. The termination of fetal life could then be defined as either direct or indirect, depending on the position which one adopts in this question.[99]

McCormick offers a different argument but arrives at the same conclusion. In his analysis, the permissible exceptions with regard to life-taking reveal that in certain cases the Catholic moral tradition allowed the termination of an individual's life *simply because in the circumstances this was considered the best solution.* These exceptions must be seen as the result of a consequentialist calculus that has identified certain situations in which the taking of human life is the lesser of two evils. McCormick therefore interprets permission to kill in capital punishment and in self-defense as formulations and concretizations of what is viewed in these instances as the lesser human evil. He is convinced that some degree of consequentialism is mandatory and that this approach is not incompatible with the Catholic tradition. Applying this to human life he concludes that man's life may be taken when doing so is the lesser of two evils and this requires, among other things, that there be a human life or an equivalent good or value at stake.[100]

Double Effect or Proportionate Reason?

I indicated in Chapter II that the American manuals presented innocent human life as inviolable "within certain reasonable limits" and that these limits were determined by the principle of double effect. It was to be expected that the subsequent debate on the morality of abortion would pay a great deal of attention to this important element of the Church's moral tradition and that Catholic moralists would reexamine the validity of the direct-indirect distinction in the light of the application of the principle to conflicts involving unborn life. The following, then, is an attempt to summarize their views on this issue. It is practically impossible to achieve a satisfactory degree of completeness or to do full justice to the insights of the individual authors; the subject has been discussed extensively, not only in the context of the abortion problem. However, it is possible to distinguish predominant themes and basic trends. The following statements can be listed as preliminary observations:

1. The traditional formulation of the principle of double effect fails to take into account the social dimension of man, as it bases its moral judgement primarily on the immediate physical effect of the act and neglects the wider constructive or destructive consequences for the well-being of the individual and of society. [101] (Cornelius J. van der Poel)

2. This emphasis on direct causality as the overriding moral factor identifies the human and moral dimension of the act with its immediate material or physical result. This approach does not pay sufficient attention to the overall intention of the agent or to the deeper reason for the act. The ultimate purpose of the act is precisely the element which makes the act human; the intrinsic structure of the act is inseparably linked with the intention of the agent through whom and in whom the material act acquires human meaning and moral significance. In every human act the end relates to the means and gives them human meaning, while the means relate to the end, translating the human meaning into concrete reality. The means, therefore, may never be evaluated on the sole basis of their material structure but only in connection with their human meaning. In the same way the end may never be judged exclusively on its own abstract merits but only as it is concretely expressed in the means. The principle of double effect treats means and end as separate entities and considers them on an individual and material basis. But the human meaning of an act cannot be understood, or its moral value assessed, if we do not examine the act in its totality. [102] (van der Poel)

3. In the admittedly rare medical situation when an abortion is the only means of preventing the death of both mother and fetus, the double effect principle enforces a choice which seems to imply that one's primary obliga-

tion consists in observing the rule rather than in protecting the human beings affected by the rule, and that the abstract demands of the law and a clear conscience must prevail over any other interest.[103] (Callahan)

4. This type of moral reasoning is based on the assumption that there exists a fixed order of goods and values which must be respected no matter what the factual consequences are. To argue that the death of both mother and fetus is merely a "physical evil" which is to be preferred to the "moral evil" of an abortion is the equivalent of pleading helplessness in the face of natural disaster and reveals a lack of moral responsibility.[104] (Callahan)

5. The literal application of the principle of double effect leads to anomalies. In ectopic pregnancies it allows the surgeon to excise that part of the tube which contains the conceptus, but he may not abort the child, leaving the organ intact, although the latter procedure does not impair the fertility of the woman. This applies also in the case of a cancerous pregnant uterus, when abortion of the fetus in conjunction with surgical therapy might save the organ and preserve the woman's fertility. The principle forbids this course of action but it permits the removal of the pregnant uterus *in toto*.[105] (Curran, Häring)

6. In complex circumstances a moral decision cannot be taken on the sole basis of the material content of the act or its immediate, physical effect. One must consider the total spectrum of the moral values that are at stake; a final judgement may only be made after all these values have been compared.[106] (Curran)

I have already paid attention to Curran's proposal to employ the traditional concept of unjust aggression in order to provide a solution for seriously distressed pregnancies. Curran himself has suggested that there might be an alternative approach which would consist in expanding the notion of "morally indirect" to cover such situations.[107] Germain G. Grisez has examined the problem from this perspective and has worked out a new formulation of the double effect principle. He finds fault not with the principle as such but with its current interpretation which in his opinion is too restrictive. The principle stipulates, he says, that the evil effect of the act may not be the means to the good effect. This is generally understood as prohibiting any activity where, in the order of physical causality, the good effect derives from the evil effect or the evil aspect of the act precedes the good result. Grisez agrees that when a single act has a good and a bad effect, the latter cannot rightly be intended by the agent, not even as the means to the good end; but, he contends, given the right motive it is irrelevant which effect or aspect of the act comes first in the order of causality. He considers that the means-end condition of the principle is fulfilled if both the good and the bad effect involved in a given action are components of a physically unified and morally indivisible process initiated by the agent. It is then immaterial which effect is prior in the course of physical causality. [108] He makes this point as follows:

> From the point of view of human moral activity, the initiation of an indivisible process through one's own causality renders all that is involved in that process equally immediate. So long as no other human act intervenes or could intervene, the meaning (intention) of the behavior which initiates such a process is no less immediate to what is, from the point of view of physical causality, a proximate effect or a secondary or remote consequence. For on the hypothesis that no other human act intervenes or could intervene, the moral agent who posits a natural cause *simultaneously* (morally speaking) posits its foreseen effects. The fact that not everything in the behavior which is relevant to basic human goods equally affects the agent's moral standing arises not from the diverse physical dispositions of the elements of the behavioral aspect of the act, but from the diverse dispositions of the agent's intention with regard to the intelligible aspects of the act. [109]

However, Grisez's relaxation of the principle applies only to the intelligible aspects of the one and indivisible act. The good and the bad effects must equally be part of that act. If the act achieves its good purpose only through additional activity either of the agent or of someone else, then the act becomes a means because the good effect arises not *concomitantly with* the evil effect but *through* the evil effect. The evil effect is then intentionally chosen for an ulterior end, and this choice enters into the agent's initial act and determines its human significance and moral value. Grisez also stipulates that, even if the act is indivisible, the agent has to accept full moral responsibility for the evil effect if this negative result is unnecessary, in the sense that it can be avoided by adopting a course of action which has the same objective but a different mode of accomplishment. Moreover, even if the procedure unfolds as a single act, and from the point of view of the agent constitutes a continuous whole, the unity of this process is merely *de facto* if it consists of phases which are not necessarily connected because one can be performed without the other. In this case the act is not really indivisible; the good intention will not cancel moral responsibility for evil aspects of the act that can be excluded but are not. [110]

On the strength of this revised version of the double effect principle Grisez justifies abortion in situations where the survival of the mother requires termination of the pregnancy as in cases of impaired heart or kidney function or a combination of these afflictions:

> The justification is simply that the very same act, indivisible as to its behavioral process, has both the good effect of protecting human life and

the bad effect of destroying it. The fact that the good effect is subsequent in time and in physical process to the evil one is irrelevant, because the entire process is indivisible by human choice and hence all aspects of it are equally present to the agent at the moment he makes his choice. [111]

If the danger to the mother's life can be averted without the destruction of the unborn child, then the protection of the mother and the death of the fetus are not necessarily linked, and the two effects of the intervention are in fact separable. If in such a case the physician does not adopt the alternative course of action which achieves the good effect without the bad effect, then the killing falls within the scope of his intention. Moreover, an abortion can be permissible only when the *physical life* of the mother is endangered. Grisez argues that no other indication will justify the intervention. Terminating a pregnancy for the sake of the mother's physical or psychological *health* implies that the unborn's total life is sacrificed in order to preserve a part of the woman's life and this is inexcusable. [112]

William E. May sponsors what he defines as "an ethics of intent + content" which takes into account means as well as ends, the "finis operis" as well as the "finis operantis." [113] He basically agrees with Grisez's position which, in his view, does not amount to an abandonment of the double effect principle nor of the fundamental distinction between the direct and the indirect effects of human acts. May feels that the traditional distinction between direct and indirect killing as applied to abortion stands in need of a correction. If a pregnancy is terminated because this is the only way of saving the mother's life, then the intervention cannot be qualified as "direct" killing because the intention of the act, and in this sense its direction, is not oriented towards the death of the fetus. There is in this case no question of a "direct" destruction of unborn life but rather of an act which is "indirect" as far as the death of the child is concerned. Like Curran, May sees parallels between this dramatic pregnancy conflict and a case of unjust aggression. The "finis operis" of the abortive act is directed not towards the death of the fetus but towards the elimination of the danger which the pregnancy poses to the mother's life. This does not mean that the abortion is justified on consequentialist grounds. [114] May emphasizes that the morality of this act is primarily determined by the intrinsic quality of the act. This quality, however, is not "deadliness" but "protectiveness":

> In order for the act to be justified as one in which human beings may rightfully engage, it is also necessary that the *activity itself,* considered from the perspective of its content or meaningful intelligibility, be truthfully describable as primarily an act of what Aquinas called a "measured force" countering a force directed against the life that is being imperilled. The act of abortion, in such instances when the death of the fetus is

"indirectly voluntary" and is only *one* aspect of an act that in its totality can properly be said to be directed to saving the life of the mother-to-be, is justifiable. [115]

Patrick J. Coffey also accepts Grisez's interpretation of the principle of double effect but tentatively proposes an additional modification which would recognize values other than the mother's physical life as legitimate reasons for abortion. A likely candidate for certification as an equivalent of body life is sanity. This amplification would permit the operation on a serious psychiatric indication, e.g., in cases where there is a definite danger of permanent and serious injury to the woman's mental health and where it is established beyond doubt that an alternative remedy is not feasible. [116]

Häring's approach is different from that of Grisez. He accepts the traditional distinction between direct and indirect killing and says that it provides a reasonable solution for problems like ectopic pregnancies. But the principle of double effect has its limitations: the policy it establishes is clearly not applicable in some cases of extreme conflict. If a direct abortion is the only way of saving the mother's life when otherwise both mother and fetus would die, the doctor should be permitted to terminate the pregnancy because his intervention does not really deprive the child of its right to life. The child would not survive in any case. [117]

Ransil goes a step further. He sees the double effect principle as a serious speculative attempt to cope with "multi-valued moral situations" —where more than one moral norm or value is involved. Although the application of the principle is limited by its subtlety, it sets a useful precedent: it represents an admission by the Church that a greater good or lesser evil may sometimes be preferred while the norm, "Thou shalt not kill," loses none of its validity. [118] McCormick develops this argument. He considers the traditional permissibility of indirect killing in the same perspective in which he views the other classical exceptions, viz., as a formulation and concretization of what in the circumstances was judged to be the lesser human evil. [119] He analyses six different modifications offered by various authors with regard to the concept of direct effect, and he comes to the conclusion that in cases of conflict it is not realistic to assess the morality of an act on the basis of its physical structure alone. [120] He recognizes the value of the traditional direct-indirect distinction but maintains that in some cases the criterion thus provided is too narrow for a moral evaluation of the act: "What was and is decisive is the proportionate reason for acting." [121] In the area of human life, actions resulting in physical evil (such as death) are permissible if there is a truly adequate reason justifying the procedure. Taking life, therefore, is wrong unless there is a commensurate reason to do so. McCormick admits that "the judgement of proportionality in conflict situations is not only a very decisive judgement; it is also a most difficult one." Moral analysis here must carefully consider all the consequences of the act, and this requires a balanced appraisal of the immediate effects as well as of "the social implications and reverberating after-effects in so far as they can be foreseen." [122]

McCormick is in agreement with the traditional view that the direct killing of noncombatant civilians in war is always evil regardless of the circumstances and consequences, but he does not adopt this position because there is question here of "direct killing" which is "intrinsically evil." He presents a more pragmatic rationale and argues that there is no proportionate reason for such killing because violence would escalate to such an exent that the undesirable consequences would far outweigh any immediate benefits derived from the attack. It is precisely the foreseen consequences that make this prohibition a "practical absolute" or "virtually exceptionless." [123] Similarly, he tends to view mercy killing as always wrong: the good effect that could be obtained by making an exception to the rule in a particular case stands in no proportion to the foreseeable ulterior consequences of this decision. [124] Dedek formulates McCormick's position and his own as follows:

> The principle of double effect in its classic expression is being reformulated in various ways, and moralists are increasingly reluctant to acknowledge moral evil in the physical make-up of any act.... Physical evil becomes moral evil only when done without a proportionate reason. Therefore the purposeful destruction of a fetus is not moral evil in the presence of a proportionate reason. One must weigh the values at stake and make a preferential choice among them. [125]

Like Curran, McCormick feels that the mother's life or its "moral equivalent" constitutes a proportionate reason justifying the direct termination of a pregnancy. A similar view is adopted by Pleasants, John F. Monagle, Mary C. Segers, Clare Boothe Luce, John Deedy, Carol A. Berger, and Patrick F. Berger. [126]

The Life of the Mother and its Moral Equivalent

It is evident that a good number of American Catholic authors regard abortion dilemmas as multidimensional moral situations in which the life of the fetus is not always the overriding value. At times other factors must be taken into consideration, such as the life of the mother or its "moral equivalent." Naturally this raises the question of how this equivalence can be determined. In order to avoid accusations of utilitarianism, these

moralists have to provide a set of guidelines indicating which individual or
social human values are comparable to man's physical life. As van der Poel
has admitted, even if the intention of the agent (the "end") shapes the
human meaning and moral value of the physical act (the "means"), it does
not follow that the realization of an end which is good justifies the use of
any means. There must be a due proportion between means and end.[127]

Using the community-building criterion van der Poel concludes that the
net result of the total act should not be harmful to society.[128] Ransil wants to
apply a similar test and stipulates that abortion decisions be taken with due
attention to the general welfare of mankind, considered individually as
well as collectively.[129] McCormick grants that the determination of the
moral equivalent of life is both difficult and dangerous. It is a complex
matter to weigh and compare human values, and the value perceptions and
criteria that will be employed will very likely have been distorted by
unrecognized cultural biases. Moreover, it is difficult to frame formulations that will resist abusive interpretation. McCormick himself is inclined
to interpret the traditional casuistry on the inviolability of human life as
supporting a narrowing rather than a broadening of the comparable values.
The judgement on moral equivalence, then, calls for "honesty and openness within a process of communal discernment, but also for further careful
studies of past conclusions and present evaluations."[130]

Several authors have indicated more precisely which reasons they consider to be proportionate with regard to abortion. James E. Krause would
allow the abortion of a seriously deformed fetus if the care of a handicapped
child would put too great a strain on the mother and her other dependents.[131]
Curran accepts as indications serious threats to the psychological health of
the woman and also "other values of a socio-economic nature in extreme
situations," adding that such cases are relatively rare.[132] Wassmer, who
favors the theory of mediate animation and the application of probabilism
to issues of human life, thinks that prior to animation an abortion could be
permitted in cases of rape, incest, or a predictably defective infant.[133]
Arguing from similar premises Schenk proposes to extend this to the
unwanted child.[134] Di Ianni, too, distinguishes between the early and the
later conceptus. During the first three or four weeks of pregnancy an
abortion could be performed for "ultra-serious" reasons of a medical,
psychological, social, or economic nature. This would include pregnancies
resulting from rape or incest, or when the mother is very young, or when
there is clear evidence that the fetus is grossly deformed. During the later
stages of gestation an abortion could only be permitted for the sake of
preserving the mother's life.[135] Dedek feels that before the beginning of the
third week an abortion could be justified in cases of rape and perhaps also

for substantial socio-economic reasons. After the third week but before viability he would require an even more serious indication such as significant danger to the mother's physical or psychological health or grave physical or mental deformity of the child.[136]

Ransil wants to judge each case on its own merits. He admits a medical indication in situations where the pregnancy poses a certain or very probable threat to the mother's physical life, but he admits that abortion is often only one of several possible therapies and that the decision to resort to this intervention is not always an obvious one. Ransil also recognizes a psychiatric indication, which in a wider sense incorporates the actual and potential deleterious effects the continuation of the pregnancy may have on the welfare of the mother and her family. In the same light he evaluates the termination of a pregnancy resulting from rape or incest; he further accepts a eugenic indication if there is a high probability that the fetus is deformed, as when the mother contracts rubella in the early stages of gestation.[137]

Maguire proposes to employ a sliding rule. He yokes the "developing personhood" theory to the principle of proportionality which he considers "a master rubric of ethical calculation in conflict situations." A sliding rule, then, is an obvious solution: a proportionately more serious reason for abortion is required with each passing day of the child's life. As the fetus approaches viability, it becomes extremely difficult (though not absolutely impossible) to visualize a reason that could warrant its expulsion from the womb.[138] Like Maguire, Dupré recognizes the "ontological significance" of the process of fetal development, though clearly favors a more restrictive moral policy, because he emphasizes that no abortion should ever be allowed unless there is a value at stake which truly compares with life itself. Thus in a case of rape of an adolescent the considerable likelihood of serious mental damage would justify the use of "abortifacient" contraception, at least during several hours after the coitus, but this permission would cease at a later stage of pregnancy. It *never* applies after sexual relations between consenting adults.[139]

Häring does not want to rule out the validity of a eugenic indication if the fetus is so defective that it is doubtful whether it represents truly human life. He would justify an abortion in this case not because of any "proportionate reasons" but because there is a difference between biological life and human or personal life:[140]

> Is a totally deformed fetus that is even lacking the biological substrate for any expression of truly human life, still to be considered a person? Is it wholly clear that we must preserve, with tremendous effort and inconvenience, a biological life born of a human mother if there is not and never will be the slightest expression of humanity? Would it be an abor-

tion in the full moral sense if the doctor, after a clear diagnosis of such a total deformation (no development of the central nervous system and human brain) would interrupt a pregnancy?[141]

Benedict M. Ashley and Kevin D. O'Rourke warn against haste in depriving the handicapped child of the benefit of the doubt, but they admit that it would be over-scrupulous to attribute personhood and human rights to a fetus that is so deformed that it will never achieve consciousness or manifest itself as a person. They seem inclined to permit an abortion if it can be established with a high degree of scientific probability that the fetus lacks the active potentiality to develop a brain and will therefore never achieve even a minimal degree of human thought and exercise of freedom.[142]

IV. The Sanctity of Life and an Ethic of Personal Responsibility

In 1970 Bernard Häring made a significant contribution to the debate by drawing attention to an element of the Catholic moral tradition which until then had not figured in the discussions at all. He pointed out that the Catholic position on abortion is milder than is generally recognized because Catholic ethics distinguish between moral theology and pastoral counselling. Moral theology is primarily concerned with the objective and abstract general principles which underlie moral judgements. Pastoral counselling, on the other hand, seeks to realize what is possible in the individual's concrete circumstances. This does not mean that pastoral prudence disregards moral rules but it does look upon moral life as a dynamic life of growth, characterized by a constant but gradual conversion. It takes into account the existential ability of a person to live up to a particular moral demand, and it seeks to maximize this potential.[143]

Abortion and Pastoral Compassion

Häring recalls that the Catholic tradition has always provided for cases where compliance with the moral law is beyond a person. It has defined this incapacity as "invincible ignorance," but this term deserves a wider exegesis, one that extends beyond difficulties of a purely intellectual nature and covers all situations where there is question of a genuine inability to cope with a particular moral obligation:[144]

> *Invincible ignorance* should not be interpreted in the sense of mere intellectualism but rather in the light of a theory on conscience, which empha-

sizes the existential totality of man. Invincible ignorance is a matter of inability of a person to "realize" a moral obligation. Because of the person's total experience, the psychological impasses, and the whole context of his life, he is unable to cope with a certain moral imperative. The intellectual difficulties of grasping the values which are behind a certain imperative are often deeply rooted in existential difficulties.... According to the very different stature and situation of people, this can be the case ... as to the concrete and existential understanding of a prohibitive moral norm.[145]

In a difficult abortion dilemma Häring excludes a pastoral approach that starts off immediately with a statement of the moral imperative. He concentrates on motivation: if the woman contemplates abortion, the counsellor will try to motivate her to comply with the moral demand. In this process it will become clear how far she can bear a concrete and definite appeal not to abort. If the counsellor comes to the conclusion that she is unable to accept the heroic solution because it is psychologically impossible for her to continue the pregnancy, then he will not force the issue by exerting undue pressure and, without condoning her decision, he will refrain from all "rigid judgement." He may leave the woman in "invincible ignorance" and entrust the judgement of her guilt to a merciful God.[146]

McCormick is in complete agreement with Häring's application of this traditional concept. He questions the use of the *term* "because of its onesidedly intellectual connotations and its aroma of arrogance." Like Häring, he distinguishes between "moral judgement and pastoral compassion, between the good that ought to be and the good that cannot be as yet, between aspiration and achievement."[147] Pastoral counselling deals with a person as he is in terms of his intellectual and volitional capacities. It tries to widen people's perspectives and maximize their strengths but it also recognizes the limits of these attempts.[148]

Dedek also wants to expand the scope of invincible ignorance. This condition is not restricted to situations where the agent lacks a theoretical knowledge of the moral law or an intellectual awareness of an objective duty. Invincible ignorance also prevails if there is a lack of emotional awareness or "evaluative knowledge, which includes the personal appropriation of the values affirmed in the law," so that the woman does not experience the obligation as a personal one. If the woman is unable to accept the objective moral prohibition as her own, then the counsellor will not insist that she does more than she is capable of doing.[149] Clare Boothe Luce has explained the difference between moral principles and pastoral care in less technical terms:

The intellectual horror with which theologians view abortion tends to dissipate when the priest, in his rectory, or confessional, is confronted by a desperate woman, who is contemplating abortion. When he fails to convince her of the gravity of the crime she is about to commit, he does not alert the police to restrain her, or to hunt her down afterward and punish her for this "heinous crime." In practice, the priest generally "leaves her to God," in whose hands she is safer than in the hands of many theologians. [150]

A Theory of Compromise

May and Curran have also considered the divergence that can exist between commandment (moral theology) and possibility (pastoral theology). May observes that there is no sin without *freedom*. He refers to Schoonenberg's theory of man's "situated liberty" and asserts that a person who tries to lead an upright moral life is not completely autonomous. Society often does not give him the necessary support, and sometimes it is even actively hostile to his endeavors. Man therefore is not always able to observe the moral law in the way that he knows he should. One must take this into account in one's moral judgement of certain abortions, even though abortion is always wrong. [151]

Curran puts even greater stress on the limitations of the human condition. He recalls that traditional moral theology tried to cater for cases of lack of freedom by distinguishing between material sin (objective sinfulness) and formal sin (subjective sinfulness) and by permitting the choice of the lesser evil if there was question of a genuine conflict of values or duties. Curran feels that these provisions are not satisfactory because they do not do justice to the very considerable problems that are caused by the social factors of man's existence and, especially, by the presence of sin in the world, which we experience so strongly today. Sin has shaped the very structures of the society to which man belongs; its disruptive and destructive influence prevents him at times from responding to moral demands in the way he wants. Sin sometimes forces him to do what he knows to be wrong and, if moral theology wants to be realistic, it may not overlook the effects which life in sinful society has on man's moral decisions. Moral assessment must seriously consider the predicament of the individual conscience as this is located in the totality of the person's condition in this world. [152]

Christian ethics, then, must develop a "theory of compromise." For Curran such a theory is a valid explication of previously accepted principles. It admits that because we live in a sinful world we sometimes find ourselves in a position where we are compelled to do something which, in normal circumstances, we would not do, since it is evil. Traditional moral theology would hold that such an act is always wrong, at least objectively so. Curran prefers to qualify it as morally good since, there and then, it represents the best man can do. However, from a different perspective the act is also evil because it reveals the presence of sin in the world, a presence which the Christian is called to overcome. Curran thinks that this theory of compromise would have been applicable to the plight of the women in Bangladesh who were raped and who would no longer have been accepted in their communities if they would have borne an illegitimate child. [153]

But none of these authors seeks to reduce the function of ethical reasoning, and McCormick adequately summarizes their views on the importance of moral science. He describes abortion as a cultural phenomenon in the sense that culture will always have something to say on abortions: it will either approve or reject them, and either change or leave intact the conditions that occasioned them. Morality thus assumes the function of a critic of society:

> One of the most important functions of morality is to provide to a culture the ongoing possibility of criticizing and transcending itself and its limitations. Thus genuine morality, while always compassionate and understanding in its meeting with individual distress (pastoral), must remain prophetic and demanding in the norms through which it invites to a better humanity (moral); for if it ceases to do this, it simply collapses the pastoral and moral and in doing so ceases to be truly human, because it barters the good that will liberate and humanize for the compromise that will merely comfort. [154]

A Decision of Conscience

Dennis J. Doherty goes a step further than Curran and states that the Catholic position on abortion leaves room for personal decision-making. He refers to the teaching of the Second Vatican Council and observes that its *Pastoral Constitution on the Church in the Modern World* condemns abortion as an "unspeakable crime." The same document, however, admits that an individual can *grow* in his ability to make *personal judgements,* and it explicitly recognizes the reality of conscience. It describes conscience as man's "most secret core and sanctuary" and states that it is conscience which impels Christians to join the rest of mankind "in the search for truth, and for the genuine solution to the numerous problems which arise in the life of individuals and from social relationships." [155] For Doherty this search for truth and for genuine solutions is the fundamental function of conscience. He recalls that the Council gave man full scope in this inquiry and that it endorsed his right to form and follow his insights in freedom. Moreover, the *Declaration on Religious Liberty* affirms that one achieves true conscience formation not by submitting to an extrinsic force but by opening oneself to the truth as the truth reveals itself and, by virtue of its own persuasive power, solicits the personal assent of man. The truth of the morality or immorality of abortion must therefore become "self-evident" to a person. [156]

In Doherty's analysis, the Catholic teaching on the inviolability of fetal life has not yet achieved complete self-evidence: there remains a modicum of doubt which the official pronouncements have not satisfactorily solved. He points to the traditional permissibility of killing in capital punishment, war, and self-defense and argues that this raises questions regarding the Church's absolute prohibition of abortion. For instance, it would seem reasonable to ask in this context what the precise implication is of such terms as direct and indirect, innocence and guilt, sanctity of life, and the right to life. It may be that just as it seems acceptable to engage in a defensive war in order to protect certain human values, we will also find a justification for inducing the abortion of what nature often spontaneously aborts. Doherty concludes that at the present stage of the debate, pending new insights, conscience is the only forum where the abortion dilemma can be resolved. Accordingly, a Catholic can conscientiously decide at times that terminating a pregnancy is morally permissible. [157]

The Sanctity of Life

Maguire welcomes McCormick's principle of proportionate reason as breaking "the absolutist bind in which many questions such as mercy killing cannot even be considered,"[158] while Callahan interprets Catholic reform efforts as a general admission that abortion dilemmas are multi-dimensional moral situations where, apart from the rights of fetal life, there may be other aspects that deserve consideration, such as the life of the mother or values of similar importance. [159] Callahan himself has elaborated a rather more innovatory moral policy. To date, his is the most explicit attempt to reformulate the Catholic position on abortion.

Callahan proposes to adopt a positive and dynamic interpretation of the Decalogue's prohibition, "Thou shalt not kill," and suggests that the principle of "the sanctity of life" be the point of departure for all moral decisions affecting human life. This principle is fundamental in the sense that it determines our basic attitude towards human life in all its aspects and asks us to respect, protect, and foster it wherever it exists. The principle is also comprehensive: it covers the "whole man," from the beginning of his life to its end, as an individual, and the subject of physical, emotional, and intellectual rights, as a member of society, and as belonging to a species. Furthermore, each of these dimensions of human life is entrusted to a set of more specific moral rules which are articulations of the general principle, and which seek to preserve and to enhance life in that particular area. These rules must be formulated in such a way that they are congruent with each other: together they must form a coherent and orderly moral policy which adequately directs the implementation of our basic commitment to human life as expressed in the fundamental principle.[160]

It is possible, of course, that a conflict arises between different sets of rules. For instance, the rules protecting the physical life of the fetus may clash with the rules which safeguard the mother's psychological integrity or right of self-determination. Callahan does not pretend that there is an easy rule of thumb with which one solves such conflicts. One solution might be to put the different human values and the corresponding sets of rules in some kind of hierarchical order which indicates the moral priorities, but this "is complicated even in theory and in practice will obviously be conditioned by changing historical circumstances." Nor can the fundamental principle itself be used as a criterion to decide which series of rules deserves precedence, for the principle only functions in the original formulation of each category and in its final assessment. The conflict exists between the rules themselves, and it must be solved at that level.[161] For instance, the basic principle of the sanctity of life undoubtedly gives rise to the moral rule that the individual's right to life must be respected, but we cannot exclude the possibility that a set of conditions develops in which this rule has to be disregarded, such as when the survival of the group or the species would be at stake. In that case the rules that guarantee the survival of the group would have to prevail.[162]

In Callahan's view, therefore, the basic principle does not bind us to a fixed series of moral obligations vis-à-vis the life of man. It rather instills in us a powerful bias in favor of human life, and it leads us to develop life-protective rules. At times, also, it forces us to ask ourselves "whether the giving of precedence to one rule or another, or the hanging on to one rule in particular, serves the respect we want to accord human life."[163] Callahan stresses that this reformulation of "Thou shalt not kill" puts the responsibility for human life firmly in the hands of man himself. Life decisions are human decisions; they are not imposed from above. It is up to man to define the terms, articulate and order the rules, examine the data and interpret them.[164]

Ransil sponsors a basic moral principle that is even more comprehensive than Callahan's and demands that life be respected *in all its manifestations*. This implies that we begin to discover the principle of ecological balance and recognize the dynamic relationship that exists among all stages and forms of life and their environments. Our concern and care must embrace

all phases of life, originating, continuing, and terminating, and this
involves the exercise of personal moral responsibility. "In a given context,
the emphasis for preservation of life may with good reason emphasize one
stage over another."[165] Ransil asks that man be given room to discharge this
responsibility. He believes that the Catholic tradition formulates its moral
policies on the presumption that if man is given a certain amount of freedom of choice he will abuse this privilege.[166] But *abusus non tollit usum:*

> Abuse or misuse of any prerogative, privilege, right or opportunity must
> be accepted as a consequence of man's freedom to choose among alterna-
> tives. To deny him this choice is to keep him forever a moral adoles-
> cent.... If a matter is seen to be morally good or at least neutral, the
> freedom to make a choice should be available to all individuals, and
> continuing effort should be directed toward preventing its abuse.[167]

Fetal Life and Personal Responsibility

I have already analysed Callahan's understanding of the conceptus as
"an important and valuable form of human life," and we have now seen
that he regards life decisions as *human* decisions. Callahan has attempted
to combine these two elements (man's individual moral responsibility and
the less-than-personal status of the fetus) into a coherent moral policy. He
states that respect for man's personal right to life is a primary implication of
the basic principle of the sanctity of life. This protection extends even to
"doubtful life" because the principle always gives life the benefit of the
doubt and bends over backwards not to destroy it:[168]

> It does not seek to diminish the range of responsibility toward life—
> potential or actual—but to extend it. It does not seek the narrowest
> definition of life, but the widest and the richest. It is mindful of individual
> possibility, on the one hand, and of a destructive human tendency, on the
> other, to exclude from the category of "the human" or deny rights to
> those beings whose existence is or could prove burdensome to others.[169]

But Callahan is quite definite that the inviolability of the fetal right to life
applies only in ordinary circumstances: it is not absolute. Respect for the
sanctity of life should incline a pregnant woman towards a general and
strong bias against abortion, i.e., "against a routine, unthinking employment of abortion."[170] But she has a right to take other factors into consideration, and these might be such that abortion becomes a responsible solution
to her problem. The decision is hers and she may decide to let other values
prevail:

> (S)he has her own rights...and her own set of responsibilities to those
> around her; that is why she may have to choose abortion.... In many

circumstances, then, a decision in favor of abortion —one which over-rides the right to life of that potential human being she carries within — can be a responsible moral decision, worthy neither of the condemnation of others nor of self-condemnation. [171]

Springer examines the claims of the women's liberation movement and comes to the same conclusion. Respect for the dignity of woman implies that the final decision should be hers:

> The abortion decision... is the mother's. The church, the state, and the medical profession have largely determined the decision for her in the past. She will continue to need the advice of her obstetrician, of course. Church and society must have norms governing abortion, and contrary to what some liberation spokespersons are claiming, the father does have a say. And the fetus's welfare must remain of paramount importance. But when all the data are in from these sources the decision is primarily the mother's. We have held her in an inferior position in the past by making the decision for her. Recognition of this right need not increase the number of abortions each year, but it does respect the dignity of woman as a person and her ability to act responsibly. [172]

V. The Multidimensional Approach: A First Assessment

In my introductory chapter I wrote that the moral issues which are at stake in the abortion debate do not belong to it exclusively, as they are a subject of discussion in other ethical contexts as well. Developments in Catholic thought on abortion are indicative of the evolution of moral theology as a whole. The new approach to abortion which I have analysed in this chapter is a reflection of a more fundamental trend in Catholic ethical thinking and is the outcome of an attempt to formulate a new moral methodology.

Curran has outlined the rationale of this new method. In his analysis, traditional moral theology argues from a substantialist epistemology and tends to see reality in terms of individual entities. It emphasizes the independence and self-sufficiency of individual beings rather than their relations with others and is concerned with their permanent substance rather than with accidentals, such as growth and change. Every substance has its own nature or principle of operation which guides its activities and determines its development. Knowledge then consists in discovering "the truth of an object." A substantialist worldview seeks objective knowledge which is achieved when the mind "conforms itself" to reality. Thus the Catholic moral tradition studied a particular substance or human faculty and tried to ascertain by an examination of the purpose inscribed in the entity itself how it was supposed to function. The purpose of the individual faculty became a moral norm—natural moral law. It stands to reason, says Curran, that this approach yields moral norms which are concrete, clear, and absolute. Moreover, it will regard the physical structure of the human act as the main constituent of the moral content of the act. [173]

Curran interprets the new moral methodology as an attempt to provide more adequately for man's personal responsibility vis-à-vis the processes of nature —processes in which through science and technology he already intervenes with great frequency so as to bring them under his dominion and humanize them. He states that the modern worldview has shifted its attention from isolated substances to relations and context. It will not consider individual beings as totally self-contained because their reality is also constituted by their relationships with other beings and with the fullness of being. Consequently, growth and development are important and their course need not be exclusively determined by a detailed plan engraved upon the substance itself. In a relationist epistemology knowledge is an active and dynamic process: man does not just discover the truth of an object by mentally conforming to it but it is man who makes reality by giving meaning to it and adding meaning to it. Curran then points out that this attitude gives rise to a new moral approach. In the perspective of the contemporary worldview, the morality of an act can no longer be defined solely in terms of the nature, natural purpose, or natural process of the individual substance or faculty that is involved, nor can the moral content of an act be completely identified with the material substratum of the act. Moral analysis has to take into account the "relations," the interests of outsiders and the effects of the act on the community. This can only be realized by an examination of the concrete conditions which surround the moral decision and by a comparison of all the values that are at stake. A relationist methodology, therefore, gives greater prominence to personal responsibility; it yields moral norms which are less absolute, and it questions the traditional rigid distinction between the direct and the indirect effects of human acts. [174]

It is not difficult to see that many of the views which have been analysed in this chapter reflect this new approach to a greater or lesser extent. Without exception the authors recognize the value of unborn life but many of them will not regard it as an absolute value. They uphold the principle, "Thou shalt not kill," but they will not define direct killing as "intrinsically evil." They hold that if in the concrete situation there is a proportionate reason for an abortion, man can in good conscience exercise his stewardship of human life and perform the intervention. There is growing emphasis, therefore, on contextuality, or the multidimensionality of moral problems, and on the wider consequentiality of human acts. The authors often point out that they argue from *within* the Catholic tradition and that their views are merely explications of previously admitted principles. Even Callahan and Ransil identify themselves with this tradition whose restrictive formulations they seek to expand. [175] Writing in a different context John G. Milhaven has characterized such attempts as "trying to engineer from within the renewal of Catholic moral theology" and achieving progress "through organic growth." [176]

It is clear that the debate has centered around three fundamental issues. The first of these concerns the quality of fetal life which seems susceptible to diverse assessments. Secondly, there is the question of the direct-indirect distinction, which in the view of a good many authors does not give man sufficient scope to safeguard life's "ecological balance" (Ransil) and discharge his responsibility towards human life in *all* its dimensions and phases of development. In my final chapter I will comment on these issues, and I will do so against the background of the opinions presented here. But there is a third problem, and I must pay attention to it now. We have seen that the wider consequentiality of human acts and the proportionality of reasons justifying abortion figure prominently in the later stages of the discussion. The relationist methodology puts less stress on natural law and intrinsic, absolute moral norms and sponsors a moral analysis which is more existential and subjective. Thus it becomes an easy target for accusations that it is situationist and no longer concerned with reality, rationality, and objectivity. The question then arises whether these charges are applicable to the positions presented in this chapter. Have the authors succeeded in developing a relational or contextual approach to abortion without falling into pure subjectivism.

They are generally agreed that abortion is a drastic course of action even in pregnancies that are seriously distressed. They insist that a decision be taken with due regard to "the general welfare of mankind considered individually as well as collectively" (Ransil), and I have registered McCormick's insistence that attention be paid not only to the immediate effects of the intervention but also to its "social implications and reverberating after-effects." The authors further advocate the principle of proportionate reason as the "master rubric of ethical calculation" (Maguire), to be applied only after an examination of all the values or interests which in the concrete circumstances of the case ask for recognition. But it is clear that no one has gone further and worked out rational and definite criteria by which the proportionality of a reason, adduced to justify an abortion, can be gauged. The debate has not provided a set of rules to help man in his evaluation of the causes that claim to necessitate the operation. McCormick has warned that the composition of such norms is "difficult and dangerous," and we have been offered sliding rules by Maguire and Dupré which remain extremely vague. Writing in 1970 Callahan stated that the criterion of proportionality with regard to abortion had not yet been found; our analysis of the subsequent literature reveals that twelve years later his statement is still applicable. Callahan wrote:

> Needless to say, given the tentativeness of the probings and the concentration upon some basic theoretical issues, there do not exist detailed efforts to work out how the different values at issue ought to be weighed and compared. About the only point which seems agreed upon is that, whatever form the balancing of values may take, they cannot scant the respect due unborn life, whether that life be adjudged fully human or only potentially human. [177]

Nor has Callahan himself filled the gap. He promises that in his final chapter he will specify which conditions in his opinion constitute serious and responsible reasons for abortion. [178] But even the most diligent examination of this chapter yields no such fruits. On the contrary, Callahan affirms there that "with the possible exception of exceedingly rare instances of a direct threat to the physical life of the mother, one cannot speak of general categories of abortion indications as *necessitating* an abortion." [179] In any case, Callahan hopes that women who have problems with their pregnancy will keep alive in their consciences a "moral tension" which will make them wary of "precipitous solutions" and of "automatic, unthinking and unimaginative" decisions either for or against abortion. But, as Callahan admits, this willingness to keep alive a moral tension presupposes that a woman wants to do what is right and that she realizes the difference between what is right and what is convenient. [180] It could validly be argued that in a permissive society such insights and attitudes can no longer be taken for granted. Consequently, one could demand that ethicists who propose to give women more moral latitude in abortion decisions should seriously consider the "reverberating after-effects" of their moral policy. [181] Or must we heed Ransil's advice and apply the old principle, *abusus non tollit usum?* I will return to this issue in my final chapter. There I will also comment on Häring's distinction between moral principles and pastoral counselling, which is as much part of the Catholic moral tradition as is the absolute prohibition of abortion.

NOTES

[1] Bernard J. Ransil, *Abortion* (Paramus, N.J.: Paulist Press Deus Books, 1969), p. 82.

[2] *Ibid.*, pp. 89-91.

[3] *Ibid.*, p. 89.

[4] *Ibid.*, pp. 89-90.

[5] *Ibid.*, p. 82.

[6] James J. Diamond, "Abortion, Animation, and Biological Hominization," *Theological Studies* 36 (1975), pp. 316-317.

[7] *Ibid.*, pp. 308-309, 315-316.

[8] *Ibid.*, pp. 314-315. Diamond distinguishes between the first differentiation (of placental cells) and subsequent differentiations (into specific human organ systems); *ibid.*, pp. 311, 314-315.

[9] *Ibid.*, pp. 308, 316.

[10] *Ibid.*, pp. 314, 315.

[11] *Ibid.*, p. 319.

[12] *Ibid.*, pp. 317-318, 319.

[13] *Ibid.*, pp. 317-318; Andre E. Hellegers, "Fetal Development," *Theological Studies* 31 (1970), p. 6.

[14] Hellegers, *op. cit.*, p. 6.

[15] *Ibid.*, p. 6.

[16] Diamond, *op. cit.*, p. 318.

[17] *Ibid.*, p. 318; Hellegers, *op. cit.*, p. 6. Before implantation no evidence of pregnancy could possibly be obtained so that one could not legally prove that an abortion had taken place; Hellegers, *ibid.*, p. 6.

[18] Diamond, *op. cit.*, pp. 320-321. This statement must be verified especially in the light of the recent Church pronouncements on abortion (Vatican II, *Humanae Vitae*, and the 1974 *Declaration on Procured Abortion*), and I will do so in my final chapter. We have seen, however, that the American bishops clearly indicate fertilization as the beginning of personal human life.

[19] Hellegers, *op. cit.*, pp. 5, 9.

[20] Diamond, *op. cit.*, pp. 321, 322. See also: John Deedy, "The Church in the World: Catholics, Abortion, and the Supreme Court," *Theology Today* 30 (1973), p. 284.

[21] Gabriel Pastrana, O.P., "Personhood and the Beginning of Human Life," *Thomist* 41 (1977), pp. 272-284; Richard A. McCormick, S.J., "Notes on Moral Theology 1977: The Church in Dispute," *Theological Studies* 39 (1978), pp. 127-128; Philip S. Keane, S.S., *Sexual Morality: A Catholic Perspective* (New York: Paulist Press, 1977), pp. 135-136; Michael V. Viola, "Abortion: A Catholic View," in E. Fuller Torrey (ed.), *Ethical Issues in Medicine* (Boston: Little, Brown and Co., 1968), pp. 94-95; Denis Cavanagh, "Legalized Abortion: The Conscience Clause and Coercion," *Hospital Progress* 52, August 1971, p. 87. Benedict M. Ashley, O.P., and Kevin D. O'Rourke, O.P., hold that the phenomenon of identical twinning does not militate against immediate hominization. They point out that every diploid cell of the human body has the basic potentiality to grow into a complete individual. In embryonic development this potentiality is inhibited in the somatic cells but it remains actualizable in the germ cells. At a very early stage of fetal life it may happen that some cells become detached and develop independently into a twin, or that the cell mass divides into two equal parts. Such events do not prove that previously no human

being existed but only that the existing human being has produced a clone asexually, or that it has ceased to exist and given rise to new twins by asexual fission. Such occurrences are accidents of development and may be due to genetic defects or environmental mishaps; *Health Care Ethics: A Theological Analysis* (St. Louis: Catholic Hospital Association, 1978), pp. 227-228. Michael A. Vaccari presents a similar explanation of twinning and states that recombination is twinning in reverse. The recombination process is dominated by the structurally superior organism which absorbs its inferior counterpart. This means that the weaker twin dies and that the stronger partner continues *his own existence* since his ability to absorb the other does not cancel his personhood; "Personhood before Implantation," *International Review of Natural Family Planning* 1 (1977), pp. 220-222. See also: Patrick Coffey, "When is Killing the Unborn a Homicidal Action?" *Linacre Quarterly* 43 (1976), pp. 91-92; William E. May, *Human Existence, Medicine and Ethics: Reflections on Human Life* (Chicago: Franciscan Herald Press, 1977), pp. 99-102; Robert E. Joyce, "Personhood and the Conception Event," *New Scholasticism* 52 (1978), p. 104. Joyce further suggests that in monozygotic twinning two separate individuals may be present from fertilization onwards but that we lack the technical know-how to identify them; *ibid.*, pp. 103-104. Coffey attributes all the essential functions of a human person to a "unified dynamic tendential act." This existential act is man's basic intrinsic principle of being and it begins to operate at fertilization. "Puzzling" biological phenomena (such as the termination of the pluripotency of the early cells by the primary organizer, and the transition of the vital activity of the unimplanted entity into that of the implanted blastocyst) arise from within the fertilizatum and are grounded in the tendential life principle which makes the person exist, and exist with an orientation to further human development and completion; *op. cit.*, pp. 85-91.

22 Daniel C. Maguire, *Death By Choice* (New York: Schocken Paperback, 1975), pp. 199-200.
23 Garth L. Hallett, S.J., "The Plain Meaning of Abortion," *America* 124 (1971), p. 633.
24 *Ibid.*, p. 633.
25 Diamond, *op. cit.*, p. 317.
26 John F. Dedek, "Abortion: A Theological Judgment," *Chicago Studies* 10 (1971), p. 321; James M. Humber, "The Case Against Abortion," *Thomist* 39 (1975), pp. 70-71. Rudolph J. Gerber admits that neither at the beginning nor at the end of human life is it possible to indicate exactly where personhood begins or ends. In such circumstances we have to follow the morally safer course; "Abortion: Two Opposing Legal Philosophies," *American Journal of Jurisprudence* 15 (1970), p. 23. On the position of Humber see Chapter III, note 80.
27 Diamond, *op. cit.*, p. 317. See also: Hellegers, *op. cit.*, p. 5.
28 Hellegers, *op. cit.*, p. 9.
29 Thomas L. Hayes, "Abortion: A Biological View," *Commonweal* 85 (1967), p. 679.
30 Hallett, *op. cit.*, p. 633.
31 Hellegers, *op. cit.*, p. 9; Dedek, *op. cit.*, p. 321.
32 Charles E. Curran, "Abortion: Law and Morality in Contemporary Catholic Theology," *Jurist* 33 (1973), p. 177.
33 *Ibid.*, p. 180.
34 Bernard Häring, "New Dimensions of Responsible Parenthood," *Theological Studies* 37 (1976), pp. 126-127.
35 Richard A. McCormick, S.J., "Notes on Moral Theology: The Abortion Dossier," *Theological Studies* 35 (1974), p. 337.

[36] Robert H. Springer, S.J., "Marriage, the Family, and Sex — A Roman Catholic View," *Perspectives in Biology and Medicine* 19 (1976), p. 188. See also: Diamond, *op. cit.*, p. 319.

[37] Joseph F. Donceel, S.J., "Immediate Animation and Delayed Hominization," *Theological Studies* 31 (1970), p. 101. He refers to the parallels between ontogeny and phylogeny and describes hominization as a gradual process which begins at conception and ends at death. However, this smooth continuity does not exclude the possibility of sudden shifts, the "thresholds" of Teilhard de Chardin. We may not be able to determine the exact location of these breakthroughs but we can definitely say when a particular quality has not yet been actualized in human life and when it has been achieved. Donceel denies that adoption of the brain criterion would deprive the seriously senile and the comatose of their personhood. In such states there are no *signs* of self-awareness but the organs required for conscious activity are present and remain potentially operative; *ibid.*, pp. 100-101. Robert H. Springer, S.J., qualifies Donceel's position as "respectable"; "Notes on Moral Theology," *Theological Studies* 31 (1970), pp. 500-501. Joseph T. Culliton is convinced that Donceel's arguments are valid but minimizes the practical implications: fetal development is strictly continuous and it does not follow from Donceel's views that before hominization the living organism is simply "fetal matter," something less than human which for a good reason may be aborted; "Rahner on the Origin of the Soul: Some Implications Regarding Abortion," *Thought* 53 (1978), pp. 208-211. For a critique of Donceel's position see: Pastrana, *op. cit.*, pp. 282-283; Joyce, *op. cit.*, p. 106; William H. Marshener, "Metaphysical Personhood and the I.U.D.," *The Wanderer* 107 (1974), October 10, p. 7.

[38] Roland M. Nardone, "The Nexus of Biology and the Abortion Issue," *Jurist* 33 (1973), pp. 153, 157-158.

[39] Roy U. Schenk, "Let's Think About Abortion," *Catholic World* 207, April 1968, p. 16.

[40] Rudolph H. Ehrensing, "When Is It Really Abortion?" *National Catholic Reporter*, May 25, 1966, p. 4. Dedek finds this argument unacceptable: the absence of brain activity in the fetus is not permanent and there is no comparison between the unborn child with its potentialities for human life and personhood, and the individual whose irreversibly nonfunctioning brain indicates that he is dead; *op. cit.*, p. 319.

[41] Häring, *op. cit.*, p. 127; id., *Medical Ethics* (revised ed.; Notre Dame, Ind.: Fides, 1975), p. 84. Curran cannot accept the brain criterion: truly spiritual activity does not take place until after birth and the rudimentary emergence of the brain in the fetus does not constitute a threshold which has qualitative significance; *op. cit.*, p. 179. See also: Germain G. Grisez, *Abortion: The Myths, the Realities, and the Arguments* (New York: Corpus Books, 1970), pp. 282-283. Ashley and O'Rourke observe that the child begins to manifest specifically human functions only after birth but they draw attention to the fact that the fetus develops *itself* in a *continuous* fashion: it possesses *from conception* all the information and active potentiality which it needs to develop a brain and to bring it to the stage of adult functioning; *op. cit.*, pp. 228-229. See also: May, *op. cit.*, pp. 96-97.

[42] Daniel Callahan, *Abortion: Law, Choice and Morality* (New York: Macmillan, 1970), p. 381.

[43] *Ibid.*, pp. 381-382. In the opinion of Ashley and O'Rourke, the phenomenon of natural fetal loss does not affect the standing of the early conceptus: through most of human history at least half of all infants failed to survive infancy but this fact has not deprived

the young child of its personhood. Moreover, there is evidence that frequently the process of fertilization is not a complete success. This means that many zygotes are only apparently such and are not proper organisms with personal-human status; *op. cit.*, p. 227. See also: Gary M. Atkinson, "The Morality of Abortion," *International Philosophical Quarterly* 14 (1974), p. 349; Vaccari, *op. cit.*, p. 222. Vaccari attributes the origin of teratomas not to zygotes but to stray cells, and describes a hydatidiform mole as a malformation which develops from the growing embryo but externally to the embryo. Since such growths are not really part of a fetal organism, they constitute no challenge to the status of unborn human life; *op. cit.*, p. 222. See also: Ashley and O'Rourke, *op. cit.*, p. 230.

[44] Callahan, *op. cit.*, p. 382. See also: Louis Dupré, "A New Approach to the Abortion Problem," *Theological Studies* 34 (1973), p. 482. Coffey advocates this safer policy; *op. cit.*, p. 87.

[45] Ransil, *op. cit.*, pp. 87-88. Joyce identifies becoming with being and defines a person as an individual with a natural capacity for rational and volitional activities. The presence of this capacity (even if it never attains a significant degree of development) is a sufficient ground for awarding the predicate of personhood because no living being can become anything other than what it already essentially is. Every potential is itself an actuality: the potential of the human conceptus to think and to talk is an actuality which the rabbit embryo does not possess; *op. cit.*, pp. 98-100, 102-103, 105-106. Arguing in a similar vein, May comes to the conclusion that the fetus is not potentially a human being but a human being with potential; *op. cit.*, pp. 102-103.

[46] Diamond, *op. cit.*, p. 322.

[47] *Ibid.*, p. 322.

[48] Albert R. Di Ianni, "Is the Fetus a Person?" *American Ecclesiastical Review* 168 (1974), p. 323. Atkinson states that even if the embryo is only potentially a person, it does not follow that it may be killed; *op. cit.*, p. 351. Larry L. Thomas makes the same point but less emphatically so: even if the fetus is only a potential person, its potentiality constitutes a morally relevant factor which rules out abortion on demand but allows abortion in certain circumstances; "Human Potentiality: Its Moral Relevance," *Personalist* 59 (1978), pp. 266-272. Grisez points to the difficulties inherent in the concept of potential personhood: it justifies infanticide as well as abortion and it obfuscates the difference between contraception and abortion; *op. cit.*, pp. 284-285.

[49] Ransil, *op. cit.*, pp. 82-83, 85-87, 95. See also: Diamond, *op. cit.*, p. 322.

[50] Maguire, *op. cit.*, pp. 200-201.

[51] *Ibid.*, p. 201.

[52] Di Ianni, *op. cit.*, pp. 323, 325.

[53] *Ibid.*, p. 325.

[54] *Ibid.*, p. 324.

[55] *Ibid.*, p. 325.

[56] Callahan, *op. cit.*, p. 368.

[57] *Ibid.*, pp. 351-364.

[58] *Ibid.*, pp. 364-368.

[59] *Ibid.*, p. 485.

[60] *Ibid.*, p. 495.

[61] *Ibid.*, p. 497.

[62] *Ibid.*, p. 389.

[63] *Ibid.*, pp. 497-498. John R. Connery, S.J., draws attention to the vagueness of this

position. It is not clear where exactly Callahan locates the beginning of actual personhood. Possibly at viability—or possibly at birth—although it is difficult to see why using such criteria he would or could draw a definite line even at birth; ''Callahan on Meaning of Abortion,'' *Linacre Quarterly* 37 (1970), p. 283. See also: Peter A. Facione, ''Callahan on Abortion,'' *American Ecclesiastical Review* 167 (1973), p. 295. May qualifies Callahan's ''developmental'' definition of personhood as basically utilitarian: it views humanity as an achievement, not as an endowment; *op. cit.*, pp. 97-98. See also: Joyce, *op. cit.*, pp. 99-100, 104-108.

64 Dupré, *op. cit.*, pp. 482-484.

65 *Ibid.*, pp. 483-484. McCormick registers Frederick Carney's critique of this argument. Carney characterizes Dupré's concept of personhood as utilitarian because its criterion is ''achievement,'' and he questions the legitimacy of this approach when basic moral rights and responsibilities are at stake; ''Notes on Moral Theology: The Abortion Dossier,'' *op. cit.*, pp. 352-353. In Joyce's analysis, Dupré fails to do justice to the actuality of potentiality; *op. cit.*, p. 100, footnote 6. Pastrana discovers a number of philosophical inconsistencies in Dupré's position; *op. cit.*, pp. 258-259.

66 Ransil, *op. cit.*, p. 91.

67 The mechanism of action of IUDs and ''morning after'' pills is still a subject of reserach and discussion; Häring, ''New Dimensions of Responsible Parenthood,'' *op. cit.*, p. 128. Thomas W. Hilgers has no doubt that IUDs do not prevent ovulation but act at the uterine level and destroy the blastocyst: their effect is abortifacient; ''An Evaluation of Intrauterine Devices,'' reprint from *International Review of Natural Family Planning* 2 (1978), no pagination given.

68 Diamond, *op. cit.*, pp. 321-323.

69 Häring, ''New Dimensions of Responsible Parenthood,'' *op. cit.*, pp. 127-129.

70 *Ibid.*, pp. 127-128.

71 H. Noldin, S.J., and A. Schmitt, S.J., *Summa Theologiae Moralis;* 23rd ed. by Godefridus Heinzel, S.J. (Innsbruck: Felizian Rauch, 1960), vol. I, pp. 219-221.

72 Thomas A. Wassmer, S.J., *Christian Ethics for Today* (Milwaukee: Bruce, 1969), pp. 200-201, referring to ''McFadden and others.''

73 *Ibid.*, p. 201.

74 Dedek, *op. cit.*, pp. 324-327, referring to Génicot, Ferreres-Mondría, Prümmer, and Mūnoyerro.

75 *Ibid.*, p. 325.

76 *Ibid.*, pp. 325-326, 331.

77 Wassmer, *op. cit.*, pp. 201-202. He adds that such abortions would be more than just the lesser of two evils: within the situation they would be morally good; *ibid.*, p. 202.

78 Dedek, *op. cit.*, p. 326.

79 *Ibid.*, p. 332.

80 *Ibid.*, p. 332.

81 *Ibid.*, p. 332. Ashley and O'Rourke question Dedek's use of probabilism and point out that he later abandoned this argument; *op. cit.*, p. 237. Cfr. John F. Dedek, *Contemporary Medical Ethics* (New York: Sheed and Ward, 1975), pp. 109-135.

82 Schenk, *op. cit.*, p. 17. Humber admits that the biological evidence is in itself inconclusive but states that it carries *some* weight and that it shifts the burden of proof to those who approve of abortion. Unless they can show that the fetus is definitely not a human person, abortion becomes a gamble and morally irresponsible. So far their arguments have not been convincing and thus their actions lack a rational warrant; *op. cit.*, pp.

70-76. Curran believes that the application of probabilism to fetal life merits further investigation; *op. cit.*, p. 180.

[83] E.F. Regatillo, S.J., and M. Zalba, S.J., *Theologiae Moralis Summa* (Madrid: La Editorial Católica, 1952), vol. I, pp. 170-201.

[84] Francis Simons, "The Catholic Church and the New Morality," *Cross Currents* 16 (1966), p. 433.

[85] *Ibid.*, pp. 433, 435, 436.

[86] *Ibid.*, pp. 438-439.

[87] *Ibid.*, pp. 436-437, 438.

[88] *Ibid.*, p. 438.

[89] *Ibid.*, p. 438.

[90] Ransil, *op. cit.*, pp. 92-95.

[91] *Ibid.*, p. 93; also pp. 93-94. See also: Robert F. Drinan, S.J., "The Jurisprudential Options on Abortion," *Theological Studies* 31 (1970), pp. 158-160. Charles P. Kindregan rejects this argument: fetal death from spontaneous abortion is no more relevant to the status of fetal life than adult death is relevant to the status of adult life; *Abortion, the Law, and Defective Children: A Legal-Medical Study* (Washington: Corpus Books, 1969), p. 7.

[92] Julian R. Pleasants, "A Morality of Consequences," *Commonweal* 86 (1967), pp. 413-414.

[93] *Ibid.*, p. 414. It is hardly necessary to indicate the weakness of this argument. McCormick rightly notes: "We may eventually be able to repair the heart pierced by a bullet, but until such happy days we shall have to continue to talk of direct killing when bullets pierce hearts and are intended to do so"; "Abortion: Aspects of the Moral Question," *America* 117 (1967), p. 719.

[94] Charles E. Curran, *A New Look at Christian Morality* (Notre Dame, Indiana: Fides, 1968), pp. 241-242; *id., Politics, Medicine, and Christian Ethics: A Dialogue with Paul Ramsey* (Philadelphia: Fortress Press, 1973), p. 122. He refers to Merkelbach (first opinion) and Lessius, De Lugo and Zalba (second opinion). See also: Dennis J. Doherty, "The Morality of Abortion," *American Ecclesiastical Review* 169 (1975), p. 43.

[95] Curran, *A New Look at Christian Morality, op. cit.*, p. 242.

[96] *Ibid.*, p. 242, quoting Merkelbach and Zalba.

[97] *Ibid.*, p. 243; *id., Politics, Medicine, and Christian Ethics, op. cit.*, p. 131.

[98] Curran, *Politics, Medicine, and Christian Ethics, op. cit.*, pp. 122-124. Cfr. Pope Pius XI, *Encyclical Letter "Casti Connubii,"* December 31, 1930, in The Monks of Solesmes (eds.), *Papal Teachings: The Human Body* (Boston: St. Paul Editions, 1960), p. 31.

[99] Curran, *Politics, Medicine, and Christian Ethics, op. cit.*, pp. 124-128. See also: Doherty, *op. cit.*, p. 43. Neither author explains why developing human life can be qualified as an aggressor, a position which David Granfield emphatically rejects; *The Abortion Decision* (revised ed.; Garden City, N.Y.: Doubleday Image Books, 1971), pp. 134-135. Ashley and O'Rourke feel that the "classical" equation of other values with human life is invalid: they cannot see how *injury* to the mother can be equivalent to the *death* of the child; *op. cit.*, p. 242.

[100] McCormick, "Notes on Moral Theology: The Abortion Dossier," *op. cit.*, pp. 345, 354. See also: Simons, *op. cit.*, pp. 437-438; James J. Diamond, "Pro-Life Amendments and Due Process," *America* 130 (1974), p. 28.

¹⁰¹ Cornelius J. van der Poel, "The Principle of Double Effect," in Charles E. Curran (ed.), *Absolutes in Moral Theology?* (Washington D.C.: Corpus Books, 1968), pp. 189-193.

¹⁰² *Ibid.*, pp. 193-198; *id.*, *The Search for Human Values* (New York: Paulist Press, 1971), pp. 51-55, 58-62.

¹⁰³ Callahan, *op. cit.*, pp. 425-426. See also: Curran, *A New Look at Christian Morality, op. cit.*, pp. 238-239.

¹⁰⁴ Callahan, *op. cit.*, pp. 424-425. Cfr. the argument of Granfield who states that two natural deaths are a lesser evil than one murder; *op. cit.*, p. 136.

¹⁰⁵ Charles E. Curran, *Medicine and Morals* (Washington: Corpus Books, 1970), pp. 5-6; Bernard Häring, "A Theological Evaluation," in John T. Noonan, Jr. (ed.), *The Morality of Abortion: Legal and Historical Perspectives* (Cambridge, Mass.: Harvard University Press, 1970), pp. 136-137.

¹⁰⁶ Curran, *A New Look at Christian Morality, op. cit.*, pp. 238-239.

¹⁰⁷ Curran, *Politics, Medicine, and Christian Ethics, op. cit.*, p. 128.

¹⁰⁸ Grisez, *op. cit.*, pp. 329-330, 333, 340.

¹⁰⁹ *Ibid.*, p. 333.

¹¹⁰ *Ibid.*, p. 334.

¹¹¹ *Ibid.*, p. 340.

¹¹² *Ibid.*, p. 341. Grisez discusses the application of the revised principle of double effect to self-defense, capital punishment, and warfare; *ibid.*, pp. 335-339. McCormick welcomes Grisez's revision as an attempt to widen the notion of indirect killing and thus accommodate those abortions of which "common sense" would approve. But he finds Grisez's approach too restrictive: it still presupposes that direct killing is intrinsically evil and that the use of evil means necessarily involves a morally reprehensible attitude; *Ambiguity in Moral Choice: The 1973 Pere Marquette Theology Lecture* (Milwaukee: Marquette University Press, 1973), pp. 40-53. In the opinion of Stanley Hauerwas, Grisez's solution is basically consequentialist, and there is no logical reason why it should only provide for the most extreme situation; "Abortion and Normative Ethics: A Critical Appraisal of Callahan and Grisez," *Cross Currents* 21 (1971), p. 414. Paul Ramsey holds that the abortions permitted by Grisez's principle are in fact direct; "Abortion: A Review Article," *Thomist* 37 (1973), pp. 211-226. Hauerwas and Ramsey write from a Protestant perspective.

¹¹³ Wiliam E. May, "Abortion and Man's Moral Being," in Robert L. Perkins (ed.), *Abortion: Pro and Con* (Cambridge, Mass.: Schenkman, 1974), pp. 25-26.

¹¹⁴ *Ibid.*, pp. 29-30.

¹¹⁵ *Ibid.*, p. 30. See also: *id., Human Existence, Medicine and Ethics, op. cit.*, pp. 103-105; Gerber, *op. cit.*, pp. 2-4.

¹¹⁶ Patrick J. Coffey, "Toward a Sound Moral Policy on Abortion," *New Scholasticism* 47 (1973), pp. 108-112. Dupré rejects efforts like Grisez's as merely verbal solutions which lead to terminological confusion: in such abortions the killing *is* the cure. He prefers to accept that abortion is an act of direct killing and then to examine under which conditions this direct killing would be permissible; *op. cit.*, pp. 485-486.

¹¹⁷ Häring, "A Theological Evaluation," *op. cit.*, pp. 137-138. See also: Ashley and O'Rourke, *op. cit.*, p. 242; Andrew C. Varga, *The Main Issues in Bioethics* (New York: Paulist Press, 1980), p.46.

¹¹⁸ Ransil, *op. cit.*, p. 60.

¹¹⁹ McCormick, "Notes on Moral Theology: The Abortion Dossier," *op. cit.*, p. 354. See

also: Mary C. Segers, "Abortion: The Last Resort," *America* 133 (1975), p. 458; Clare Boothe Luce, "Two Books on Abortion and the Questions They Raise," *National Review* 23 (1971), p. 32.

[120] McCormick, *Ambiguity in Moral Choice, op. cit.,* pp. 7-67.

[121] *Ibid.,* p. 84.

[122] *Ibid.,* p. 95.

[123] *Ibid.,* pp. 86-87.

[124] Richard A. McCormick, S.J., "Notes on Moral Theology," *Theological Studies* 34 (1973), pp. 70-74.

[125] Dedek, "Abortion: A Theological Judgment," *op. cit.,* p. 331. Over the years McCormick has developed and refined his position on the distinction between direct and indirect effects of human acts. This process is reflected in his annual "Notes on Moral Theology" in *Theological Studies.* For recent statements of his view on this issue see his "A Commentary on the Commentaries," in Richard A. McCormick, S.J., and Paul Ramsey (eds.), *Doing Evil to Achieve Good: Moral Choice in Conflict Situations* (Chicago: Loyola University Press, 1978), pp. 193-267; "Reflections on the Literature," in Charles E. Curran and Richard A. McCormick, S.J. (eds.), *Moral Norms and Catholic Tradition* (Readings in Moral Theology, No. 1; New York: Paulist Press, 1979), pp. 294-340. May questions McCormick's approach and affirms his support of that of Grisez; "Ethics and Human Identity: The Challenge of the New Biology," *Horizons* 3 (1976), pp. 17-37; "The Moral Meaning of Human Acts," *Homiletic and Pastoral Review* 79, October 1978, pp. 10-21.

[126] Pleasants, *op. cit.,* p. 414; John F. Monagle, "The Ethics of Abortion," *Social Justice Review* 65 (1972), p. 115; Segers, *op. cit.,* p. 458; Luce, *op. cit.,* pp. 28, 32; Deedy, *op. cit.,* p. 284; Carol A. Berger and Patrick F. Berger, "The Edelin Decision," *Commonweal* 102 (1975), pp. 77-78. See also: Hallett, *op. cit.,* p. 633. John T. Noonan, Jr., discusses the traditional solution to the cancerous pregnant uterus and the ectopic pregnancy and he disputes that an abortion in these situations is "indirect." He prefers to regard these cases simply as exceptions where the ordinary rule does not apply because the fetus endangers the life of the mother who is then permitted to kill in self-defense. We may therefore presume that Noonan would not object to other (direct) abortions which save women's lives; "Responding to Persons: Methods of Moral Argument in Debate over Abortion," *Theology Digest* 21 (1973), pp. 295-297.

[127] van der Poel, "The Principle of Double Effect," *op. cit.,* p. 205.

[128] *Ibid.,* p. 209. McCormick considers this criterion too "ultimate" and too vague; *Ambiguity in Moral Choice, op. cit.,* pp. 31-32. See also: Grisez, *op. cit.,* pp. 332-333.

[129] Ransil, *op. cit.,* p. 99.

[130] McCormick, "Notes on Moral Theology: The Abortion Dossier," *op. cit.,* p. 355.

[131] James E. Krause, "Is Abortion Absolutely Prohibited?" *Continuum* 6 (1968), p. 439.

[132] Curran, *Politics, Medicine, and Christian Ethics, op. cit.,* p. 131.

[133] Wassmer, *op. cit.,* p. 201. See also: Thomas, *op. cit.,* pp. 271-272; Viola, *op. cit.,* p. 97; William Jacobs, *The Pastor and the Patient: An Informal Guide to New Directions in Medical Ethics* (New York: Paulist Press, 1973), pp. 36-39; Gary L. Chamberlain, "The Abortion Debate is Revealing our Values," *New Catholic World* 215 (1972), p. 208.

[134] Schenk, *op. cit.,* p. 17.

[135] Di Ianni, *op. cit.*, pp. 323, 325. He does not explain how fetal deformity can be ascertained during the first few weeks of pregnancy.

[136] Dedek, "Abortion: A Theological Judgment," *op. cit.*, p. 332.

[137] Ransil, *op. cit.*, pp. 99-101.

[138] Maguire, *op. cit.*, p. 202.

[139] Dupré, *op. cit.*, pp. 486-488. McCormick rightly qualifies Dupré's position as undecided and ambiguous. It is not clear which factor decides the abortion dilemma: the equivalence to life of the indication or the degree of fetal development? "Notes on Moral Theology: The Abortion Dossier," *op. cit.*, pp. 351-352. Keane accepts the principle of proportionate reason in theory but he is reluctant to apply it to problematic pregnancies (except in the life vs. life case) because he feels that more work has to be done on the question of what values can be considered proportionate to human life; *op. cit.*, p. 138. See also: John R. Connery, S.J., "Eugenic Abortion," in William C. Bier, S.J. (ed.), *Human Life: Problems of Birth, of Living, and of Dying* (The Pastoral Psychology Series, No. 9; New York: Fordham University Press, 1977), p. 110.

[140] Häring, "A Theological Evaluation," *op. cit.*, pp. 138-139.

[141] *Ibid.*, p. 138. William J. Tobin seems to doubt that such total deformation in fact occurs; *Jurist* 31 (1971), p. 570.

[142] Ashley and O'Rourke, *op. cit.*, pp. 230-231. See also: Leo O. Farley, "The Meaning of Life and Divine Transcendence," *The Catholic Theological Society of America: Proceedings of the Twenty-Third Annual Convention, Washington, D.C., June 17-20, 1968* 23 (1968), p. 116; Berger and Berger, *op. cit.*, p. 77; Rudolph J. Gerber, "Abortion: Parameters for Decision," *International Philosophical Quarterly* 11 (1971), p. 565; Drinan, *op. cit.*, pp. 160-161.

[143] Häring, "A Theological Evaluation," *op. cit.*, pp. 139-140.

[144] *Ibid.*, pp. 140-141.

[145] *Ibid.*, p. 140.

[146] *Ibid.*, pp. 141-142. See also: Charles E. Curran, *Issues in Sexual and Medical Ethics* (Notre Dame: University of Notre Dame Press, 1978), pp. 144-147.

[147] McCormick, "Notes on Moral Theology: The Abortion Dossier," *op. cit.*, p. 341.

[148] *Ibid.*, p. 355.

[149] Dedek, "Abortion: A Theological Judgment," *op. cit.*, pp. 332-333.

[150] Luce, *op. cit.*, p. 33. See also: Doherty, *op. cit.*, p. 45; Connery, "Eugenic Abortion," *op. cit.*, pp. 110-111; Keane, *op. cit.*, p. 139; Jacobs, *op. cit.*, pp. 167-174.

[151] William E. May, "Abortion as Indicative of Personal and Social Identity," *Jurist* 33 (1973), p. 216.

[152] Curran, *A New Look at Christian Ethics*, *op. cit.*, pp. 170-172. The Catholic moral tradition does allow a "perplexed conscience" to choose the lesser evil but it does not follow that the evil act is justified at the level of the objective moral order. See: Noldin and Schmitt, *op. cit.*, p. 203; Regatillo and Zalba, *op. cit.*, pp. 315-317.

[153] *Ibid.*, pp. 171-173; *id.*, "Abortion: Law and Morality in Contemporary Catholic Theology," *op. cit.*, p. 182. See also: Doherty, *op. cit.*, p. 44; Dupré, *op. cit.*, p. 485; Berger and Berger, *op. cit.*, pp. 77-78; Daniel Callahan, "Abortion: Thinking and Experiencing," *Christianity and Crisis* 32 (1973), p. 298; Daniel C. Maguire, "The New Morality in Focus," in Mary Perkins Ryan (ed.), *Toward Moral Maturity: Religious Education and the Formation of Conscience* (Paramus, N.J.: Paulist Press Deus Books, 1968), pp. 8-9. William E. May is critical of Curran's theology of compromise because it so alters the objective moral order that an evil act becomes

morally justifiable; *Becoming Human: An Invitation to Christian Ethics* (Dayton, Ohio: Pflaum, 1975), pp. 127-132.

[154] McCormick, "Notes on Moral Theology: The Abortion Dossier," *op. cit.*, p. 356. See also: *id.*, "Notes on Moral Theology: 1976," *Theological Studies* 38 (1977), pp. 112-114.

[155] Doherty, *op. cit.*, pp. 39, 46; *Pastoral Constitution on the Church in the Modern World*, *"Gaudium et Spes,"* nos. 16, 51, 59.

[156] Doherty, *op. cit.*, pp. 39-40, 41-42; *Declaration on Religious Liberty*, *"Dignitatis Humanae,"* nos. 1-3.

[157] Doherty, *op. cit.*, pp. 37, 41, 42-43, 44-45, 46-47, footnote 9.

[158] Maguire, *Death by Choice, op. cit.*, p. 71.

[159] Callahan, *Abortion: Law, Choice and Morality, op. cit.*, p. 433.

[160] *Ibid.*, pp. 307-334.

[161] *Ibid.*, p. 335.

[162] *Ibid.*, pp. 335-338.

[163] *Ibid.*, p. 338.

[164] *Ibid.*, pp. 339-341. Connery indicates the difference between Callahan's approach and the traditional Catholic position; "Callahan on Meaning of Abortion," *op. cit.*, pp. 281-282.

[165] Ransil, *op. cit.*, pp. 18-19.

[166] *Ibid.*, p. 37.

[167] *Ibid.*, p. 37.

[168] Callahan, *Abortion: Law, Choice and Morality, op. cit.*, p. 498.

[169] *Ibid.*, p. 498.

[170] *Ibid.*, p. 498; see also p. 497.

[171] *Ibid.*, p. 498. See also: *id.*, "Abortion: Some Ethical Issues," in David F. Walbert and J. Douglas Butler (eds.), *Abortion, Society, and the Law* (Cleveland: Case Western Reserve University, 1973), p. 91. Callahan criticizes the traditional Catholic solution of abortion dilemmas because of its one-dimensionality in the sense that the welfare of the fetus always takes precedence; *Abortion: Law, Choice and Morality, op. cit.*, pp. 409-426, 438-441. Connery rejects this criticism: the Catholic Church opposes without compromise the killing not only of the child but also of the mother; "Callahan on Meaning of Abortion," *op. cit.*, pp. 282-283. Noonan, who allows an abortion for the sake of the life of the mother, argues that even if one adopts a multidimensional approach to a distressed pregnancy one will not be able to justify the intervention for a less serious reason. At stake in the decision is not just a single value, fetal life, against which the suffering of the woman may be balanced. There are other values that prevail or perish with the child: parental responsibility and fidelity, the physician's commitment to life, the State's care for its citizens. A decision which subordinates these values to personal interests (the mother's self-determination) and social interests (population control) is unbalanced; "Responding to Persons," *op. cit.*, pp. 299-301. McCormick feels that Callahan's approach is not sufficiently prophetic: a true morality of abortion must aim at the expansion of an individual's perspectives and value commitments; "Notes on Moral Theology: The Abortion Dossier," *op. cit.*, pp. 347-348.

[172] Springer, "Marriage, the Family, and Sex — A Roman Catholic View," *op. cit.*, p. 194.

[173] Curran, *A New Look at Christian Ethics, op. cit.*, pp. 234-236, 237.

[174] *Ibid.*, pp. 234-239. Writing from a non-Catholic perspective, Harry W. Rudel *et al.*

present a similar analysis; *Birth Control: Contraception and Abortion* (New York: Macmillan, 1973), p. 296.

[175] Callahan, *Abortion: Law, Choice and Morality, op. cit.,* p. 433.

[176] *Theological Studies* 35 (1974), p. 101.

[177] Callahan, *Abortion: Law, Choice and Morality, op. cit.,* p. 433.

[178] *Ibid.,* p. 430.

[179] *Ibid.,* p. 496.

[180] *Ibid.,* p. 500.

[181] Ashley and O'Rourke question the application of the proportional method to abortion dilemmas: its supporters believe that the advantages to the mother sometimes outweigh the value of the life of the child but they never explain how this calculation can be made. Ashley and O'Rourke feel that this problem of evaluation is incapable of an objective solution. Those therefore who employ the proportional method will either fall into mere utilitarianism or they simply have to leave the decision in the hands of the mother; *op. cit.,* pp. 241-242. For similar observations see: David Little, "Abortion: Law, Choice and Morality," *Commonweal* 93 (1970), p. 74; Leonard F.X. Mayhew, "Abortion: Two Sides and Some Complaints," *Ecumenist* 5, July-August 1967, p. 77. McCormick notes that Callahan's moral policy falls short in moral reasoning because it fails to establish the necessity or desirability of abortion in terms of competitive values and available alternatives; "Notes on Moral Theology: The Abortion Dossier," *op. cit.,* pp. 347-348.

SECTION II

ABORTION AS A LEGAL POLICY

Chapter Six

The Inheritance from the Past:
Human Law in the Traditional Manuals
of Catholic Ethics

My analysis of American Catholic thinking on the morality of abortion took as its point of departure the traditional manuals which yielded a good amount of material. However, when we examine the same authors on the subject of abortion legislation, there is not a similar abundance of information. Considering the abortion problem exclusively from the point of view of the individual moral decision, they pay no attention to the legal aspects of that decision. An exception is Francis J. Connell who wrote in 1955 that abortion liberalization is opposed to the natural moral law:

> The Catholic legislator may not approve of any measure opposed to the natural law. An example of this would be legislation authorizing the establishment of birth-control clinics or the spreading of information helpful to contraception. The same principle would hold regarding proposed measures to prescribe or permit "eugenic" sterilization, or to legalize what is known as "therapeutic" abortion. In casting their votes against such proposals, Catholic legislators need have no fear that they are imposing distinctively Catholic tenets on their fellow citizens. They are simply condemning violations of the natural law, which is binding on all men without exception, irrespective of their religious beliefs.[1]

Four years later Joseph T. Tinnelly is one of the first Catholic authors to refer to the implications of the American Law Institute's *Model Penal Code*. The Institute had published a tentative draft of a revised abortion statute earlier that year.[2] Tinnelly argues that criminal law must respect the moral law:

> The statement of the case against justification of abortion is simple and concise. Direct and voluntary abortion is intrinsically wrong since it is the direct killing of an innocent human being. It is never justifiable because the person who is killed has not been guilty of any crime or unlawful aggression on account of which he could be said to have forfeited his right to live. The State does not have, nor can it ever have, the right to kill an innocent person.
> Other problems in the Penal Code are much less clear cut and require an

application of principles derived from the science of ethics. The penal law cannot and should not attempt to enforce the moral law in every last detail but it cannot ignore, much less violate, that law.[3]

The first official Church pronouncement on abortion legislation was issued on February 12, 1967, when the bishops of New York State expressed their opposition to a liberalization of the New York statute. They said in their declaration, which was their first joint pastoral letter, that permissive abortion laws violate the unborn child's God-given right to life:

> The right of innocent human beings to life is sacred and inviolable. It comes from God Himself. . . .
> Since laws which allow abortion violate the unborn child's God-given right, we are opposed to any proposal to extend them. We urge you most strongly to do all in your power to prevent direct attacks upon the lives of unborn children.[4]

To arrive at a proper understanding of such early statements we have to refer again to the manuals because these formulations employ the concepts and the language of the classical ethical tracts.

I. Natural Law and Natural Rights

The traditional handbooks of Catholic ethics present a virtually identical exposé of the *ratio fundamentalis* of human law. Their discussion of this question is basically Thomistic in outlook and invariably takes God's eternal law as its point of departure.[5] Celestine N. Bittle summarizes their argument as follows:

> Eternal law, natural law, and positive law are closely related. They have their ultimate source in the reason and nature of God. Without the eternal and natural law, positive law would lack a rational foundation and would have no power to enforce obedience on the part of the human will. Because man is a rational being, a social being, and a creature of God, he has the natural and moral obligation to submit his will to the precepts of the eternal, natural and positive law.[6]

The manuals emphasize that natural law exists independently of the human will and that it is the source and criterion of all human law. In this context they point out that the theories of positivism present a completely unacceptable analysis of human law, especially from the human rights viewpoint. In the perspective of positivism the State is the creator of all rights, and this means that human rights owe their existence exclusively to human consent or social customs. Political philosophy is thus reduced to an empirical science.[7] In contrast to this the manuals sponsor a "theistic conception of the universe" which alone is able to provide a satisfactory explanation of law and rights.[8]

The traditional authors define natural law as a body of moral principles which reason itself discovers and which are binding for all men. This law is formulated not through any special promulgation but by a natural process of human reasoning which identifies the intentions of the Creator by analysing the "nature of things" and, in the first place, human nature. Man reflects upon his natural inclinations and expresses his obedience to God by ordering these to their proper ends. This "ordering" results in a dictate of practical reason, and it is this dictate which constitutes the essence of the natural law.[9]

The manuals explain that natural law is dependent on and inferior to God's eternal law. The latter exists in the mind of God: it does not depend on any other law, and it orders the whole of the cosmos. Natural law, on the other hand, exists in the minds of men as a reflection of the eternal law, and it regulates only part of creation: man and his conduct. However, since it is based on the nature of rational man, it is universal and unchangeable. None of its precepts can be abrogated because the necessities of nature are not subject to change. Moreover, natural law takes precedence over all human law. The latter must be a deduction from, or a determination of, the former.[10] Natural law is binding on all men, both as individuals and as members of society, and it obliges them to strive for the perfection which is proper to rational life. Moral goodness thus consists in the conformity of an action with rational human nature: an act is morally good if it is in accordance with the true end of man, morally bad if it is not.[11]

The manuals further say that, independently of any human laws or human conventions, there exist natural rights which are direct concessions to man from natural law. Nature not only endows man with rational faculties, his intellect and will, but also gives him an opportunity to use them. This implies that man is given an area of personal independence, to exercise his powers and thereby attain in a befitting and rational manner his ultimate aim: the perfection proper to his nature. His freedom is not absolute: it is qualified by the counterclaims of others who have similar spheres of freedom. However, since man has the responsibility of attaining final perfection, he should not be interfered with in his reasonable pursuit of this goal. This is another way of saying that nature has endowed man with certain rights.[12]

The Christian tradition has always upheld the existence of natural rights founded upon the basic requirements of human nature itself. These rights safeguard the inviolability of the human person who is to be respected as a rational, self-active, and independent being. As self-active, he must be allowed to be the master of his own actions and carry responsibility for what he does. As independent, he may not be considered part of any other being nor be treated as inferior to any other man in the essentials of his nature and his end.[13] To secure his end he must have at his disposal a number of internal and external goods. By conferral of natural rights nature commands that the person and his necessary adjuncts be respected. The human person is inviolable and so is that which belongs to him.[14]

An individual, therefore, has natural rights, not merely by virtue of his membership in the community or because he is a citizen of the State, but because of his status as a human being endowed with reason and free will, and obliged to strive towards his final end. Natural rights derive from the natural law and are antecedent to any organization of men into civil society. They are not created by the State: they are established before the State begins to exist. They impose themselves by their own evidence since their source is human nature itself.[15] The manuals emphasize that basic among these natural rights is the right to life.[16] E.J. Ross has indicated the various implications of this human right:

> (a) A man has the right to be born; hence abortion is murder. (b) A man has also the right to individual and private self-defense; hence intentional slaying can only be lawful in self-defense; infants have a right to their life being preserved by their parents; war is justified only for social and public self-defense; capital punishment is justified only when the offense is very grave, when the offender's guilt is clearly established, and when it is necessary for the public good (e.g., to deter others from committing a similar heinous crime). (c) No man has the right to end his own life; hence suicide is never justified; God is the only author and master of life, and He alone may end it directly or by legitimate authority.[17]

II. Natural Law and Human Law

Under this heading the manuals point out, first of all, that human legislation as such is valid. No precept of natural law may be abrogated but additions to it can be made. God can add to natural law by his positive laws; so can the Church and the State which may make legal provisions for that which natural law permits, or determine and confirm what it prohibits. These amplifications by human law must remain in harmony with natural law.[18]

The authors explain why such amplifications are necessary. Although in a general way natural law is clear to all men, it still has to be applied to concrete circumstances. The human condition is subject to change, and there are often profound differences between various communities or groups. Not everyone is in a position to apply natural law in the complicated situations arising in any society; therefore there is need of human legislation which interprets natural law in the light of the actual circumstances of a particular community at a particular time. Furthermore, the common good requires that laws be enforced, and the only way of achieving this is by the application of sanctions. This aspect of law and legislation can only be provided for by the civil authorities. [19]

In order that laws be genuine and impose a real moral obligation on the wills of citizens, the manuals require as a primary condition that their contents or objectives do not conflict with the natural law. A human law is legitimate only in so far as it conforms with the principles grounded in the rational nature of man. A human law is a moral law only in so far as it has been derived from the natural law. [20] The authors give two reasons for this restriction. Firstly, the natural law is the fundamental criterion of human conduct, and rational man must comply with it if he wants to arrive at his ultimate end: the perfection of his nature. Every human law, then, must conform to this law and must in one way or another be derived from it: it must perfect rational beings. [21] Secondly, nature has ordered that men live in community. Man has been created as a social being; therefore he can reach perfection only by being a member of society. Civil society requires that an authority directs the cooperative activity of its members towards the common good. Man's very nature, then, implies that he subject himself to civil authority which has been entrusted with directing citizens in their observance of natural law and leading them to their common end. This direction, obviously, must be based on the precepts of natural law. [22]

Genuine human legislation is not an arbitrary affair: it is an authoritative expression and application in concrete cases of the general requirements of natural law. [23] Human law, therefore, must respect the moral law. It cannot validly command the nonobservance of obligations imposed by natural law nor may it impose duties which violate that law. [24] It also follows that human law must respect natural rights. These are absolute and universal; thus no one can abolish or modify them. They are necessary for individual and social life, and it is the function of the State to see to it that these rights are safeguarded. [25]

Human law must be *moral*. The manuals add that it must also be *just*. For a law to be just, its object must be *possible*, that is, citizens must be physically and morally capable of fulfilling the obligations it imposes. Human law may not place too heavy a burden on the subject. Here also the principle applies: *ad impossibile nemo tenetur.* Heroic actions cannot generally be the object of human legislation.[26]

This does not mean that human legislation should limit itself to some vague generalities which do not really interfere with one's personal freedom. Without any restrictive human law at all, vice and chaos would be the order of the day. On the other hand, the lawgiver should not occupy himself with every detail of men's lives by translating the whole of the natural law into State law. The manuals insist that human legislation must limit its sphere of operations to the order which ought to exist in social relationships. By regulating these it should secure the necessary cooperation among citizens and thus promote their moral perfection. The purpose of the State is the promotion of the external good of society, and therefore only that which affects public welfare favorably or unfavorably falls in some manner under its jurisdiction. State law should neither try to enforce the practice of all virtues nor attempt to eliminate all vice and iniquity by a complete control of even the private lives of the citizens. It may not interfere with their private lives, their families, their professional and business activities, except when this is required by the common good.[27] Offenses against morality need not necessarily involve another person: they can be directed against God or against oneself. Blasphemy and drunkenness and many other vices are expressly condemned by the moral law but this does not imply that human law must also forbid them. If they are forbidden, their prohibition is based on their harmful effects on society, and not because they are destructive of spiritual or eternal values.[28] It is evident, then, that the traditional authors do not grant the State the right to regulate private morality that is really private and does not affect the common good. Private morality is an affair of the individual and not of the State.[29]

When it comes to interpreting natural law, the manuals place the Church in a privileged position. The Pope, as the shepherd of the flock of Christ, is divinely constituted to interpret natural law, and he does so authentically and infallibly.[30] Yet the traditional authors do not appoint the Church as the supreme judge of civil law nor do they demand that ecclesiastical interpretations of the requirements of natural law be translated into State legislation. The relationship between Church teaching and State law is expressed in a different manner. Discussing the role of the Catholic legislator, Connell states that he must realize that his primary consideration should be the common good of the State or of mankind as a whole. The Catholic legislator is then *aided* in making just decisions and passing appropriate legislative measures by the definite and comprehensive norms of right and wrong proposed by his Church:

(A)nyone who is sincerely convinced that the Catholic Church is protected and guided in its teaching office by the Spirit of God must realize
that Catholic principles, properly applied, will necessarily promote the
best interests of society.... (I)t is utterly absurd to claim that the Catholic
legislator is manifesting a bias in favor of his own religion when he allows
such teachings of his Church to influence his decision in matters of
statesmanship. He is simply applying the principles of the natural law,
principles of the soundest political wisdom, the observance of which
affords the best safeguard of the vitality and the peace of any nation.[31]

Connell therefore adopts the a priori argument that there can be no
contradiction between the dictates of natural law, as authentically interpreted by the Church, and wholesome State legislation. As soon as human
legislation departs from or contradicts natural law, it ceases to be sound and
no longer serves the common good. Its evil effects upon the community can
be empirically assessed, and the law can then be challenged on these
grounds, also by the Church. Augustine J. Osgniach discusses the legalization of divorce in similar terms:

It has been retorted that divorce under certain circumstances, as in cases
of adultery, desertion, etc., serves as a suitable means for restoring peace
and happiness to the family. True, divorce may obviate a great many
inconveniences, but this cannot be a guiding criterion for lawmakers who
before all else must take into account the moral lawfulness of an act as
well as its consequences. Divorce does at times avoid certain evils, but as
a general rule it opens wide the doors to greater and numberless other
evils....

The so-called arguments against the indissolubility of marriage are
sophistries devoid of value and tending to foment sinful passions and to
legalize conjugal infidelity. Once legalized, divorce will accomplish its
nefarious task. Neither legislator nor magistrate will succeed in saving
the family and society from utter disintegration.... A breach in the
indissolubility of marriage will inevitably lead to the abolition of marriage itself. Divorce does not, as is often asserted, indicate an advance in
culture and civilization, but rather a retrogression to barbarism and
immorality.[32]

Osgniach's argument on the legalization of artificial birth control runs
parallel to his proposition on divorce:

For man any sort of artificial birth control is not only unnatural but gravely
sinful. The Catholic doctrine on this matter is clearly stated by Pius XI in
his encyclical letter on "Christian Marriage."
...Birth control is not merely an individual problem, it is a national
problem, for it harms the individual, physically and morally, and

menaces public morality by undermining the State. In this connection it is well to remember that the State does not legislate on or interfere with the purely private actions of individuals, but as soon as any action has social consequences it comes within the competency of the State, and this from the standpoint of its relation to the moral law.[33]

The handbooks present natural law, itself grounded on God, as the foundation of all true human laws and rights. They define a genuine human law as one which is *moral, possible,* and *concerned with the common good as such*.

III. The Argument of the Manuals and the Subsequent Debate

It is not difficult to see that the traditional tracts on natural law and human law were completely inadequate from the point of view of the political debate which developed after the publication of the ALI *Model Penal Code* in 1962. The manuals clearly lack explicitness on the subject of abortion legislation. Only one author, Connell, refers to the legal aspects of the abortion issue, and this only in passing. He states that the Catholic legislator must cast his vote in accordance with the dictates of natural law and that these rule out the legalization of abortion.[34] None of the others we have considered refers to the legal aspect of abortion, directly or indirectly. Under the heading "The Right to Life," Osgniach's book deals with self-defense, suicide, duelling, lynching, euthanasia, and capital punishment, and elsewhere considers the ethico-juridical aspects of divorce, artifical birth control, and sterilization of mental defectives but he never at all refers to abortion or abortion laws.[35] In his 1960 publication *We Hold These Truths,* John Courtney Murray discussed several contemporary conflicts between Church and State but kept clear of the abortion issue.[36] In 1961, Norman St. John-Stevas published a study on the relationship between law and Christian morals in the English and American legal systems. While he dealt with the legal aspects of contraception, artificial insemination, sterilization, homosexuality, sucide, and euthanasia, he mentioned the word "abortion" just once.[37]

Clearly, the whole issue was considered self-evident or at least not sufficiently urgent to be included in the tracts. It is equally manifest that American Catholicism was ill-prepared to face the reform movement which gained such momentum in the 1960s. However, we know by inference what the position of the manuals would have been if they had

expressed it: (1) abortion violates the human rights of the fetus and, therefore, natural law; consequently it cannot be legalized; (2) moreover,
liberalization will have disastrous social consequences. This inferred argument is relevant. We will meet it again in the subsequent Catholic debate,
as some will formulate the position of the Catholic Church in kindred
concepts and terms.

Theism and Teleology

In the context of the Catholic theological view on creation, the traditional proposition on the relationship between natural law, natural rights,
and human law certainly does not lack internal logic and coherence. However, it clearly presupposes a theistico-teleological understanding of the
cosmos and of man. This is admitted very plainly by Osgniach who asserts
that "the right to life is founded and rests upon the theistico-teleological
conception of the universe."[38] He states further that the "denial of a
personal God is the cause of the chief difficulties in modern . . . political
philosophy."[39] Moreover, the manuals place the Church in a privileged
position with regard to the understanding and interpretation of natural law,
even if they do not always do so explicitly.

It goes without saying that a political and legal argument based on such
"parochial assumptions"[40] is less than effective in a secular society, and
especially so if the morality of the individual act is presented in terms of
intramural values. I have discussed this in Chapter II where I drew attention
to the limitations of an anthropology which is onesidedly theistic and
teleological. Man is seen as subject to nature which reveals the divine will
and which he has to obey in order to reach his last end—God. This may
result in an attitude of passive resignation. The Secular City takes a more
existentialist and active view of man and emphasizes the need of personal
responsibility and initiative.

The Common Good

We have seen that in the perspective of the traditional authors the
demands of natural law and the requirements of the common good necessarily coincide. Consequently, an immoral law will invariably have
adverse social repercussions. The liberationists, however, will later claim
to have empirical evidence that, as far as abortion is concerned, the common good requires in fact a liberal legal code, irrespective of the dictates of
any natural law. They will refer to such problems as illegal abortions,
unwanted children, and the population explosion which, in their view,
would be alleviated by less restrictive statutes. Not all liberationists will
advocate such a step because of ideological considerations: a good number

of them will support it only as a lesser evil, without reference to women's rights or similar arguments.[41] Daniel Callahan has formulated this element of the reformist argument as follows:

> The worst possible laws on abortion are those which are highly restrictive. They lead to a large number of illegal abortions, hazardous enough in affluent countries, but all the more so in underdeveloped countries. If they succeed in keeping down the overall number of abortions, they do so at too high a price. Unenforced and unenforceable, they bring the law into disrepute. They have proved to be discriminatory. In a pluralistic society, they offend the conscience of many. They take from a woman's hands the possibility of making her own decision, thus restricting her freedom —but in doing so offer no compensatory or justifying gain for the common good. As a means of symbolizing a society's respect for unborn life, they are poor, too widely disregarded and known to be disregarded to give the symbol any real power. Society ought to have a high regard for nascent life, seeking to protect it and further it, but restrictive abortion laws have not proved an effective way of exhibiting this regard.[42]

Not the Handmaid of Morals

Whatever position the American Catholic Church later adopted on the issue of abortion legislation and whatever arguments it employed to justify its stand, it is important to note that the manuals had not appointed human law as a mere handmaid of morals. In the view of the traditional handbooks, human legislation must be moral, i.e., it may not violate natural law or natural rights. But as a further condition they stipulate that a law must be just or "possible," i.e., it may not put an impossible burden on its subjects. Furthermore, human legislation must restrict itself to that which is strictly necessary for the common good. In other words, the manuals recognize the distinction between public and private morality. Richard A. McCormick has pointed out that St. Thomas Aquinas' theory of law (which is the tradition of the handbooks) lays much more stress on "possibility" or "feasibility" as a criterion of human legislation than on the moral content or public character of the acts in question:

> (W)ithin Thomas' perspectives, all acts, whatever their nature, whether private or public, moral or immoral, if they have ascertainable public consequences on the maintenance and stability of society, are a legitimate matter of concern to society, and consequently fit subjects for the criminal code. But it is feasibility that determines whether they *should be* in the penal code, and this cannot be collapsed into the private-public distinction. Therefore, while Thomas does not tell us whether abortion ought to be in the criminal code, his philosophy of law tells us what questions to ask.[43]

Now the liberationist movement will hold that restrictive laws, in fact, place an "impossible" burden on many pregnant women, and it will devise a list of indications or "criteria of impossibility."[44] Moreover, it will claim that restrictive codes are also socially and legally "impossible." A lawgiver must be in a position to enforce effectively the legislation which he has enacted, otherwise the legal system itself will fall into disrepute. Since public opinion is becoming increasingly permissive of abortion, and since the abortion procedure does not readily lend itself to criminal investigation and prosecution, the movement claims that the legislator at the present time has no hope of enforcing rigid codes. In order to be "just" and, especially, prudent, he should repeal such legislation. In this context it should also be noted that the argument of the handbooks lacks the dimension of social justice. None of the authors discusses the thesis that laws cannot be "just" or "possible" if socio-economic conditions are such that their observance in fact constitutes too heavy a burden for the citizens.

The distinction between private and public morality will be gratefully employed by the liberationists who, in the best tradition of the manuals, will emphasize the citizen's right to freedom without unnecessary interference by the legislator. They will hold that the woman's abortion decision is a matter of private moral choice which in no way affects the common good. The lawgiver should not intervene in what is essentially a private moral option.

Negativity

Ironically, then, the traditional tracts on human law contain several elements which, if developed and accentuated sufficiently, would seem to give a certain amount of support to the liberationist position. The situation is not aided by the fact that the exhortations the manuals address to the human legislator are invariably formulated in a negative way and concentrate upon what the lawgiver should not do rather than on what he should do. He has the power to make laws but should not legislate against natural law. He is not to interfere with natural rights. His legislation should not extend beyond what is strictly necessary for the common good. One seldom finds an explicit enumeration of those elements of natural law and of those natural rights which he *must* translate into State legislation. The following statement is typical:

> The law must always ordain a prescription of right reason. No law may contradict the Natural Law. Thus an edict forbidding a father to bequeath money to his children would be void. Nor may civil law contradict positive divine law as did the laws of England which forbade the Mass. Negatively, civil law must not contravene the law of any higher authority.

Positively, it must be either necessary or useful to the common good. Frivolous or silly measures, or measures which benefit only the ruler or a small class, cannot be valid laws.[45]

The lawgiver is given a certain amount of freedom to determine which areas of human activity should be covered by legislation. Thus it could conceivably be argued that the lawgiver has no positive duty to enact restrictive abortion legislation. The common good is a reality which is subject to a certain amount of empirical assessment and the lawgiver might conclude that a partial or complete legislative withdrawal from the area of abortion might serve the common good better than the enforcement of a restrictive code. This would not necessarily imply that the State recognizes the woman's right to an abortion or that it denies the fetus' right to life. Complete or partial repeal of the law is not by definition the equivalent of moral approval of the practice. It merely implies nonprosecution or withdrawal of penal sanctions. At the same time it must be admitted that the law undoubtedly has some didactic function and that repeal would be interpreted by many as a form of approval at public level.[46]

Undemocratic

Finally, it must be noted that the arguments of the traditional authors are not geared in any way at all to the contemporary process of lawmaking. Their approach reflects a socio-political situation which no longer exists: the theocratic or monarchic or oligarchic Christian State in which legislation was enacted by one person or a restricted group of persons who were able to be inspired by the dictates of natural law, and whose legislative and judicial activities were in no way hampered by the political requirements of a pluralist democracy.[47] In the Christian State, ideology was indeed the determinant of law.

Charles E. Curran will later point out that in a pluralistic society lawmaking will always have a pragmatic aspect.[48] In a democratic political structure which is complex, almost by definition, and which often has to accommodate conflicting ideologies, legislation is enacted on the basis of political consent and, in practice, this usually involves a good deal of compromise. Politics has now become the art of achieving the possible and sometimes this implies settling for the lesser evil. It is clear that the handbooks hardly cater to the democratic situation.

The Secularization of the Catholic Position

Evidently, the nationwide debate which followed the publication of the ALI *Model Penal Code* found American Catholic theology unprepared.

The arguments of the manuals on natural law and human law were not really helpful in the present controversy because they were associated with a theistic and teleological conception of the universe. Moreover, they had some inherent ''weaknesses'' as far as the liberationist contentions were concerned and, last but not least, they made no mention of the requirements of democracy. Consequently, the natural law argument did not figure prominently in the later American Catholic tradition on abortion, although we do find references to it in episcopal pronouncements. The American hierarchy declared in its official statement on the 1973 Supreme Court decision:

> We find that [the] majority opinion of the Court is wrong and entirely contrary to the fundamental principles of morality. Catholic teaching holds that, regardless of the circumstances of its origin, human life is valuable from conception to death because God is the Creator of each human being, and because mankind has been redeemed by Jesus Christ.... No court, no legislative body, no leader of Government, can legitimately assign less value to some human life. Thus, the laws that conform to the opinion of the Court are immoral laws, in opposition to God's plan of creation and to the Divine Law which prohibits destruction of human life at any point of its existence. Whenever a conflict arises between the law of God and any human law, we are held to follow God's law. [49]

The bishops have repeatedly stated that this view on the function of human law is part of the philosophical and theological traditions from which the Declaration of Independence and the Constitution emerged. These include belief in God, a perception of natural law as an expression of divine law, and a realization that natural rights derive from the plan of the Creator and must be respected by individuals and by the Government. [50] But, as we will see, the bishops did not restrict themselves to natural law or divine law arguments and presented a variety of other considerations besides.

The Catholic tradition as a whole went in search of a new approach and would concentrate on two elements which had already been suggested by the manuals: man's personal right to life and the disastrous social consequences of liberal abortion codes. The natural law argument would be dropped.

NOTES

[1] Francis J. Connell, C.SS.R., *Morals in Politics and Professions: A Guide for Catholics in Public Life* (Westminster, Maryland: Newman Press, 1955), p. 17.

[2] Germain G. Grisez, *Abortion: The Myths, the Realities, and the Arguments* (New York: Corpus Books, 1970), pp. 236-237.

[3] Joseph T. Tinnelly, C.M., "Abortion and Penal Law," *Catholic Lawyer* 5 (1959), pp. 190-191.

[4] Bishops of New York State, "Declaration on Abortion—February 12, 1967," in Daughters of St. Paul (eds.), *Yes to Life* (Boston: St. Paul Editions, 1977), pp. 199-200. New York practically repealed its traditional statute in 1970. See also: "Statement of Cardinal Francis McIntyre," *The Tidings* (Los Angeles), May 5, 1967. p. 1; cited by Daniel Callahan, *Abortion: Law, Choice and Morality* (New York: Macmillan, 1970), p. 4. The California statute was liberalized in 1967.

[5] *Summa Theologica*, I-II, qq. 93-97.

[6] Celestine N. Bittle, O.F.M.Cap., *Man and Morals: Ethics* (Milwaukee: Bruce, 1950), p. 212. See also: Augustine J. Osgniach, O.S.B., *The Christian State* (Milwaukee: Bruce, 1943), p. 156; Austin Fagothey, S.J., *Right and Reason: Ethics in Theory and Practice* (3rd edition; St. Louis: C.V. Mosby, 1963), p. 158. Positive law in this context refers to laws enacted by man; Fagothey, *op. cit.*, pp. 121-122.

[7] Osgniach, *op. cit.*, pp. 136-137; Fagothey, *op. cit.*, pp. 212-216.

[8] Osgniach, *op. cit.*, p. 156. See also: Fagothey, *op. cit.*, p. 216.

[9] John A. McHugh, O.P., and Charles J. Callan, O.P., *Moral Theology: A Complete Course. Based on St. Thomas Aquinas and the Best Modern Authorities;* revised and enlarged edition by Edward P. Farrell, O.P. (vols. I-II; New York City: Joseph F. Wagner, 1958); vol. I, pp. 99-100; Osgniach, *op. cit.*, pp. 156-158; Fagothey, *op. cit.*, pp. 128-131.

[10] McHugh and Callan, *op. cit.*, vol. I, pp. 100, 104-105; Fagothey, *op. cit.*, pp. 136-137, 145-146, 340-341.

[11] Osgniach, *op. cit.*, pp. 158-159; Fagothey, *op. cit.*, pp. 131-135.

[12] Fagothey, *op. cit.*, pp. 211-216; Thomas J. Higgins, S.J., *Man as Man: The Science and Art of Ethics* (Milwaukee: Bruce, 1949), p. 233; McHugh and Callan, *op. cit.*, vol. II, p. 113.

[13] Osgniach, *op. cit.*, p. 161; Higgins, *op. cit.*, p. 233.

[14] Higgins, *op. cit.*, pp. 233-234.

[15] Osgniach, *op. cit.*, pp. 167, 207-208; Fagothey, *op. cit.*, pp. 213-216.

[16] Bittle, *op. cit.*, p. 368; McHugh and Callan, *op. cit.*, vol. II, p. 113; Fagothey, *op. cit.*, p. 235; Osgniach, *op. cit.*, pp. 208, 209.

[17] E.J. Ross, *Basic Sociology* (Milwaukee: Bruce, 1953), p. 319.

[18] McHugh and Callan, *op. cit.*, vol. I, pp. 107-108; Higgins, *op. cit.*, p. 231; Osgniach, *op. cit.*, pp. 168-169; Fagothey, *op. cit.*, pp. 340-341.

[19] Michael V. Murray, S.J., *Problems in Ethics* (New York: Henry Holt, 1960), pp. 281-283; Fagothey, *op. cit.*, pp. 340-341; Osgniach, *op. cit.*, pp. 169-170.

[20] Osgniach, *op. cit.*, pp. 164-165; Murray, *op. cit.*, p. 284; Fagothey, *op. cit.*, p. 341. Nor may human law contradict divine positive law; Higgins, *op. cit.*, p. 479; McHugh and Callan, *op. cit.*, vol. I, p. 134.

[21] Higgins, *op. cit.*, p. 321; Murray, *op. cit.*, p. 284.

[22] Murray, *op. cit.*, p. 284; Fagothey, *op. cit.*, p. 343.

[23] Murray, *op. cit.*, p. 284; Fagothey, *op. cit.*, pp. 340-341.

[24] Ross, *op. cit.*, p. 317; Higgins, *op. cit.*, p. 479; Osgniach, *op. cit.*, pp. 174-176.

[25] Osgniach, *op. cit.*, p. 176; Fagothey, *op. cit.*, p. 213.

[26] Bittle, *op. cit.*, p. 212; McHugh and Callan, *op. cit.*, vol. I, p. 135; Higgins, *op. cit.*, p. 480.

[27] Murray, *op. cit.*, pp. 286-287; McHugh and Callan, *op. cit.*, vol. I, pp. 134-135; Fagothey, *op. cit.*, pp. 350-352.

[28] Murray, *op. cit.*, pp. 290-291; McHugh and Callan, *op. cit.*, vol. I, pp. 134-135; Osgniach, *op. cit.*, pp. 171-174.

[29] Bittle, *op. cit.*, pp. 582-584.

[30] McHugh and Callan, *op. cit.*, vol. I, pp. 108-110. However, natural law does not admit of emendatory interpretations ("epieikeia"); *ibid.*, p. 109. In his Encyclical Letter *Humanae Vitae* (1968), Pope Paul VI confirmed the authority of the Church with regard to the interpretation of natural law; *Acta Apostolicae Sedis* 60 (1968), p. 483.

[31] Connell, *op. cit.*, pp. 11-12.

[32] Osgniach, *op. cit.*, pp. 276-277.

[33] *Ibid.*, p. 281; see also pp. 281-283. Cf. Pope Pius XI, *Casti Connubii, Acta Apostolicae Sedis* 22 (1930), pp. 550-556.

[34] Cf. *supra*, note 1.

[35] Osgniach, *op. cit.*, pp. 208-214, 275-279, 280-283, 330-344.

[36] John Courtney Murray, S.J., *We Hold These Truths: Catholic Reflections on the American Proposition* (New York: Sheed and Ward, 1960).

[37] Norman St. John-Stevas, *Life, Death and the Law: Law and Christian Morals in England and the United States* (Bloomington: Indiana University Press, 1961), p. 87. In a later publication he questions the alleged social benefits of liberalization and states that in any case these would be heavily outweighed by the damage done to society's respect for the sanctity of life; *The Right to Life* (New York: Holt, 1964), pp. 32-35.

[38] Osgniach, *op. cit.*, p. 209.

[39] *Ibid.*, p. 156.

[40] Callahan, *op. cit.*, p. 15.

[41] I will discuss the liberationist arguments and motivation in Chapter VIII.

[42] Callahan, *op. cit.*, pp. 486-487. He comes to this conclusion after an extensive analysis of the social effects of restrictive, moderate, and liberal codes; *ibid.*, pp. 123-302. See also: Burton M. Leiser, *Liberty, Justice and Morals: Contemporary Value Conflicts* (New York: Macmillan, 1973), pp. 95-111. The argument will be elaborated in Chapter VIII.

[43] Richard A. McCormick, S.J., "Notes on Moral Theology: The Abortion Dossier," *Theological Studies* 35 (1974), pp. 322-323. He refers to an article by Paul J. Micallef, "Abortion and the Principles of Legislation," *Laval Théologique et Philosophique* 28 (1972), pp. 267-303. See also: McCormick, "Abortion," *America* 112 (1965), p. 880; J.C. Murray, *op. cit.*, pp. 166-167.

[44] These have been considered in Chapter III.

[45] Higgins, *op. cit.*, p. 479.

[46] Callahan, *op. cit.*, pp. 501-502.

[47] The title of Osgniach's book is precisely *The Christian State; op. cit.*

[48] Charles E. Curran, "Abortion: Law and Morality in Contemporary Catholic Theology," *Jurist* 33 (1973), pp. 164-165.

[49] "Pastoral Message of the Administrative Committee, National Conference of Catholic

Bishops," in Daughters of St. Paul, *op. cit.*, p. 262. See also: "U.S. Bishops' New Pastoral Plan for Pro-Life Activities," *ibid.*, p. 283; Paul V. Harrington, "Abortion: Part IV," *Linacre Quarterly* 34 (1967), pp. 72, 73.

50 Bishops of Missouri, "Statement on Abortion—December, 1970," in Daughters of St. Paul, *op. cit.*, pp. 226-227; Bishops of Massachusetts, "Statement on Abortion—March, 1971," *ibid.*, p. 233; Indiana Catholic Conference, "Declaration on Abortion—December, 1972," *ibid.*, pp. 256-257; "Pastoral Message of the Administrative Committee, National Conference of Catholic Bishops," *ibid.*, p. 262; Bishops' Committee for Pro-Life Activities, National Conference of Catholic Bishops, *Respect Life! The 1976 Respect Life Handbook* (Washington, D.C.: Respect Life Committee NCCB, 1976), pp. 15, 16.

Chapter Seven

The Function of Law
and the Right to Life of the Unborn

The call for a new approach came from across the Atlantic. It came from England in 1966, a few months before Colorado, on April 25, 1967, became the first American State to enact an abortion statute along the lines suggested by the ALI *Model Penal Code*. Norman St. John-Stevas, an English Catholic and member of Parliament, who was taking an active part in the abortion debate in his country,[1] warned American Catholics that they would have to employ a new argument and adopt a new strategy if their contribution to the discussions on the ALI proposal was to remain ideologically relevant and politically effective.

Analysing popular feelings on the termination of pregnancy, St. John-Stevas distinguishes three different attitudes. The official Catholic view rules out all abortions with the exception of those that are "indirect." The liberationists argue that it is the right of every woman to have an abortion if she wants one, and they therefore urge that the intervention be made available on request. The vast majority of people, however, are not swayed by either of these "extreme" positions, and since it is this large middle group that will ultimately decide the legal issue, it is to them that the appeals must be addressed. Consequently, Catholics must formulate the case against abortion in a different manner. They must abandon their theistic exposés, seek common ground with other Christians and with all men of good will, and propose an argument which is likely to gain wider comprehension and support. In the view of St. John-Stevas, this new proposition should concentrate on "the sanctity of life" or "the right to life," and it should present this right as a value which is fundamental to society because it constitutes the premise not only of liberty but also of equality and fraternity. Public opinion must be persuaded that a liberal abortion policy undermines the very foundation of society and that legal protection of the fetus is self-protection.[2]

St. John-Stevas suggests that the new proposition can be based on principle or on pragmatism or on both.[3] In this chapter we will examine the new argument on *principle* which American Catholic authors developed in the

171

late 1960s and early 1970s. The next chapter will be devoted to their *pragmatic considerations*.

I. Justice: The Principal Concern of Law

The Catholic argument first of all reaffirms the traditional distinction between law and morality, and admits that morality *as such* should not be enforced by law. Positive laws are not simply deductions from moral laws or from a set of moral ideals. Even a homogeneous society which finds itself in unanimous agreement on the validity of a particular moral precept should provide more than merely ethical considerations to justify the enactment of a corresponding law. A valid general principle is: Liberty is in possession; law must be justified. The presumption, therefore, favors freedom: legal limitations of the personal liberty of citizens are undesirable, and the burden is on the legislator to prove that such restrictions are necessary. Moral norms by themselves do not constitute a sufficient reason for legislation, and liberty remains in possession until legislation is warranted by something more than purely ethical interests.[4]

Human law possesses criteria of its own. The primary criterion of its validity is necessity, and this necessity is determined by the public interest or the common good. Individual citizens and private groups must be allowed to pursue their own objectives in a manner they see fit, and the legislator should not intervene except when the interests of others or of society as a whole are affected. His area of concern is that aspect of the common good which is called public morality, or public order and decency.[5] Therefore, in the words of Germain G. Grisez, "law should not attempt to enforce moral standards as such, but it should enforce moral standards insofar as they bear on the goods common to the civil society, affect these goods in a direct and substantial way, and admit of enforcement without damage to the common good."[6] Moral standards can be made legal standards for *appropriate reasons,* not because they are moral but because they are necessary. In establishing this necessity, morality neither coerces nor disqualifies.[7]

This does not mean that the Catholic position sponsors a purely pragmatic concept of human law. From a pragmatic point of view, a society which permits "simple" homicide (such as abortion or infanticide) could very well survive. In such communities law would simply be a convalidation of the rights of the stronger.[8] But law is more than "merely an expression of the minimum pragmatic conditions without which there can be no society at all."[9] Negatively, the law must *respect* the liberty of all its subjects by not interfering unnecessarily with their private lives and enterprises. Positively, it must *protect* the liberty of all without exception. [10]

All men are equal before the law. This equality constitutes a fundamental and necessary restriction on individual liberty: the freedom of each citizen is conditioned by the freedom of others. The law therefore must provide equal liberty to all citizens and put equal restrictions on the liberty of each citizen. By the imposition of penal sanctions it must ensure that all its subjects have equal opportunities for the free development of their potential. Its basic function is to establish and safeguard the equal rights of every person and to determine what cannot be inflicted on any person. This is what is meant by justice. [11] Law, then, is not simply the outcome of public consent or of a majority vote. The Catholic argument rejects "democratic absolutism" and points out that the essential duty of the law is to secure justice for all. Liberty and equality are fundamental and inalienable human rights, and these must be protected by human legislation. [12]

In an obvious reference to unborn human life, many Catholic authors stress that the law, although it must protect all citizens, has special obligations towards "the young, the weak, the inexperienced, the dependent — all those who are not adequately able to protect themselves from exploitation, corruption, and death." [13] Grisez puts it this way:

> In fact, the whole point of law is to make the naturally unequal sufficiently equal that they can cooperate as persons in a common life, not become exploiter and victim, master and slave. He who is too weak to defend himself is given the armor of the law; he who is too easily seduced to keep his freedom is liberated by legal keys from the captivity into which he has been led; he who is too stupid to keep his possessions is protected from the fraud of the wily by the accounting the law demands. [14]

In this way premises have been established to support the conclusion that human life must be protected by law. An acceptance of liberty and equality as fundamental personal and legal values necessarily implies the recognition of the right to life of everyone in the community. Human life is the beginning and end of everything, and if liberty and equality are basic human rights, then their foundation must constitute an absolute right. [15] Catholic authors frequently mention that this concept of human law and civil rights is clearly reflected in the Declaration of Independence: "We hold these truths to be self-evident, that all men are created equal, that they are endowed by their Creator with certain inalienable Rights, that among these are Life, Liberty and the pursuit of Happiness." This emphasis on human dignity and human equality they find preserved and articulated in the United States Constitution, especially in the Fifth and Fourteenth Amendments which guarantee due process of law and equal protection of the laws to all persons.[16] Every human being has "natural" rights, chief among them the right to life. This right is not conferred by society: it is man's own, in the strict sense of the word, because it derives directly from his very nature. Man's right to life is therefore universal, inviolable, and inalienable, and the State has an irremissible duty to protect it.[17]

Rudolph J. Gerber and Donald DeMarco have pointed out that the contemporary trend toward liberalizing abortion statutes reveals a completely different understanding of law and human rights. They have characterized this approach as "sociologism" or "sociological jurisprudence." Sociologism accentuates the importance of human relationships in the development of the individual and claims that it is society which humanizes man: without the benefit of social interaction, man is considered either prehuman (presocialized) or subhuman (unsocialized). This emphasis on the role of society in the life of man further manifests itself in a preoccupation with the welfare of the community, to the extent that the "common good" takes precedence over any good of any one individual. Thus it is the task of the lawgiver to register the social interests or claims of individual citizens and of groups of citizens, and to secure these by legislation. When such interests overlap or when he is faced with conflicting demands, he must accede to the request of the greater number and sacrifice the interests of the minority to those of the majority.[18]

In this philosophical and moral perspective, the legislator does not establish human rights by a logical deduction from biological facts or metaphysical postulates. His lawmaking is primarily an empirical and inductive process: he examines the sociological data which reflect the social interests of his subjects, and he sanctions the wishes of the majority. In a sociological jurisprudence, the lawgiver seeks to provide the greatest happiness for the greatest number and constantly readjusts his laws to fit the contours of an ever-changing society. There is no question of natural and inalienable human rights: an individual possesses only those rights that have been granted to him by man-made laws.[19]

The implications of sociologism for the fetus are obvious. Humans who are unborn cannot be counted and their interests and wishes do not figure in sociological surveys and public opinion polls. The lawgiver may well decide that in the public interest he should grant the request of a vociferous liberationist majority and suppress the rights of a presocial and silent minority.[20] It is clear that a sociological jurisprudence is irreconcilable with the "natural rightism" of the Catholic position, and the American bishops have repeatedly drawn attention to this divergency. The bishops of Indiana wrote in 1972:

Each man and woman in our state has certain fundamental rights —to life, to freedom, and to an opportunity for happiness. These rights do not depend upon that person's condition, his stage of development, and certainly not upon his value to society. They do not depend upon the whim of the state, which might deny such rights to particular individuals because they are "non-productive," weak, poor, ignorant, or voiceless. [21]

The philosophical-juridical foundation of the Catholic defense of unborn human life has now been established but it is evident that the crucial question has not yet been answered. In the controversy about laws which forbid or permit abortion, the primary issue is not just the function of law but also, and more specifically, the legal status of the fetus. The legal debate centers around the question whether or not the unborn are "legal persons" in the sense that their right to life must necessarily be protected by law. This question has two aspects. The first one is theoretical: *should* the law regard the unborn as persons entitled to the same degree of protection as is extended to postnatal human beings? The second one is a factual one: *does* the law, and in this case the law of the United States, in fact recognize the unborn as such legal persons? An answer to the latter question involves an examination of the American legal tradition on the status of the human conceptus.

An analysis of the American Catholic abortion literature reveals that the theoretical question has been answered in a twofold way. I will first present these answers; later I will examine the Catholic view on the actual legal position of the fetus.

II. The Fetus, a Legal Person: The Arguments from Philosophy and Biology

Grisez has attempted to establish on philosophical grounds that fetal life must be accorded full legal protection from fertilization onwards. He explains first that even for purely practical reasons the law has no option but to regard every human conceptus, irrespective of the degree of its development, as a legal person. If the lawgiver were to decide not to recognize conception as the determinant of legal personhood, he would have to provide an alternative criterion. In practice this would be highly problematic. [22]

Birth does not constitute a single moment in time; accepting the severing of the umbilical cord as decisive is unrealistic. Establishing a point of demarcation at some stage of gestation prior to birth is questionable too. Quickening has no special significance for fetal development: it is a subjective and variable event since it depends on the relative size of the infant and the mother, and the sensitivity and experience of the mother. Viability is equally variable because it is subject to such enigmatic factors as the child's race; also it is determined to some extent by the quality of the care that will be available to the prematurely delivered fetus. Therefore, unless the abortion is performed at a very early stage of pregnancy, one can never predict with certainty that the child will not survive. An earlier dividing line, e.g., after twelve weeks of gestation, is unsatisfactory from the point of view of possible technological innovations such as the artificial placenta. This criterion would make the legal status of the fetus dependent on the progress of medical techniques. The only possibility which remains is that the law consistently regard the unborn as persons from the very outset of pregnancy.[23]

Grisez maintains that this is more than just "the only remaining practical alternative." The law *must* adopt this principle. The legislator must have a definite and consistent standard of personhood, for he must know who the recipients are of the rights he seeks to guarantee. It is clear that he cannot formulate his criteria on the basis of popular feelings or "common sense": subjective impressions are never a sound foundation for lawmaking. Nor should the problem be resolved by majority vote: "If majority opinion is to be decisive, then the rights of the minority —of every minority —are in principle undermined, for what is at issue is the criterion according to which one will be able to remain a *person* —a subject of rights —though in the minority."[24] Moreover, the legislator must establish his definition of personhood without committing himself to any particular worldview, as he must provide for a heterogeneous society. He would violate democratic principles if he would adopt denominational philosophical concepts or moral tenets as the official norms of his public policies.[25]

Grisez then presents his theory of "presumed fetal option." Since the lawgiver cannot validly apply any sectarian criterion of personhood, he must take the position of the potential victim and express the view which the fetus itself would presumably adopt. The lawgiver must then assume that the unborn child, if it would be given the ability and opportunity to speak, would claim to be a legal person with a legal right to life and to equal protection of the laws. The law, therefore, should speak for the unborn and should claim for them what they would claim for themselves, if they would be able to make their demands known. This implies that the law must commit itself to the biological or comprehensive definition of personhood: a being with a human genetic code is man. If the legislator adopts restrictive standards, such as consciousness or rationality, he attributes to the fetus a theory of personhood which we cannot plausibly assume it would share. [26] Grisez adds that no true liberal will accept a narrow definition of personality. A true liberal is intent on recognizing human life in all its forms, and he willingly extends human rights to all who conceivably qualify. There is nothing liberal about the liberationist attempt to restrict human rights and facilitate the disposal of the unborn by distinguishing between persons and nonpersons. [27]

Grisez's theory of "presumed fetal choice" is unique; no Catholic author or hierarchical statement has elaborated his proposition or even supported it. [28] Indeed, on the issue of the legal status of the unborn child the Catholic argument as a whole has shied away from philosophical syllogisms and has opted instead for more "factual" proofs. After our analysis of the official position on the moral aspect of the abortion dilemma it is not difficult to predict the general trend of Catholic thought on the legal question. On the moral issue Catholic authors had turned to biology, and they did so again in their legal considerations.

Their legal argument is a logical development of their moral views. Having established that the biological individuality and autonomy of the fetus is the primary factor in the individual moral decision, they saw no reason not to adopt the same "objective" approach in the legal debate. Their answer to the legal question is thus short and simple: the law must accept the recent discoveries of biology. It has no choice but to recognize the unborn as legal persons who are entitled to full legal protection. Paul V. Harrington wrote in 1968:

> One must keep in mind that the law and legal jurisprudence necessarily depend upon the medical sciences for the knowledge and information which is required for the determination and verification of conception, the beginning of human life, the nature, growth and development of intrauterine life, the duration of pregnancy, the problems and complications of pregnancy and the entire process of delivery. [29]

On this premise the biological status of the fetus features prominently in the legal arguments of moralists as well as of the hierarchy. The bishops of New Jersey declared in the same year:

> (W)e must clearly voice our protest to any relaxation of the abortion statute.
>
> As to whether the unborn child is, indeed, human, we refer to the great weight of scientific testimony which clearly states that life begins at the moment of conception, and from that moment on we are dealing with the life development of a new human being.
>
> The significant fact is that although the unborn child is dependent on its mother during the time of gestation, science regards this child in the womb as a separate human individual. [30]

The American hierarchy condemned the 1973 Supreme Court decision on theological, historical, and scientific grounds.[31] Referring to the Court's declaration that prior to viability the life of the unborn child is not to be considered of any compelling value, the bishops formulated their scientific critique as follows:

> The Court has apparently failed to understand the scientific evidence clearly showing that the fetus is an individual human being whose prenatal development is but the first phase of the long and continuous process of human development that begins at conception and terminates at death.[32]

The law therefore must recognize the findings of biology. In a parallel argument, reminiscent of the "morally safer course" in the manuals, a number of authors claim that the burden of proof does not lie with the party that is trying to protect the unborn but with the liberationists who seek the right to destroy fetal life. Those who support the legalization of abortion have a great responsibility to prove beyond reasonable doubt that the life they want to liquidate is not human or does not have sufficient dignity to warrant protection by the law. The authors invariably observe that such proof has not been given.[33]

III. The Fetus, a Legal Person: The Juridical Argument

It is clear that in the Catholic view the abortion decision is not a private matter. The termination of pregnancy is regarded as nothing less than a question of civil rights, and of the most fundamental civil right: the right to life. In this perspective it is incumbent on all members of the community, regardless of their religious persuasion or private moral convictions, to respect and protect the human conceptus.[34]

For their position on the legal status of the fetus Catholic moralists derive additional justification from American law itself. They observe that in the United States constitutional and statutory law and jurisprudential judgement have granted the unborn significant legal rights. In other words American jurisprudence has recognized, or is in the process of recognizing, the fetus as a legal person. This means that the Catholic emphasis on the civil rights of the unborn is neither a sectarian idiosyncrasy nor a juridical innovation. On the contrary, it is clearly representative of, and in harmony with, the American legal tradition which has developed, over the years, a remarkable degree of respect for the human conceptus. The Catholic argument on the actual status of the unborn in United States law can be summarized as follows:

1. Laws of property and decedents' estates have always guaranteed the right of the unborn to inherit and to own property without imposing any restrictions requiring a certain degree of fetal development.[35]

2. In tort law the legal status of the fetus has significantly improved. Until well into the twentieth century most legal decisions denied recovery in tort to the human offspring injured during pregnancy but since 1946 the right of the fetus to sue for prenatal injuries has been generally accepted. Initially some courts required that the unborn child had reached the stage of viability at the time the injuries were inflicted, but the modern trend has been to discard this criterion. Other areas of tort law have also recognized the rights of the unborn. Thus the fetus has been allowed to bring an action for the death of his father where the death occurred prior to the child's birth. In cases of fetal death resulting from negligent injuries to the conceptus, a majority of courts have held that an action for the wrongful death of the unborn child is maintainable.[36]

3. Child support laws uphold the right of the unborn to care and support. The fetus is legally entitled to exact support from his father through a guardian.[37]

4. Criminal law has always defended the fetus' right to life. The traditional abortion statutes were designed to protect the lives of the unborn, not the lives of the mothers. In common law quickening was required but subsequent statutory law eliminated this condition.[38]

5. Various legal decisions have upheld the unborn's right to life over certain constitutional rights of the parents.[39]

American law, then, identifies the legal with the natural personality. It has consistently and progressively recognized the rights of the unborn by setting up an adequate legal structure for their protection and compensation, and in doing so it has granted them legal personality in areas where they need it. The liberalization of abortion clearly contradicts this development because a permissive code deprives the fetus of the most basic right which positive law has accorded to it. Legalization of abortion constitutes an outright denial of the legal personality of the unborn.[40]

It is in this perspective that Grisez qualifies liberal abortion laws as an "intolerable anomaly."[41] He argues that the law must be consistent in whom it regards as a "person." Admittedly, a legal term need not have the same implication in all statutes or in all fields of law but there can be no such fluctuation in the meaning of "person." While a person is undoubtedly a subject of the law, in the sense that he is one of the "things" with which the law deals, he is at the same time above the law because he is a member of the community from which the law originates. He is also a member of the community whose welfare the law seeks to secure and to promote. Persons are not made for the law: the law is made for persons and by persons. The person in a sense stands outside the legal system with its fictions and devices, and above it. The law, says Grisez, cannot dispose of him by its own fiat, and it must be consistent in its recognition of legal personhood: it cannot confer personality on an individual and then withdraw it again at its own behest. In American jurisprudence the unborn *are* persons. The laws of the land have accepted the legal rights of the fetus, and the courts are in the process of extending these rights. If the same law were to adopt a liberal abortion code, such statutes would seriously conflict with traditional as well as contemporary legal attitudes. The fetus would then be declared a nonperson. This would be incompatible with the evolving legal personality of the unborn which is manifest in the American legal tradition.[42] In 1969 Trinkaus *et al.* made this point before the California Supreme Court where they argued that it would be illogical for the law not to protect the fetus' life:

> It is conceded by all that a conceived, but unborn child (under any appellation one may select) is entitled to a substantial number of rights, including property rights, inheritance rights, and the right to be free of injury. It seems to follow with irresistible logic that if a being is recognized as a person for the possession of *any* rights, the right to *life* cannot be ignored as though the concept were entirely irrelevant.[43]

Consequently, Trinkaus *et al.* rejected the contention that American society is powerless under the Constitution to legislate *any* controls over abortion:

> The right to life is a sacred one, deemed inalienable by the Declaration of Independence and protected, insofar as applicable here, by the Fourteenth Amendment to the United States Constitution. In these circumstances, in view of the status the law has recognized as applying to a conceived, but unborn child, from property rights, to the right to be free of injury, to the right to life itself, it is submitted that the action by the legislature to protect that right to life in its prohibition against abortion is immune from attack.[44]

In 1971 William J. Maledon referred to the abortion statute revisions of the previous years and emphasized that these are inconsistent with American law, not only from a logical but also from a juridical point of view. Liberalization has created a legal maze by introducing unprecedented incongruities into the law,[45] as is evident from the following examples:

> The unborn child, under the law of property in most jurisdictions, can, among other things, inherit and own an estate, be a tenant-in-common with his own mother, and be an actual income recipient prior to birth. The new liberalized abortion laws, however, present a dilemma in this area. Is it a crime for a woman to misappropriate the estate of her unborn child,

and yet no crime for her to kill that child? Can a woman, who has inherited an estate as a tenant-in-common with her unborn child, increase her own estate 100 percent simply by killing the child? Will the law which has recognized the unborn child as an actual income recipient prior to birth allow the child's heir (the mother) to kill the child for her own financial gain? Will the law that has specifically said that an unborn child's *estate* cannot be destroyed where the child has not been represented before the court allow the child himself to be destroyed without being represented before the court?

. . . The law of torts provides even more striking examples. Will the pregnant woman who is hit by a negligent driver while she is on her way to the hospital to have an abortion still have a cause of action for the wrongful death of her unborn child? If so, how is it possible for the law to say that a child can be wrongfully killed only hours before he can be rightfully killed? Absurd as it may seem, this is the present state of the law in some jurisdictions.

. . . Is the unborn child any less a person when, instead of being killed by an automobile, he is killed by a doctor in the performance of an abortion? Seldom has the law been confronted by such an obvious contradiction.[46]

In the opinion of many Catholic authors the growing emphasis in American law on the legal rights of the fetus and its legal personality cannot be attributed to the influence of any metaphysical or religious dogma. This development is entirely due to the fact that the courts gradually came to accept the discoveries of modern biology which show that biologically the infant in the womb is an independent human being.[47]

From the Catholic viewpoint the legalization of abortion is not just a logical inconsistency or a legal anomaly, implying more than merely a disregard for recent legal trends and a reversal of juridical precedents which have subordinated the civil rights of the parents to the right to life of their unborn offspring.[48] Liberalization is nothing less than a violation of the Constitution of the United States because every indication points towards the conclusion that the fetus is a "person" under constitutional law. Scientifically it is a *fact* that the unborn child is an autonomous human being. Legally it is a *fact* that in every area where the courts have had to decide whether fetal life is the subject of legal rights, they have consistently regarded the conceptus as a person vested with civil rights.[49] Therefore, as a "constitutional person" the fetus must be given the protection of the "due process" clause of the Fifth Amendment and the "equal protection" and "due process" clauses of the Fourteenth Amendment. Like all other persons' lives, the unborn's life is entitled to equal protection under law, and it can be taken only with due process of law.[50] If the State were to adopt a liberal abortion code and allow the life of the child to be taken at the will of the parent, then such withdrawal of legal safeguards would clearly constitute a discriminatory act and a denial of "equal protection."[51] Furthermore, as Grisez has pointed out, a permissive statute violates the "due process" requirement because "due process" means more than that the law is properly enacted by the legislature and the governor:

> It means an open hearing, with suitable warning beforehand, before a properly constituted tribunal. The one whose life, liberty, or property is to be taken must have legal representation, who must be allowed to hear the opposing case, examine the evidence, cross-examine witnesses, and present the case against the projected deprivation. Finally, there must be an opportunity for appeal.[52]

Clearly, a liberal abortion code fails to provide due process. Under such a statute the justification for the intervention is formulated in a private judgement without a judicial inquiry and without representation of the interest of the unborn child, of its father, or of the community.[53] David W. Louisell and John T. Noonan, Jr., adequately summarize the Catholic legal argument:

> Easy legal abortion presents a genuine and disturbing reversal of the law's steady progress toward recognition of the dignity, value, and essential equality of human life. It is a negation of the constitutional guarantee of equal protection of the law. It is a loveless act offensive to the conscience of our common law tradition.[54]

IV. The Didactic Function of Law

We have seen that in the Catholic conception of law the lawgiver has an irremissible duty to render justice in matters of civil rights. If he enacts a permissive abortion statute which allows the massive destruction of human lives, he fails in his most fundamental obligation, which is to recognize, preserve, and protect the right to life of all citizens.[55] Many Catholic authors draw attention to a further dimension of legislation and liberalization, pointing out that law is more than merely a system of sanctions designed to prevent external actions which are harmful to society. Law has a didactic as well as a coercive function: it channels action and thereby shapes behavior and inculcates attitudes. It teaches that certain activities are good and should be encouraged, and that others are wrong or dangerous for society and should be discouraged.[56]

Noonan explains that man does not make his moral decisions as a disembodied spirit or in a private area of his personality which is so insulated from the community that the social judgements formulated in law do not affect his decision-making. Man lives in society, and his moral notions are partly formed by the law. The public teaching embodied in the law tells the uncertain man—and everybody is at times uncertain—what is the right thing to do. For example, legislation which enforced slavery systematically shaped the moral attitudes of American whites towards the black population, while the court decisions which imposed desegregation created new attitudes for blacks and whites.[57] Therefore, in the words of Cardinal Shehan:

> The law is a teacher. It establishes the moral tone of the community it regulates. The legal prohibition of a specific act assists the citizen in assessing its propriety.[58]

The traditional abortion statutes expressed society's recognition of the value of unborn human life. If these laws are now relaxed, this will have a substantial and negative impact on the moral consciousness of Americans. By withdrawing protection from the fetus the law will profess that human life in its earliest stages need not be respected.[59] The American bishops have warned that such disregard for unborn human life will extend to born human life. Unless the law expresses an irrevocable commitment to safeguarding the lives of all, it teaches that life is a relative value, one which can be denied.[60] A law which allows the destruction of any unwanted life unavoidably teaches that all life is cheap.[61] The bishops of Pennsylvania wrote in 1970:

> Law is an educator. Society's proudest heritage has been its development through law of an atmosphere of respect and concern for human life.
> Pro-abortion laws, however, can create an anti-life atmosphere in society which will lead to a general disregard for life. Accepting abortion as a solution to one problem implies that human life and dignity need not be respected in the face of other social problems.[62]

Grisez dismisses a popular argument which compares restrictive abortion codes with the Prohibition laws. The contention is that such statutes should be repealed because they have proved to be ineffective; they are unenforced and unenforceable as is evident from the large number of illegal abortions that are performed, in spite of the very explicit teaching of these laws. Grisez maintains that the comparison with Prohibition as an example of obsolete legislation is not valid because the issue in abortion is the right to life, and this was not the issue in Prohibition. Where basic human values are at stake, the validity of a law must be assessed by other criteria than its mere effectiveness in preventing crime.[63] If there are voices, even if they are the majority, which propose to define a certain group as "nonpersons," thus depriving these of their most fundamental right, that design should be resisted as far as possible since it threatens the inner structure of the community itself.[64] For Grisez the abortion issue is "a testing ground for justice in a pluralistic society. If the test is not passed here, we must face the grim possibility that it may be failed altogether."[65] David Granfield makes the same point:

> The recognition of the right to life of everyone in the community is fundamental to democracy. If the lives of the minority are not sacred and immune from violation, then no one is safe, for everyone is a member of some kind of minority. In fact, in our personal uniqueness, each one of us forms a minority of one. Our democratic ideals are impossible of full realization if the life of any minority member is in jeopardy simply because he is a member of a minority. Little comfort is given to the American Negro, whose race puts him in this precarious position. Indeed, the same unsettling realization should sooner or later dawn upon the American male who, since universal adult suffrage, finds himself politically outnumbered.[66]

The right to life then is a *moral* value, but at the same time its recognition and protection are *necessary* for the common good:

> (M)orality is enforceable only if the common good of society requires it. Our constitutional democracy is structured on an essentially *moral component of the common good* —the equal dignity of all men before the law. Fundamental to our political ideology is the proposition that in a society of equals no man is expendable. Our society cannot assimilate the Nazi notion of "useless mouths." Nor can it play the diabolical game of marking undesirables for extinction. The thrust of liberal abortion is to the heart of the democratic community. "If we are to keep our democracy," Judge Learned Hand insisted, "there must be one commandment: Thou shalt not ration justice."[67]

Commenting on the 1973 Supreme Court decision, the American hierarchy declared that the Court, by denying the right to life to the unborn child, had committed an error which attacked the very foundation of human society; it had rent the fabric of human law whereby the inherent worth of every man is recognized.[68] Clearly, it is an oversimplification to say that in the Catholic view the ultimate rationale of restrictive abortion codes is morality. It is necessity. Such laws are considered to be necessary for the common good: if they are repealed, justice is threatened and the basis of a just society undermined.

In the first section of this book I analysed the development of American Catholic thinking on the moral aspects of abortion. We observed that in the course of the debate on the ALI proposals the authors abandoned the theistic considerations of the manuals and adopted an empirical, and therefore nonsectarian, approach to the phenomenon of nascent human life. We have now seen that a similar development took place in the argument on the legal aspects of the abortion issue. The emphasis is no longer on the eternal and natural laws as the foundation of true positive laws and rights. In their search for a nonsectarian presentation of the Church's position on the legal problem, the authors turned to a secular and "neutral" discipline: juridical science.

If we compare the new legal argument with the teaching of the manuals, we find that the authors have reaffirmed and further developed an element which was already present in embryo in the handbooks: that law is not the handmaid of morals. The distinction between private and public morality has been underlined, and the common good has now firmly been established as the criterion of a just law. At the same time we observe that the authors reject a purely pragmatic and utilitarian view of law. They state that the law must dispense justice and that therefore it must protect the fundamental rights of all citizens. If these rights are not secure, society itself is in danger. The authors argue in a variety of ways that the law, and particularly American law, must consistently recognize the unborn as legal persons. It cannot exclude their lives from its equal protection, just as it cannot make an exception of infants and others who are too weak to protect themselves.[69] Liberal abortion laws are a violation of civil rights and a threat to the basis of the civil community. Legal protection of the fetus becomes self-protection.

This is the legal argument on principle which Catholic moralists developed in the late 1960s and early 1970s. Few people would question their philosophical and juridical premises if these were to support legislation which seeks to terminate racial or economic discrimination or promote the emancipation of women. But when the same principles are used to sustain an anti-abortion stand, we find that they fail to convince and that they raise a great many questions and objections. It is to these that we must now turn our attention.

NOTES

[1] The British Abortion Act was passed in 1967 and became effective in 1968.

[2] Norman St. John-Stevas, "Abortion Laws," *Commonweal* 85 (1966), pp. 164-165. See also: *id.*, "Abortion: The English Experience," *America* 117 (1967), p. 709; "Abortion, Catholics, and the Law," *Catholic World* 206 (1968), p. 150. Cf. also: Betty Sarvis and Hyman Rodman, *The Abortion Controversy* (New York: Columbia University Press, 1973), pp. 21-23.

[3] St. John-Stevas, "Abortion Laws," *op. cit.*, pp. 164-165.

[4] David Granfield, *The Abortion Decision* (revised edition; Garden City, N.Y.: Doubleday Image Books, 1971), pp. 140-141; Rudolph J. Gerber, "Abortion: Parameters for Decision," *International Philosophical Quarterly* 11 (1971), p. 578; Editorial, "On Imposing Catholic Views on Others," *America* 116 (1967), p. 273; Bishops of Maryland, "Statement on Abortion," *Catholic Mind* 66, March 1968, p. 2. Arguing from the same perspective Germain G. Grisez concludes that the law ought not to regard fornication, adultery, and homosexual acts in themselves as criminal but he does not infer that *existing* legislation prohibiting such acts should be repealed; *Abortion: The Myths, the Realities, and the Arguments* (New York: Corpus Books, 1970), pp. 358-360.

[5] Granfield, *op. cit.*, pp. 141-143; Grisez, *op. cit.*, p. 357; Gerber, *op. cit.*, p. 578; William J. Kenealy, S.J., "Law and Morals," *Catholic Lawyer* 9 (1963), pp. 203-204.

[6] Grisez, *op. cit.*, p. 358.

[7] Granfield, *op. cit.*, p. 141. Consequently, a law cannot be considered invalid just because it happens to coincide with a moral tenet of some religious denomination; *ibid.*, p. 141; Grisez, *op. cit.*, pp. 347-355, 436-437; Walter R. Trinkaus *et al.*, "Abortion Legislation and the Establishment Clause," *Catholic Lawyer* 15 (1969), pp. 109-110. Liberationists often accuse their opponents of imposing a sectarian morality on society at large and of violating thereby the establishment and freedom of religion clauses of the Constitution. The issue will be discussed in Chapter VIII. Not all Catholic authors support a rigid distinction between law and morals. In the view of Joseph E. Hogan, C.M., legality and morality are not identical or coextensive but they overlap: they are interrelated and interdependent. Issues of public morality are not settled by moral principles alone but they cannot be decided without reference to these principles; "The Conscience of the Law," *Catholic Lawyer* 21 (1975), pp. 190-196. See also: John T. Noonan, Jr., "Introduction," in John T. Noonan, Jr. (ed.), *The Morality of Abortion: Legal and Historical Perspectives* (Cambridge, Mass.: Harvard University Press, 1970), pp. x-xi; John M. Finnis, "Three Schemes of Regulation," *ibid.*, pp. 203-207; Robert M. Byrn, "Abortion-on-Demand: Whose Morality?" *Notre Dame Lawyer* 46 (1970), pp. 34-36; "U.S. Bishops' New Pastoral Plan for Pro-Life Activities—November 20, 1975," in Daughters of St. Paul, *Yes to Life* (Boston: St. Paul Editions, 1977), p. 283. At an early stage of the debate *America* adopted a similar position; Editorial, "Morality and Policy," *America* 112 (1965), pp. 280, 351, 450, 520-521, 747. Grisez sees a close relationship between law and morality but he does not equate them: the criterion of law is necessity and this necessity is determined by the common good; *op. cit.*, pp. 357-358.

[8] Grisez, *op. cit.*, pp. 421-422. He distinguishes between *murder* which attacks healthy and mature persons and which is bound to disturb the social order, and *simple homicide* (abortion, infanticide, and euthanasia) which destroys human life but need not have the

same social effects; *ibid.,* p. 415. See also: Edward J. Lauth, Jr., "Liberal Abortion Laws: The Antithesis of the Practice of Medicine," *Linacre Quarterly* 34 (1967), pp. 372-373.

9 Grisez, *op. cit.,* p. 422.

10 Granfield, *op. cit.,* pp. 142-143.

11 *Ibid.,* p. 143; Grisez, *op. cit.,* p. 422; Kenealy, *op. cit.,* p. 209.

12 Granfield, *op. cit.,* p. 143; Grisez, *op. cit.,* p. 355; "Testimony of United States Catholic Conference on Constitutional Amendment Protecting Unborn Human Life before the Sub-Committee on Constitutional Amendments of the Senate Committee on the Judiciary—March 7, 1974," in National Conference of Catholic Bishops, United States Catholic Conference, *Documentation on the Right to Life and Abortion* (Washington, D.C.: Publications Office USCC, 1974), pp. 16-18.

13 Granfield, *op. cit.,* p. 143.

14 Grisez, *op. cit.,* p. 422. See also: Trinkaus *et al., op. cit.,* p. 113; Gordon C. Zahn, "A Religious Pacifist Looks at Abortion," *Commonweal* 94 (1971), p. 281; Charles P. Kindregan, *Abortion, the Law, and Defective Children* (Washington: Corpus Books, 1969), p. 40; Bishops of Massachusetts, "Joint Statement on Abortion—February, 1972," in Daughters of St. Paul, *op. cit.,* p. 253; Bishops' Committee for Pro-Life Activities, National Conference of Catholic Bishops, *Respect Life! The 1976 Respect Life Handbook* (Washington, D.C.: Respect Life Committee NCCB, 1976), p. 18.

15 Granfield, *op. cit.,* pp. 143-144; Grisez, *op. cit.,* pp. 421-422; Robert M. Byrn, "The Abortion Amendments: Policy in the Light of Precedent," *Saint Louis University Law Journal* 18 (1974), pp. 394, 404-405; Donald DeMarco, *Abortion in Perspective: The Rose Palace or the Fiery Dragon?* (Cincinnati: Hiltz & Hayes, 1974), pp. 54-58; Bishops of Illinois, "Statement on Abortion—March 20, 1969," in Daughters of St. Paul, *op. cit.,* pp. 204-205; Bishops of Pennsylvania, "Declaration on Abortion— September, 1970," *ibid.,* p. 218.

16 Granfield, *op. cit.,* p. 155; Grisez, *op. cit.,* pp. 421-423; Robert M. Byrn, "Abortion-on-Demand: Whose Morality?" *op. cit.,* p. 19; Bishops of Illinois, *op. cit.,* p. 205; Bishops of Pennsylvania, *op. cit.,* p. 216; Bishops of Missouri, "Statement on Abortion—December, 1970," in Daughters of St. Paul, *op. cit.,* pp. 226-227.

17 Bishops of New York State, "Declaration on Abortion—March 19, 1970," in Daughters of St. Paul, *op. cit.,* pp. 210-211; Bishops of Missouri, *op. cit.,* pp. 226-227; "Pastoral Message of the Administrative Committee, National Conference of Catholic Bishops— February 13, 1973," in Daughters of St. Paul, *op. cit.,* pp. 260-261; "U.S. Bishops' New Pastoral Plan for Pro-Life Activities," *op. cit.,* pp. 276-277, 279.

18 Rudolph J. Gerber, "Abortion: Two Opposing Legal Philosophies," *American Journal of Jurisprudence* 15 (1970), pp. 9-11; DeMarco, *op. cit.,* pp. 17-18.

19 Gerber, "Abortion: Two Opposing Legal Philosophies," *op. cit.,* p. 11; DeMarco, *op. cit.,* pp. 17-18.

20 Gerber, "Abortion: Two Opposing Legal Philosophies," *op. cit.,* pp. 11-12; DeMarco, *op. cit.,* pp. 18-19, 23-28, 67-71.

21 Indiana Catholic Conference, "Declaration on Abortion—December, 1972," in Daughters of St. Paul, *op. cit.,* p. 257. See also: Catholic Bishops of Texas, "Open Letter on Abortion—April, 1971," *ibid.,* pp. 242-243, 244. In the view of Grisez, this conception of law and the right to life does not necessarily imply that the law is obliged to forbid suicide and voluntary euthanasia: these acts are undoubtedly immoral but they violate no one's fundamental rights since a person does not have rights against himself.

However, there may be valid *social* grounds for maintaining the legal prohibition; *op. cit.*, p. 421.

[22] Grisez, *op. cit.*, pp. 412-413.

[23] *Ibid.*, pp. 413-415. See also: "Testimony of United States Catholic Conference on Constitutional Amendment Protecting Unborn Human Life....," *op. cit.*, p. 26.

[24] Grisez, *op. cit.*, p. 418. See also: Trinkaus *et al.*, *op. cit.*, pp. 112-114. Grisez admits that in law there is a certain amount of arbitrariness, e.g., a person legally remains an infant until his 21st birthday when suddenly he becomes competent to make contracts, to sue, and to vote. However, the interests here at stake are not of the order of fundamental and inalienable rights; *op. cit.*, p. 414.

[25] Grisez, *op. cit.*, pp. 416-418.

[26] *Ibid.*, pp. 418-420. See also: St. John-Stevas, "Abortion Laws," *op. cit.*, p. 165.

[27] Grisez, *op. cit.*, p. 420. See also: Gerber, "Abortion: Parameters for Decision," *op. cit.*, p. 577; DeMarco, *op. cit.*, pp. 59-63; Jay Newman, "An Empirical Argument Against Abortion," *New Scholasticism* 51 (1977), pp. 384-395.

[28] James M. Humber considers Grisez's approach artificial. Psychologically we find it very difficult to identify with a zygote or embryo and even if we are able to force ourselves into this empathic relationship, where do we stop? We could also force ourselves to identify with cattle and thus give up eating steak; "The Case Against Abortion," *Thomist* 39 (1975), p. 82. Gerber qualifies Grisez's argument as hypothetical and weak but has discovered some legal precedent for attributing precisely this sort of option to the unborn; "Abortion: Parameters for Decision," *op. cit.*, p. 574.

[29] Paul V. Harrington, "Abortion—Part X: A Legal Review," *Linacre Quarterly* 35 (1968), p. 190. See also: Trinkaus *et al.*, *op. cit.*, p. 115; Kenealy, *op. cit.*, p. 208; Robert J. Henle, S.J., "Georgetown University Statement on Abortion," *Catholic Mind* 71, September 1973, pp. 9-10; James A. Kearns, "Case Comment," *Notre Dame Lawyer* 48 (1973), pp. 725-726; Richard R. Romanowski, "Abortion—A Fetal Viewpoint," *Linacre Quarterly* 34 (1967), pp. 277-278. Granfield is not totally convinced by this biological argument: "(T)he law is not simply a vehicle for legislating moral evaluations or scientific conclusions"; *op. cit.*, p. 146. Grisez believes, as we have seen in Chapter III, that the definition of "person" is essentially a matter of metaphysics or theology; *op. cit.*, p. 416.

[30] Bishops of New Jersey, "Pastoral Letter on Abortion," *Catholic Mind* 66, June 1968, p. 5.

[31] "Statement of the Committee for Pro-Life Affairs of the National Conference of Catholic Bishops—January 24, 1973," in Daughters of St. Paul, *op. cit.*, p. 259.

[32] "Pastoral Message of the Administrative Committee, National Conference of Catholic Bishops," *op. cit.*, p. 261. See also: Indiana Catholic Conference, *op. cit.*, pp. 257-258; "Testimony of United States Catholic Conference on Constitutional Amendment Protecting Unborn Human Life....," *op. cit.*, pp. 4-16, 22-23, 25, 26.

[33] Trinkaus *et al.*, *op. cit.*, pp. 114-115; Lauth, *op. cit.*, p. 372; William J. Tobin, "Ethical and Moral Considerations Concerning Abortion," *Homiletic and Pastoral Review* 67 (1967), p. 1031; Robert M. Byrn, "Abortion: A Legal View," *Commonweal* 85 (1967), p. 680; Bishops of Pennsylvania, *op. cit.*, p. 217; Bishops of Maryland, "Statement on Abortion—January 27, 1971," in Daughters of St. Paul, *op. cit.*, p. 229.

[34] Dennis J. Horan *et al.*, "The Legal Case for the Unborn Child," in Thomas W. Hilgers and Dennis J. Horan (eds.), *Abortion and Social Justice* (New York: Sheed and Ward, 1972), p. 105.

[35] Kenealy, *op. cit.*, p. 206; David W. Louisell and John T. Noonan, Jr., "Constitutional Balance," in Noonan (ed.), *op. cit.*, pp. 220-223; Granfield, *op. cit.*, pp. 146-147; Grisez, *op. cit.*, pp. 362-365; Horan *et al.*, *op. cit.*, pp. 109-111; Kindregan, *op. cit.*, pp. 27-28.

[36] Kenealy, *op. cit.*, p. 206; Louisell and Noonan, *op. cit.*, pp. 226-230; Granfield, *op. cit.*, pp. 147-149; Grisez, *op. cit.*, pp. 365-373; Kindregan, *op. cit.*, pp. 28-31; Horan *et al.*, *op. cit.*, pp. 111-114. On the notion of "wrongful life" and its relevance to the abortion issue, see the discussion of the famous *Gleitman* v. *Cosgrove* case decided by the New Jersey Supreme Court in March 1967 in: Granfield, *op. cit.*, pp. 149-151; Grisez, *op. cit.*, pp. 397-402; Kindregan, *op. cit.*, pp. 31-32, 34-37. Horan *et al.* admit that in some jurisdictions some of the property and tort rights are not recognized unless the child is born alive but they claim that this restriction does not negate the child's legal existence prior to birth: "There can be no right to enforce at birth if the person was not in legal existence at the time of the injury or the time the property right first arose"; *op. cit.*, p. 114. On this issue see further: Granfield, *op. cit.*, p. 145.

[37] Louisell and Noonan, *op. cit.*, pp. 245-246; Grisez, *op. cit.*, pp. 373-374; Kindregan, *op. cit.*, pp. 27, 28.

[38] Louisell and Noonan, *op. cit.*, pp. 223-226; Granfield, *op. cit.*, p. 147; Grisez, *op. cit.*, pp. 374-397; Kindregan, *op. cit.*, p. 32; Robert M. Byrn, "Demythologizing Abortion Reform," *Catholic Lawyer* 14 (1968), pp. 182-183. Horan *et al.* maintain that the traditional statutes were intended to protect the mother as well as the unborn child; *op. cit.*, pp. 120-127. The original intent of the traditional statutes is a point of dispute. See: Chapter I, notes 50 and 51.

[39] Louisell and Noonan, *op. cit.*, pp. 244-245; Grisez, *op. cit.*, p. 374; Horan *et al.*, pp. 115-117; Kindregan, *op. cit.*, pp. 27, 32-33.

[40] Granfield, *op. cit.*, pp. 145-146, 151-152; Kindregan, *op. cit.*, p. 26; Lauth, *op. cit.*, p. 368; Romanowski, *op. cit.*, p. 276; A. James Quinn and James A. Griffin, "The Rights of the Unborn," *Jurist* 31 (1971), pp. 606-607; Bishops of New Jersey, "Pastoral Letter on Abortion—March, 1970," in Daughters of St. Paul, *op. cit.*, p. 212; Indiana Catholic Conference, *op. cit.*, p. 258.

[41] Grisez, *op. cit.*, p. 406.

[42] *Ibid.*, pp. 402-411. See also: Horan *et al.*, *op. cit.*, p. 113. Granfield generally concurs with Grisez's position but places less emphasis on the need of consistency in the attribution of legal personality. Natural personhood cannot always be equated with legal personhood. To grant legal personality to the fetus does not necessarily imply that the child is a human person, because legislation is not merely a translation of moral values or scientific findings. A legal personality is a creature of the positive law: it means what the law intends it to mean, namely, that certain interests of the individual will be legally protected. On the other hand, legal personality is not usually a mere fiction: it is based on factual realities and it implies a value judgement. Therefore a consistent and increasing acceptance of fetal rights forcefully argues that the community recognizes an underlying human personality; *op. cit.*, pp. 145-146. See also: Kindregan, *op. cit.*, pp. 33-34; John M. Finnis, "Three Schemes of Regulation," in Noonan (ed.), *op. cit.*, pp. 199-200.

[43] Trinkaus *et al.*, *op. cit.*, p. 122. This article is the text of an amici curiae brief submitted to the California Supreme Court in *People* v. *Belous* (1969) which challenged the state's traditional abortion statute.

[44] *Ibid.*, p. 123. See also: James A. Fitzgerald, "Abortion on Demand," *Linacre Quarterly* 37 (1970), p. 185; Paul V. Harrington, "Abortion—Part XI," *Linacre Quarterly* 35

(1968), pp. 276-279; *id.*, "Abortion—Part XV," *Linacre Quarterly* 37 (1970), pp. 132-133; John T. Noonan, Jr., "Amendment of the Abortion Law: Relevant Data and Judicial Opinion," *Catholic Lawyer* 15 (1969), pp. 129-130.

[45] William J. Maledon, "The Law and the Unborn Child: The Legal and Logical Inconsistencies," *Notre Dame Lawyer* 46 (1971), p. 369.

[46] *Ibid.*, p. 369. See also: Louisell and Noonan, *op. cit.*, pp. 230, 246; Grisez, *op. cit.*, pp. 409-411; Gerber, "Abortion: Parameters for Decision," *op. cit.*, p. 573; Robert F. Drinan, S.J., "The Jurisprudential Options on Abortion," *Theological Studies* 31 (1970), pp. 151-152.

[47] Louisell and Noonan, *op. cit.*, pp. 226, 230, 251-253; Grisez, *op. cit.*, p. 411; Kenealy, *op. cit.*, pp. 205-206; Harrington, "Abortion—Part X: A Legal Review," *op. cit.*, p. 194; Indiana Catholic Conference, *op. cit.*, p. 258.

[48] Grisez, *op. cit.*, p. 412.

[49] Louisell and Noonan, *op. cit.*, pp. 244-246, 251-254, 258; Horan *et al.*, *op. cit.*, p. 132; Kindregan, *op. cit.*, pp. 26, 33-34; "Testimony of United States Catholic Conference on Constitutional Amendment Protecting Unborn Human Life....," *op. cit.*, pp. 4-16, 19-20.

[50] Horan *et al.*, *op. cit.*, pp. 130-133; "Testimony of United States Catholic Conference on Constitutional Amendment Protecting Unborn Human Life....," *op. cit.*, p. 20.

[51] Louisell and Noonan, *op. cit.*, pp. 246-247; Granfield, *op. cit.*, pp. 154-157.

[52] Grisez, *op. cit.*, p. 426.

[53] Louisell and Noonan, *op. cit.*, pp. 247-250; John B. Gest, "Comment on Fr. Drinan's Article on Abortion Laws," *Catholic Lawyer* 14 (1968), p. 328; Harvey J. Johnson, "Is Embryonic or Fetal Life Human Life?" *Social Justice Review* 60 (1968), p. 421; James V. McNulty, "The Therapeutic Abortion Law: A Fight for Life," *Linacre Quarterly* 33 (1966), p. 342; Romanowski, *op. cit.*, p. 278; Quinn and Griffin, *op. cit.*, pp. 608-609; "Testimony of United States Catholic Conference on Constitutional Amendment Protecting Unborn Human Life....," *op. cit.*, pp. 20-21.

[54] Louisell and Noonan, *op. cit.*, p. 258. On the justifiability of the legal distinction between "abortion" (the murder of an unborn child) and "homicide" (the murder of someone outside the womb), see: Louisell and Noonan, *op. cit.*, p. 247; Grisez, *op. cit.*, p. 427.

[55] "Testimony of United States Catholic Conference on Constitutional Amendment Protecting Unborn Human Life....," *op. cit.*, pp. 16-18; Bishops' Committee for Pro-Life Activities, *op. cit.*, pp. 10, 18-19.

[56] Noonan, "Introduction," *op. cit.*, pp. x-xi; Grisez, *op. cit.*, p. 447; "Testimony of United States Catholic Conference on Constitutional Amendment Protecting Unborn Human Life....," *op. cit.*, p. 18.

[57] Noonan, "Introduction," *op. cit.*, pp. x-xi.

[58] Cardinal Shehan, "Pastoral Letter on Abortion," *Catholic Mind* 69, March 1971, p. 10. See also: Byrn, "Abortion-on-Demand: Whose Morality?" *op. cit.*, pp. 36-37.

[59] Noonan, "Introduction," *op. cit.*, p. xi; Louisell and Noonan, *op. cit.*, p. 258; Gerber, "Abortion: Two Opposing Legal Philosophies," *op. cit.*, pp. 20-21.

[60] "Testimony of United States Catholic Conference on Constitutional Amendment Protecting Unborn Human Life....," *op. cit.*, pp. 18-19.

[61] Bishops of New Jersey, "Pastoral Letter on Abortion—March, 1970," *op. cit.*, p. 213; National Conference of Catholic Bishops, "Statement on Abortion—April, 1970," in Daughters of St. Paul *op. cit.*, p. 214.

[62] Bishops of Pennsylvania, *op. cit.*, p. 217. See also: Byrn, "Abortion-on-Demand:

Whose Morality?'' *op. cit.*, pp. 37-39; Gerber, ''Abortion: Two Opposing Legal Philosophies,'' *op. cit.*, p. 24.

[63] Grisez, *op. cit.*, pp. 447-448. See also: Editorial, ''Morality and Policy,'' *op. cit.*, p. 521; Robert M. Byrn, ''The Abortion Question: A Nonsectarian Approach,'' *Catholic Lawyer* 11 (1965), p. 322; Kenealy, *op. cit.*, pp. 202-203.

[64] Grisez, *op. cit.*, pp. 446-447. A 1964 editorial of *The Catholic Lawyer* issues a warning to Catholic politicians: ''In theological terminology, to vote for the liberalization of the present abortion laws would be material cooperation, and anyone who cooperates in an abortion incurs a canonical penalty. Material cooperation in a sin is licit when the action of the one who cooperates is not evil and there is proportionately a grave reason. But as long as the canonical limitation on cooperation remains, it would seem that even if there was a grave reason for so doing, a Catholic legislator would be prohibited from voting for a more liberal abortion law''; ''Note: The Current Trend to Liberalize Abortion Laws—An Analysis and Criticism,'' *Catholic Lawyer* 10 (1964), p. 173.

[65] Grisez, *op. cit.*, p. 447.

[66] Granfield, *op. cit.*, pp. 143-144.

[67] *Ibid.*, pp. 163-164, emphasis supplied. See also: Lauth, *op. cit.*, pp. 372-373; Editorial, ''Public Policy and Abortion Laws,'' *America* 120 (1969), p. 240; Bishops of Maryland, ''Statement on Abortion,'' *Catholic Mind* 66, March 1968, p. 2.

[68] ''Testimony of United States Catholic Conference on Constitutional Amendment Protecting Unborn Human Life. . . .,'' *op. cit.*, p. 16.

[69] Grisez, *op. cit.*, p. 422; Bishops of Illinois, ''Statement on Abortion—February 3, 1971,'' in Daughters of St. Paul, *op. cit.*, pp. 231-232.

Chapter Eight

Pragmatic and Apologetic Considerations

When calling for a different style and strategy in the Catholic presentation of the case against abortion liberalization, Norman St. John-Stevas suggested that the new proposition could be based on principle or pragmatism or both.[1] In the previous chapter I analysed the new argument about principle which Catholic authors propounded in defense of restrictive abortion codes. We saw that they characterized permissive statutes as a threat to the heart of the democratic community.[2] The authors have specified this assertion by describing in some detail how such laws would endanger the social fabric. The first section of this chapter will be devoted to these pragmatic observations with which they support their philosophical-juridical position.

They further point out that the objections presented by the abortion reform movement against the maintenance of the traditional statutes are largely unfounded and that the alleged benefits of liberalization are illusory. Moreover, they believe that the basic ideology of the movement is unsound and that its tactics are objectionable. These apologetical arguments will be listed in Sections II and III. Finally, they maintain that the abortion problem will not be solved by a liberalization of the law but by social reform. I will discuss their social recommendations in Section IV.

I. The Threat to the Social Fabric

In the view of many Catholic authors, as well as in that of the bishops, liberalization of abortion will have disastrous consequences for society. The following is a summary of the multitudinous observations with which the Catholic argument substantiates its definition of a permissive legal code as a decadent and destructive force.

1. *Liberalization will have a profound psychological effect on society and will lead to an erosion of respect for human life.*

(a) The law is a teacher. It affects the attitudes of individual citizens and therefore influences the outlook of the whole community. If it allows the destruction of unwanted life, it unavoidably teaches that life is cheap. The enactment of permissive abortion statutes will create a general disregard for human life.[3]

(b) Abortion assigns a relative rather than an absolute value to human life on the basis of some social or utilitarian criterion. This selective treatment of human life undermines the fundamental moral and legal equality of all human beings and violates basic principles of justice as we have understood these in Western society. Liberal abortion laws are contrary to the Judeo-Christian tradition, which is inspired by love for life, and to the Anglo-Saxon legal tradition which protects life and the person. Abandoning this philosophy will have enormous implications and in the long run this infringement of the fundamental human right to equal treatment is a more serious threat to the community than the birth of numerous children will be.[4]

(c) Accepting abortion as a solution to one problem implies that human life and dignity need not be respected in the face of other social problems. Once men subordinate life in the early stages of its development to another value, they will forfeit any future appeal to a legal system that can logically protect human life at any other point.[5]

2. *Liberal abortion laws will create an abortion-minded society, and this will result in an increase in the number of abortions.*

(a) Once a permissive code has been introduced, there is an immediate and significant increase in the number of requests for abortion because the social stigma attached to the intervention disappears. Women who never contemplated it before now want to have their pregnancy terminated, and unmarried mothers come under social pressure to get rid of their child. This is the chief negative effect of a liberalized law.[6]

(b) Permissive statutes are a step on the road to human degradation and totalitarianism. As the clamor for compulsory fertility control increases, it is quite possible that governments will decide to enforce abortions legally under certain circumstances. It is frighteningly plausible that the sequence might be: legal abortion in particular cases, legal abortion upon simple request, removal of the choice from the mother to a medical board, to a social worker, to the State.[7]

3. *This lack of respect for unborn life will extend to born life and will lead to other moral and social calamities.*

(a) Abortion liberalization is simply the camel's nose in the tent. If we legalize abortion, it is only a small step from, and a few years to, pleas for unrestricted sterilization, euthanasia, the killing of the handicapped and the mentally retarded, and other measures which seek to elevate the *quality* of human existence rather than to protect every *instance* of humanity. It would be only one more step to the extermination of all groups in society which are causing trouble and which we cannot handle conveniently.[8]

(b) This downward trend is already evident in the current debate about experimentation on fetuses and children. It is argued that there should be no restrictions on fetal research, especially when the fetus is already earmarked for abortion, because such investigations will yield information about fetal development and fetal defects which will be useful in the treatment of other unborn children. On similar grounds some medical scientists seek permission to conduct experiments on infants who are born with a specific weakness or disease.[9]

(c) Permissive abortion policies go hand in hand with the erosion of family values. In a society that frequently resorts to abortion children will become aware that parental love is lacking, and this will affect their psychological security. Parents who are grossly disappointed or irritated by a child may regret that they did not have it aborted; such feelings may lead to mental and physical cruelty. This will result in parent-child alienation and family breakdown.[10]

(d) Permissive statutes further threaten the family and society in general, contributing to the contemporary rise in juvenile sex, with its inevitable psychological reverberations in the form of emotional and mental disturbances.[11]

4. *Liberalization will have an adverse effect on the practice of contraception.*

Anyone experienced with women seeking abortions knows that, when this operation can be readily obtained, women become careless about contraception because there is an easy solution to contraceptive failure. Wherever the laws have been relaxed, it has been found that the return rate for another abortion is high. Liberal laws create an abortion habit and foster the acceptance of this intervention as just another means of birth control.[12]

5. *Liberalization will have a negative effect on medical science and on the medical profession, and will place a strain on hospital facilities and medical care.*

(a) Liberal abortion codes threaten the basic orientation of medicine because such statutes discourage research to discover methods of treating the complications of pregnancy and childbirth; it will be more expedient to abort. Medical science will learn little about fetal defects resulting from disease, drugs, or trauma, if we are continually killing fetuses which are thus affected.[13]

(b) Abortion is the antithesis of the practice of medicine. The sole and exclusive function of the medical profession is the reasonable maintenance of life. The physician taking care of a pregnant woman is medically and morally responsible for the health and welfare of *two* patients: the mother and the child. Therefore abortion is repulsive to most doctors and other medical staff.[14]

(c) Unless a permissive statute is very clear, physicians will have great difficulty interpreting when an abortion is legal. Moreover, any medical practitioner will recognize that his training and competence are inadequate for the Solomon-like decisions required in the recommendations for abortions on the basis of social or economic conditions.[15]

(d) The public image of the medical profession will be damaged if doctors take to abortion. If they abandon the Hippocratic Oath, and if the medical profession is no longer exclusively the protector of life but equally the purveyor of death, the relationship between doctors and their patients will be adversely affected. The patient will no longer know in which capacity the doctor approaches. A girl whose pregnancy has been terminated by a doctor will not return to him when she is pregnant again and wants the child because she looks upon him as an abortionist and not as a doctor.[16]

(e) The doctor-patient relationship will further suffer because of the dishonesty involved in the use of social indications as medical indications. Doctors who perform abortions on nonexistent grounds will resort to similar manipulations to justify other unnecessary surgery. Moreover, under a permissive statute women will conclude that they have a right to have their pregnancy terminated, and they will pressure the doctor into performing the operation even if this goes against his better medical judgement.[17]

(f) Since liberalization will lead to a great increase in the demand for abortion, and since the intervention should take place in a hospital, serious problems are likely to arise in the field of medical care. In many States there is already a severe shortage of medical facilities and personnel. Unless hospitals can afford to set aside special beds for abortion patients, reserve operating rooms for them, and provide medical and paramedical staff, liberalization can only be implemented at the expense of genuine medical and surgical patients or by a lowering of the medical standards for safe abortions.[18]

6. *Liberalization may lead to abortion rackets and to migratory abortion.*

Under a permissive statute some members of the medical profession will succumb to the temptation of larger profits and will attempt to exploit the commercial potential of abortion. Women who cannot get an abortion in their own country will come to the United States to avail themselves of the local facilities. This will further increase the demand for the intervention, and there is a danger of unscrupulous operators taking advantage of this situation.[19]

7. *Liberalization will result in an undesirable decline in the birth rate.* In countries which have already taken this step, such as Hungary and Japan, there is growing concern about the effect of a rapidly declining birth rate on the national economy and the labor supply.[20]

II. Challenging the Liberationist Claims

The Catholic argument also questions the various reasons which the abortion reform movement presents to justify its demand for permissive legal codes. In this section I will list the principal liberationist propositions and, using these as headlines, I will register the respective refutations formulated by Catholic authors.

Argument 1. Restrictive codes and moderately liberal codes do not make provision for certain indications which are recognized as valid by the medical profession.

Refutations:

(a) The liberationists have created the impression that abortion is morally acceptable to the medical profession and that there is a general consensus regarding the proper indications for therapeutic abortion. Admittedly, there are many physicians who favor some degree of liberalization but it is incorrect to state that the medical profession as a whole supports abortion on demand.[21]

(b) The traditional statutes already cater for what most physicians would regard as valid medical indications. These laws permit an abortion if the intervention is necessary to preserve the mother's life. Judicial interpretation has extended this permission to the preservation of maternal *health* in situations where ill health would affect the duration of the woman's life.[22]

(c) The traditional codes need not be liberalized to provide for cases of rape. If a victim of rape presents herself immediately for medical treatment, the doctor is able to perform a uterine scraping or any other procedure which he deems advisable. This is well within the traditional law.[23]

(d) A community which legalizes abortion in cases of rape places its confidence in revenge and destruction instead of goodness and love. Any legislation which is based on the conviction that evil is stronger than goodness and that faith in love is naïve must necessarily have a demoralizing effect on society.[24]

(e) A law which recognizes a eugenic indication presupposes that one human being is able to judge whether the life of another is worth living. Such legislation abandons the use of clear and objective criteria, and it confers a license to kill without definite limiting terms, a power that has never been granted by Anglo-American law.[25]

(f) Abortion on demand will not remove the *causes* of rape, of incest, of mental disorder, and of fetal defects. Physicians arguing in favor of permissive laws reveal a defeatist attitude on their own part and in those segments of scientific medicine which support them.[26]

(g) Hard cases make bad law: we cannot use exceptions and cases on the fringe of the ordinary as criteria for legislation. Difficult situations such as incestuous and forceful assault pregnancies deserve consideration and compassion, but if we make legal provisions on the basis of marginal cases and not of ordinary ones, we will have great difficulty in controlling the effects on society as a whole.[27]

Argument 2. The abortion decision is a private decision and belongs to the sphere of private morality. Many respectable people sincerely believe that abortion is a legitimate solution to distressed pregnancies. The ethical values of a particular section of the population should not be imposed on the whole nation by means of penal law. Such legislation conflicts with the United States Constitution which prohibits the establishment of any religion in order to allow for the freedom of all.

Refutations:

(a) Abortion is not a private moral issue because the unborn child is not the private possession of the mother. The father and the State also have rights and duties. The fetus has public value, primarily as organized human life, and therefore its destruction requires public justification. Abortion is a legitimate area of concern for every citizen.[28]

(b) It is true that there are honorable and respectable men who favor the legalization of abortion. But honorable and respectable men cooperated in the enactment and enforcement of the laws that legalized slavery and the slave trade, and the killing and spoliation of the American Indians. Hitler could not have led Germany to the shame of the Holocaust if decent and respectable men had not cooperated.[29]

(c) Even if the majority of the population were to support liberalization this would not automatically justify the enactment of permissive statutes, because the wishes of the majority are not necessarily legitimate. As American history sadly attests—the Prohibition laws, the abomination of racial discrimination, the segregation of Japanese in concentration camps during World War II—the majority can be both stupid and brutal.[30]

(d) The anti-abortion stand which is belittled as a mere private religious belief has a longer standing in public tradition than has the liberationist position.[31]

(e) The appeal to religious liberty in order to justify permissive abortion laws is a clever rhetorical device which diverts attention from the real issue (sound legal policies) to the religious convictions of the opposing party.[32]

(f) This argument allows people to follow their religious and moral convictions in the private sector of their lives, yet prevents them from voicing such beliefs in the public forum of a pluralistic community. In our society, though, individual citizens and groups of citizens have the right and the duty to urge the adoption of whatever legal policies they sincerely believe to be in the best interest of the general welfare. Every citizen is free to argue for or against the legalization of marijuana, for or against the private possession of firearms, for or against a change in the divorce laws, for or against the death penalty, etc. We do not have to check our consciences at the door before we vote against a particular law and persuade others to do likewise.[33]

(g) It is certainly true that the Catholic Church and many other churches condemn abortion, just as they reject racial discrimination, exploitation of the poor, and all injustice and injury to others. On these issues religious doctrine powerfully confirms the human commitment to human rights. The abortion decision affects a basic human right which transcends sectarian moral insights. To claim that abortion belongs to private morality is to ignore that the unborn child has a right to life, that society has a duty to defend its members against those who would kill them, and that individual citizens have the right and the duty to be concerned about the humaneness of the laws that regulate the life of their community. The right to life is not an invention of the Catholic Church or any other church. The churches which oppose liberalization are motivated to do so by their respect for human rights, and not by a desire to impose denominational morality on the whole nation.[34]

(h) A criminal law does not become invalid just because there are concurring thoughts on the issue in the field of religion or morals. The legal prohibitions of theft and murder are not rendered null and void by the fact that they are coincidentally forbidden by the Decalogue. Our founding fathers expressed their belief in human dignity and the right to life in religious terms: ''We hold these truths to be self-evident, that all men are created equal, that they are endowed by their Creator with certain unalienable rights...'' Are we now going to reject the principles on which this republic was founded simply because they reflect convictions which were rooted in religious as well as secular tradition? Moreover, if the liberationist argument were to be followed to its logical conclusion, then the civil rights laws and the large body of legislation authorizing assistance to the poor, the sick, the aged, the disabled, and other disadvantaged groups would have to be revoked on constitutional grounds because the churches have always supported these public welfare programs and have actively contributed to them.[35]

(i) If a law could only be enacted when there was universal agreement on its validity, the statutes of the land would have to limit themselves to such general injunctions as "do good and avoid evil" or "act lovingly."[36]

(j) This argument has been cleverly contrived to appeal to our constitutional neutrality towards denominational moral tenets but it serves a purpose (abortion on demand) which itself reflects a sectarian ideology: the "new morality" of utilitarianism. If the statement that prenatal life is inviolable conflicts with the religious clauses of the First Amendment, then also the antithesis of this assertion must be taken as contrary to the Constitution. It is not fair to silence one side to the debate by stigmatizing its position as religious, while it is permissible and constitutional to hold the opposite view. One can validly argue that a State which legally endorses abortion on demand violates the rights of conscience of those of its citizens who are opposed to abortion. Moreover, once abortion has been legalized the State will be asked to guarantee that the operation will be available to any woman who asks for it. This will affect its social policies and its public assistance and welfare programs to such an exent that these not only approve abortion but in some cases also subtly coerce women into terminating a pregnancy which others consider undesirable. There will be pressure on the State to fund abortion services for all who want them, and hospitals will be required to perform their equitable share of the interventions. This inappropriate exercise of State power would be a violation of the religious liberty of those who do not wish to support, perform, or pay for permissive abortions.[37]

(k) There are those who believe that a child does not acquire humanity until the severance of the umbilical cord or that it is not fully human, because not fully rational, until some later age. Nevertheless, it cannot be seriously suggested that a law prohibiting the killing of a child at the moment of birth or forbidding infanticide is an unconstitutional invasion of religious liberty.[38]

(l) Convictions so deep as those of the opponents of abortion have to be taken into consideration if they are not to be wholly alienated from the body politic.[39]

Argument 3. The traditional statutes need to be liberalized because they are disregarded by so many, and this leads to disrespect for the legal system. Moreover, criminal law cannot effectively operate in the area of abortion since all activity of this nature is surreptitious. Abortion, like fornication and adultery, is not an appropriate subject for criminal law.

Refutations:

(a) One does not deal with crime by discarding the penal code.[40]

(b) If the statutes were really so ineffective, there would not be such strong pressure by those who disagree with them to have them repealed.[41]

(c) This argument seems to assume that what is done by a good many people cannot be evil. This presupposition is often employed when sexual behavior is evaluated, but it is rarely favored when racial discrimination or war is discussed.[42]

(d) The true criterion of the efficacy of an abortion law is not how many people it punishes but how many abortions it prevents. To legalize abortion is to increase the number of abortions.[43]

(e) It is not at all certain that the traditional statutes are ineffective. No one knows how often they are violated, and how often they are observed by those who would otherwise resort to abortion. The crime of abortion is admittedly difficult to detect and prosecute successfully, but that is no reason to brush aside the right to life of the unborn. Infanticide and involuntary euthanasia also occur frequently without being discovered. Does this breakdown of law enforcement mean that these practices should no longer be forbidden by law?[44]

(f) It is true that the principal aim of a criminal law is to prevent undesirable conduct, but this does not mean that all statutes which fail to realize this objective should be repealed. There are many criminal laws that are relatively ineffective: laws against speeding, against perjury, against theft. But no one concludes from the enormous number of violations of the law against larceny that there is something wrong with the statutes, that the real problem lies with the victims whose property is taken, and that we should reform the law to provide for contemporary moral standards.[45]

(g) Criminal law has symbolic power. It establishes a public policy which gives certain interests official protection. It indicates that in the judgement of the community certain activities are socially harmful. Restrictive abortion codes commit society to a high regard for unborn life. A nation which treats abortion as a crime and as culpable homicide communicates a public censure of abortion. Similarly, if the community removes the termination of pregnancy from the penal code and makes it a private medical matter, it communicates a neutral and even favorable attitude towards the intervention.[46]

Argument 4. Under restrictive or moderately permissive codes the wealthy can get an abortion more easily than the poor. These statutes therefore discriminate against the economically disadvantaged and they should be repealed.

Refutations:

(a) With equal logic one could argue that because some men are wealthy enough to move to a Muslim country and marry four wives, we must change our bigamy laws because they discriminate against the poor. Undoubtedly, persons who are poor are less likely to secure the services of a sympathetic physician who will detect a legal reason for a therapeutic abortion, and they find it more difficult to travel to a place where the intervention is available on request. But we surely cannot facilitate the doing of evil in order to give everyone equal opportunities in this respect. Many criminal laws are in practice more severe on the poor than on the wealthy. This discrimination must be rectified by reforming the administration of criminal justice, not by a selective repeal of statutes.[47]

(b) This statement must be seen in its proper historical context. In the 1920s and early 1930s the proponents of birth control urged that contraception be made available to lower class women, whose unrestricted breeding jeopardized society and culture. In later years this argument was reformulated but the underlying motivation has remained and this eugenic concern surfaces again in propositions which qualify traditional abortion statutes as discriminatory.[48]

Argument 5. The traditional statutes are unconstitutionally vague because they do not clearly define the prohibited act and lack the precision which is necessary in a penal law to make due process possible.

Refutations:

(a) History proves that the usual statutory phrase "necessary to preserve life" is sufficiently clear. These statutes have existed in substantially the same form for decades. They have been interpreted by judicial decisions and have been applied to countless cases without the courts ever adverting to the vagueness of their formulation.[49]

(b) Under the traditional statutes no physician had the slightest doubt regarding the conditions on which he could legally induce an abortion. If the intervention was performed openly in a hospital by a licensed physician who acted with the approval of his colleagues, the law would not intervene. The law never forbade a physician to terminate a pregnancy if there was a genuine medical indication.[50]

(c) The uncertainty that surrounds these statutes has been intentionally created by determined efforts to widen the very limited possibility of abortion originally envisaged by the law. But laws are not invalidated simply because those who violate them are not sure how far they can proceed without getting into trouble.[51]

(d) The notion of vagueness itself is none too clear.[52]

Argument 6. The law must be liberalized because physicians feel like hypocrites when they perform abortions for reasons that are not in accordance with the exact letter of the law. A physician should be free to terminate any pregnancy within the framework of the doctor-patient relationship.

Refutations:

(a) The comfort or discomfort of the physician is entirely irrelevant if the law which he has to observe is written for the protection of some common good. In fact, the destruction of an unborn child should never be a comfortable matter.[53]

(b) A physician's claim to privacy in his relationship with an abortion-seeking woman is conditional to the validity of the woman's claim that she has the right to kill her child.[54]

(c) When a doctor treats a pregnancy, he has two patients: the mother and her child. Therefore restrictive abortion codes do not intrude upon the physician-patient relationship. On the contrary, such statutes remind the doctor of his obligations towards his unborn client.[55]

(d) It could be argued with equal logic that the homicide laws make hypocrites of physicians who favor the disposal of defective babies and senile senior citizens.[56]

(e) The notion that a physician should be allowed to perform any abortion he chooses within the context of the doctor-patient relationship has no precedent in any other profession. Does the lawyer demand that he be granted the right to change the laws and adapt them to his client's needs? The State is fully entitled to regulate the practice of medicine so as to protect the health and general welfare of all its citizens.[57]

(f) The idea that a doctor should be free from legal restrictions when making "professional" decisions is dangerous indeed, as many medical issues have socio-moral implications. The law must protect the human rights of its citizens when the medical profession engages in experimentation on humans, research on dangerous drugs, vital organ transplantation, etc.[58]

(g) In abortion decisions judgements have to be made which are not really medical, e.g., when humanitarian and socio-economic factors are involved. A doctor may know how to do an abortion but he does not necessarily know when it should be done.[59]

(h) It is preferable to keep the responsibility governing abortion within the legal profession, which is somewhat removed from the pressures inherent in the doctor-patient relationship.[60]

(i) Prosecution of physicians for abortions performed in *bona fide* hospitals has been extremely rare. The law never forbade physicians to terminate a pregnancy if there was a genuine medical indication. Those who have taken the law into their own hands and performed abortions which were not medically necessary are hardly likely to refrain from doing so if some further indications are permitted. The hypocrisy will remain.[61]

(j) There is no unanimity among medical professionals on the morality of abortion. Under a permissive law getting an abortion would depend on no more than the woman's ability to find the liberal practitioner or hospital. She needs only to persist in her search and eventually she will find someone who will "authorize" her request. Or perhaps the decisive factor will just be her wealth.[62]

(k) If society would emphasize the freedom of the medical practitioner rather than the protection of unborn human life, some medical professionals might conclude that the community was willing to follow professional ethics no matter how these developed. Such conclusions might inspire them to revise medical ethics, not in the light of objective medical and moral norms but in accordance with presumptions about "social opinion."[63]

Argument 7. A woman has a right of privacy which implies that she should not be forced to bear a child against her will. She has a right to dispose of her unborn child because her body is hers and hers alone.[64]

Refutations:

(a) There is no more justification in putting the life in the womb at the disposal of the mother than there is in putting the life of the child after birth at her disposal. The life of the unborn child is human life. The woman's rights must be considered in the light of the child's right to life, her own maternal responsibilities, and the rights and duties of the child's father.[65]

(b) This argument assumes that a pregnant woman enjoys complete personal autonomy with no obligations to anyone but herself. But all human beings hold and exercise their rights in a social context, and the pregnant woman does so in a special way. Pregnancy and childbirth have great social ramifications; they entitle the woman to the help and support of others. A pregnant woman who asserts her personal independence and who claims sovereignty over all aspects of her reproductivity disrupts the bonds she has established with her husband, with her family, and with her unborn child. Her attitude reflects a highly individualized and ultimately antisocial understanding of human rights.[66] Only in a culture which attaches such great significance to private ownership could a woman regard her body as her own property.[67]

(c) Even if the fetus were merely part of the woman's body, it would not follow that she has the right to destroy it. The right over one's body is not absolute because it does not extend to suicide, euthanasia, sterilization, mutilation of the body, submission to dangerous experimentation, and similar activities which society condemns.[68]

(d) The abortion decision cannot be left to the mother. Of all persons, under such stress of circumstances that she contemplates abortion, she is least likely to make an objective and dispassionate assessment of the dignity and the rights of the child she is carrying.[69]

(e) The law obliges the father to support his children even before they are born. It is unjust to impose this duty on him and at the same time deny him any voice as to whether the object of his obligation—the child—shall live or die.[70]

(f) Restrictive abortion statutes enhance the freedom of women by protecting them from male pressures. Public opinion surveys show that men are more favorable to abortion liberalization than women. The fact seems to be that men who are faced with the problem of an unwanted child are more likely to want an abortion than the women who would have to undergo the intervention—even if abortion is legal.[71]

Argument 8. There are 1,200,000 illegal abortions in the United States each year and 5,000 or 10,000 women die as a result of them.

Refutations:

(a) Professional demographers have discredited the surveys from which these statistics were derived. These figures are employed for their propaganda effect, not because they are accurate.[72]

(b) Illegal abortions are less dangerous than is often supposed because the vast majority of clandestine interventions are performed by competent medical professionals. Maternal death due to septic criminal abortion is rare.[73]

(c) Such evidence as there is shows that widening the legal grounds for abortion does not reduce the illegal rate, which may even increase. Unless the statutes become extremely liberal, making abortion available free of charge, there will always be women who will turn to illegal or self-induced abortion if the law does not provide for their situation. Halfway measures merely make abortion culturally acceptable and create a larger clientele for the black market operator.[74]

(d) This argument seems to presume that after liberalization the illegal interventions are simply replaced by legal ones. But legal approval of abortion encourages women who would not have sought an illegal abortion to obtain a legal one. Liberalization leads to a marked increase in the total number of abortions and creates an abortion-minded society. The cure is worse than the disease.[75]

Argument 9. Abortions performed under hospital conditions are very safe procedures.

Refutations:

(a) Even for an expert working in the best conditions the removal of a pregnancy can be difficult and is not infrequently accompanied by serious complications. Apart from the operative mortality connected with abortion, nonfatal serious complications do occur and morbidity rates are considerable. Medical sequelae of therapeutic abortion include a two percent sterility rate, and there is evidence that subsequent pregnancies result in a significantly higher rate of prematurity which is a primary cause of physical and mental retardation in newborns. Abortion is particularly hazardous if the woman is pregnant for the first time. For women who have a serious medical indication for termination of pregnancy, induction of abortion is definitely dangerous, and its risks have to be weighed carefully against those involved in leaving the pregnancy undisturbed.[76]

(b) When therapeutic abortion is performed for psychiatric reasons, about one-fourth to one-half of the women undergoing the operation will have psychiatric sequelae related to the intervention. About one-tenth of the women who undergo an abortion for nonpsychiatric reasons will have similar problems.[77]

Argument 10. Abortion is a solution to such social problems as poverty and illegitimacy.

Refutations:

(a) The poor do not have abortions to the extent that the middle classes do.[78]

(b) The medical profession must resist any attempt to apply a medical solution to problems that are essentially social and economic.[79]

(c) Abortion does solve problems—but only in the sense in which war, famine, and disease can be said to solve population problems.[80]

(d) If abortion is justifiable to protect the social and economic interests of the mother and her family, is not the intervention all the more permissible when it achieves a similar purpose for the wider community? If these justifications become legally acceptable indications, will the individual woman have a right to refuse an abortion which others deem necessary for the common good? Do not the reasons which are given to justify abortion on demand also justify involuntary abortion?[81]

(e) The pragmatic vision of this argument is essentially flawed because the most basic fact of all is systematically overlooked: that each abortion kills an innocent human being. Are we going to improve the social situation of the poor by providing them with the means of killing their unborn children if these are potentially burdensome?[82]

(f) Abortion is a nonsolution. It does nothing to correct the social and economic conditions which cause women to seek abortions. A liberal abortion code permits and even encourages the community to evade the responsibility of making alternatives to abortion readily available. But if the law forbids abortion with a clear voice, society will find it much easier to set assistance programs in motion.[83]

Argument 11. Rigid safeguards will be written into the law to prevent abuse, e.g., well-defined indications, residence requirements, and the establishment of abortion boards. Abortions will be performed on nonviable fetuses only.

Refutations:

(a) Medical and legal terminology will always be subject to varying interpretations by individual physicians and psychiatrists. Just as there are liberal doctors, there will be liberal boards.[84]

(b) Residence requirements can easily be circumvented.[85]

(c) Viability is a relative and vague term.[86]

(d) Moderately liberal codes are inherently illogical. If abortions performed under such statutes can be defended as somehow not violating the right to life, then how can other abortions still remain legally felonious or medically unethical?[87]

(e) Less restrictive codes are simply a first step towards completely permissive codes.[88]

Argument 12. Unwanted pregnancies produce unwanted children and should be terminated.

Refutations:

(a) It is true that a child has a right to be born into a family where it is wanted, just as it has a right to be born into a family not burdened with poverty and not living in a slum and not subject to discrimination and oppression. But this does not mean that the life of the unborn child can be taken so that it will not have to live in deprivation of these rights. Social and economic problems must be solved, but not by taking the lives of those who are the victims of these situations.[89]

(b) Arguments which refer to unborn children as "unwanted" divert attention from the fact that it is the *parents* who do not want the fetus. This creates the impression that the lack is in the fetus and that the fetus is in some way responsible for this. But the lack resides in the "unwanting" parents. It is difficult to see how this parental shortcoming can justify the killing of the unborn child.[90]

(c) If the fetus has a right to be *born* loved, the born child must have a right to *be* loved. If the unborn child may be killed because it *will* not be loved, why may the born child not be killed if it *is* not loved?[91]

(d) There is a good deal of arrogance in the claim that one knows what makes human life meaningful and happy and in the verdict that a person whose life does not meet these requirements may be killed.[92]

(e) If a child is unwanted before conception, science has provided sufficient means for preventing tahe beginning of the life process.[93]

(f) In view of the large number of couples desiring but unable to adopt a child it is correct to say that many of the fetuses who are aborted are by no means unwanted.[94]

(g) It is common for women to have feelings of great emotional distress about an unplanned or unwanted conception but most of them accept the new reality fairly soon in pregnancy.[95]

(h) An unwanted child may be able to overcome this handicap and become a happy adult and a valuable member of society.[96]

III. Exposing the Liberationist Ideology and Tactics

In order to present the full range of anti-abortion arguments formulated by American Catholic authors, I must also refer to the observations they have made regarding the fundamental ideology of the reform movement and the strategy it employs to realize its objective. The accusations which these authors have levelled against the liberationists are so numerous that a complete registration is not feasible. I will therefore not consider their general assertions, such as those which regard the materialism, secularism, liberalism, and situationism purportedly espoused by the movement. I will restrict myself to those criticisms which affect the new abortion ethos in a more direct and specific manner. This critique can be summarized as follows:

1. *The Übermensch philosophy*. The liberalization movement is part of a much wider scheme designed to produce a super race of men. There is a growing group of scientists who believe that what science can do, it must do. These humanists maintain that the human race is destroying itself by an epidemic of unrestrained breeding, and they have set out to improve man's lot by raising "the quality, not the quantity of human life." They want to achieve this by widespread fertility control, compulsory if necessary, through abortion and abortifacient contraception, other methods of contraception, sterilization, euthanasia, artificial insemination, and genetic engineering.[97]

2. *The technological mentality*. The abortion reform movement clearly reflects the technological approach which modern man adopts towards any problem which confronts him. As technology advances and as man extends his mastery over his environment, he increasingly wishes to control his

future through rational planning, and he becomes less willing to accommodate himself to the unplanned or unforeseen. To have one's designs upset by a pregnancy which can easily be terminated seems senseless self-denial. Moreover, in this perspective abortion becomes a necessary technique if population growth is to be kept in check, without recourse to more drastic measures. In this world view the final arbiter of morality is the technician.[98]

3. *The rejection of the costing principle.* The real motive of the reform movement is not a desire to find a human solution for cases of exceptional hardship like incest, rape, or deformity. Its rationale is basically one of expediency. The liberationist thrust is provided by the articulate, drifting middle classes who want the laws to be relaxed simply because they are no longer willing to put up with unwanted pregnancies which they find too inconvenient, too time-consuming, too life-upsetting.[99]

4. *The cult of perfection.* The argument that abortion should be allowed on eugenic indication is inspired by a cult of perfection which finds the imperfect unpalatable and which considers life not worth living unless it is free of handicaps. This mentality does not accept irregularities, misfortunes, and accidents as part of man's existence, and it seeks to eliminate whatever is "impure" or "waste."[100]

5. *The utilitarian ethic.* Many of the arguments presented in support of permissive abortion statutes are based on a utilitarian theory of morality. On the principle that the moral good or evil of a human act is determined by the consequences of the act rather than by the act itself, abortion is first proposed as a legitimate solution in cases of extreme hardship, as when the intervention is necessary to save the life of the mother. Subsequently it is judged acceptable in the more common instances as when the mother's health or the welfare of the family or society is at stake.[101]

6. *The rejection of sexual moral codes.* The liberationist movement is a logical consequence of the contemporary trend towards rejecting all codes of morality, especially sexual codes, as an undue infringement of personal liberty. In order to be a complete success the sexual revolution needs not only unrestricted access to contraceptives but also a supplementary and foolproof method of postconceptive fertility control. The unspoken premise of this trend is found in a new attitude towards human procreation. The reproductive system and the life which it generates is regarded as something merely biological, a purely physiological phenomenon which deserves no particular respect.[102]

7. *The emotionalist appeal.* The liberationist argument addresses itself primarily to people's emotions. It concentrates on cases of extreme hardship, illustrating the plight of individuals in face of objective, "impersonal" moral standards. In this way it prevents people from dispassion-

ately considering alternative solutions to these problems and from recognizing the potential consequences of permissive statutes. Many proponents of abortion reform have switched from an emphasis on tragic cases and the need to reduce the incidence of illegal interventions to the argument that a woman has a right to terminate her pregnancy, and even that abortion is just another and more efficient means of birth control. In its campaign the movement makes skillful use of the mass media.[103]

8. *The strategy of evasion.* The liberationist position is couched in such terms as freedom of choice, women's rights, the tragedy of the unwanted child, and the hazards to man and milieu of overpopulation. Its arguments reflect an almost exclusive preoccupation with the needs and rights of those who want abortions and with society, which allegedly stands to benefit from a permissive statute. Notably absent, as a subject of concern, is the being whose life is to be extinguished. The liberationist therefore evades the fundamental debate which seeks to assess the relative rights of the mother and her child, and he transforms the abortion problem into a civil rights struggle between the supporters of liberalization and their opponents. This reduces the moral discussion to the political issue of religious liberty or respect for minority opinion. Once the abortion dilemma has been successfully reformulated in terms of personal freedom, the political and legal outcome of the debate is predictable.[104]

9. *Semantic camouflage.* The evasiveness of the liberationists is further manifested in their medical and moral euphemisms which attempt to gloss over the fact that a very young child is being killed, or which make this unpleasant event a little more palatable, a little more positive, and dignified. For instance, "expectant mother" becomes "client," "pregnancy" becomes "problem," "abortion" is replaced by "termination," and "unborn child" becomes "the product of conception" or "fetal tissue."[105]

IV. The Need for a Consistent Pro-life Ethic

It is clear that in the Catholic view permissive abortion laws are not a legitimate solution to the medical, social, and economic problems of individual women or of society at large. Germain G. Grisez qualifies a liberal abortion code as "a cowardly expedient, which discharges social responsibilities by dispatching part of those for whom we are responsible rather than by intelligence, work, and sacrifice."[106] David Granfield also rejects liberalization as a nonsolution, because it merely cures symptoms and does not eliminate the social evils of rape and incest, of poverty and ill-health, and whatever else makes pregnancies unwanted.[107]

These statements are a first indication that the Catholic response to the liberationist proposition has not been a merely negative one. While arguing that permissive abortion statutes are morally and legally unjustifiable and socially disastrous, Catholic authors have also recognized that at the root of many abortion dilemmas lies a genuine human problem; those who do not accept a liberal legal code as a remedy to these difficulties are under a grave obligation to put forward other solutions. Granfield states that opponents of abortion who attempt to thwart the liberalization movement without offering viable alternatives are guilty of irresponsible obstructionism. Those who reject permissive statutes must work out realistic solutions to distressed pregnancies and offer assistance which not only preserves the life of the child but also eliminates the conditions that occasioned the demand for its destruction. [108]

For the anti-abortion movement this means first of all, and as a matter of fundamental principle, that its concern with human life should not restrict itself to unborn life. An anti-abortion position that is not part of a total pro-life attitude and an expression of a wide commitment to intervene in defense of human life whenever that is threatened will not be convincing and will be dismissed by many as hypocritical. In a homily which he preached in 1971 Archbishop Humberto S. Medeiros eloquently pleaded for such an authentic pro-life ethic. He emphasized that all human life is at once indivisible and interdependent:

> (It is) indivisible, in the sense that each man is unique, and his life is a delicate thread that runs with chronological continuity from the womb to the tomb; and interdependent, in the sense that every man's life is lived on a sacred spectrum of life that is tied to other men's lives by bonds of mutual trust and common respect. [109]

It follows that an attack on human life at any one point on the spectrum of life constitutes a threat to human life as such, to all human life:

> (A)ll isolated and indiscriminate attacks upon life, or the quality of life, serve only to destroy the bonds of mutual respect and common reverence that are necessary for men who wish to live together in security and in civil peace. Thus, to be vitally concerned about the rights of innocent human life at one point, as in the case of war, while being quite indifferent to the destruction of innocent lives in the case of abortion, is evidence of our inability to see the unity of those bonds of trust and respect that support a consistent ethic of life. The converse is also true. [110]

Gordon C. Zahn has underscored that "the converse is also true." Referring to the Church's silence on the United States war policy in Vietnam he says:

No one who publicly mourns the senseless burning of a napalmed child should be indifferent to the intentional killing of a living fetus in the womb. By the same token, the Catholic, be he bishop or layman, who somehow finds it possible to maintain an olympian silence in the face of government policies which contemplate the destruction of human life on a massive scale, has no right to issue indignant protests when the same basic disregard for human life is given expression in government policies permitting or encouraging abortion. [111]

Zahn adds that a wide commitment to human life is not just a matter of consistency: in a very real sense it represents the choice of integrity over hypocrisy. [112] Archbishop Medeiros makes the same point when he states that an ethic of life in order to appeal to the conscience of contemporary society must be comprehensive in scope and consistent in substance:

It must be comprehensive, in order to speak with concern to all issues where life is threatened today; and it must also be consistent, sufficiently refined and sophisticated so as to speak with precision to the different kinds of problems which touch upon the value of life today. [113]

It stands to reason that a consistent pro-life ethic will address itself with compassion to the problem of distressed pregnancies and that it will concretely manifest its concern not only with the lives of the children but also with the lives of the mothers. In Granfield's analysis, the social crisis which gives rise to the demand for abortion cannot be resolved by a single solution, but there is a combination of remedies that together form the viable alternative to permissive statutes. [114] This aspect of the abortion problem has received a great deal of attention from Catholic authors, and it constitutes a major theme in the declarations and pastoral letters of the bishops. The practical initiatives which they have suggested can be summarized as follows:

1. *Medical measures.* Against the liberationist assertion that permissive abortion codes are necessary in order to safeguard maternal life and health and avoid the birth of defective children, Catholic authors have made several recommendations in the field of medical care:

(a) An obvious alternative to therapeutic abortions performed to preserve the life or health of the mother is greater medical expertise. [115]

(b) The area of psychiatric indications stands in need of further research to establish the exact relationship between pregnancy and mental illness. Relevant in this connection are the psychiatric sequelae of abortion. Is the cure worse than the disease? [116]

(c) We should encourage and support medical research and therapeutic care which seek to minimize the incidence of defective children. This includes the development of centers for genetic counselling, gene therapy, and neo-natal intensive care. [117]

(d) Our techniques and facilities for the education and rehabilitation of handicapped children should be improved. [118]

(e) The parents of defective children could receive assistance under the welfare program of the State so that their heavy financial burden is alleviated. [119]

(f) Parents or potential parents with transmissible defects could be advised to practice contraception or undergo sterilization. [120]

2. *Social measures.* Against the liberationist argument that less restrictive codes are necessary to provide for pregnancies resulting from crime (incest and rape) and illegitimate pregnancies, Catholic authors have suggested a number of social initiatives:

(a) Society must seek to reduce the incidence of criminal and illegitimate pregnancies. This could be achieved through early sex education which aims at inculcating reverence for sex and for the human person and which includes realistic information about birth control. Counselling and psychiatric help must be available to those whose behavior patterns suggest that they need this assistance. [121]

(b) Victims of rape are entitled to prompt and humane medical treatment. If pregnancy occurs, society should recognize its liability and compensate the woman for the lack of adequate protection by the community of her personal security. [122]

(c) Society must do everything possible to persuade the unmarried pregnant woman not to terminate her pregnancy. Assistance to unmarried mothers should include the availability of maternity homes and foster homes, welfare assistance, legal aid, medical aid, counselling and psychiatric help, and rehabilitation programs. Paternity laws need tightening and adoption procedures must be simplified. [123]

(d) Above all, the community must change its attitude towards the unmarried mother. She is entitled to sympathy and help and her child should be sheltered from social stigmas. All legal discrimination against illegitimates must be eliminated, including the provisions of Canon Law which bar illegitimates from ecclesiastical offices. [124]

3. *Socio-economic measures.* Against the liberationist contention that permissive abortion laws contribute to the solution of economic problems, the Catholic argument insists on the need for socio-economic reform. The American bishops strongly endorse initiatives of this nature and they repeatedly pledge the support of the Church to all endeavors in this field. [125] The various recommendations can be summarized as follows:

(a) Improved socio-economic planning and more effective poverty prevention programs. [126]

(b) Uniform minimum wages and family allowances.[127]
(c) Better housing conditions.[128]
(d) Adequate child welfare laws.[129]
(e) Improved education, especially for women, including sex education and preparation for family living.[130]
(f) Wider employment opportunities, with an emphasis on part-time jobs so that married women can supplement the family income.[131]
(g) Child care centers for working mothers.[132]
(h) Family counselling and budget guidance.[133]
(i) Adequate prenatal, obstetrical, and postnatal care for the mother, including psychiatric help, and nutritional and pediatric care for the child.[134]
(j) Counselling centers which provide encouragement, advice, and support for women who face difficulties related to pregnancy.[135]

The American bishops have stressed that an essential element of the battle against abortion is a thorough education of society to sexual values with the purpose of assisting people in their marriage and family life and promoting responsible sexual behavior.[136] Gregory Baum has developed this theme of responsibility in sexual relations and has concluded that the Catholic position on abortion calls for a new attitude to contraception. In Baum's analysis, the traditional Catholic view on marriage concentrated on the biological-procreative aspect of sexuality; it was in this perspective that contraception was defined as an undue interference with the order of nature. The Second Vatican Council initiated a new trend of thought in the Catholic tradition: it abandoned the view that procreation is the primary end of marriage and recognized that sexuality, apart from its reproductive purpose, has an important function in the building up of love in the family. Furthermore, Vatican II wholeheartedly adopted the ideal of responsible parenthood and encouraged people to assume full responsibility for their procreative role. Baum argues that Catholics should accept the implications of this new approach and promote a sexual morality which acknowledges "man's quest for sexual freedom within the bounds of reason and love" and "the right and duty of men and women to choose with responsibility the form and pattern of their sexual lives."[137] Catholics therefore should not link their fight against abortion to a purely biological-procreative view of sexuality and the traditional moral code corresponding to it. Their opposition to abortion should include an endorsement of man's personal responsibility for his sexual life, and this implies that Catholics promote the diffusion of sexual information, facilitate access to contraceptives, and affirm enlightened attitudes which recognize people's individual responsibility in their sexual relations.[138] Granfield also is positive about the role of contraception in relation to the abortion problem. He observes that concern about the population explosion is one of the factors underlying agitation for permissive statutes.[139] He foresees that the easy availability of reliable contraceptives will allay the fear of overpopulation:

> Tremendous advances over the last few years in developing chemical or hormonal means of inhibiting the ovulatory function have already radically transformed the life of the woman in American society. A continuance of the same rate of scientific and medical research make imminent the breakthrough discovery of the "perfect contraceptive." A safe, foolproof, long-lasting, and inexpensive contraceptive, channeled through a well-funded counseling and medical service, could largely eliminate the fear of overpopulation and most unwanted pregnancies without recourse to abortion, but it would not eliminate all of the abortion problems.[140]

Baum draws attention to a further implication of a consistent pro-life ethic and demands that those who oppose abortion liberalization be willing to engage in a critical analysis of the social and cultural conditions through which the problem arises. He points out that moralists in church and society, when discussing moral and social evils such as theft, robbery and drug addiction, tend to put the burden of guilt on the individual person, his selfishness and bad will. Such conclusions, however, are incomplete and one-sided; they overlook the fact that man's moral consciousness is influenced by the social and cultural conditions in which he lives. Therefore the antiliberalization argument should not restrict itself to individualistic denunciations and moralizations but should adopt a wide approach, recognize abortion as a symptom of social ills, and submit the social system to a critical examination.[141] In Baum's own analysis contemporary society features two forms of oppression which favor abortion. The first is the present economic system which fosters a consumeristic mentality:

> First and foremost, it seems to me, is the alienation imposed on people, especially, though not exclusively, on the underprivileged, by the money- and profit-oriented, maximizing economic system. The present system, through its various institutions, tries to make people into customers. From childhood on people are taught to dream of buying goods and symbolizing affluence through ostentatious consumption. As they become part of the world of consumers, be it only in their dreams, they become estranged from the deep things of life, from love, truth and fidelity. Institutionally summoned to a false life, they fall into emotional and sexual chaos. The confusion, isolation and terror created among the urban dispossessed, coupled with an authentic desire for ecstasy, traps vast numbers of women in unwanted pregnancies. And while they are quite incapable of looking after themselves, society expects them to look after their children.[142]

A second factor in the growing demand for abortion is the revolution of women against male oppression:

> A second contradiction, operative in another section of the population, is the oppression of women. In our generation women have discovered that much of the emphasis that they are mothers, and achieve their highest fulfillment as mothers looking after a family, is an ideology that prevents them from experiencing the self-realization that is open to men. They sense that what is involved in much of the opposition to abortion is the hidden trend of the male-dominated society, endorsed by many women, to keep the power relations between men and women as they are. The women struggling for their liberation regard any form of unwanted motherhood as an unjust imposition of society. [143]

Baum concludes that arguments repudiating permissive abortion statutes should reflect a detailed critique of society and should be formulated in such a manner that they "do not strengthen the oppressions working in the social order but promote social change and the liberation of men and women." [144] The rejection of abortion as a means of birth control should be expressed in a statement which "is politically and culturally responsible and raises the consciousness of the community in regard to the contradictions operative in it." [145]

V. The Official Position of the Catholic Church

The philosophical-juridical proposition, outlined in the previous chapter, together with the pragmatic and apologetic observations which have been listed in the present chapter, can be said to constitute the "official" or "orthodox" Catholic position on the legality of abortion liberalization, and it reflects the teaching of the American bishops until today. It is evident that the Catholic argument on the legal aspects of abortion developed along the same lines as did the argument on the moral side of the issue. At an early stage of the moral debate the emphasis shifted from theology to biology, from speculative to empirical considerations. We have now seen that a similar change took place in the legal deliberations. The authors have abandoned the traditional emphasis on natural moral law as the criterion for human legislation. They have transferred the discussion to a secular level and formulated a pragmatic argument which draws on juridical philosophy, sociology, individual and social psychology, and individual and social medicine. They oppose the introduction of permissive legal codes not primarily on moral grounds but for legal, social, medical, and psychological reasons. Their intention is clear: they want to show that the case against

abortion liberalization can be cogently stated without recourse to ecclesiastical or theological presuppositions.

The Threat to the Social Fabric

The theme of the quality of unborn human life dominates the demonstra-
tions and refutations. The Catholic argument persists in its refusal to allow
any discrimination between prenatal and postnatal persons and demands
that the child in the womb be given the same social consideration and legal
recognition as the born infant. The Catholic position also attaches great
significance to the didactic function of law and warns that liberal abortion
statutes will lead to a general erosion of respect for human life because
abortion is contagious: if people are permitted to commit fetal homicide,
they will inevitably be led to greater, nonfetal homicide. Liberalizing
abortion becomes the equivalent of signing the death warrant for unwanted
infants, the physically handicapped, the mentally retarded, comatose
patients, and senile senior citizens.

Not everybody is convinced of the validity of the socio-psychological
part of the argument. At the 1967 Harvard-Kennedy International Conference on Abortion it was observed that it is practically impossible to assess
the effects that liberal abortion laws have on society in terms of popular
attitudes and behavior. One must assume that a relaxation of the law will
result in an increase in the number of women who seek a termination of
their pregnancy. But we cannot state with any certainty that this will lead to
an erosion of reverence for nonfetal human life. Much will depend on the
popular understanding of abortion. If people generally feel that the operation kills a defenseless human being, then there might be negative effects
for born human life. If it is felt that up to a certain point of fetal development abortion does not represent the taking of life, then there might not be
such undesirable consequences.[146]

Writing in 1969 Bernard J. Ransil became the first Catholic author to
question the validity of the "opening wedge" argument. In his opinion,
this proposition is based on "the naive and erroneous notion that moral law
is made up of an interdependent (as differentiated from interrelated) set of
norms possessing the stability of a row of dominoes or a house of cards:
knock one down and all the rest come tumbling after."[147] One year later
Daniel Callahan drew attention to the uniqueness of the abortion situation
where, in his analysis, we are dealing with *potential* human life. Therefore
we cannot justifiably extrapolate from attitudes towards fetal life attitudes
towards *actualized, existing* human life. Moreover, for the socio-
psychological argument to be valid it has to be *proved* that a policy of
abortion on demand poses a threat to extrauterine human life. But in

Callahan's observation there is no evidence from countries where the law has been liberalized that such statutes imperil the lives of those that have been born.[148]

In this context it is interesting to note the admission by many Catholic authors that, while contemporary society certainly favors abortion on demand, there is no question of a general disregard for human life in the world today. On the contrary, the authors find substantial evidence that modern man treasures human life and seeks to enhance its quality wherever he can. We witness an almost universal desire for peace, for disarmament, for an effective international agency for peaceful mediation. The death penalty is now widely questioned as too severe a punishment for even the most serious crimes. Society appreciates and supports the efforts of scientists and doctors to relieve pain and to extend life, efforts which even involve heart transplants. Great attempts are being made all around the globe to improve the human condition, not only in the area of physical and mental health but also from a social and economic point of view.[149] It is clear that any "slippery slope" arguments will have to account for this massive social affirmation of life which is as manifest in contemporary society as is the effort to liberalize abortion laws. One cannot really state without further qualifications that abortion liberalization will inevitably lead to a legalization of other forms of arbitrary killing and to widespread moral decay. Abortion and infanticide are not necessarily ideological twins.

Callahan has warned against another oversimplification. He admits that a relaxation of the law will lead to a sustained and continuing rise in the number of legal abortions, and that not all of this increase is due to a shift from the illegal to the legal sector. Under a permissive statute more women will make a choice in favor of abortion; they will feel that the moral bias against the intervention has disappeared and that society now approves and supports their decision. However, it would not be correct to attribute the increase in the number of abortions solely to the fact that the law has become more permissive.[150] Callahan explains that it is the growing social acceptance of abortion which causes the laws to be relaxed in the first place:

> It is very rare for laws to be changed solely out of a concern for procedural questions of freedom and due process. They are usually changed because of a shift in the thinking or the attitudes of the public toward the substantive issues at stake. Laws are rarely passed, changed or repealed independently of public opinion; on the contrary, the changes they undergo will reflect that opinion to a considerable degree. This will be true of abortion laws as well.[151]

It is correct to say that the introduction of permissive statutes will increase the total number of abortions, but one must add that it is the increased public acceptability of abortion which led to the change in the laws. [152]

The Liberationist Motivation and the Social Justice Solution

There is another theme which emerges in the Catholic contributions to the debate on abortion legislation. We found it repeatedly suggested that many decisions to terminate a pregnancy are inspired by selfishness or expediency, and I have presented a whole list of inferior or immoral motives which are attributed to the proponents of abortion reform. However, not all Catholic authors support these allegations and some have offered corrections on this point. Callahan states that the success of the liberalization movement is due to one central fact: that many couples in many different parts of the world want to have fewer children than their ancestors had. When that decision has been taken and when effective methods of contraception are not available, people turn to abortion as a means of birth control. [153]

In Callahan's view, one cannot justifiably qualify the abortion liberation movement as a massive genocidal plot or present it as the ultimate proof of the decadence of contemporary society. Such statements ignore the motives of those couples who choose abortion out of a sense of responsibility to their living children. Nor do these accusations do justice to the intentions of those who seek to affirm the right of women to control their own lives—a lofty goal. [154] William E. May also believes that many advocates of liberalization are motivated by a genuine concern for human welfare. They accept the destruction of fetal life not for the sake of sheer destruction but because frequently this loss of life provides a solution to real human needs, securing authentic individual and social goods, as it does in cases where the continuation of the pregnancy would adversely affect the physical or mental health of the mother, or the socio-economic or psychological well-being of the family. [155] The American bishops have repeatedly expressed their appreciation of the very tragic conditions that can surround an unwanted pregnancy, of the pressures which may drive a woman to consider having an abortion, of the fear, the loneliness, the despair, which may make abortion seem the only solution. [156] Nor do the bishops wish to impute evil motives to those who seek to justify abortion at a legal level. Cardinal Terence Cooke said in 1976:

> Let me begin by expressing respect for those who in good faith oppose the conviction which we have concerning the evil of abortion. It is not my intention to question their sincerity. Indeed, I share the concern of many

of them for the poor and the underprivileged, for those who feel the stab
of hunger's pain, for those ravaged by war, for those who will never see
the inside of a school or explore the wonders in the pages of a book. With
you and with all my fellow Americans, I dream of a better world and I
wish to share in building it. [157]

But the Cardinal adds that in his conviction the way of abortion is not the
path to this better world. [158] Nor does David Granfield accuse the reform
movement of wickedness or cruelty or insensitivity, and he recognizes that
in the ranks of those who promote liberal abortion there are many men and
women who are acutely aware of the sufferings of mankind. But they have
grown so sensitive to the pain and hardship of their neighbors that they are
willing to pay any price to overcome the world's distress, even the price of
killing members of the very community they are so determined to assist.
Thus they betray their finest ideals. [159] In this perspective the liberationist
proposition is no longer a devilish genocidal plot but rather a "tragic
inconsistency" [160] or, in the words of the American bishops, "a tragic error
which cries out for correction." [161]

The Catholic argument clearly recognizes that there is no simple solution
to the abortion problem and that apologetics alone will not solve it. Consequently, while the Catholic Church insists on the maintenance of the traditional restrictive statutes, it equally emphasizes the need for social reform
measures. It proposes to identify the underlying causes of the abortion
phenomenon through a critical analysis of society and to cure the evil at its
source through education and social action. These insights represent a
significant development in Catholic thinking on the termination of pregnancy. As I mentioned in Chapter VI, the traditional manuals did not refer
in any way at all to this aspect of law enactment and law enforcement.

No one will deny that the remedies which have been suggested are valid
and useful. A consistent and wide implementation of these proposals will
undoubtedly help to reduce the demand for abortion and to modify the
dimensions of the problem. At the same time it would be naïve to assume
that these initiatives will be realized overnight — if ever they are realized at
all. Thus the "social solution" does not provide an answer for those who,
right now, find themselves in conditions in which they can see no alternative but abortion. Callahan draws attention to another limitation of the
social argument. He states that to attribute the abortion problem solely to
the social and economic injustice prevailing in society is to ignore two
facts. Firstly, there are many women who choose abortion not because of
social or economic pressure but simply because they want to shape and live
a life of their own, not dominated by unwanted children or upset by
unplanned pregnancies. Secondly, there is the reality of contraceptive fail-

ure which can and does occur irrespectively of economic or social circumstances. Until such time as the perfect contraceptive is universally and
perfectly used, a good number of women, against their intentions, will
become pregnant.[162]

It is only realistic to say that the abortion problem will be with us for a
long time to come and that women will continue to demand abortions.
These they will get—legally if the statutes are liberalized, illegally if they
are not. However, the social argument is not invalidated by its limitations.
Its basic thesis is perfectly sound: abortion must be treated with action
rather than with rhetoric. Even if the laws are liberalized the battle has not
been lost, and there is much that can still be achieved for unborn children—
and for their parents. But, as Grisez observed, this requires intelligence,
work, and sacrifice.[163] Discipleship here, as everywhere, is costly.

We have seen that some authors want to include in the list of social
desiderata a more open policy on the part of the Catholic Church towards
contraception and even sterilization. It is important to note that this particular suggestion cannot be considered an element in the "official" position.
Pope Paul VI forbade the use of any artificial method of birth control in his
1968 Encyclical Letter *Humanae Vitae,* and the American hierarchy supported this prohibition in their collective pastoral letter *Human Life in Our
Day,* which was published a few months after the papal pronouncement.[164]
I will return to this issue in my final chapter.

One could argue, I think, that the American Catholic statement of the
case against abortion liberalization is not altogether free from oversimplifications, amateur psychologizing, and *ad hominem* argumentation. It
would be possible to indicate other flaws. For instance, it is rather odd that
the Catholic proposition minimizes the medical sequelae of clandestine
abortions but makes the most of the negative physiological and psychological effects of legal interventions. But such a critique merely affects a
number of peripheral arguments and does not really touch the core of the
Catholic position: that abortion kills an innocent human being and that the
law must protect the right to life of all citizens.

NOTES

¹ Norman St. John-Stevas, "Abortion Laws," *Commonweal* 85 (1966), pp. 164-165. Julian R. Pleasants also advocated a more pragmatic approach and urged Catholics to find the basis for a political consensus in a "morality of consequences"; "A Morality of Consequences," *Commonweal* 86 (1967), pp. 415-416. See also: Thomas A. Wassmer, S.J., *Christian Ethics for Today* (Milwaukee: Bruce, 1969), p. 196.

² David Granfield, *The Abortion Decision* (revised ed.; Garden City, N.Y.: Doubleday Image Books, 1971), p. 164.

³ John M. Finnis, "Three Schemes of Regulation," in John T. Noonan, Jr. (ed.), *The Morality of Abortion: Legal and Historical Perspectives* (Cambridge, Mass.: Harvard University Press, 1970), pp. 200-202, 207; Rudolph J. Gerber, "Abortion: Parameters for Decision," *International Philosophical Quarterly* 11 (1971), p. 578; Bishops of New Jersey, "Pastoral Letter on Abortion—March, 1970," in Daughters of St. Paul, *Yes to Life* (Boston: St. Paul Editions, 1977), p. 213; Bishops of Pennsylvania, "Declaration on Abortion—September, 1970," *ibid.*, p. 217; Cardinal Shehan, "Pastoral Letter on Abortion," *Catholic Mind* 69, March 1971, p. 10.

⁴ Karen A. Lebacqz, "Prenatal Diagnosis and Selective Abortion," *Linacre Quarterly* 40 (1973), pp. 126-127; Norbert J. Rigali, S.J., "Catholics and Liberalized Abortion Laws," *Catholic World* 213 (1971), p. 284; Bishops of Illinois, "Statement on Abortion—March 20, 1969," in Daughters of St. Paul, *op. cit.,* p. 203; Bishops of Pennsylvania, *op. cit.,* p. 216.

⁵ National Conference of Catholic Bishops, "Statement on Abortion—April, 1970," in Daughters of St. Paul, *op. cit.,* p. 214; Bishops of Pennsylvania, *op. cit.,* pp. 216, 217; Bishops of New Jersey, *op. cit.,* pp. 212-213.

⁶ Norman St. John-Stevas, "The Tragic Results of Abortion in England," *Linacre Quarterly* 39 (1972), pp. 32-33; Andre E. Hellegers, "Law and the Common Good," *Commonweal* 86 (1967), pp. 422-423; Germain G. Grisez, *Abortion: The Myths, the Realities, and the Arguments* (New York: Corpus Books, 1970), pp. 253-256, 263; Finnis, *op. cit.,* pp. 180-184; National Conference of Catholic Bishops, *op. cit.,* p. 214. See also: Daniel Callahan, *Abortion: Law, Choice and Morality* (New York: Macmillan, 1970), pp. 501-502.

⁷ Frank J. Ayd, Jr., "Liberal Abortion Laws," *America* 120 (1969), pp. 130, 132; Edward J. Lauth, Jr., "Liberal Abortion Laws: The Antithesis of the Practice of Medicine," *Linacre Quarterly* 34 (1967), p. 373; Robert M. Byrn, "Abortion-on-Demand: Whose Morality?" *Notre Dame Lawyer* 46 (1970), pp. 29, 31; Bishops of Illinois, *op. cit.,* pp. 208-209; "U.S. Bishops Protest Program against 'Right to Life'," in Daughters of St. Paul, *op. cit.,* pp. 219-220.

⁸ St. John-Stevas, "The Tragic Results of Abortion in England," *op. cit.,* p. 31; Paul J. Weber, "Perverse Observations on Abortion," *Catholic World* 212 (1970), p. 77; Rudolph J. Gerber, "Abortion: Two Opposing Legal Philosophies," *American Journal of Jurisprudence* 15 (1970), pp. 21, 23-24; Richard A. McCormick, S.J., "Abortion," *America* 112 (1965), p. 878; Bishops of New York State, "Declaration on Abortion—December 2, 1970," in Daughters of St. Paul, *op. cit.,* p. 222; Bishops of Missouri, "Statement on Abortion—December, 1970," *ibid.*, p. 227. On euthanasia of defective newborns, see: National Conference of Catholic Bishops, United States Catholic Conference, *Documentation on Abortion and the Right to Life II* (Washington, D.C.: Publications Office USCC, 1976), pp. 19-20; Bishops' Committee for

Pro-Life Activities, National Conference of Catholic Bishops, *Respect Life! The 1976 Respect Life Handbook* (Washington, D.C.: Respect Life Committee NCCB, 1976), p. 19.

⁹ *Documentation on Abortion and the Right to Life II*, *op. cit.*, pp. 16-18; Bishops' Committee for Pro-Life Activities, National Conference of Catholic Bishops, *op. cit.*, p. 19. However, this committee allows *some* research under appropriate circumstances on infants and fetuses in need of exceptional but risky therapy, and also on dead infants and fetuses in order to seek ways of overcoming the diseases which killed them; *ibid.*, p. 19.

¹⁰ Robert M. Byrn, "Demythologizing Abortion Reform," *Catholic Lawyer* 14 (1968), pp. 186-187; Russell Shaw, *Abortion on Trial* (Dayton, Ohio: Pflaum, 1968), p. 131; Pleasants, *op. cit.*, p. 416; Grisez, *op. cit.*, p. 450; Bishops of New York State, "Declaration on Abortion—March 19, 1970," in Daughters of St. Paul, *op. cit.*, p. 210.

¹¹ Ayd, *op. cit.*, p. 131.

¹² Frank J. Ayd, Jr., "Liberal Abortion Laws: A Psychiatrist's View," *American Ecclesiastical Review* 158 (1968), pp. 83, 90; Grisez, *op. cit.*, pp. 256, 261-263. See also: Callahan, *op. cit.*, pp. 289-291, 501-502; *id.*, "Abortion: Thinking and Experiencing," *Christianity and Crisis* 32 (1973), p. 297.

¹³ Lebacqz, *op. cit.*, p. 126; Ayd, "Liberal Abortion Laws: A Psychiatrist's View," *op. cit.*, p. 90; Editorial, "Public Policy and Abortion Laws," *America* 120 (1969), p. 239; Lauth, *op. cit.*, p. 371; Grisez, *op. cit.*, p. 96.

¹⁴ St. John-Stevas, "The Tragic Results of Abortion in England," *op. cit.*, p. 33; Robert J. Henle, S.J., "Georgetown University Statement on Abortion," *Catholic Mind* 71, September 1973, p. 10; Byrn, "Demythologizing Abortion Reform," *op. cit.*, p. 186; Grisez, *op. cit.*, pp. 86-87.

¹⁵ Ayd, "Liberal Abortion Laws: A Psychiatrist's View," *op. cit.*, pp. 78-79, 90; Editorial, "Abortion and Mental Health," *America* 116 (1967), p. 239; Finnis, *op. cit.*, p. 192.

¹⁶ James A. Fitzgerald, "Abortion on Demand," *Linacre Quarterly* 37 (1970), p. 187; Paul V. Harrington, "Human Life and Abortion," *Catholic Lawyer* 17 (1971), p. 29; Thomas A. Lane, "Population and the Crisis of Culture," *Homiletic and Pastoral Review* 75, April 1975, p. 64.

¹⁷ Harrington, *op. cit.*, pp. 29, 30; Byrn, "Abortion-on-Demand: Whose Morality?" *op. cit.*, p. 33.

¹⁸ Ayd, "Liberal Abortion Laws: A Psychiatrist's View," *op. cit.*, pp. 80-81; Paul Marx, O.S.B., *The Death Peddlers: War on the Unborn* (Collegeville, Minn.: St. John's University Press, 1971), pp. 12-14; Harrington, *op. cit.*, p. 29.

¹⁹ Harrington, *op. cit.*, p. 29; St. John-Stevas, "The Tragic Results of Abortion in England," *op. cit.*, p. 33; Fitzgerald, *op. cit.*, p. 188; James V. McNulty, "The Therapeutic Abortion Law: A Fight for Life," *Linacre Quarterly* 33 (1966), pp. 341-342; Bishops of New York State, "Declaration on Abortion—December 2, 1970," *op. cit.*, p. 222.

²⁰ Harrington, *op. cit.*, pp. 25, 29; Finnis, *op. cit.*, p. 202; Richard P. Vaughan, S.J., "Abortion and the Law," *Homiletic and Pastoral Review* 66 (1966), p. 647; Ayd, "Liberal Abortion Laws: A Psychiatrist's View," *op. cit.*, p. 90; Grisez, *op. cit.*, pp. 196-200, 253-254, 256. In Callahan's analysis, such declining birth rates cannot be attributed solely to abortion liberalization. Moderate and permissive codes did not

initiate this decline: they merely confirmed and accelerated an already existing trend which had been brought about by a variety of other factors; *Abortion: Law, Choice and Morality, op. cit.,* pp. 291-292.

[21] Walter R. Trinkaus *et al.,* "Abortion Legislation and the Establishment Clause," *Catholic Lawyer* 15 (1969), pp. 117-121; Grisez, *op. cit,* pp. 77-81.

[22] Ayd, "Liberal Abortion Laws," *op. cit.,* p. 130; Grisez, *op. cit.,* pp. 75-76; David W. Louisell and John T. Noonan, Jr., "Constitutional Balance," in Noonan, *op. cit.,* pp. 230-231.

[23] Fitzgerald, *op. cit.,* p. 184; Lauth, *op. cit.,* p. 371; John T. Noonan, Jr., "Responding to Persons: Methods of Moral Argument in Debate over Abortion," *Theology Digest* 21 (1973), p. 294. Granfield discusses the incidence of rape-induced pregnancy and concludes that it is very small. He suggests that a traditional statute which allows abortion to preserve maternal health could take care of this category; *op. cit.,* pp. 106-108. On the legal complexities of the rape and incest provisions of moderately liberal codes, see: *ibid.,* pp. 182-187.

[24] Donald DeMarco, *Abortion in Perspective: The Rose Palace or the Fiery Dragon?* (Cincinnati: Hiltz & Hayes, 1974), pp. 86-88. DeMarco's legal argument follows logically from his moral position which I presented in Chapter III, note 111.

[25] St. John-Stevas, "Abortion Laws," *op. cit.,* p. 165.

[26] Lauth, *op. cit.,* pp. 367, 371.

[27] Weber, *op. cit.,* p. 75; Noonan, "Responding to Persons. . . .," *op. cit.,* pp. 293-295.

[28] Richard Stith, "A Secular Case Against Abortion on Demand," *Commonweal* 95 (1971), pp. 152-153; Gary L. Chamberlain, "The Abortion Debate Is Revealing Our Values," *New Catholic World* 215 (1972), pp. 206-208; Joseph P. Witherspoon, "Impact of the Abortion Decisions upon the Father's Role," *Jurist* 35 (1975), pp. 32-65; DeMarco, *op. cit.,* pp. 72-75; National Conference of Catholic Bishops, "Statement on Abortion—April, 1970," *op. cit.,* pp. 214-215.

[29] Grisez, *op. cit.,* p. 446; Finnis, *op. cit.,* p. 204; Cardinal O'Boyle, "Pastoral Letter on Abortion," *Catholic Mind* 69, March 1971, p. 8.

[30] Grisez, *op. cit.,* p. 355; Joseph E. Hogan, C.M., "The Conscience of the Law," *Catholic Lawyer* 21 (1975), pp. 192-193. See also: Noonan, "Responding to Persons. . . .," *op. cit.,* p. 304.

[31] Stith, *op. cit.,* p. 153; Francis Canavan, S.J., "The Church's Right to Speak on Public Issues," *Catholic Mind* 65, April 1967, pp. 14-15; Rigali, *op. cit.,* pp. 284-285; Harrington, *op. cit.,* p. 11.

[32] Grisez, *op. cit.,* pp. 347-348.

[33] Hogan, *op. cit.,* p. 192; DeMarco, *op. cit.,* p. 164; Clare Boothe Luce, "Two Books on Abortion and the Questions They Raise," *National Review* 23 (1971), p. 30; National Conference of Catholic Bishops, United States Catholic Conference, *Documentation on the Right to Life and Abortion* (Washington, D.C.: Publications Office USCC, 1974), pp. 36-37. Grisez concurs with this argument but states that there are matters of religious doctrine and ritual, such as Sunday observance, which cannot be translated into State law; *op. cit.,* pp. 353-354, 360-361.

[34] Robert M. Byrn, "Abortion: The Future in America," *America* 117 (1967), pp. 712-713; Grisez, *op. cit.,* pp. 348-353; Rigali, *op. cit.,* pp. 283-284; Bishops of Maryland, "Statement on Abortion—January 27, 1971," in Daughters of St. Paul, *op. cit.,* pp. 229-230; "Testimony of United States Catholic Conference on Constitutional Amendments Protecting Unborn Human Life before the Subcommittee on Civil

and Constitutional Rights of the House Committee on the Judiciary—March 24, 1976," in *Documentation on Abortion and the Right to Life II, op. cit.,* p. 23; "Statement of Archbishop Joseph L. Bernardin," *ibid.,* pp. 38-39, 40.

[35] Hellegers, *op. cit.,* p. 421; Robert M. Byrn, "The Abortion Question: A Nonsectarian Approach," *Catholic Lawyer* 11 (1965), p. 322; Trinkaus *et al., op. cit.,* pp. 109-110; Grisez, *op. cit.,* pp. 347, 353-354, 360, 437; Bishops' Committee for Pro-Life Activities, National Conference of Catholic Bishops, *op. cit.,* p. 16; "Testimony of United States Catholic Conference....," *op. cit.,* pp. 24, 25-26; "Statement of Archbishop Joseph L. Bernardin," *op. cit.,* pp. 38-39.

[36] James J. Diamond, "Abortion, Animation, and Biological Hominization," *Theological Studies* 36 (1975), pp. 306-307.

[37] Trinkaus *et. al., op. cit.,* p. 116; Rigali, *op. cit.,* pp. 284-285; Hogan, *op. cit.,* p. 192; Albert Broderick, O.P., "A Constitutional Lawyer Looks at the *Roe-Doe* Decisions," *Jurist* 33 (1973), pp. 123-133; "Testimony of United States Catholic Conference....," *op. cit.,* pp. 25-27; Joseph M. Boyle, "That the Fetus Should Be Considered a Legal Person," *American Journal of Jurisprudence* 24 (1979), pp. 63, 69-71.

[38] Trinkaus *et al., op. cit.,* p. 114; Louisell and Noonan, *op. cit.,* p. 251; Gary M. Atkinson, "The Morality of Abortion," *International Philosophical Quarterly* 14 (1974), pp. 360-362; Bishops of Maryland, *op. cit.,* pp. 229-230.

[39] Stith, *op. cit.,* p. 153.

[40] Eugene F. Diamond, "The Physician and the Rights of the Unborn," *Linacre Quarterly* 34 (1967), p. 180; Ayd, "Liberal Abortion Laws: A Psychiatrist's View," *op. cit.,* p. 83; Rigali, *op. cit.,* p. 284.

[41] John T. Noonan, Jr., "Amendment of the Abortion Law: Relevant Data and Judicial Opinion," *Catholic Lawyer* 15 (1969), p. 132.

[42] Noonan, "Responding to Persons....," *op. cit.,* p. 304.

[43] Granfield, *op. cit.,* pp. 167, 168.

[44] Grisez, *op. cit.,* p. 447.

[45] Noonan, "Amendment of the Abortion Law....," *op. cit.,* pp. 132-133; Louisell and Noonan, *op. cit.,* pp. 241-244; Granfield, *op. cit.,* pp. 167-168; Finnis, *op. cit.,* pp. 179-180, 182; Charles P. Kindregan, *Abortion, the Law, and Defective Children: A Legal-Medical Study* (Washington: Corpus Books, 1969), p. 6; Grisez, *op. cit.,* p. 447.

[46] Granfield, *op. cit.,* pp. 169-170; Finnis, *op. cit.,* pp. 184, 203.

[47] Hellegers, *op. cit.,* p. 421; St. John-Stevas, "The Tragic Results of Abortion in England," *op. cit.,* p. 34; Louisell and Noonan, *op. cit.,* pp. 236-237; Robert M. Byrn, "The Abortion Amendments: Policy in the Light of Precedent," *Saint Louis University Law Journal* 18 (1974), pp. 399-400; Grisez, *op. cit.,* p. 436. Writing in 1970, Grisez admits that the private services of hospitals perform many more abortions than the ward services but he observes that abortion is related to status-striving and is therefore less sought by the poorer classes. Thus a major reason for the lower incidence of "therapeutic" abortion in this group is a lower demand for the intervention. Moreover, the "discrimination" suffered by the poor patient in abortion services is related to a much wider pattern of real discrimination. Grisez adds that since abortion is rarely necessary from a medical point of view, ward patients will find it more difficult to have this unnecessary operation than will private patients who generally get what they want because they can pay for it; *ibid.,* pp. 76-77, 436. Callahan presents similar observations but insists that restrictive laws are *de facto* discriminatory; *Abortion: Law, Choice and Morality, op. cit.,* pp. 130, 136-139, 289.

[48] Grisez, *op. cit.*, p. 76.

[49] Louisell and Noonan, *op. cit.*, p. 240; Grisez, *op. cit.*, p. 435; Dennis J. Horan *et al.*, "The Legal Case for the Unborn Child," in Thomas W. Hilgers and Dennis J. Horan (eds.), *Abortion and Social Justice* (New York: Sheed and Ward, 1972), pp. 118-119. Finnis admits that some restrictive codes lack the necessary precision and are inconsistently applied by police and prosecutors; *op. cit.*, p. 196.

[50] Lauth, *op. cit.*, pp. 368-369; Grisez, *op. cit.*, pp. 435, 436, 449; Louisell and Noonan, *op. cit.*, pp. 230-231, 239-240; Horan *et al.*, *op. cit.*, p. 119.

[51] Grisez, *op. cit.*, p. 435.

[52] *Ibid.*, p. 435. For an explanation of "unconstitutional vagueness," see: Louisell and Noonan, *op. cit.*, pp. 237-239; Horan *et al.*, *op cit.*, pp. 117-119.

[53] Hellegers, *op. cit.*, p. 421; Lauth, *op. cit.*, p. 369.

[54] Byrn, "The Abortion Amendments: Policy in the Light of Precedent," *op. cit.*, p. 404.

[55] Byrn, "Abortion-on-Demand: Whose Morality?" *op. cit.*, pp. 23, 24.

[56] *Ibid.*, p. 24; Grisez, *op. cit.*, p. 449.

[57] Eugene F. Diamond, "The Humanity of the Unborn Child," *Catholic Lawyer* 17 (1971), p. 179; Byrn, "The Abortion Amendments....," *op. cit.*, p. 404; DeMarco, *op. cit.*, p. 164.

[58] Byrn, "Abortion-on-Demand: Whose Morality?" *op. cit.*, p. 23; Finnis, *op. cit.*, p. 195.

[59] Grisez, *op. cit.*, pp. 449-450; Eugene F. Diamond, "Who Speaks for the Fetus?" *Linacre Quarterly* 36 (1969), p. 61.

[60] Lauth, *op. cit.*, p. 369; Hellegers, *op. cit.*, p. 419.

[61] Lauth, *op. cit.*, pp. 368-369; Grisez, *op. cit.*, p. 449. Callahan accepts that restrictive statutes are hypocritical: they are openly violated in numerous hospitals but the authorities show little interest in prosecution; *Abortion: Law, Choice and Morality, op. cit.*, pp. 138-139.

[62] Finnis, *op. cit.*, pp. 190-191.

[63] *Ibid.*, pp. 194-195.

[64] The 1973 Supreme Court decision upheld a woman's right to abort her child on the ground that her right to privacy takes precedence over the child's right to life. See David Granfield, "The Legal Impact of the *Roe* and *Doe* Decisions," *Jurist* 33 (1973), pp. 113-122.

[65] St. John-Stevas, "The Tragic Results of Abortion in England," *op. cit.*, p. 35; Louisell and Noonan, *op. cit.*, pp. 235-236; Horan *et al.*, *op. cit.*, pp. 107-109; Byrn, "Abortion-on-Demand: Whose Morality?" *op. cit.*, pp. 19-22; National Conference of Catholic Bishops, "Statement on Abortion—April, 1970," *op. cit.*, p. 214; Bishops of Pennsylvania, *op. cit.*, p. 218.

[66] DeMarco, *op. cit.*, pp. 7-10, 13-15, 118-121; Richard A. McCormick, S.J., "Notes on Moral Theology: The Abortion Dossier," *Theological Studies* 35 (1974), p. 317; Bishops' Committee for Pro-Life Activities, National Conference of Catholic Bishops, *op. cit.*, p. 19. Callahan also concludes that the rights of women are not the sole rights at issue in abortion decisions; *Abortion: Law, Choice and Morality, op. cit.*, pp. 460-468.

[67] Chamberlain, *op. cit.*, p. 206.

[68] Ayd, "Liberal Abortion Laws," *op. cit.*, p. 130; DeMarco, *op. cit.*, p. 163; Gary D. Glenn, "Abortion and Inalienable Rights in Classical Liberalism," *American Journal of Jurisprudence* 20 (1975), pp. 62-80; Atkinson, *op. cit.*, pp. 352-353.

[69] Trinkaus *et al.*, *op. cit.*, p. 113.

[70] David W. Louisell and Charles Carroll, "The Father as Non-Parent," *Catholic World* 210 (1969), pp. 109-110; DeMarco, *op. cit.*, p. 164; Witherspoon, *op. cit.*, pp. 32-65; "Pastoral Message of the Administrative Committee, National Conference of Catholic Bishops—February 13, 1973," in Daughters of St. Paul, *op. cit.*, p. 263.

[71] Grisez, *op. cit.*, pp. 450-451. See also: Callahan, "Abortion: Thinking and Experiencing," *op. cit.*, p. 297.

[72] Lauth, *op. cit.*, pp. 369-370; Hellegers, *op. cit.*, pp. 421-422; Louisell and Noonan, *op. cit.*, pp. 231-232, 241-243; Grisez, *op. cit.*, pp. 35-42, 67-72; "Testimony of United States Catholic Conference....," *op. cit.*, p. 9. In Callahan's analysis, the data on illegal abortions lack any real accuracy and do not enable either side in the debate to make a solid case. However, even if the lowest estimates are closest to the truth, they still are figures worthy of considerable concern; *Abortion: Law, Choice and Morality, op. cit.*, pp. 132-136. See also: Kindregan, *op. cit.*, pp. 1-2.

[73] Diamond, "Who Speaks for the Fetus?" *op. cit.*, p. 61; Ayd, "Liberal Abortion Laws: A Psychiatrist's View," *op. cit.*, pp. 84-85; Grisez, *op. cit.*, pp. 48-51, 67-72; "Testimony of United States Catholic Conference....," *op. cit.*, p. 10.

[74] Hellegers, *op. cit.*, pp. 422-423; Diamond, "The Physician and the Rights of the Unborn," *op. cit.*, pp. 179-180; Robert M. Byrn, "Abortion: A Legal View," *Commonweal* 85 (1967), p. 680; Bishops' Committee for Pro-Life Activities, National Conference of Catholic Bishops, *op. cit.*, p. 17; "Testimony of United States Catholic Conference....," *op. cit.*, p. 9.

[75] St. John-Stevas, "The Tragic Results of Abortion in England," *op. cit.*, p. 35; Grisez, *op. cit.*, pp. 263, 450; Finnis, *op. cit.*, pp. 182-184, 202; Bishops' Committee for Pro-Life Activities, National Conference of Catholic Bishops, *op. cit.*, pp. 17-18; "Testimony of United States Catholic Conference....," *op. cit.*, pp. 9-10.

[76] Ayd, "Liberal Abortion Laws: A Psychiatrist's View," *op. cit.*, pp. 81-83; id., "Liberal Abortion Laws," *op. cit.*, p. 131; Fitzgerald, *op. cit.*, pp. 185, 186-187; Hellegers, *op. cit.*, p. 423; DeMarco, *op. cit.*, pp. 46-50; Thomas W. Hilgers, "The Medical Hazards of Legally Induced Abortion," in Hilgers and Horan (eds.), *op. cit.*, pp. 57-75; "Testimony of United States Catholic Conference....," *op. cit.*, pp. 14-15.

[77] Diamond, "The Physician and the Rights of the Unborn," *op. cit.*, p. 178; Richard R. Romanowski, "Abortion—A Fetal Viewpoint," *Linacre Quarterly* 34 (1967), p. 280; DeMarco, *op. cit.*, p. 48; Hilgers, *op. cit.*, pp. 75-77. Noonan points out that the trauma and sense of guilt which have been found associated with abortion could be due to social conditioning or personal predispositions; "Responding to Persons....," *op. cit.*, p. 304. Callahan admits that there is an element of medical risk in the abortion procedure but considers that the risks are not unacceptable if the abortion is necessary or desirable. He is less definite about the psychiatric sequelae; *Abortion: Law, Choice and Morality, op. cit.*, pp. 42-43, 67-75. See also: Kindregan, *op. cit.*, p. 3.

[78] Denis Cavanagh, "Legalized Abortion: The Conscience Clause and Coercion," *Hospital Progress* 52, August 1971, p. 86; Grisez, *op. cit.*, pp. 76-77, 436; Bishops of Illinois, *op. cit.*, p. 208. See also: Callahan, "Abortion: Thinking and Experiencing," *op. cit.*, p. 297.

[79] Diamond, "The Physician and the Rights of the Unborn," *op. cit.*, p. 180.

[80] Stith, *op. cit.*, p. 154; Byrn, "The Abortion Amendments....," *op. cit.*, p. 398; Bishops' Committee for Pro-Life Activities, National Conference of Catholic Bishops, *op. cit.*, p. 20.

[81] Granfield, *The Abortion Decision, op. cit.*, pp. 113-114; Byrn, "The Abortion Amendments....," *op. cit.*, p. 401.

[82] Byrn, "The Abortion Amendments....," *op. cit.*, pp. 397, 399-400; *id.*, "Abortion-on-Demand: Whose Morality?" *op. cit.*, p. 26; DeMarco, *op. cit.*, pp. 17-20, 82-84, 139; "Testimony of United States Catholic Conference....," *op. cit.*, p. 15.

[83] Finnis, *op. cit.*, p. 207; Byrn, "The Abortion Amendments....," *op. cit.*, p. 400; DeMarco, *op. cit.*, pp. 29-33; Chamberlain, *op. cit.*, pp. 207-208; Patrick J. Coffey, "Toward a Sound Moral Policy on Abortion," *New Scholasticism* 47 (1973), p. 112; Edward J. Ryle, "Some Sociological and Psychological Reflections on the Abortion Decisions," *Jurist* 33 (1973), p. 229; "Testimony of United States Catholic Conference....," *op. cit.*, pp. 11, 15-16.

[84] Byrn, "Abortion: The Future in America," *op. cit.*, p. 711; McNulty, *op. cit.*, pp. 340-341; Finnis, *op. cit.*, pp. 190-191.

[85] Byrn, "Abortion: The Future in America," *op. cit.*, p. 711.

[86] Gordon C. Zahn, "A Religious Pacifist Looks at Abortion," *Commonweal* 94 (1971), pp. 280-281; James J. Diamond, "Humanizing the Abortion Debate," *America* 121 (1969), pp. 37, 38. The relevance of viability was discussed in Chapter III.

[87] Thomas J. O'Donnell, S.J., "Current Medical-Moral Comment: Contrasts," *Linacre Quarterly* 35 (1968), p. 35; Diamond, "Humanizing the Abortion Debate," *op. cit.*, p. 38; Gerber, "Abortion: Parameters for Decision," *op. cit.*, p. 562.

[88] Gerber, "Abortion: Two Opposing Legal Philosophies," *op. cit.*, p. 13; Grisez, *op. cit.*, pp. 448-449.

[89] Trinkaus *et al.*, *op. cit.*, p. 117; Zahn, *op. cit.*, p. 281; Atkinson, *op. cit.*, p. 355; Harrington, *op. cit.*, p. 44; DeMarco, *op. cit.*, pp. 105-110.

[90] Atkinson, *op. cit.*, pp. 354-355.

[91] *Ibid.*, p. 355.

[92] *Ibid.*, p. 355.

[93] Zahn, *op. cit.*, p. 281; Louisell and Noonan, *op. cit.*, p. 236.

[94] Atkinson, *op. cit.*, p. 355.

[95] Ayd, "Liberal Abortion Laws: A Psychiatrist's View," *op. cit.*, p. 86; Diamond, "Who Speaks for the Fetus?" *op. cit.*, pp. 60-61; DeMarco, *op. cit.*, pp. 160-161.

[96] Marx, *op. cit.*, p. 183; Harrington, *op. cit.*, p. 43. See also: Callahan, "Abortion: Thinking and Experiencing," *op. cit.*, pp. 297, 298. Grisez suggests that the availability of legal abortion will result in larger numbers of unwanted children; *op. cit.*, p. 450. William E. May points out that many children, desperately wanted by their parents before conception and during pregnancy, become unwanted after birth for a variety of reasons. Even if some unwanted children are aborted, it does not follow that all born children will be wanted; "Abortion as Indicative of Personal and Social Identity," *Jurist* 33 (1973), p. 207. Callahan carefully evaluates the unwanted child argument and discovers a number of inconsistencies and ambiguities; *Abortion: Law, Choice and Morality, op. cit.*, pp. 451-460.

[97] Ayd, "Liberal Abortion Laws: A Psychiatrist's View," *op. cit.*, pp. 90-91; *id.*, "Liberal Abortion Laws," *op. cit.*, pp. 130, 131; William J. Tobin, "Ethical and Moral Considerations concerning Abortion," *Homiletic and Pastoral Review* 68 (1967), p. 55; DeMarco, *op. cit.*, pp. 133-135. Gary L. Chamberlain remarks that even Hitler could be said to have been concerned with the quality of (Aryan) life; *op. cit.*, p. 207. See also: Harrington, *op. cit.*, pp. 41-43.

[98] John T. Noonan, Jr., "Introduction," in Noonan (ed.), *op. cit.*, pp. xi-xvii; Stith, *op.*

cit., p. 154; Byrn, "Abortion-on-Demand: Whose Morality?" *op. cit.*, pp. 25, 26; Granfield, *op. cit.*, pp. 114-116; DeMarco, *op. cit.*, pp. 138, 139, 140-141; Mary C. Segers, "Abortion: The Last Resort," *America* 133 (1975), p. 457.

[99] Weber, *op. cit.*, pp. 74-75; St. John-Stevas, "The Tragic Results of Abortion in England," *op. cit.*, p. 35; DeMarco, *op. cit.*, pp. 80-81, 93-94, 113-117, 140; Walter Reinsdorf, "Occasional Homily: On Human Life," *Homiletic and Pastoral Review* 75, January 1975, p. 68; Richard Stith, "The World as Reality, as Resource, and as Pretense," *American Journal of Jurisprudence* 20 (1975), pp. 141-153; "Statement of Archbishop Joseph L. Bernardin," *op. cit.*, p. 39.

[100] Diamond, "Who Speaks for the Fetus?" *op. cit.*, p. 60; Chamberlain, *op. cit.*, p. 208; DeMarco, *op. cit.*, pp. 124-126, 133-135.

[101] Editorial, "Growing Consensus on Abortion," *America* 114 (1966), p. 219; Grisez, *op. cit.*, pp. 287-297; Marx, *op. cit.*, p. 182.

[102] Noonan, "Introduction," *op. cit.*, pp. xv-xvi; Marx, *op. cit.*, p. 182; Editorial, "Abortion Law Reform," *America* 112 (1965), p. 703; DeMarco, *op. cit.*, pp. 67-71, 141; Reinsdorf, *op. cit.*, p. 67.

[103] Grisez, *op. cit.*, p. 290; Ayd, "Liberal Abortion Laws," *op. cit.*, p. 131; Byrn, "Abortion: The Future in America," *op. cit.*, p. 711; Editorial, "The Abortion Debate," *Commonweal* 92 (1970), p. 132; Noonan, "Responding to Persons....," *op. cit.*, pp. 293-295.

[104] Paul V. Harrington, "Abortion—Part XV," *Linacre Quarterly* 37 (1970), p. 117; DeMarco, *op. cit.*, pp. 155-157; Bishops of Texas, "An Open Letter on Abortion—April, 1971," in Daughters of St. Paul, *op. cit.*, pp. 237-239.

[105] DeMarco, *op. cit.*, pp. 146-147, 171-172; Chamberlain, *op. cit.*, pp. 207, 208; Atkinson, *op. cit.*, p. 362; "Testimony of United States Catholic Conference on Constitutional Amendment Protecting Unborn Human Life before the Sub-Committee on Constitutional Amendments of the Senate Committee on the Judiciary—March 7, 1974," in *Documentation on the Right to Life and Abortion, op. cit.*, pp. 13-14. See also: Callahan, "Abortion: Thinking and Experiencing," *op. cit.*, p. 295. DeMarco presents a very sharp critique of the liberationist strategy and style; *op. cit.*, pp. 146-154.

[106] Grisez, *op. cit.*, p. 464.

[107] Granfield, *The Abortion Decision, op. cit.*, p. 199. See also: Indiana Catholic Conference, "Declaration on Abortion—December, 1972," in Daughters of St. Paul, *op. cit.*, p. 258.

[108] Granfield, *The Abortion Decision, op. cit.*, p. 199. See also: May, *op. cit.*, p. 216; Kevin D. O'Rourke, O.P., "Some Theological and Ethical Perspectives of the Teachings of the Catholic Church in Regard to Abortion," in Claude U. Broach (ed.), *Seminar on Abortion: The Proceedings of a Dialogue Between Catholics and Baptists* (Charlotte, N.C.: The Ecumenical Institute, 1975), p. 65; DeMarco, *op. cit.*, pp. 64-66; Bishops of Texas, *op. cit.*, p. 247.

[109] Archbishop Humberto S. Medeiros, "A Consistent Ethic of Life and the Law," *Catholic Mind* 70, May 1972, p. 38.

[110] *Ibid.*, p. 38. See also: DeMarco, *op. cit.*, pp. 100-104; Rigali, *op. cit.*, p. 284.

[111] Zahn, *op. cit.*, p. 282. See also: Chamberlain, *op. cit.*, p. 207; Medeiros, *op. cit.*, p. 42; Pleasants, *op. cit.*, p. 414.

[112] Zahn, *op. cit.*, p. 282.

[113] Medeiros, *op. cit.*, p. 37. See also: O'Rourke, *op. cit.*, pp. 65-66; Rigali, *op. cit.*, p.

284; Robert Edelstein *et al.*, "Moral Consistency and the Abortion Issue," *Commonweal* 100 (1974), pp. 59-61.

[114] Granfield, *The Abortion Decision*, *op. cit.*, p. 199.

[115] *Ibid.*, p. 202; Thomas W. Hilgers *et al.*, "Is Abortion the Best We Have to Offer?" in Hilgers and Horan (eds.), *op. cit.*, p. 190; Bishops of New Jersey, *op. cit.*, p. 213; "U.S. Bishops' New Pastoral Plan for Pro-Life Activities—November 20, 1975," in Daughters of St. Paul, *op. cit.*, p. 282.

[116] Granfield, *The Abortion Decision*, *op. cit.*, p. 202; Ryle, *op. cit.*, pp. 223-229. See also: Callahan, *Abortion: Law, Choice and Morality*, *op. cit.*, pp. 81-82.

[117] Granfield, *The Abortion Decision*, *op. cit.*, p. 203; Grisez, *op. cit.*, p. 464; Hilgers *et al.*, "Is Abortion the Best We Have to Offer?" *op. cit.*, pp. 182, 190-191; Kindregan, *op. cit.*, pp. 39-40; "U.S. Bishops' New Pastoral Plan....," *op. cit.*, p. 282.

[118] Granfield, *The Abortion Decision*, *op. cit.*, pp. 203-204; Grisez, *op. cit.*, p. 464; Kindregan, *op. cit.*, p. 40; Bishops of Illinois, *op. cit.*, p. 204; Bishops of New Jersey, *op. cit.*, p. 213.

[119] Granfield, *The Abortion Decision*, *op. cit.*, p. 204; Grisez, *op. cit.*, pp. 464-465; Chamberlain, *op. cit.*, p. 208; Kindregan, *op. cit.*, p. 40; Bishops of Illinois, *op. cit.*, p. 204.

[120] Granfield, *The Abortion Decision*, *op. cit.*, p. 204; Kindregan, *op. cit.*, p. 40; Hilgers *et al.*, "Is Abortion the Best We Have to Offer?" *op. cit.*, p. 182.

[121] Granfield, *The Abortion Decision*, *op. cit.*, p. 205.

[122] *Ibid.*, p. 205; Grisez, *op. cit.*, p. 464; Hilgers *et al.*, "Is Abortion the Best We Have to Offer?" *op. cit.*, p. 182; "U.S. Bishops' New Pastoral Plan....," *op. cit.*, p. 282.

[123] Granfield, *The Abortion Decision*, *op. cit.*, pp. 207-208; Stith, "A Secular Case Against Abortion on Demand," *op. cit.*, p. 153; Grisez, *op. cit.*, p. 465; Hilgers *et al.*, "Is Abortion the Best We Have to Offer?" *op. cit.*, pp. 182-185; Bishops of Illinois, *op. cit.*, p. 204; "U.S. Bishops' New Pastoral Plan....," *op. cit.*, p. 282.

[124] St. John-Stevas, "Abortion Laws," *op. cit.*, p. 166; Granfield, *The Abortion Decision*, *op. cit.*, pp. 205-208; Grisez, *op. cit.*, p. 465; Hilgers *et al.*, "Is Abortion the Best We Have to Offer?" *op. cit.*, pp. 182-184; Bishops of Illinois, *op. cit.*, p. 204; "U.S. Bishops' New Pastoral Plan....," *op. cit.*, p. 282.

[125] National Conference of Catholic Bishops, "Statement on Abortion," *op. cit.*, p. 215; Bishops of Maryland, *op. cit.*, pp. 230-231; "U.S. Bishops' New Pastoral Plan....," *op. cit.*, p. 282.

[126] Romanowski, *op. cit.*, p. 280; Diamond, "Humanizing the Abortion Debate," *op. cit.*, p. 39; Hilgers *et al.*, "Is Abortion the Best We have to Offer?" *op. cit.*, pp. 191-193; Bishops of New Jersey, *op. cit.*, p. 213.

[127] Romanowski, *op. cit.*, p. 280; Bishops of Illinois, *op. cit.*, p. 204.

[128] Romanowski, *op. cit.*, p. 280.

[129] Diamond, "Humanizing the Abortion Debate," *op. cit.*, p. 39.

[130] *Ibid.*, p. 39; Hilgers *et al.*, "Is Abortion the Best We Have to Offer?" *op. cit.*, pp. 189-190; Bishops of Illinois, *op. cit.*, p. 204; "U.S. Bishops' New Pastoral Plan....," *op. cit.*, p. 281.

[131] Stith, "A Secular Case Against Abortion on Demand," *op. cit.*, p. 153; Segers, *op. cit.*, p. 458; Bishops of Illinois, *op. cit.*, p. 204.

[132] Chamberlain, *op. cit.*, p. 208; Segers, *op. cit.*, p. 458.

[133] Romanowski, *op. cit.*, p. 280; Bishops of Illinois, *op. cit.*, p. 204.

[134] Romanowski, *op. cit.*, p. 280; Diamond, "Humanizing the Abortion Debate," *op. cit.*,

p. 39; Chamberlain, *op. cit.*, p. 208; Segers, *op. cit.*, p. 458; "U.S. Bishops' New Pastoral Plan. . . .," *op. cit.*, p. 282.

[135] Hilgers *et al.*, "Is Abortion the Best We Have to Offer?" *op. cit.*, pp. 180-182; Segers, *op. cit.*, p. 458; Chamberlain, *op. cit.*, p. 208; Bishops of Illinois, *op. cit.*, p. 204; "U.S. Bishops' New Pastoral Plan. . . .," *op. cit.*, p. 282.

[136] Bishops of Illinois, *op. cit.*, p. 208; Bishops of New Jersey, *op. cit.*, p. 213.

[137] Gregory Baum, O.S.A., "Abortion: An Ecumenical Dilemma," *Commonweal* 99 (1973), p. 234. He refers to the Council's *Pastoral Constitution on the Church in the Modern World, "Gaudium et Spes"*, nos. 47-52.

[138] Baum, *op. cit.*, p. 234. But no. 51 of *"Gaudium et Spes"* excludes methods of family planning which are unacceptable to the Church.

[139] Granfield, *The Abortion Decision, op. cit.*, pp. 208-209.

[140] *Ibid.*, p. 211. See also: Hilgers *et al.*, "Is Abortion the Best We Have to Offer?" *op. cit.*, p. 188; Segers, *op. cit.*, p. 458; Editorial, "The Abortion Debate," *op. cit.*, p. 132; James A. Coriden, "Church Law and Abortion," *Jurist* 33 (1973), p. 198. James M. Humber, "Abortion: The Avoidable Moral Dilemma," in James M. Humber and Robert E. Almeder (eds.), *Biomedical Ethics and the Law* (New York: Pflaum Press, 1976), p.91.

[141] Baum, *op. cit.*, pp. 234-235.

[142] *Ibid.*, p. 235. See also: McCormick, "Notes on Moral Theology: The Abortion Dossier," *op. cit.*, pp. 333-334.

[143] Baum, *op. cit.*, p. 235.

[144] *Ibid.*, p. 235.

[145] *Ibid.*, p. 235. See also: Chamberlain, *op. cit.*, p. 208; Editorial, "The Abortion Decision," *Commonweal* 97 (1973), p. 436.

[146] Robert E. Cooke *et al.* (eds.), *The Terrible Choice: The Abortion Dilemma. Based on the Proceedings of the International Conference on Abortion Sponsored by the Harvard Divinity School and the Joseph P. Kennedy Jr. Foundation* (New York: Bantam Books, 1968), pp. 65-66. In the view of Betty Sarvis and Hyman Rodman, most people take a middle position on abortion: they do not consider the fetus a human being but neither do they recognize the woman's right to do whatever she wishes to her unborn child. A human fetus has special status and therefore abortion is permissible under certain circumstances and up to a certain stage of pregnancy; *The Abortion Controversy* (New York: Columbia University Press, 1973), pp. 21-23.

[147] Bernard J. Ransil, *Abortion* (New York: Paulist Press Deus Books, 1969), p. 38. See also: Daniel Callahan, "Abortion: Some Ethical Issues," in David F. Walbert and J. Douglas Butler (eds.), *Abortion, Society, and the Law* (Cleveland: Case Western Reserve University, 1973), p. 94.

[148] Callahan, *Abortion: Law, Choice and Morality, op. cit.*, pp. 474-475. See also: *id.*, "Abortion: Some Ethical Issues," *op. cit.*, pp. 93-94; Granfield, *The Abortion Decision, op. cit.*, pp. 157-158. But Granfield warns that the arguments which are used to justify permissive abortion policies can just as readily justify other kinds of eugenic and socio-economic killing; *ibid.*, p. 158. See also: Atkinson, *op. cit.*, pp. 361-362.

[149] Trinkaus *et al.*, *op. cit.*, p. 108; Lauth, *op. cit.*, p. 372; Thomas G. Dailey, "The Catholic Position on Abortion," *Linacre Quarterly* 34 (1967), p. 218; Bishops of Illinois, *op. cit.*, pp. 206-207; Cardinal Shehan, *op. cit.*, p. 10.

[150] Callahan, *Abortion: Law, Choice and Morality, op. cit.*, pp. 501-502.

[151] *Ibid.*, p. 501.

[152] *Ibid.*, p. 502.

153 *Ibid.*, p. 285. See also: Grisez, *op. cit.*, pp. 54-58; Leonard F.X. Mayhew, "Abortion: Two Sides and Some Complaints," *Ecumenist* 5, July-August 1967, p. 76; Sebastian MacDonald, C.P., "The Meaning of Abortion," *American Ecclesiastical Review* 169 (1975), pp. 302-305.

154 Callahan, "Abortion: Some Ethical Issues," *op. cit.*, pp. 95, 100-101.

155 May, *op. cit.*, pp. 202-203. Stanley Hauerwas, who writes from a Methodist perspective, is critical of Grisez's "not too subtle *ad hominems* against the pro-abortionist"; "Abortion and Normative Ethics: A Critical Appraisal of Callahan and Grisez," *Cross Currents* 21 (1971), p. 400.

156 Bishops of Illinois, *op. cit.*, pp. 204, 209; Bishops of New Jersey, *op. cit.*, pp. 212-213; Bishops of Missouri, *op. cit.*, p. 224.

157 "Statement of Terence Cardinal Cooke," in *Documentation on Abortion and the Right to Life II, op. cit.*, p. 41. See also: John Cardinal Krol, "Testimony," in *Documentation on the Right to Life and Abortion, op. cit.*, p. 37; Medeiros, *op. cit.*, p. 40; Bishops of Illinois, *op. cit.*, p. 205; Editorial, "Political Responsibility and Abortion," *America* 134 (1976), p. 173.

158 "Statement of Terence Cardinal Cooke," *op. cit.*, p. 41.

159 Granfield, *The Abortion Decision, op. cit.*, pp. 137-138, 115-116.

160 *Ibid.*, p. 138.

161 John Cardinal Krol, *op. cit.*, p. 37. Catholic authors remain divided on this point. Some recognize the honorable intentions of many supporters of abortion reform and point to their good record on other issues involving human life. See, e.g.: *The New Technologies of Birth and Death: Medical, Legal and Moral Dimensions. Proceedings of the Workshop for Bishops of the United States and Canada, Dallas, January 28-31, 1980* (St. Louis: Pope John XXIII Medical-Moral Research and Education Center, 1980), pp. 81, 88-89. Others are very critical of the liberationist motivation and ideology, though in a dignified way, and uphold the validity of the "slippery slope" argument: John T. Noonan, Jr., *A Private Choice: Abortion in America in the Seventies* (New York: Free Press, 1979); James V. Schall, S.J., *Christianity and Life* (San Francisco: Ignatius Press, 1981), pp. 15-34; James T. Burtchaell, C.S.C., *Rachel Weeping and Other Essays on Abortion* (Kansas City: Andrews and McMeel, 1982). See also: Richard A. McCormick, S.J., "Abortion: A Changing Morality and Policy?" *Hospital Progress* 60, February 1979, pp. 42-44. These authors develop many of the arguments which I have listed in a more concise manner in this chapter. A number of these issues were also discussed at two conferences on abortion organized by the University of Notre Dame in 1975 and 1979 where a serious attempt was made to initiate a nonpolemical dialogue between representatives of various disciplines and of diverse moral and political persuasions on abortion. See: Edward Manier *et al.* (eds.), *Abortion: New Directions for Policy Studies* (Notre Dame, Ind.: University of Notre Dame Press, 1977); James T. Burtchaell, C.S.C. (ed.), *Abortion Parley: Papers Delivered at the National Conference on Abortion Held at the University of Notre Dame in October 1979* (Kansas City: Andrews and McMeel, 1980).

162 Callahan, "Abortion: Some Ethical Issues," *op. cit.*, p. 97.

163 Grisez, *op. cit.*, p. 464.

164 Pope Paul VI, *Encyclical Letter "Humanae Vitae"*, (Washington, D.C.: United States Catholic Conference, 1968); United States National Conference of Catholic Bishops, *Human Life in Our Day: A Collective Pastoral Letter of the American Hierarchy Issued November 15, 1968* (Washington, D.C.: Publications Office U.S. Catholic Conference, 1968).

Chapter Nine

Human Law: Prophetic or Pragmatic?

This chapter will conclude our analysis of American Catholic thinking on the juridical-ethical aspects of the abortion problem. It will be devoted to the attempts of those who have felt the need of adjustments or changes in the Church's position as it has been described in the previous pages. Each phase of the moral and legal debates so far examined featured not just an abundance of literature but a good number of extensive and consistent arguments with definite conclusions on the various elements of the ethical or juridical question. The same cannot be said of the legal reform efforts which are under consideration now. Robert F. Drinan, one of the principal protagonists at this stage of the discussions, admits that he regards his own proposition as tentative, and this observation is applicable to most of the other contributions. Drinan writes:

> The foregoing makes it abundantly clear that the tangled web of abortion and the law yields very few clear questions about the problem and virtually no answers. The dilemmas surrounding the issue of abortion and the law involve aspects of genetics, medicine, sexuality, morality, jurisprudence, and in the ultimate analysis one's view of the nature and purpose of any human existence...
>
> This author has no easy solutions or ready options for the Catholic legislator, jurist, or spokesman on the question of abortion and the law.[1]

Whatever the reasons are, it is clear that relatively few authors have developed a complete and sustained rationale in support of a reformulation of the Church's stand on the legal issue. Speculation here has been less intense and systematic: there is some agreement on the questions that should be asked but the answers that are offered lack the persuasive force of unanimity and sometimes even that of individual conviction.

232

I. Facing Facts and a Strategy of Compromise

At an early stage of the debate on the moral implications of abortion legislation, Robert H. Springer injects a carefully measured dose of political realism into Catholic thinking on the issue. Writing in 1967 when the discussions centered around the moderate statute proposed by the American Law Institute, he draws attention to the demands of political reality and argues that the opposition of Catholics to liberalization will be ineffective if they reject even a modicum of compromise in the area of fertility control. He recalls that Vatican II envisaged a Church which would be open to the world and to its needs. Moral pluralism is a dominant feature of society today, and political initiatives which truly have the common welfare at heart will only realize this objective if they stem from a public consensus and are launched from a widely supported platform. Springer feels that in the abortion debate Catholics could obtain such backing if they would modify their position on public family planning services. If they would be prepared to consider a number of social provisions for contraceptive needs, other citizens would be assured that Catholics are willing to discuss objectively and amicably which social and legal measures are best suited to preserve respect for human life in American society.[2]

This political realism is reflected in other publications. Again in 1967 an editorial in *America* asked the Church to adopt a more flexible attitude and more active approach to abortion law reform, given the hard fact that changes were going to come, and come quickly, whether Catholics opposed them or not.[3] Almost ten years later, *Commonweal* writes on the occasion of the third anniversary of the 1973 Supreme Court decision:

> (I)t seems to us that there is so strong a national consensus supporting the woman's "right" to abortion during the early stages of pregnancy that those Catholics who are absolutely opposed to abortion will have to learn to live with some of the evil that has followed from the Supreme Court decision as part of the cost of living in a pluralistic and secular state.[4]

Writing prior to the Supreme Court decision, Germain G. Grisez warns that on the abortion issue the margin for political compromise is very narrow indeed. A genuine pro-life strategy consists, first of all, in strong and unrelenting opposition to any liberalization of the statutes, including a moderate relaxation. Even if the passage of a more permissive bill is inevitable and further resistance would seem to be fruitless, there is no room for political bargaining in order to obtain amendments that would mitigate the evil effects of the new law. Grisez rules out any form of cooperation in abortion liberalization, not even for the sake of avoiding greater evils, because society is not faced with an ordinary conflict of interests for which it is possible to work out several just solutions. The issue at stake is the most fundamental one, involving the right to life. Those who feel inclined to compromise should first ask themselves where they will stop and where they think those who collaborated with the Nazis should have stopped. Grisez emphasizes that even a moderate bill has to be fought tooth and nail because also a limited relaxation of the law implies a repudiation of the only premise on which complete liberalization can be resisted —that the unborn child is a legal person. Once this principle has been breached, the restrictions of the law will be stretched, torn, and discarded, and this will be done in the courts because this type of abortion statute is susceptible to charges of vagueness and discrimination. Outside the courts a moderate law will make everyone familiar with legal abortion and will make it "normal." It is only *after* the bill has been passed and *after* relaxation has become a fact that the opponents of liberalization may attempt to introduce restrictive amendments, but always on the condition that they are able to do this without lending any support to the law itself. Grisez approves of such legislative efforts on the ground that they might save at least some lives.[5]

Grisez is not opposed to the legalization of a strictly therapeutic indication, where an abortion is necessary to save the life of the mother. Of course the legislator could not justify his recognition of this exception with theological or ethical arguments: Grisez maintains, as we have seen in Chapter VII, that the juridical system must be metaphysically and ethically neutral. It has no option but to protect the unborn as legal persons with the very same rights as adults. However, in conditions of extreme conflict the law could permit an abortion as a form of "justifiable homicide." An obvious instance of legally justifiable homicide would be a situation where the killing of one or some is necessary to prevent the death of more or all, where the person or persons thus killed would not have lived in any case. From Grisez's ethical perspective, this solution is utilitarian and unacceptable as a general moral principle, but he admits that almost everybody regards killing under these circumstances as permissible. Likewise in public opinion an abortion is acceptable when otherwise both mother and child would die. In these rare cases the law may employ commom judgement as the criterion by which life is to be saved or sacrificed.[6] For the same reason Grisez has no *legal* objections to the termination of a pregnancy resulting from rape, in spite of the fact that the intervention is immoral:

> (I)n the present situation, I would hestitate to condemn as unjust a legal provision which permitted victims of *forcible rape who subsequently conceived as a consequence of that rape* to obtain an abortion. Many

people believe that there is in this situation a conflict of rights more severe than that between the life of the unborn and the health of the mother. Granted that such fundamental rights are in conflict here, as people seem to believe, a legal system such as ours must establish a rule of resolution not on the basis of any single moral or religious theory but on the general consensus of reasonable people.[7]

Grisez is prepared to make a further allowance. Since the law must respect the fetus as a legal person, it must extend to unborn life a consistent "equal protection." One could argue that the law must regard the vast majority of abortions as homicide and punish them as emphatically as the killing of born human life. But Grisez is willing to distinguish between prenatal and postnatal murder: the latter crime not only destroys human life but also undermines the social order, while abortion does not seem to have these social repercussions. The termination of pregnancy may thus be treated as "simple homicide" as distinct from "murder" or "homicide of born persons." Both crimes must be punished as violations of the right to life but the degree of punishment may be different because of the social factor.[8]

David Granfield adopts the same policy as Grisez, and he does so on the same grounds. He rejects a policy of political compromise because it would be naïve to think that settling for a moderate bill will keep complete liberalization indefinitely at bay. Moreover, one cannot logically approve of a limited destruction of fetal life without recognizing in principle the expendability of all human life, born as well as unborn. Once relaxation seems inevitable, the anti-abortion forces should concentrate their efforts on the practical implications of the proposed law and insist on adequate medical standards and clearly spelled-out procedural formalities. This is a normal and indispensable aspect of all law enactment. The anti-abortion forces must ensure that the law in its final formulation will not grant the equivalent of abortion on demand and that *within its own limits* it will be fair and reasonable.[9] Granfield, Grisez, and James V. McNulty each recommend to the attention of the anti-abortion movement a number of restrictive amendments and procedural safeguards. Their suggestions can be summarized as follows:

1. Abortion services must be kept strictly separate from social welfare programs.

2. The criteria of justification for the intervention should be as clear and reasonable as possible. "Mental health" and "fetal defect" must be accurately defined. Something more than the physician's "belief" in the authenticity of an indication should be required for its legal validity. Instances of rape and incest must be legally certified.

3. The operating surgeon or physician must be duly licensed and a provision be made that he performs the intervention personally. Mere supervision should not be enough.

4. Abortions should be performed only in accredited or licensed hospitals, not in doctors' offices where supervision and inspection are difficult.

5. All abortions must be subjected to the approval of a special hospital board.

6. Before an abortion is performed, it must be established that the woman's consent is free and informed. The consent of the husband must also be obtained, or of the parents or guardian in the case of minors.

7. There should be a time limit, as early as possible, beyond which no abortions are permitted except those that are necessary to save the life of the mother.

8. Since the unborn are legal persons and are therefore entitled to full legal protection, their lives cannot be taken without due process of law. This means that a request for an abortion must be argued in an open hearing before a court of law after the appointment of a guardian *ad litem* and with the opportunity of cross-examination of witnesses and a right of appeal.

9. A hospital must keep official and complete records of all abortions that are performed. These records should be checked regularly by the State medical department.

10. A "conscience clause" must protect the rights of hospitals, doctors, and other hospital employees to refuse to permit, or to perform, or to cooperate in an abortion.

11. Strict penalties should be applied to violations of the abortion statutes. [10]

Writing in 1967 Drinan took a more positive view of political compromise and expressed the opinion that such a policy is not irreconcilable with the Catholic position on the morality of abortion. He observes that American Catholics invariably object to any lessening of the moral content of the law and are reluctant to cooperate in the enactment of "immoral" legislation. [11] But the limitations of political circumstances may warrant a compromise which meets the opposition halfway, in order to secure the lesser evil. Analysing the strategy of the liberationists Drinan points out that they use the hard and rare cases, such as rape, incest, and grave fetal defect, as an argument for abortion on demand. He urges the anti-abortion movement to adopt a less obstructionist approach and work for the enactment of a law which would provide for these exceptional situations. This would take the sting out of the propaganda efforts for complete liberalization. Catholics should be prepared to settle for the lesser evil and accept the legal authorization of abortion in the rare instances of a threat to the life of the mother, rape, incest, or a predictably deformed infant. [12]

Norman St. John-Stevas is convinced that a strategy of compromise is justified. He recognizes that Catholics have the same right as everybody else in society to articulate their moral views and work for their legal implementation but he advises them to combine prophecy with prudence. Prudence requires that they consider feasibility and give up the idea that they can permanently block relaxation of the law in the prevailing climate of moral opinion. This means that their attitude towards abortion law reform should become more pragmatic and constructive. In a democratic society law enactment is determined by public opinion and on the abortion issue public opinion is middle-of-the-road. It favors a certain degree of relaxation but at the same time it wants to preserve the community's respect for life. Thus it opposes abortion on demand:[13]

> In the middle is found a mass of people with no theological presupposi-
> tions, who want to relieve human suffering, who see that abortions are
> being carried out under insanitary conditions, who feel that the law binds
> the poor but can be evaded by the rich, who, in other words, think the
> present law capricious and unjust, but who nevertheless see that relaxa-
> tion of the law raises wider ethical and social issues, and who, while
> stopping short of attributing to the fetus the rights of a fully developed
> human person, nevertheless feel that as the potential from which a fully
> human person could develop, it should not be treated merely as waste
> matter to be disposed of as a matter of convenience in a hospital
> incinerator. In a democracy it is these middle people who matter and who
> ultimately decide the legal issue.[14]

Catholics then must join forces with the "middle people" and form a common front against the extremists who seek abortion on demand. They should accept some relaxation and aim at a law which provides limited scope for abortion and which is carefully drafted. St. John-Stevas argues that such a compromise is more than merely a choice of the lesser evil. By linking up with other pro-life groups and by insisting that the value of unborn life is a serious moral issue, Catholics will exert a unifying and moralizing influence on society. In this way they will make a significant contribution to the national consensus and to the welfare of modern man.[15]

II. Morality and Law: The Tradition of the Church

A reconsideration of a theological or ethical tenet necessarily involves an examination of its historical roots; it seeks to determine to what extent the present supposition has been shaped by events or socio-cultural condi-tions of the distant or more recent past. In the American Catholic debate on the morality of abortion legislation there has been little effort to investigate the historical aspect of the Church's teaching on the subject. Charles E. Curran is the only author who has given the matter much thought.

Natural Law and Civil Legislation

Curran detects a certain ambivalence in ecclesiastical attitudes towards civil law: the Church does not exactly equate human law with moral law but it does tend to establish a firm link between the two. This policy is the outcome of a long process of theological reflection on three interrelated topics: the relationship between Church and State, the origin and purpose of the State, and the function of civil law.[16] In his analysis of the Church's traditional view of these issues Curran makes the following observations:

1. The theocratic ideology of the Middle Ages distinguished two different orders in this world: the temporal order which was entrusted to the authority of the State (the *Regnum*) and the spiritual order which was governed by the Church (the *Sacerdotium*). Each order had its own specific end but the end of the temporal order was considered subordinate to that of the spiritual order. Human government should reflect the pattern of divine government. This political outlook naturally did not recognize religious freedom and did not grant Jews and other infidels the right to practice their religion in public. However, it was felt that the civil authorities could tolerate divergent cults if suppressing them would cause greater problems for society. When the Church in the nineteenth and twentieth centuries decided that non-Catholics could be granted external religious liberty, it still did so in terms of acquiescence in a lesser evil. It was only at the Second Vatican Council that the Church adopted a more positive attitude.[17]

2. In the Catholic tradition the proximate norm for human law is natural law. Natural law is the criterion of validity of any civil law, and it gives civil laws their moral binding force. But this tradition does not identify human law with moral law, nor crime with sin. Civil law is supposed to restrict its concern to the protection and promotion of the *common good*. This means that the lawgiver is only allowed to enforce those acts of moral virtue which are necessary for the welfare of society. Similarly, it should not attempt to suppress all vices but only those which are harmful to others and whose prohibition is required by the common good. Thus the law can decide to tolerate prostitution and regulate it.[18]

The Catholic political-moral tradition recognized that civil law and natural law are not *identical* but it did stress the *relationship* between human law and moral law. Even in recent history, says Curran, Catholics have urged that moral problems such as contraception, divorce, homosexual relations, abortion, and social justice be regulated by civil law in accordance with the demands of natural law. While they carefully avoided equating the two, they argued that violations of natural law will ultimately have negative consequences for society and should therefore be prohibited by the legislator.[19] Daniel Callahan reflects more specifically on the contemporary Catholic position on abortion laws. He offers a similar explanation of the Church's acceptance, on the one hand, of the distinction between law and morality, and its determination, on the other, to impose by law on the whole population what would seem to be a moral belief. The Church's case against abortion is based on the natural law proposition, and since it considers this law to have universal validity, it does not view its conviction as a merely sectarian one which binds Catholics only. Furthermore, the Church's insistence that abortion is "the killing of the innocent" enables it to formulate a social argument and depict liberalization of the law as a disaster for the community. Once the case against abortion is presented in these terms, the issue naturally can no longer be settled by private belief, majority vote, or medical opinion.[20] James J. Diamond states that this juridical-ethical outlook is typical of those who oppose any relaxation of abortion statutes:

> The antiabortionist wants his national jurisprudence to be a moral one. He equates justice with morality by observing that true justice cannot be immoral and true immorality cannot be just.... (T)his is the generalized endpoint for which the antiabortionist is working.[21]

Bernard Häring has a different exegesis of the Church's interest in the moral content of State law. In homogeneous and closed societies, and especially in their less developed strata, approved customs and legislation were important factors in the formation of moral conscience.[22] He cites an admonition to the State by Pope Pius XI which refers to this moralizing effect of human legislation. The Pope charged the State

> in legislating to take into account what is determined by the divine law and by Church legislation, and to proceed with penal sanction against those who have sinned. For there are people who think that whatever is allowed by civil legislation or not subject to penal sanctions may also be allowed according to the moral law; or they may put it into practice even against their conscience, since they do not fear God and would not have to fear anything from human legislation.[23]

In Häring's analysis, it is this didactic function of law that accounts for the Church's insistence on the relationship between civil law and moral law. He grants that even in a modern pluralistic society human legislation affects moral decisions, but he adds that the moralizing factor of law is in decline.[24]

Drinan confirms his earlier statement that the Church tends to evaluate civil law by the application of a moral criterion and explains that this attitude has made Catholics wary of the utilitarian or sociological jurisprudence of Jeremy Bentham (1748-1833) and John Stuart Mill (1806-1873), which has exerted considerable influence on American understanding of the function of law. To the lawgiver of a pluralistic society Bentham and Mill assign a minimal role in the preservation of morality and only grant the right to interfere with individual liberty if the welfare of others is at stake.[25]

Dialogue and Liberty: The Mind of Vatican II

The teaching of the Second Vatican Council, particularly its documents on the Church, ecumenism, and religious liberty, has perceptibly shaped the views of some authors on the relationship between law, morality, and the liberalization of abortion statutes. At an early stage of the debate Springer felt that the spirit of Vatican II authorized a new approach to the legal-moral aspects of abortion. He notes the Council's statement that "from the moment of its conception life must be guarded with the greatest care, while abortion and infanticide are unspeakable crimes," but recalls that Vatican II also emphasized the need for "sincere and prudent dialogue" with other churches and with secularists for the sake of the betterment of the world. Springer observes that there are groups outside the Catholic Church which have a genuine respect for human life even if they favor a mitigation of the abortion laws.[26] Dennis J. Doherty develops this argument. He refers to the *Decree on Ecumenism* and quotes a passage which has "far-reaching implications":

> And if in moral matters there are many Christians who do not always understand the gospel in the same way as Catholics, and do not admit the same solutions for the more difficult problems of modern society, nevertheless they share our desire to cling to Christ's word as the source of Christian virtue.... Hence, the ecumenical dialogue could start with discussions concerning the application of the gospel to moral questions.[27]

In Doherty's view, dialogue implies genuine communication, an openness to the other's point of view, and a willingness to listen and to learn. If a person enters into a "dialogue" but has a prior and unshakable commitment to his own opinion and merely seeks to convert his partner, his contribution is essentially a monologue. This can hardly be what the Council had in mind. Ecumenical dialogue, especially when it is concerned with serious moral problems, involves a sincere consultation of "the insights of fellow Christians both of one's own and other communions and, by extension, those of non-Christians (as well as non-religious humanists)."[28]

Drinan draws attention to the Council's *Declaration on Religious Lib-*

erty and states that this document has implications for one's definition of the State's role in the preservation of public morality.[29] He cites the following passage as particularly relevant:

> The usages of society are to be the usages of freedom in their full range. These require that the freedom of man be respected as far as possible, and curtailed only when and in so far as necessary.[30]

Drinan believes that this accentuation of freedom, which may be restricted only "when and in so far as necessary," is a rediscovery of a traditional element in the Church's politico-moral thought. It contains a "new and profound principle which is capable of bringing about the most profound shifts in Catholic thinking about legal-moral problems."[31] Curran comes to the same conclusion. After the *Declaration on Religious Liberty* the Catholic emphasis on the relationship between law and morality must be modified, and the traditional definition of the function of civil law must be revised. The Council's concept of religious liberty involves "the immunity from external coercion in civil society in the worship of God, so that no one is forced to act contrary to his religious beliefs and individuals are not restrained from acting in accord with their consciences in religious matters."[32] The Council therefore affirms the dignity of the individual person and shows a deep awareness of the rights of his conscience. This has consequences, says Curran, for one's interpretation of the role of civil law: in the area of personal morality the lawgiver must safeguard the freedom of the individual, and he may restrict that freedom only when this is necessary.[33] In the same *Declaration* Drinan finds support for the contention that Catholics should not attempt to enforce their moral beliefs upon those who do not accept them. He quotes:

> (I)n spreading religious faith and in introducing religious practices, everyone ought at all times to refrain from any manner of action which *might seem* to carry a *hint* of coercion or of a kind of persuasion that would be dishonorable or unworthy. . . . [34]

If those who oppose liberalization are in fact imposing a moral policy which in the last analysis is Christian and sectarian, then the Council's firm prohibition of all forms of coercion becomes operative.[35] Drinan thinks that this is indeed the case. He compares the Catholic abortion argument to that of the liberation movement and concludes that the controversy is not primarily about the quality of fetal life but rather about the quality of the reasons which justify the termination of that life. The crucial point is the Catholic principle which upholds "the transcendence of any human or potentially human being over the health or happiness of an older or more powerful human being." The question then arises whether Catholics can be so certain about the validity of their priorities in this area that they may translate their hierarchy of values into civil law.[36]

Doherty answers this question in the negative. He admits that there is no doubt where the Church stands regarding the morality of abortion, but he points out that its teaching on this issue is not an article of faith and is not taught infallibly. Moreover, abortion remains a complicated moral problem, and the validity of the Church's position is not self-evident to many non-Catholics, especially since the taking of human life is sometimes permissible. Persons of good will can and do have different opinions on doctrinal and moral issues, and this in spite of ecclesiastical pronouncements. In such cases of doubt there is need for dialogue, and as long as the doubt persists there should be no legal compulsion:[37]

> What is legal is clearly not necessarily moral, but at the same time, especially in a society characterized by religious pluralism, it may not be moral for some to use the power of the ballot to make something illegal for all.[38]

Thomas A. Wassmer makes the same point:

> Where men of good will and ethical integrity disagree is it always prudential for Catholics to try to impose their "traditional" answers on other citizens by way of a general civil law? Is it not the best index of a man's love of freedom that he respects the freedom of others, ethically perceptive and morally sensitive of the freedom of Catholics? This responsibility is of course reciprocal.[39]

Writing some years after the 1973 Supreme Court decision Mary C. Segers expressed the same opinion in a more definite manner. The law should not pronounce on abortion because public opinion is divided on this issue:

> [Abortion] is not a matter to be decided by law or by the government. This does not mean that society has no interest in the matter. It means that, in a pluralistic society, government ought not to enforce or legislate an anti-abortion moral position, when that position is so seriously questioned by members of the society that it is improper to speak of any social consensus on the matter.[40]

Häring affirms that a moral norm *as such* cannot be translated into civil legislation and observes that the Church's teaching on the morality of abortion is often formulated in terms of natural and divine law. These premises are undoubtedly valid for Catholics but they do not make sense to those who are their partners in the dialogue on liberalization. If the Church wants to get its view across it will have to present a rationale that is convincing also to sincere and intelligent people who are not under its authority. Häring suggests that a search be initiated for *the best legal solution*. This would involve an examination of the *social consequences* of relaxation or liberalizaton, and this will require responsible and responsive discussions:[41]

> The state preparing new legislation on abortion should study with great care the foreseeable impact on the common good, on respect for another person's life, and on all other values that could be affected by changes being considered; but this is not the duty of the legislators alone. It is likewise the responsibility of members of the Church, of Church authorities, and of ethicists who wish to make concrete suggestions about the content of a law, to study on all levels the matter of probable consequences.[42]

It is clear that these authors are willing to engage in a dialogue about the desirability of liberalization and the extent to which it should be implemented. This willingness does not stem from a political pragmatism which is prepared to bargain for the sake of the lesser evil but from the conviction that legislative activity in a pluralistic society must respect individual freedom and personal conscience. Richard A. McCormick made this point early in the debate when he wrote in a report on the 1967 Harvard-Kennedy Conference on Abortion:

> Perhaps the most immediately pressing question raised was that of learning to live with our disagreements on abortion. This itself is an important moral issue. It is the moral issue of our growth as a community. . . .
>
> The spirit of this conference must be read as an insistence that every moral point of view on the meaning of sanctity of life has a right to be stated in the public forum. . . . The sincerity evidenced in this conference contains an implicit message. It invites all to a cease-fire on talk about imposition of one's views on others, whether these others be fetuses or adults. It invites all to a renewal of responsibility in public debate.[43]

III. Morality and Abortion Laws: The Prophetic Approach

It is evident that in the opinion of some authors the Catholic tradition overemphasized the relationship between human law and moral law. Curran believes, as we have seen, that the Church should reformulate its position on this issue. On the strength of Vatican II's *Declaration on Religious Liberty*, which affirms the freedom of the individual conscience and limits the interventions of the State to those that are "necessary," he proposes the following distinctions:

1. *The distinction between the spiritual and the temporal order of*

human life. The secular has its own finality. It is not dependent on the sacred and is not subordinate to it.

2. *The distinction between the common good of society and the public order which is the proper area of concern of the State.* The common good of society comprises all the material and spiritual values pursued by its members, and the State has been instituted to help the people in their efforts to achieve this common good. The State realizes this objective if it protects the public order which is a narrower concept than the common good. It is not the function of civil law to direct the life and work of each citizen and relate these to the general welfare. Individual citizens must be allowed maximum freedom and creativity so that they can serve the good of the community in their own way; the State may only interfere when this is necessary for the public order.

3. *The distinction between private morality and public or social morality.* Private morality refers to acts of individuals which do not significantly affect other members of the community, while public morality comprises activities which have consequences for others. [44]

On the basis of the Council's affirmation of freedom and these differentiations, Curran offers the principle of "freedom under the law" as the fundamental legal-moral norm: "Let there be as much freedom, personal and social, as is possible; let there be only as much restraint and constraint, personal and social, as may be necessary for the public order." [45] At the same time Curran asserts that the State has a definite duty to maintain a genuine public peace as well as an order of justice which protects the rights of all citizens and provides for a fair settlement when these rights conflict. Another concern of the State is the preservation of a public morality, meaning a basic morality which covers the essentials of human coexistence but allows for pluralism on more specific moral issues. [46] Legislation therefore is more than a mere canonization of the established convictions and life styles of the community. At times the law must assume the role of a teacher and transform the moral outlook of society. This applies especially in questions of social justice, such as racial integration and minimum wage laws. [47]

But Curran allows the State to adopt a prudential and pragmatic approach to its lawmaking and law enforcement. In a constitutional democracy respect for the rights of individuals is a fundamental value. If a section of the population is convinced that the object of a particular law belongs to the area of private morality, then the lawgiver must take this into consideration, all the more so because legislation in these circumstances might be futile or have a divisive effect on the community. In such a situation the legislator could opt for a compromise solution. Similarly, if he is not in a position to enforce the law or if the law *de facto* discriminates against a

particular group or class it should not be enacted. A law which is ineffective or discriminatory does not really fulfil its task in society and causes
disregard for the legal system.[48] Curran clearly assigns a didactic, ideal-
istic, or prophetic function to the law: it must promote peace, justice, and
an order of morality. But there is also a pragmatic aspect to human legislation, and the lawgiver must walk a middle path between prophecy and
pragmatism:

> [In this understanding of law] there is also the recognition of the rights of
> freedom of individuals and at the same time the recognition of prudential
> and pragmatic judgments about the effectiveness and function of law
> itself. In this way the danger of an idealistic approach, which does not
> give enough importance to freedom and considerations of feasibility, is
> avoided as is the danger of a purely pragmatic approach, which sees law
> as totally distinct from considerations of justice and peace and merely
> accepting the mores of a particular society at any given time.[49]

Law and morality then are different but "not totally dichotomous."[50]
Curran concludes that the Catholic Church must revise its traditional
politico-moral outlook and relinquish the idea that the primary function of
civil law is the confirmation and implementation of natural law. Nor should
the Church always insist that its doctrinal pronouncements be enforced by
the laws of the State.[51]

Applying this modified concept of human law to the abortion issue,
Curran admits that Catholics and others who define the intervention as the
destruction of an innocent human life are justified in opposing liberalization on the ground that the criterion of public order involves an order of
justice which must safeguard the rights of individuals. But in the light of
prudential and pragmatic considerations, such as the moral freedom of
citizens in a pluralistic State, the importance of social consensus in legislation, the problem of clandestine abortions, the unenforceability and discriminatory effect of restrictive laws, these same persons could also adopt
the position that abortion should be available on demand. The distinction
between human law and moral law implies that one's stand on the legal
issue is not a logical and necessary deduction from one's moral or religious
beliefs. Someone who is convinced that abortion is morally wrong could
still support a moderate or permissive law and, if he is a member of the
legislature, vote for different types of statutes. His decision would depend
not only on his moral opinions but also on a prudential and pragmatic
judgement.[52] Curran summarizes his views as follows:

> An understanding of the above criteria and their application to the ques-
> tion of legislation in the matter of abortion indicates that one who believes
> that human life is present even from the moment of conception could

adopt a number of different approaches to the question of the law concerning abortion. In practical terms this means that for Roman Catholics
there is no such thing as *the* one Roman Catholic approach to abortion
legislation. The existence of the prudential and the feasible aspect in law
argues against the possibility of any immediate and necessary translation
of a moral teaching into a matter of law. Roman Catholics and those in
society who believe that human life is present from the moment of conception can very well argue there should be a law against abortion. On the
other hand, in light of some of the considerations of prudence and feasibility in a pluralistic society, one might argue that there should be no law
against abortion.[53]

Curran thinks that, in view of the conflicting opinions in the United
States on the morality of abortion, he could do justice to the prophetic as
well as the pragmatic functions of law by allowing some type of accommodation. This would take the form of a moderately restrictive code (such as
the one suggested by the American Law Instiuute) or a statute which would
limit the operation to the first ten or twelve weeks of pregnancy. Thus the
law would emphasize the rights of the fetus and proclaim the value of
unborn life and, at the same time, it would recognize a greater number of
problem situations in which abortion is a legally permissible solution.[54]

McCormick accepts Curran's analysis of the relationship between law
and morality in a pluralistic society and agrees that a democratic legislator
must steer a middle course between the "idealist" tradition (which simply
translates natural law into civil law and only tolerates deviations) and a
purely pragmatic legal policy (which merely reflects and confirms the
mores of the community). McCormick compares law enactment to pastoral
counselling. Like pastoral care, law should consider not only the moral
ideal but also the social reality, and it should ask itself what is feasible in a
given community at a particular time. On the other hand, just as the
counsellor seeks to widen the horizon and maximize the strengths of his
client, so the law must also fulfil its didactic task instead of merely bowing
to popular opinion.[55]

McCormick feels that in the United States the necessary ingredients for a
good abortion law are lacking, as not only is there a difference of opinion
on the feasibility of such legislation, but the very ideal which the law is
supposed to serve is a subject of debate. There is no public consensus on the
value of unborn life. A law cannot be good if it is not rooted in the solid
moral convictions of the majority of the population. In these circumstances
there is only a choice between two legal evils. A prohibitive or moderately
permissive law has obvious social disadvantages, such as "a degree of
unenforceability, clandestine abortions, less than total control over fertility," but a very liberal law will allow and encourage "enormous bloodlet-

ting.'' McCormick admits that, in spite of the difference between law and morality, it is one's moral perspective that will greatly determine what one accepts as a tolerable legal compromise. Personally he would opt for a law which ''protects fetal life but exempts abortion done in certain specified conflict situations from legal sanctions.'' The lawgiver then should decide not to punish abortion in some exceptional cases.[56]

Daniel A. Degnan also recognizes the intrinsic limitations of law: it depends on public consensus for its enactment, enforcement, and observance, and often it realizes its objective only imperfectly. A law therefore must be ''possible.'' But it must also be *just*; law has a prophetic function and its area of concern is the common good which it must promote by ensuring that justice is done. Its primary duty is the protection of the right to life, and it should extend this to unborn life because ''the human fetus, especially in its later development, shares too many of the characteristics of human existence to leave its life or death solely to choice of private persons.''[57] If the law does not protect fetal rights it fails to render justice and undermines respect for human life which is the foundation of society. Consequently, abortion statutes must reflect our recognition that fetal life is entitled to legal security. In effect these statutes must seek to reduce the destruction of that life.[58]

Degnan observes that in the United States a very restrictive law would lack necessary public support. In any case, it would not be right for the law to forbid all abortions because not all such interventions are morally unjustified. He admits that the conceptus has a moral claim at any stage of its development but he detects a qualitative difference between the early and the late fetus (the theory of developing personhood) and argues that abortion dilemmas may involve other values apart from the unborn's right to life (the principle of proportionate reason). On the other hand, he finds the 1973 Supreme Court decision unacceptable because by affirming that the mother's constitutional right to privacy prevails over the claims of the child, the Court has declared that unborn life has little value. This verdict has made abortion socially and morally respectable. Degnan therefore proposes to seek a consensus for a moderately restrictive law which would be rooted in the common moral awareness that abortion affects the sanctity of life, especially when the operation is performed at a later stage of gestation. By rejecting the taking of life on demand this type of law would proclaim that fetal life has a right to legal protection, that abortions should be restrained, not encouraged, and that the termination of pregnancy is a serious issue and requires a grave reason. At the same time this moderate statute would concede areas of private decision in the early months of pregnancy and would allow abortion of the more developed fetus if there are serious reasons for doing so.[59]

In 1968 the Queens Chapter of the Catholic Lawyers Guild of the Diocese of Brooklyn had already decided to support a moderately restrictive statute. Like Degnan, the chapter rejected complete liberalization because a permissive law proclaims that the lives of the unborn are outside the legitimate interest and concern of the community. Such an evaluation of life is so casual that it is "fundamentally abhorrent and clearly adverse to the common good of society, if not the public order."[60] At the same time it was agreed that the Church's teaching on the morality of abortion does not require Catholics to oppose all attempts to relax the penal laws in this area. The chapter justified this conclusion as follows:

> The precise issue of principle relates to the office and purpose of human law, in particular the penal law, and resolution of that basic issue will always depend upon considerations of the public order and common good of society.[61]

The chapter, however, insisted that the legal indications for abortion be delimited clearly so as to allow the least possible extension in practice. It also asked for procedural safeguards which would ensure the observance of the law and protect the rights of all interested parties, including society.[62]

Diamond places considerable emphasis on the prophetic function of legislation and states that the law has to render justice:

> We must remember that jurisprudence is not an exercise in mere legality. It is an attempt to bring the state close to the moral, the good, the just and the right. It is man's intellect seeking truth within the confines of a legal system. A right act is one that is better than its opposite or all other options. A right law is one that is better than its opposite or all other options. In jurisprudence, the elusive term "better" means "more likely to yield justice and equity" or "likely to yield more justice and equity."[63]

Diamond does not wish to imply that a just and equitable law could not allow any abortions. He points out that even if the State recognizes the fetus as a legal person with full constitutional rights, it does not follow that its life becomes absolutely inviolable. The State will protect its right to life no less but also no more than that of adults. Since the State may deprive its subjects of their legal right to life if they have committed a lethal crime, a case can be made for a clause permitting abortion to save the life of the mother. The State may also inflict capital punishment for nonlethal crimes, which are equivalent to murder, such as rape, mutiny in war, treason, sabotage, espionage, and diabolical torture. Similarly, it may expose its soldiers to hazards to protect its citizens' lives as well as to defend values which are comparable to life. It could be argued that also in circumstances which are *comparable* to "life-threatening situations" the law should permit an abortion.[64] Diamond clarifies this criterion as follows:

The key word here would be circumstances "comparable" to life-threatening, e.g., a context objectively demonstrable as being, or irremediably threatening to be, so humanly devastating to the mother that reasonable people, committed legally and philosophically to guarding all life, cannot see daylight between "devastation" and the actual death of the mother.[65]

It is clear that Diamond favors limited relaxation, not only for purely political or pragmatic motives but also for philosophical-juridical reasons. Gary D. Glenn presents a similar argument. He defends the inalienability of the right to life and explains that this right is not a "subjective" reality since it is not conferred by convention, custom, or law. It is an "objective" reality which is bestowed by nature and which must be protected by legislation.[66] However, the right to life is not absolute because circumstances may arise which make it impossible for society to protect it. The cases of capital criminals and soldiers during war are instances when society withdraws its protection from some of its citizens. This withdrawal is justifiable because it is inspired by strict necessity, viz., the defense of the community against domestic or foreign enemies.[67] The law then may not provide abortion on demand but this does not mean that it should forbid all abortions: society decided a long time ago to permit the intervention for the sake of the mother's life. Glenn admits that other indications such as rape and incest are somewhat more controversial but thinks that their legal recognition should prove acceptable. These relatively narrow grounds are indeed exceptions to the general principle that abortion is prohibited. Since they are "reasonable and specific" they do not subvert that principle and are not inconsistent with the inalienability of the right to life.[68]

IV. Morality and Abortion Laws: The Pragmatic Approach

The proposal to support the enactment of a moderately restrictive abortion statute as the best or the least unsatisfactory compromise between the prophetic task of civil legislation and its practical limitations does not appeal to all American Catholic authors. We have seen that for some even a modicum of political accommodation is out of the question, but others feel that a moderate code is not an adequate solution to the social and legal problems associated with the practice of abortion, and they plead for complete liberalization. Defining this more radical view as pragmatic may be overstating its case. On the subject of the function of law in society these authors do not seem to sponsor a theory fundamentally different from that of the "prophetic school." It is difficult to substantiate this because none of them has expounded his position on the basic legal issue. I think it is correct to say that from an ideological point of view the pragmatists would subscribe to the politico-moral philosophy of Curran and McCormick. The divergence arises in the pragmatists' analysis of the American abortion problem, especially in its social aspects, and in their selection of criteria for the best legal solution which include such factors as public opinion, enforceability, equity, and other considerations of a factual and practical nature. Here it becomes evident that they attach less significance to the symbolic value of restrictive laws and give greater prominence to the unfeasibility of such statutes. At the same time they wish to take seriously the freedom of conscience of the individual citizen. Thus their position has a definite prophetic element.

The Case for Abortion on Demand

Drinan is the earliest exponent of the pragmatic school. His point of departure is the same as Curran's. He states that there is no such thing as *the* Catholic view on the morality of abortion legislation:

> The position that an individual or a church takes regarding the *morality* of abortion does not necessarily determine the individual's or the church's position with respect to the *legality* of abortion. One's position on abortion and the law cannot be resolved simply by affirming the right of the fetus to be born. [69]

Consequently, Catholics could advocate any one of the options which are available: strict legal prohibition, a moderate code, or abortion on demand. Drinan insists that the abortion phenomenon must be studied in all its dimensions —moral, social, and legal. If after a thorough analysis of the total problem Catholics came to the conclusion that a very restrictive law would be the best overall solution, they would then at least be able to present some factual and effective objections against liberalization, instead of their traditional propositions that simply take for granted the correlation of criminality with immorality. [70] Daniel Callahan is the most outspoken representative of this pragmatic approach. He tries "to take seriously and employ the distinction between law and morality." [71] He does so on the strength of the Catholic legal-moral tradition which "provides ample precedent for a use of this distinction to tolerate as law or sanctioned practice what might be considered morally offensive, not only to a few but even to a large number." This "sets the stage" for a change in the traditional attitude towards abortion laws. [72]

The pragmatists then are convinced that the welfare of American society requires a repeal of the *penal* laws against abortion, and they urge that the operation be made available on request. However, they do not want the law to withdraw completely from this area. They propose to make the practice of abortion the object of *regulatory* laws, protecting the interests of the community when the termination of pregnancy relates to the common good. Their argument for the abolition of criminal sanctions comprises the following considerations:

1. *The freedom of conscience of the individual citizen*

(a) A significant section of the population believes that abortion is not immoral; abortion liberalization has the support of many sincere and responsible people who desire facilities for pregnancies when contraceptive techniques have failed. Many women feel that prohibitive laws unduly restrict their freedom, and they demand the right of control over their procreative faculties. Those who maintain that the destruction of intrauterine life is tantamount to murder will find this claim repulsive. But they are not entitled to deny women this freedom unless they can demonstrate that abortion affects not only the fetus but the welfare of the whole community. There is no evidence that this form of killing (which is *sui generis* because it destroys prenatal life) has adverse effects on the lives of those outside the womb. Without such factual proof the law cannot impose a decision on pregnant women in distress. It must step aside and recognize the mother's right to control her fertility.[73] (Drinan; Callahan; Segers; Peter A. Facione; Raymond G. Decker)

(b) The question of when human life should be granted full legal protection cannot be resolved. Under these circumstances the benefit of the doubt should be given to the mother and not to the fetus.[74] (Callahan; Donald P. Doherty)

(c) Fetal life is not personal human life and therefore abortion is not murder. In certain conditions the interruption of pregnancy is morally justified. Consequently the law must give women the opportunity to exercise their personal responsibility in this matter.[75] (Roy U. Schenk; Bernard J. Ransil; Springer)

2. *The negative social impact of unenforceable statutes*

(a) Experience shows that there never has been public pressure to enforce restrictive abortion laws; illegal abortionists and their clients have rarely been brought to trial. Moreover, prosecution of clandestine practitioners is difficult both in principle and in practice because all activity of this nature is underground and secretive. The fact of abortion is hard to prove because evidence of the operation is quickly concealed. The natural prosecutor (the victim) is dead and its guardian (the mother) is an accomplice in the crime.[76] (Callahan; Drinan)

(b) At the present time the traditional statutes no longer have public support because the social censure of abortion is diminishing. This creates a political and a legal problem. People demand abortion services, and there is a general unwillingness to use restrictive laws as a means of limiting the practice.[77] (Callahan)

(c) Prohibitive laws are frequently transgressed and known to be transgressed; this nullifies their symbolic and didactic significance. A statute which is unenforceable and widely violated breeds disregard and contempt of the legal system. Consequently, society will have to express its concern for nascent life in a different manner.[78] (Drinan; Callahan)

3. *The problem of illegal abortions*

(a) Restrictive laws limit the incidence of legal abortion but do not decrease the demand for the intervention. The result is a large number of clandestine operations. Liberalization leads to a dramatic increase in legal abortions but significantly reduces the number of illegal interventions. Even if under a liberal law the total number of abortions (legal and illegal) is greater than under a restrictive code, the injury and death rate associated with the activities of clandestine practitioners, even in developed countries, is a valid reason to bring the *de facto* practice under medical supervision.[79] (Callahan; Segers)

(b) Under restrictive codes safe abortions are expensive: the rich can afford them but the poor cannot. These statutes confirm the economic imbalance in society and are discriminatory in effect. Such discriminatory laws do not foster respect for the legal system.[80] (Callahan; Segers)

4. *The nonsolution of moderate laws*

(a) A moderate statute does not realize the primary objective which abortion law reform is meant to achieve: it will not significantly reduce the number of illegal operations. Even with the range of the indications widened, these statutes will not provide for many women who will ask for the intervention and get it, illegally if necessary. Indeed, there is reason to believe that moderate statutes increase the incidence of clandestine abortion.[81] (Callahan; Drinan)

(b) The acceptance of a moderate code with specific indications constitutes a *de facto* recognition of the right of the State to determine which unhealthy or inconvenient persons may be killed, thus establishing standards as to who may live and who should die. Since this may have long-range consequences of a most undesirable nature, the law should not pronounce on the value of fetal life but leave the abortion decision to the woman.[82] (Drinan)

(c) In a pluralistic society doctors and hospitals will adopt different interpretations of a moderately restrictive statute and, in practice, will establish different medical policies. It will be difficult to administer such a law equitably.[83] (Callahan)

5. *The advantages of a liberal legal policy*

(a) The repeal of penal laws which prohibit abortion except in rare circumstances and the easy availability of the intervention through doctors and hospitals would facilitate the legal prosecution of clandestine practitioners. If the illegal practice of abortion could be ended, at least one part of the social problem would be solved.[84] (Drinan)

(b) Allowing the practice of abortion to come out into the open will enable the authorities to assess the extent of the problem; this will help them in their attempts to solve it.[85] (Drinan)

(c) If abortion is not automatically a criminal offense, a woman seeking the termination of her pregnancy can be approached genuinely, not as a potential criminal but as a person in an agonizing dilemma. She needs and deserves adequate counselling instead of a threat of legal prosecution and, if she is offered meaningful assistance, she may well change her mind and decide to bring the child to term.[86] (Drinan)

6. *Practical considerations*

(a) The pro-life forces must face facts. Liberalization is here to stay, and it will be impossible to reverse this trend. From a political point of view the anti-abortion position is a weak one. It cannot claim to represent majority opinion. It is vulnerable to the charge that it seeks to impose sectarian beliefs on society at large—an accusation which is highly effective in legislatures and courts. Nor can the anti-abortionists pose as an oppressed minority group whose rights are ignored; pluralistic societies will only support minorities that want restrictions removed, not kept. Furthermore, in a country where public opinion is sensitive to arguments for social justice and where discriminatory laws are being repealed, it will be almost impossible to maintain restrictive abortion statutes because of their discriminatory effect.[87] (Callahan)

(b) The repeal of abortion laws may be inevitable because chemistry and pharmacology might well produce new abortifacients which make a surgical intervention unnecessary in the majority of cases. This development would complicate further the detection and prosecution of clandestine abortions.[88] (Drinan)

Regulatory Laws and Social Initiatives

While advocating the withdrawal of penal sanctions and the availability of abortion on request, the pragmatic school has recommended a set of parallel measures of a legal and social nature. These seek not only to regulate the granting of abortions but also to reduce the need for them and to counteract whatever negative influence a liberal abortion policy might have on society. Callahan explains the desirability of regulatory legislation and points out that such laws do not constitute an infringement of the rights of women. It is true that abortion cannot be shown to be dangerous to society and that in principle the final decision rests with the mother, but the liberal practice of abortion does have ascertainable social consequences. From this point of view it becomes a legitimate matter of concern for the community and a valid object of legislation.[89] Callahan defines the interest of society as follows:

1. *Liberalization leads to an increase in the number of legal abortions.* The community may try to reduce this number by persuading women that the interruption of pregnancy is a serious matter.[90]

2. *Abortion affects the health of women.* Society may express its desire to limit the number of late and repeated abortions where the health of the woman becomes a concern.[91]

3. *Abortion affects the dignity of women.* Society may be concerned about the conditions and equality of induced abortions and insist that women who seek the intervention be treated humanely.[92]

4. *Abortion affects the rights of others.* Apart from the pregnant woman there are others who are involved in an abortion: hospital authorities, doctors, and other medical personnel. Their rights must also be legally protected.[93]

5. *Liberalization affects the freedom of women.* Under permissive abortion laws women will be pressured into having an abortion which they do not want or need: the new freedom will rapidly become a new social compulsion. The lawgiver may seek to protect women from undue coercion by introducing legislation to ensure that the decision to abort is a free one.[94]

6. *Liberalization affects the use of contraceptives.* Society may try to forestall a primary reliance on abortion for birth control purposes rather than contraception.[95]

Callahan and Drinan insist that it is perfectly in order for the State to *regulate* the practice of liberal abortion and with the assistance of voluntary agencies to take social initiatives so as to minimize the incidence of fetal death. A primary consideration should be that liberalization will be interpreted by many in terms of legal, social, and moral approval and that many women will demand an abortion who would otherwise have made a different decision. Furthermore there is need for safeguards to anticipate any possible erosion of public respect for life.[96] The following is a summary of the legal and social measures suggested by various authors:[97]

1. *The incidence of abortion.* Prior to the operation the law should offer formal counselling by at least one trained person other than the attending surgeon. This might convert an unwanted pregnancy into a wanted one or

at least prevent the woman from becoming a repeater.[98] Such counselling should comprise the following:

(a) The nature of the medical procedure will be explained to the woman, and she will be informed about any possible medical consequences.[99]

(b) An attempt should be made to ascertain whether the woman's professed wish reflects her real wish.[100]

(c) She should be offered viable alternatives to abortion. This would include any assistance she needs in order to bear and raise the child: psychiatric therapy, marriage counselling, financial help, domestic assistance after delivery, assistance in finding better housing, or adoption facilities.[101]

2. *Late abortions.* Since after the first trimester of pregnancy the medical sequelae of the operation become a subject of concern, the law should permit abortion on request up to that time. A later intervention would require a more serious reason. The decision would not be left completely to the woman although her wish should remain the most important consideration.[102]

3. *Repeated Abortions.* The law should require a contraceptive counselling and assistance process after an abortion has been performed so that another unwanted pregnancy is less likely to occur.[103]

4. *Contraception.* The availability of contraceptives does not automatically lead to a reduction in the number of abortions nor are liberal abortion laws conducive to a wider or more efficient use of contraception. In order to limit the greater number of abortions that can be expected under a permissive code and to prevent abortion from becoming the primary method of birth control, extensive family planning programs are necessary. These should include adequate sex education that begins with the young child, the development and distribution of effective and cheap contraceptives, and information campaigns which are also addressed to teenagers and the unmarried.[104]

5. *Anti-abortion campaigns.* Once the restrictions of the law have been removed the abortion decision reverts to the forum of personal conscience. There can be no doubt that permissive laws have a symbolic effect and make abortion socially acceptable. Society should try to counteract this influence by maintaining steady pressure against the formation of an abortion habit. Everything possible must be done to persuade people that the destruction of nascent human life requires very serious thinking.[105] The following points deserve particular attention:

(a) The biological facts of fetal development must be widely publicized. These make it perfectly clear that the "product of conception" does bear a remarkable resemblance to a human person.[106]

(b) The fundamental issue of the humanity of the fetus and of its conse-
quent right to life must be persistently kept in the mind of the public.[107]
(c) The abortion operation must be described in suitable language. It
must avoid, on the one hand, an emotional overemphasis on the plight of
distressed pregnancies and, on the other, the use of technical jargon
which is impersonal and does not adequately express what actually
occurs.[108]
(d) Abortion must be presented not merely as a private moral dilemma
but as a social problem of the first order. The abortion issue reflects the
quality of the society in which we live, and it will be solved only when
that quality improves. True abortion reform begins with social reform.
Adequate social services including a good maternal welfare system will
give pregnant women the type of support they need so that they no longer
see abortion as the only way out of their difficult situation.[109]
(e) The anti-abortion argument should be addressed more specifically to
women. While the abortion dilemma is a moral and legal problem, the
experience itself is uniquely female. The emotions and motivations of
women must therefore be given the fullest attention. This will require a
less intellectual and magisterial approach, one that is not exclusively
oriented to the fetus but gives due consideration to the fact that the lives
and the welfare of women are important values too. Women are particularly sensitive to a comprehensive and consistent pro-life proposition
which does not onesidedly concentrate on the quality of fetal life but
affirms the dignity of human life in all its dimensions.[110]
(f) All who are convinced that certain measures are necessary to protect
the life of the fetus should realize the importance of public opinion on
this issue and master the various techniques of influencing it.[111]
6. *Specific tasks of the Church*
(a) Since the abortion decision will become a private moral choice, the
Church must invigorate the sense of personal moral responsibility of its
faithful. It must work for a deeper formation of their consciences and
give them a better understanding of the various levels of moral values
and the corresponding obligations.[112]
(b) Since the new legal freedom may degenerate into social pressure, the
Church must help women to make a personal moral decision, free from
any coercion by their social milieu or their physician. Those women
especially who are not convinced by the Church's position on abortion
and who are not likely to be persuaded by arguments from authority must
be helped to unravel the pressures that are upon them so that they come to
understand the values that are at stake. This will help them to recognize
that inconvenience, social embarrassment, or economic discomfort are
insufficient reasons for a decision to abort.[113]

(c) The growing acceptance of abortion is one of the signs that the Catholic view on sexuality, love, marriage, and the family is becoming increasingly unpopular. In this area the Catholic community has a primary responsibility towards its own young people: it has to keep the Christian ideal before their eyes and instill into them a corresponding sense of self-respect, discipline, and reverence for life, no matter how unfashionable these have become. [114]

(d) The Church has to adopt a prophetic stand against egoism in government, Church, and culture. [115]

(e) The Church must promote new social attitudes towards unmarried mothers. [116]

7. *The conscience clause.* The law must protect the human and professional rights of doctors and other medical personnel. They should not be forced to perform abortions against their conscience or against their medical judgement. [117]

Drinan summarizes the pragmatic argument and at the same time tries to ease the Catholic conscience. He states that it would be wrong to look upon Catholic acquiescence to a liberal regulation of abortion as the surrender or abdication of a system that "worked" and solved the problem. On the contrary, Drinan seems many advantages and opportunities in a legal arrangement which does not stigmatize a woman seeking an abortion as a criminal. [118]

V. The Abortion Ethos: New Analyses

In the previous chapter I presented a number of analyses by American Catholic authors of the psychology of the abortifacient society and the ideology of the liberationist movement. We saw that they tended to associate the social and legal acceptance of abortion with a general lessening of respect for individual human life, a development which they feared would be reinforced and accelerated by legalization of abortion on demand. At a later stage of the debate there has been further speculation on this important aspect of the abortion problem. Some new insights have been offered which must now be listed.

Nonidentification with Fetal Life
In the opinion of James M. Humber, an inability or unwillingness to accept fetal life as personal human life often derives from sentiment rather than from intellectual conviction. He observes that people who justify the destruction of prenatal life before it has reached a certain stage of development, such as viability or birth, very often cannot explain satisfactorily

why they select that particular point as the moment of hominization rather than any other. It would seem that their moral attitude is not founded on "hard facts" or objective intellectual insights; it should be traced to an emotional inability to empathize with the prenatal organism before it has achieved certain adult characteristics. At the same time the advocates of abortion do not find it difficult to identify themselves with pregnant women in distress. [119] Humber writes:

> Why do so many believe that they may assume by arbitrary definition that pre-natal organisms are not human? It is not just that the status of these beings is unsure; rather, the abortion advocate finds it difficult to *feel* that such organisms are human. First, they are not usually seen. And when they are seen, they do not have human form. Further, they are not (at least in the earlier stages of development) conscious. On the other hand, a mother who threatens suicide if she must bear another child *is* seen, she *is* identified with. This is why the "reasons" cited by those favoring arbitrary definition seem to have force, even though they carry no logical weight. [120]

Humber states that many a nurse who initially favored abortion changed her mind after she had actually assisted in the operation and had been exposed to the realities of fetal life and death:

> When *she* was the one handed a six month old wriggling fetus, when *she* was the one who dropped it into a basin where it slowly turned blue and suffocated, she somehow began to feel party to a crime. Why? Quite clearly, to actually see the fetus die is a shocking experience. She found, to her horror, that she could empathize with it—that she could feel the fetus was human, despite her earlier views. Obviously her attitudes and feelings were here determining her beliefs as to what is and what is not human. [121]

Humber therefore maintains that very few people who now define the unborn child as nonhuman would not change their mind if they would witness the abortion of a six-month-old conceptus. [122] John G. Milhaven has also discussed the phenomenon of nonidentification with nascent human life. Unlike Humber, he does not explain it in terms of basic psychology but attributes it to modern man's understanding of human nature and of his task in the world. In Milhaven's analysis, the debate on the value of fetal life is a reflection of a more fundamental controversy: the real conflict exists between two different world views—the traditional Christian and the modern. The traditional Christian experience of reality is based on the Hellenistic-medieval outlook on the world relating all human events to the afterlife and evaluating them according to the degree to which they brought man closer to the beatific vision after death. This classical mentality did recognize the dignity of man but explained his value primarily in the supernatural terms of the afterlife. Man had to be respected because he was the image of God and the object of divine providence. Human fulfilment was also principally celestial. Man was destined in the first place for a life with God after death, and terrestrial values were therefore a secondary concern. Moral principles were derived from the conjectured intentions of the divine legislator who had wisely preordained the good of the human species and prearranged its development. Such rules, obviously, were absolute and unchangeable.[123]

Milhaven contrasts this classical view of man and reality with the present day secular outlook. Modern man no longer believes that the afterlife and the wisdom of a divine lawgiver should be his criteria of good and evil. He concentrates on his own worldly experience which he tries to analyse in order to understand what he is. He has his doubts about any speculation on the human which tries to influence his experience of himself but which he cannot experimentally verify. He adopts a new attitude towards nature. He no longer regards it as fixed and absolute or as reflecting the intentions of the Creator, but he shapes it responsibly and creatively in order to exploit its potential. For Milhaven this is the essence of man's new awareness of himself and of his task on earth.[124] Man sees himself as autonomous and responsible, as ''self-legislating and self-creating, and thus legislating and creating for all men as persons and ends in themselves.''[125] It is this concentration on experience and self-creation as the fundamental characteristics of man which explains why the modern mind finds it difficult to grant full human status to the unborn child. The fetus gives no evidence of awareness and reaction, of activity, of humanness.[126]

In Milhaven's opinion the modern world view has many positive aspects. It has resulted in a new moral sensitivity that has brought about fundamental changes in Western society, especially in the field of social justice.[127] The contemporary acceptability of abortion stems from the same philosophy. This moral position must be respected, and this respect be expressed in law:

> The position of abortionists in our society could be seen as an inseparable component of a total outlook, held by many people and to be with us for a long time. There is no reason to doubt that people who have this outlook share in universal human weakness and, like the rest of men, will show themselves at times hypocritical, superficial, selfish, choosing the easy way out. But their position on abortion arises organically out of their strength, a responsible, intelligent, moral synthesis that has served the nation well, whatever be its limitations and drawbacks. The laws of the

nation should treat these men with their views as a mature segment of a pluralistic society. The law should not prohibit their carrying out their basic moral convictions. [128]

Sexuality, Contraception, and Abortion

In Milhaven's analysis, the present trend towards easy abortion is a reflection of secular man's self-awareness. William E. May and Sebastian MacDonald have offered supplementary insights. They have related the abortion ethos to the contemporary understanding of human sexuality.

May distinguishes two different attitudes towards sexual relationships. The first view recognizes that sexual activity has a twofold dimension, viz., the unitive and the procreative aspect or lovemaking and baby-making, and it accepts both functions as fundamental constituents of sexual intercourse. This does not mean that this view rules out all use of contraception. It considers contraceptive *acts* permissible under certain circumstances but there is no question here of a contraceptive *mentality*; in principle union and procreation are seen as indissolubly linked even when *in fact* they are disconnected. Those who sponsor this concept of sexuality agree with the supporters of an abortion ethos that no woman should become pregnant against her will, but they also point out that intercourse is a matter of human choice. This choice must take into consideration the possibility that the act of love will generate new life, and this awareness of personal responsibility will put an "intelligent restraint" on sexual relationships. May describes the second view as a "contraceptive mentality." It separates *in principle* the unitive and procreative dimensions of sexuality which are brought together only when the partners decide to do so. For such people the only moral criterion of sexual intercourse is the mutual exchange of love and tenderness. Contraception becomes a way of life, and conception and birth are regarded as the price which may have to be paid for the expression of love between a man and a woman. May states that this attitude will easily lead to a social and moral acceptance of abortion. Abortion simply becomes another form of birth control, "post-conceptive birth control." [129]

MacDonald also believes that the abortion problem must be seen in the perspective of present-day attitudes towards contraception. He notes that the Church treats the liberal practice of abortion as a symptom of an anti-life mentality prevalent in society today. But this approach attributes to those who practice or defend abortion a meaning and a motive which very often are not theirs; in American society the interruption of pregnancy is understood *contraceptively*. [130] MacDonald makes the same point as May and argues that in the United States the Church is confronted with a basic identification of two very different forms of birth control. For the majority of women there is a causal connection between contraception and abortion. This mechanism becomes operative when contraception has failed, and they are faced with an unwanted pregnancy. The imperative to use contraception translates itself into a decision to terminate the pregnancy. Abortion becomes a corrective or supplementary measure which belatedly achieves the birth prevention originally contemplated by the application of contraceptives. American society therefore views abortion primarily as a drastic form of *contraception*. Due to this correlation popular moral analysis fails to do justice to the unique anti-life character of the operation.[131]

I mentioned in the previous chapter that Callahan also defines the abortion ethos as basically a contraceptive ethos. He observes that many people in many different parts of the world want smaller families than their forefathers did. He attributes this development to a combination of economic and social factors:

> There are any number of reasons for this shift in attitude. Among the most important are the advance of industrialization and technology, with their accompanying social, cultural, economic and often political changes; increasing urbanization, invariably a concomitant of industrialization; improvements in medicine and public health, which have drastically cut death rates generally and infant mortality particularly; and finally, in some areas, a shortage of food because of the population squeeze. These developments, characteristic of modern society, are interwoven in complex patterns that appear in slightly different forms in different parts of the world. But one result is the same: smaller families, fewer children, are desired or believed necessary.[132]

When such a social trend gains momentum, while the availability and effectiveness of methods of contraception leave much to be desired, people will turn to abortion as a means of birth control.[133] MacDonald concludes that if the Church wants its message on the value of unborn life to make sense, it must first of all begin to speak on abortion as it is commonly understood, and not relate the abortion ethos to an anti-life or anti-child mentality. The practice of abortion reflects instead a preoccupation with the *wanted* child.[134]

VI. Prophecy or Pragmatism: A First Evaluation

This chapter has described the whole scale of positions adopted by American Catholic authors on the morality of abortion liberalization. Some authors reject any form of political and legal compromise with the reform movement, but others are willing to lend support to the enactment of a moderately restrictive code because they consider this a lesser evil than abortion on demand. Others again utilize the insights of Vatican II and conclude that the Church cannot insist on an automatic translation of sectarian morality into civil law. The "prophetic school" employs the traditional distinction between law and morality and favors a moderate statute, while the pragmatists argue from the same premise but advocate abortion on request. A wide variety of views, therefore, but with one common denominator: the Catholic tradition. In Chapter V, which described the Catholic reform efforts concerning the moral aspects of the abortion issue, I pointed out that all authors presented their views as legitimate explications of principles which tradition, at least implicitly, admitted. A similar conviction characterizes the parallel stage of the legal debate.

It must be noted that those who, on the ground of pluralism or pragmatism, have pleaded for a new Catholic approach to abortion legislation have without exception avoided the question of the legal status of the fetus. Yet this remains the fundamental legal —and moral —problem. Even if one accepts the emphasis placed by the pragmatic school on the feasibility of civil legislation and is also willing to pay attention to such factors as personal freedom and equity, it still largely depends on one's assessment of the quality of fetal life whether one is prepared to let practical considerations prevail over prophetic function. In other words, people who (rightly or wrongly) believe that the fetus is a human person, entitled to the full protection of the law, are naturally extremely reluctant to surrender on its behalf in the legal battle, merely because the legal enactment and enforcement of its right to life is difficult in a pluralistic society. We saw in Chapter VII that the American legal tradition does not treat the fetus as a nonentity or as protoplasm. On the contrary, the fetus enjoys a significant and a *growing* degree of legal protection. I have registered the arguments of those who point to the ambiguities or inconsistencies of a juridical system that recognizes the unborn child's right to inherit and to receive compensation for injuries but does not protect the same child against total destruction. In 1970 Drinan believed that the opponents of liberalization tended to exaggerate the relevance of the rights which the conceptus has acquired. He admitted, however, that in American law the unborn child is *sui juris* capable of possessing at least inchoate rights and that so far the proponents of abortion on demand have not felt obliged to explain the legal logic of what would seem to be a complete reversal of a definite legal and jurisprudential trend.[135] A decade has passed since then but there has been no great effort on the part of the Catholic reformists to clarify this aspect of their position. It is remarkable, for instance, that Callahan's extensive and profound examination of the abortion problem completely neglects the question of the legal status of the fetus and argues from the premise that legality and morality are not identical —a postulate which he more or less takes for granted.[136]

Some authors have used the teaching of Vatican II as the basis for a new legal-moral policy. Without wanting to question the validity of their explications of the various conciliar statements, I must point out that their conclusions are *extrapolations* and certainly do not reflect what the Council directly had in mind. Vatican II declares that life must be protected with the utmost care from the moment of conception and that abortion and infanticide are unspeakable crimes.[137] At the same time "the protection and promotion of the inviolable rights of man ranks among the essential duties of government."[138] If the Council had explicitly pronounced on the morality of abortion liberalization, it is not hard to conjecture what its verdict would have been.[139]

The pragmatic school argues that restrictive laws have little symbolic value as far as society's respect for life is concerned. They are unenforced, unenforceable, and discriminatory and, as such, even have negative effects on the community. Yet we are also warned that their repeal will be interpreted by many in terms of legal, social, and moral approval and will result in an increase not only in the number of legal abortions but perhaps even in the *total* number of abortions (legal and illegal). There would seem to be a contradiction here: if the *repeal* of a restrictive code makes an impact on social attitudes, surely the *maintenance* of these statutes has social significance.[140]

Various authors have recommended a number of legal and social initiatives which will reduce the demand for abortion. Few people will deny the value of these suggestions but, as I pointed out in the previous chapter, it is easier to picture ideals than to put them into practice. Diamond admits this, perhaps unintentionally, when he outlines the legal and social measures which would be needed to solve the problem of abortion:

> I envisage [a solution] that is comprehensive, one that bows in all directions: it will contain enough law to protect the future and the unborn child; enough aggressive sociology to prevent incest, rape and hardship pregnancies; enough aggressive scientific research to prevent deformities; enough medical and sex education to annihilate ignorance about pregnancy; enough common sense to develop the theology of love and the ethics of situationism with insight into both the fallibility and capability of mere humans; enough discipline to develop character; enough liberty to permit growth.[141]

Finally, a sense of political realism pervades the arguments at this stage of the debate. Even those who oppose any form of political compromise seem to accept that liberalization in the United States is now a fact and that it may not be possible to reverse this trend and reenact the traditional statutes. This awareness is also reflected in the statements issued by the American hierarchy in the wake of the 1973 Supreme Court decision. For instance, in their 1975 *Pastoral Plan for Pro-Life Activities* the bishops launched a comprehensive program of legislative action which included the following elements:

(a) Passage of a constitutional amendment providing protection for the unborn child *to the maximum degree possible.*

(b) Passage of federal and state laws and adoption of administrative policies that will restrict the practice of abortion *as much as possible.*

(c) Continual research into the *refinement* and precise interpretation of *Roe* and *Doe* and subsequent court decisions. [142]

The bishops, therefore, seem to admit that a reenactment of the traditional statutes may not be feasible from a political point of view. They appear not to rule out the possibility of a compromise solution — and this in spite of their conviction that "a just system of law cannot be in conflict with the law of God," and that the Court's decisions "violate the moral order." [143] This became evident again in November 1981 when they endorsed a constitutional amendment which would rule out a constitutional right to abortion and empower Congress and then the individual States to adopt laws regulating and prohibiting abortion. The bishops preferred this compromise measure to a so-called human rights amendment which would impose an outright ban on virtually all abortions but would have no chance of mustering sufficient political support. [144]

NOTES

[1] Robert F. Drinan, S.J., "The Jurisprudential Options on Abortion," *Theological Studies* 31 (1970), p. 168.

[2] Robert H. Springer, S.J., "Notes on Moral Theology," *Theological Studies* 28 (1967), pp. 334-335. Note that Springer wrote prior to the encyclical *Humanae Vitae* which was published the following year. In my final chapter I will refer to the Catholic position on contraception.

[3] Editorial, "The Abortion Question: Life and Law in a Pluralistic Society," *America* 117 (1967), p. 706.

[4] Editorial, "Politics and Abortion," *Commonweal* 103 (1976), p. 132.

[5] Germain G. Grisez, *Abortion: The Myths, the Realities, and the Arguments* (New York: Corpus Books, 1970), pp. 458-460.

[6] *Ibid.*, pp. 429-430. Grisez's ethical perspective on this issue has been presented in Chapter V. David Granfield explains why the traditional statutes allowing an abortion to save the life of the mother were not incompatible with the constitutional principles of liberty, equality, and the right to life. The law did not consider the fetus an unjust

aggressor but rather the unfortunate victim of circumstances beyond human control. The legal ground of the abortion was one of duress of circumstances, without any imputation of even material culpability of the child; *The Abortion Decision* (revised ed.; Garden City, N.Y.: Doubleday Image Books, 1971), p. 144. See also: A. James Quinn and James A. Griffin, "The Rights of the Unborn," *Jurist* 31 (1971), pp. 606-607; David W. Louisell and John T. Noonan, Jr., "Constitutional Balance," in John T. Noonan, Jr. (ed.), *The Morality of Abortion: Legal and Historical Perspectives* (Cambridge, Mass.: Harvard University Press, 1970), pp. 230-233; Editorial, "Public Policy and Abortion Laws," *America* 120 (1969), p. 240; Robert M. Byrn, "Abortion in Perspective," *Duquesne University Law Review* 5 (1966), pp. 134-138.

[7] Grisez, *op. cit.*, p. 430. See also: Granfield, *op. cit.*, p. 108.

[8] Grisez, *op. cit.*, p. 427. Clare Boothe Luce qualifies this distinction as ambiguous: it reveals a conviction that abortion is not *really* equivalent to murder; "Two Books on Abortion and the Questions They Raise," *National Review* 23 (1971), pp. 30, 33. See also: Donald P. Doherty, "Constitutional Law: Abortion Statute as Invasion of a Woman's Right of Privacy," *Saint Louis University Law Journal* 15 (1971), pp. 647-648. The issue was discussed at the 1967 Harvard-Kennedy Conference on Abortion. See: Robert E. Cooke *et al.* (eds.), *The Terrible Choice: The Abortion Dilemma. Based on the Proceedings of the International Conference on Abortion Sponsored by the Harvard Divinity School and the Joseph P. Kennedy Jr. Foundation* (New York: Bantam Books, 1968), p. 94.

[9] Granfield, *op. cit.*, pp. 190-192.

[10] Grisez, *op. cit.*, pp. 431, 460-463; Granfield, *op. cit.*, pp. 192-193; James V. McNulty, "The Therapeutic Abortion Law: A Fight for Life," *Linacre Quarterly* 33 (1966), pp. 342-343. See also: Louisell and Noonan, *op. cit.*, pp. 254-258; Thomas L. Shaffer, "Abortion, the Law and Human Life," *Valparaiso University Law Review* 2 (1967), p. 106; Michael V. Viola, "Abortion: A Catholic View," in E. Fuller Torrey (ed.), *Ethical Issues in Medicine* (Boston: Little, Brown and Co., 1968), p. 101. McNulty stipulates in addition that no abortion be approved on social or other nonmedical grounds; *op. cit.*, pp. 342-343.

[11] Robert F. Drinan, S.J., "Strategy on Abortion," *America* 116 (1967), p. 179. He refers to Catholic attitudes towards laws on divorce and on the public promotion and distribution of contraceptives.

[12] *Ibid.*, pp. 178, 179. As we will see, Drinan will gradually adopt a more liberal position. Viola believes that relaxation of the statutes is "reasonable" if it allows abortion when the mother's physical or mental health is seriously endangered, if it is very likely that the child will be gravely handicapped, or if the pregnancy is the result of rape or incest; *op. cit.*, p. 101. Patrick Coffey is willing to accept some relaxation of the law (e.g., a legalization of abortion during the first trimester) as long as it is perfectly clear that there is question here of a political compromise and not of a morally justifiable concession; "When Is Killing the Unborn a Homicidal Action?" *Linacre Quarterly* 43 (1976), p. 92.

[13] Norman St. John-Stevas, "Abortion: The English Experience," *America* 117 (1967), p. 709.

[14] Norman St. John-Stevas, "Abortion, Catholics, and the Law," *Catholic World* 206 (1968), p. 151.

[15] *Ibid.*, p. 151; *id.*, "Abortion: The English Experience," *op. cit.*, p. 709. See also: Raymond Tatalovich and Byron W. Daynes, "The Trauma of Abortion Politics," *Commonweal* 108 (1981), pp. 648-649.

[16] Charles E. Curran, *Ongoing Revision: Studies in Moral Theology* (Notre Dame, Ind.: Fides, 1975), pp. 110-111. Curran's analysis is mainly concerned with the teaching of St. Thomas Aquinas.

[17] *Ibid.*, pp. 111-113.

[18] *Ibid.*, pp. 119-121. My analysis of the traditional manuals in Chapter VI yielded similar conclusions. See also: Granfield, *op. cit.*, p. 142.

[19] Curran, *op. cit.*, pp. 121-124.

[20] Daniel Callahan, *Abortion: Law, Choice and Morality* (New York: Macmillan, 1970), pp. 434-435.

[21] James J. Diamond, "Pro-Life Amendments and Due Process," *America* 130 (1974), p. 28.

[22] Bernard Häring, "A Theological Evaluation," in Noonan (ed.), *op. cit.*, p. 142.

[23] Pius XI, "Casti Connubii," *Acta Apostolicae Sedis* 20 (1930), p. 589; Häring, *op. cit.*, pp. 142-143. Häring adds that the context of this exhortation is the 1929 Concordat with the Italian State to which the Pope explicitly refers as a hopeful agreement; *ibid.*, p. 143, footnote 37.

[24] Häring, *op. cit.*, p. 143.

[25] Robert F. Drinan, S.J., "Catholic Moral Teaching and Abortion Laws in America," *The Catholic Theological Society of America: Proceedings of the Twenty-Third Annual Convention, Washington, D.C., June 17-20, 1968* 23 (1968), pp. 118-119.

[26] Springer, *op. cit.*, pp. 334-335; *Pastoral Constitution on the Church in the Modern World, "Gaudium et Spes,"* nos. 21, 51. We will see that Springer would eventually adopt a very liberal position.

[27] Dennis J. Doherty, "The Morality of Abortion," *American Ecclesiastical Review* 169 (1975), p. 40; *Decree on Ecumenism, "Unitatis Redintegratio,"* no. 23.

[28] Dennis J. Doherty, *op. cit.*, p. 40. See also: Thomas A. Wassmer, S.J., *Christian Ethics for Today* (Milwaukee: Bruce, 1969), p. 196; Editorial, "Abortion and U.S. Protestants," *America* 128 (1973), pp. 156-157; Robert F. Drinan, "Abortion: Contemporary Protestant Thinking," *America* 117 (1967), p. 715; *id.*, "The Jurisprudential Options on Abortion," *op. cit.*, pp. 155-158.

[29] Drinan, "Catholic Moral Teaching and Abortion Laws in America," *op. cit.*, p. 119.

[30] *Declaration on Religious Liberty, "Dignitatis Humanae,"* no. 7; Drinan, "Catholic Moral Teaching....," *op. cit.*, p. 119.

[31] Drinan, "Catholic Moral Teaching....," *op. cit.*, p. 119. Grisez questions Drinan's use of the conciliar text. The passage forms the end of a paragraph in which the Council stipulates that even in the exercise of religious freedom certain moral standards must be observed and that the State may enact *just* legislation in order to ensure this. *For the rest*, the usages of society..., *i.e.*, liberty should prevail. If the passage is read in its context it is difficult to see how it paves the way for a liberalization of abortion laws; *op. cit.*, pp. 452-453.

[32] Curran, *op. cit.*, pp. 124-125; *"Dignitatis Humanae,"* nos. 2-3.

[33] Curran, *op. cit.*, pp. 125-129.

[34] Drinan, "Catholic Moral Teaching....," *op. cit.*, p. 123; *"Dignitatis Humanae,"* no. 4, emphasis supplied by Drinan.

[35] Drinan, "Catholic Moral Teaching....," *op. cit.*, p. 123.

[36] *Ibid.*, p. 121. See also: *id.*, "The State of the Abortion Question," *Commonweal* 92 (1970), p. 109; John Deedy, "The Church in the World: Catholics, Abortion, and the Supreme Court," *Theology Today* 30 (1973), p. 283. Grisez questions the application of this conciliar text to the abortion issue. He observes that there is coercion in any

criminal law and that the Council did not prohibit legal coercion in general but only as an instrument of spreading religious faith or introducing religious practice; *op. cit.*, p. 453.

[37] Dennis J. Doherty, *op. cit.*, pp. 37, 41-42.

[38] *Ibid.*, p. 42.

[39] Wassmer, *op. cit.*, p. 201. See also: Raymond G. Decker, "The Abortion Decision: Two Years Later: More Christian than its Critics," *Commonweal* 101 (1975), pp. 384-386.

[40] Mary C. Segers, "Abortion: The Last Resort," *America* 133 (1975), p. 457. See also: Decker, *op. cit.*, pp. 386-387; Peter Steinfels, "The Search for an Alternative," *Commonweal* 108 (1981), pp. 662-664. Frank J. Ayd, Jr., seems to accept without question that law is no more than the expression of the moral consensus of society. If the majority believe that there should be abortion on request, then the law should permit it. The only problem is how to determine what the majority believe; "Liberal Abortion Laws: A Psychiatrist's View," *American Ecclesiastical Review* 158 (1968), p. 81.

[41] Häring, *op. cit.*, pp. 143-145.

[42] *Ibid.*, p. 145. See also: Editorial, "The Abortion Question: Life and Law in a Pluralistic Society," *op. cit.*, p. 706. Richard T. De George presents as essential functions of law the protection of individual liberty and the prohibition of acts that are seriously harmful to the community. Immorality by itself is not a sufficient ground for legal sanctions: law should only enforce those morals that are necessary for the common good. Whether it is necessary for American society that abortion be made illegal is a question that still remains undecided. Legislation prohibiting the termination of pregnancy should be enacted not on the basis of the moral beliefs of part of the population but "on the basis of the considered majority opinion about the social effects of doing so as opposed to not doing so"; "Legal Enforcement, Moral Pluralism and Abortion," in *Philosophy and Civil Law: Proceedings of the American Catholic Philosophical Association* 49 (1975), p. 179.

[43] Richard A. McCormick, S.J., "Conference Without Consensus," *America* 117 (1967), p. 321.

[44] Curran, *op. cit.*, pp. 124-129. Curran utilizes the writings of John Courtney Murray on religious freedom and the relationship between Church and State.

[45] Curran, *op. cit.*, pp. 126-127. Curran points out that the acceptance of this legal-moral policy would constitute a significant development in Catholic social thought. Medieval society which co-determined the formation of the Church's view on the function of law was theocratic, not democratic, and paid little attention to the political freedom and civil rights of its citizens. Moreover, Catholic moral theology traditionally emphasized the existence of a hierarchical order throughout the universe which has been established by God and which must be observed by man under the direction of those who in some way take God's place—a framework which left little scope for individual freedom; *ibid.*, pp. 111, 113-119, 128, 129-131.

[46] *Ibid.*, pp. 131-132; *id.*, "Abortion: Law and Morality in Contemporary Catholic Theology," *Jurist* 33 (1973), pp. 165-166.

[47] Curran, *Ongoing Revision....*, *op. cit.*, pp. 127-129; *id.*, "Abortion: Law and Morality....," *op. cit.*, pp. 164-165.

[48] Curran, *Ongoing Revision....*, *op. cit.*, pp. 132-134; *id.*, "Abortion: Law and Morality....," *op. cit.*, p. 166.

[49] Curran, *Ongoing Revision....*, *op. cit.*, pp. 133-134.

[50] Curran, "Abortion: Law and Morality....," *op. cit.*, p. 168.

[51] Curran, *Ongoing Revision....* , *op. cit.*, pp. 136-139, 142-143. See also: Drinan, "Catholic Moral Teaching....," *op. cit.*, pp. 124-125, 129-130.

[52] Curran, *Ongoing Revision....*, *op. cit.*, pp. 134-135.

[53] *Ibid.*, p. 135. See also: Gordon C. Zahn, "A Religious Pacifist Looks at Abortion," *Commonweal* 94 (1971), p. 279; Drinan, "Catholic Moral Teaching....," *op. cit.*, pp. 121-122, 124, 129.

[54] Curran, *Ongoing Revision....* , *op. cit.*, pp. 135-136, 138-139; *id.*, "Abortion: Law and Morality....," *op. cit.*, p. 167. Curran disagrees with the arguments which the Supreme Court adopted in its 1973 decision but he can understand why the Court came to its final conclusion: in American jurisprudence there is the tendency to give the benefit of the doubt to the freedom of the individual; *Ongoing Revision....* , *op. cit.*, pp. 139-141.

[55] Richard A. McCormick, S.J., "Notes on Moral Theology: The Abortion Dossier," *Theological Studies* 35 (1974), pp. 323, 356-357.

[56] *Ibid.*, pp. 357-358. He refers to a joint statement by the Catholic bishops and the Council of the Evangelical Church in Germany which recommends this legal solution; *ibid.*, pp. 328, 358. Rudolph J. Gerber also distinguishes between the didactic and coercive functions of law but he does not commit himself to a specific position on the legal issue; "Abortion: Parameters for Decision," *International Philosophical Quarterly* 11 (1971), p. 578.

[57] Daniel A. Degnan, S.J., "Law, Morals and Abortion," *Commonweal* 100 (1974), pp. 305-307.

[58] *Ibid.*, pp. 306-307.

[59] *Ibid.*, pp. 306-308. Steinfels adopts a similar position and suggests that the fetus be given effective legal protection after eight weeks of gestation; *op. cit.*, pp. 663-664. Richard Stith also seems in favor of some degree of relaxation; "A Secular Case Against Abortion on Demand," *Commonweal* 95 (1971), p. 153.

[60] Wilfred R. Caron, "New York Abortion Reform—A Critique," *Catholic Lawyer* 14 (1968), p. 212.

[61] *Ibid.*, p. 200.

[62] *Ibid.*, p. 213. The chapter clearly opted for the lesser evil. In 1968 the New York State legislature was considering the "Blumenthal Bill" which proposed to legalize abortions performed on specific statutory indications. The chapter had serious reservations about this bill because of its legal deficiencies (a vague and loose terminology) and because *in practice* it would establish a policy of abortion on demand; *ibid.*, pp. 199-200, 212-213. In a statement issued in August 1977 the Leadership Conference of Women Religious emphasized that the feasibility of abortion legislation is particularly problematic because there is no public consensus regarding the nature and dignity of unborn human life. This means that the social climate for a really good abortion law is lacking and that at the present time it would be unwise to attempt to enact legislation in this area. First there must be an articulate and intelligent dialogue which keeps the abortion issue in the public arena in order to create a greater awareness of the value of fetal life; "Choose Life: Promoting the Value and Quality of Life," *Origins* 7 (1977-1978), pp. 166-167. See the critique of this statement by Msgr. James McHugh, director of the Committee for Pro-Life Activities of the National Conference of Catholic Bishops: "Official Reacts to 'Choose Life' Text," *Origins* 7 (1977-1978), p. 317. Benedict M. Ashley, O.P., and Kevin D. O'Rourke, O.P., feel that Catholics should be practical rather than "fanatical" in their defense of

fetal rights. They should work for legislation that achieves as much as possible for prenatal life, and they should not eschew political or legal compromises if these are necessary to generate social initiatives in favor of the unborn child; *Health Care Ethics: A Theological Analysis* (St. Louis: The Catholic Hospital Association, 1978), pp. 263-264.

[63] Diamond, *op. cit.*, p. 28.

[64] *Ibid.*, pp. 27-28.

[65] *Ibid.*, p. 28. Arguing along similar lines Donald A. Giannella would legalize the termination of a pregnancy which threatens the life or the physical or mental health of the woman, but only if the threat results from the pregnancy itself, not if it stems from prospective problems after delivery. However, if the legislator feels that he can only muster political support and public respect for a law that is more permissive, he should seek to enact legislation which pragmatically meets the most insistent demands of the public but prophetically affirms the human value of the fetus and its right to equal protection. Such statutes would also provide for pregnancies resulting from rape and would generally permit abortions during the first trimester on specific therapeutic or eugenic indications; "The Difficult Quest for a Truly Humane Abortion Law," *Villanova Law Review* 13 (1968), pp. 280-289, 301-302.

[66] Gary D. Glenn, "Abortion and Inalienable Rights in Classical Liberalism," *American Journal of Jurisprudence* 20 (1975), pp. 62-80.

[67] *Ibid.*, p. 66.

[68] *Ibid.*, pp. 76-77.

[69] Drinan, "Abortion: Contemporary Protestant Thinking," *op. cit.*, p. 715.

[70] *Ibid.*, p. 715; *id.*, "Catholic Moral Teaching. . . .," *op. cit.*, pp. 122, 129.

[71] Callahan, *op. cit.*, p. 478.

[72] *Ibid.*, p. 438. Callahan bases his position largely on the arguments of Drinan; *ibid.*, pp. 435-438. It is not clear what laws or practices he has in mind.

[73] Drinan, "Catholic Moral Teaching. . . .," *op. cit.*, p. 127; Callahan, *op. cit.*, pp. 473-475, 479; *id.*, "Abortion: Thinking and Experiencing," *Christianity and Crisis* 32 (1973), p. 297; Segers, *op. cit.*, pp. 457, 458; Peter A. Facione, "Callahan on Abortion," *American Ecclesiastical Review* 167 (1973), pp. 296-297; Decker, *op. cit.*, pp. 384-388. The legal position of Callahan clearly reflects his moral view which was presented in Chapter V. Ashley and O'Rourke argue that abortion liberalization does not enhance the freedom of women. On the contrary, permissive statutes encourage and even force them to act against deep-seated instincts, and there is no reason to suppose that the social approval expressed in the law will do more than cover up the trauma which easy abortions inflict upon women's self-respect and upon society's appreciation of the dignity of womanhood; *op. cit.*, p. 240.

[74] Callahan, "Abortion: Thinking and Experiencing," *op. cit.*, p. 297; Donald P. Doherty, *op. cit.*, pp. 648-650.

[75] Roy U. Schenk, "Let's Think About Abortion," *Catholic World* 207 (1968), p. 17; Bernard J. Ransil, *Abortion* (Paramus, N.J.: Paulist Press Deus Books, 1969), pp. 101-102; Robert H. Springer, S.J., "Marriage, the Family, and Sex—A Roman Catholic View," *Perspectives in Biology and Medicine* 19 (1976), p. 194. The moral perspectives of Schenk, Ransil, and Springer have been presented in Chapter V.

[76] Callahan, "Abortion: Thinking and Experiencing," *op. cit.*, p. 297; *id., Abortion: Law, Choice and Morality, op. cit.*, pp. 468-469; Drinan, "Catholic Moral Teaching. . . .," *op. cit.*, p. 124.

[77] Callahan, *Abortion: Law, Choice and Morality, op. cit.*, p. 469.

[78] *Ibid.*, pp. 472, 486-487; Drinan, "Catholic Moral Teaching....," *op. cit.*, p. 128. Grisez observes that respect for the legal system will wane even further if the law will not even attempt to protect the fundamental rights of the weakest; *op. cit.*, pp. 457-458.

[79] Callahan, *Abortion: Law, Choice and Morality, op. cit.*, pp. 285-289, 472-473, 490; Segers, *op. cit.*, p. 457.

[80] Callahan, *Abortion: Law, Choice and Morality, op. cit.*, pp. 136-140, 289, 472; Segers, *op. cit.*, p. 457. Noonan qualifies *permissive* statutes as discriminatory and oppressive because they enable society to dispense itself from its real obligations to the pregnant poor by providing a cheap alternative: abortion. The enactment of these laws has deprived the poor of assistance for their unborn children and has intensified pressure on them to destroy their offspring; *A Private Choice: Abortion in America in the Seventies* (New York: The Free Press, 1979), pp. 64-65, 190. See also: Ashley and O'Rourke, *op. cit.*, p. 240.

[81] Callahan, *Abortion: Law, Choice and Morality, op. cit.*, p. 487; Drinan, "Catholic Moral Teaching....," *op. cit.*, pp. 126-127. A moderate code does not alleviate the discrimination between the rich and the poor. See: Editorial, "The Abortion Debate," *Commonweal* 92 (1970), p. 131.

[82] Drinan, "The Jurisprudential Options on Abortion," *op. cit.*, pp. 165-166, 167; *id.*, "The State of the Abortion Question," *op. cit.*, pp. 108-109; Editorial, "The Abortion Debate," *op. cit.*, pp. 131-132. Drinan feels that complete withdrawal of the law would not have such dangerous implications; the law would then adopt a "neutral" attitude—as it does on many moral issues; "The Right of the Fetus to Be Born," mimeograph distributed at the 1967 Harvard-Kennedy Conference; cited by Grisez, *op. cit.*, p. 454. Grisez maintains that the repeal of a restrictive abortion statute is not a "neutral" act because it implicitly confirms the position of those who deny that the fetus has moral and legal rights. Moreover, the law simply cannot be neutral on the issue of the right to life: by permitting the unborn to be killed the law would in fact declare that they are not legal persons; *ibid.*, p. 455. Segers formulates another reason why the State should not legislate on abortion: an official statement on the legality or illegality of abortion may lead to an abdication of personal moral responsibility on the part of individual citizens; *op. cit.*, p. 457.

[83] Callahan, *Abortion: Law, Choice and Morality, op. cit.*, p. 487.

[84] Drinan, "Catholic Moral Teaching....," *op. cit.*, p. 128; *id.*, "The Jurisprudential Options on Abortion," *op. cit.*, p. 166. Grisez fails to see how the legalization of abortion would facilitate the detection and prosecution of clandestine operations; *op. cit.*, pp. 456-457.

[85] Drinan, "Catholic Moral Teaching....," *op. cit.*, p. 128. Grisez points out that once abortion is legalized it is no longer regarded as a social problem: the community will then have less of an incentive to do something about its solution; *op. cit.*, p. 457.

[86] Drinan, "Catholic Moral Teaching....," *op. cit.*, p. 128; Drinan, "The Jurisprudential Options on Abortion," *op. cit.*, pp. 166-167. Grisez feels that such counselling would not save many fetal lives unless it would include an offer of substantial social and economic support. But legalization of abortion is hardly conducive to better welfare programs; *op. cit.*, p. 457. The American bishops question the factual validity of many of the advantages that are attributed to permissive abortion policies. Moreover, the pragmatism of these arguments is invalidated by the fundamental fact that each abortion kills an innocent human being. There are other ways in which society can secure the various desired social goods. See: "Testimony of United States Catholic Conference on

Constitutional Amendments Protecting Unborn Human Life Before the Sub-Committee on Civil and Constitutional Rights of the House Committee on the Judiciary — March 24, 1976," in National Conference of Catholic Bishops, United States Catholic Conference, *Documentation on Abortion and the Right to Life II* (Washington, D.C.: Publications Office USCC, 1976), p. 15; "Statement of Terence Cardinal Cooke," *ibid.*, p. 43.

[87] Callahan, *Abortion: Law, Choice and Morality, op. cit.*, pp. 11-12.

[88] Drinan, "Catholic Moral Teaching....," *op. cit.*, p. 128. Grisez suggests that the law should forbid the manufacture of such drugs. Moreover, the availability of pharmacological abortifacients does not necessitate the repeal of laws against abortion; *op. cit.*, p. 457. In 1971 the bishops of Texas declared themselves opposed to relaxation or liberalization of the State's abortion statutes. They added, however, that if a change is inevitable the law should totally withdraw from the area of abortion and be completely silent and neutral on the issue rather than attempt to regulate the practice and thus express approval of it; "Open Letter on Abortion — April, 1971," in Daughters of St. Paul (eds.), *Yes to Life* (Boston: St. Paul Editions, 1977), p. 246. Several authors agree with Grisez (cf. note 82 *supra*) that withdrawal by the law would not imply "neutrality." Repealing a law is tantamount to approving what is no longer forbidden. Moreover, the State's inaction regarding the protection of the civil rights of one class of its people is in fact an act of discrimination against the group which is thus deprived of legal security; Louisell and Noonan, *op. cit.*, pp. 246-247; Gerber, *op. cit.*, p. 578. See also: Daniel Callahan, "Abortion: Some Ethical Issues," in David F. Walbert and J. Douglas Butler (eds.), *Abortion, Society, and the Law* (Cleveland: Case Western Reserve University, 1973), p. 93.

[89] Callahan, *Abortion: Law, Choice and Morality, op. cit.*, pp. 478-479.

[90] *Ibid.*, p. 478.

[91] *Ibid.*, pp. 478, 488.

[92] *Ibid.*, p. 478. See also: Drinan, "Catholic Moral Teaching....," *op. cit.*, p. 127.

[93] Callahan, *Abortion: Law, Choice and Morality, op. cit.*, p. 478. Noonan describes how the 1973 victory of private choice has led to a massive coercion of conscience of those who respect fetal life. College administrators force students to contribute towards the costs of abortions performed on their fellow students. Hospitals and doctors face lawsuits for refusing to terminate pregnancies. Students are interrogated about their moral position on abortion before gaining admission to medical schools. Judges and governors have forced their citizens to pay for operations repugnant to their consciences. Noonan concludes: "The dynamism of the liberty does not allow for neutrality. He or she who does not conform must be made to cooperate"; *A Private Choice....*, *op. cit.*, p. 191; see also pp. 64, 80-89.

[94] Callahan, *Abortion: Law, Choice and Morality, op. cit.*, pp. 213, 217, 478; *id.*, "Abortion: Thinking and Experiencing," *op. cit.*, p. 296.

[95] Callahan, *Abortion: Law, Choice and Morality, op. cit.*, p. 478.

[96] *Ibid.*, pp. 501-505; *id.*, "Abortion: Thinking and Experiencing," *op. cit.*, p. 296; Drinan, "Catholic Moral Teaching....," *op. cit.*, pp. 127, 129; *id.*, "The Jurisprudential Options on Abortion," *op. cit.*, pp. 167-168.

[97] Not all authors whose proposals are listed below are explicit supporters of the pragmatic approach. Some of them argue from the premise that liberalization is unavoidable or that permissive statutes are now a fact.

[98] Callahan, *Abortion: Law, Choice and Morality, op. cit.*, p. 488; Drinan, "The Jurisprudential Options on Abortion," *op. cit.*, p. 167.

[99] Callahan, *Abortion: Law, Choice and Morality, op. cit.*, p. 488.

[100] *Ibid.*, p. 477.

[101] *Ibid.*, pp. 477, 488; Curran, *Ongoing Revision.* . . . , *op. cit.*, p. 136; Drinan, "The Jurisprudential Options on Abortion," *op. cit.*, p. 167; Editorial, "The Abortion Decision," *Commonweal* 97 (1973), p. 436.

[102] Callahan, *Abortion: Law, Choice and Morality, op. cit.*, p. 488; *id.*, "Abortion: Some Ethical Issues," *op. cit.*, p. 91. Drinan draws the line at viability; "Catholic Moral Teaching. . . .," *op. cit.*, p. 129.

[103] Callahan, *Abortion: Law, Choice and Morality, op. cit.*, p. 488.

[104] Drinan, "Catholic Moral Teaching. . . .," *op. cit.*, p. 127; Callahan, "Abortion: Thinking and Experiencing," *op. cit.*, pp. 296-297; *id., Abortion: Law, Choice and Morality, op. cit.*, pp. 289-291, 490-491, 501-504; Segers, *op. cit.*, pp. 457-458; Viola, *op. cit.*, p. 102; Editorial, "Politics and Abortion," *op. cit.*, p. 131. Bishop Denis E. Hurley writes: "We could possibly come to terms with forms of contraception not involving abortion. In actual fact, this seems to have happened already for the majority of Catholics in developed countries and the practice looks like spreading progressively to Catholics in developing countries. . . . "; "Population Control and the Catholic Conscience: Responsibility of the Magisterium," *Theological Studies* 35 (1974), p. 162.

[105] Callahan, *Abortion: Law, Choice and Morality, op. cit.*, pp. 11-12; *id.*, "Abortion: Thinking and Experiencing," *op. cit.*, p. 298; David Goldenberg, "The Right to Abortion: Expansion of the Right to Privacy Through the Fourteenth Amendment," *Catholic Lawyer* 19 (1973), p. 57; McCormick, "Notes on Moral Theology: The Abortion Dossier," *op. cit.*, p. 339; Segers, *op. cit.*, pp. 457-458; Degnan, *op. cit.*, p. 308.

[106] Callahan, "Abortion: Thinking and Experiencing," *op. cit.*, p. 298.

[107] Editorial, "Abortion: Deterrence, Facilitation, Resistance," *America* 128 (1973), pp. 506-507.

[108] Callahan, *Abortion: Law, Choice and Morality, op. cit.*, p. 499. Noonan has provided this description. He depicts the various operations and their consequences and lists a number of abuses associated with the practice of easy abortion: experimentation on fetuses, homicide of viable infants, medical malpractice, pecuniary motivations. He also analyses the semantic camouflage that surrounds the realities of abortion on demand; *A Private Choice.* . . . , *op. cit.*, pp. 119-171, 191-192.

[109] Callahan, *Abortion: Law, Choice and Morality, op. cit.*, p. 504; "Abortion: Thinking and Experiencing," *op. cit.*, p. 298; Häring, *op. cit.*, p. 144; McCormick, "Notes on Moral Theology: The Abortion Dossier," *op. cit.*, pp. 328, 359; Editorial, "Politics and Abortion," *op. cit.*, p. 132. Drinan feels that indigent women who elect to terminate their pregnancy are entitled to Medicaid assistance to pay for the abortion; "Abortions on Medicaid? The Bartlett Amendment," *Commonweal* 102 (1975), p. 103. For a critical examination of the liberationist argument favoring public funding of abortions, see: Charles E. Curran, *Transition and Tradition in Moral Theology* (Notre Dame, Ind.: University of Notre Dame Press, 1979), pp. 230-250; Mary C. Segers, "Political Discourse and Public Policy on Funding Abortion: An Analysis," in James T. Burtchaell, C.S.C. (ed.), *Abortion Parley: Papers Delivered at the National Conference on Abortion Held at the University of Notre Dame in October 1979* (Kansas City: Andrews and McMeel, 1980), pp. 267-297.

[110] Luce, *op. cit.*, p. 28; Editorial, "Abortion: The Catholic Presentation," *America* 124 (1971), p. 62; Donald DeMarco, *Abortion in Perspective: The Rose Palace or the Fiery Dragon?* (Cincinnati: Hiltz & Hayes, 1974), pp. xiii-xiv.

111 Häring, *op. cit.*, p. 143.

112 *Ibid.*, p. 143.

113 Editorial, "Abortion and the Church," *America* 128 (1973), pp. 110-111.

114 Editorial, "Political Responsibility and Abortion," *America* 134 (1976), p. 173. In Noonan's analysis, the Supreme Court decisions on the woman's "right of privacy" with regard to abortion constituted an assault on the family. They made the woman autonomous but by doing so separated her from her partner in procreation. They destroyed a father's responsibility for his offspring and authorized the reverse of a mother's care of her helpless child; *A Private Choice....*, *op. cit.*, pp. 90-95, 190-191. Ashley and O'Rourke also point out that contemporary abortion policies degrade the father as a person. Moreover, in an abortifacient society children lack the important psychological assurance of unconditional parental acceptance; *op. cit.*, p. 240.

115 Editorial, "The Abortion Decision," *op. cit.*, p. 436.

116 *Ibid.*, p. 436.

117 Callahan, *Abortion: Law, Choice and Morality*, *op. cit.*, p. 489; Häring, *op. cit.*, pp. 144-145; James T. McHugh, "Commentary," *Hospital Progress* 54, March 1973, pp. 88-89; Richard A. McCormick, S.J., "Commentary," *Hospital Progress* 54, March 1973, p. 85.

118 Drinan, "Catholic Moral Teaching....," *op. cit.*, pp. 128-129.

119 James M. Humber, "The Case Against Abortion," *Thomist* 39 (1975), pp. 74-75, 77-80, 81-82.

120 *Ibid.*, p. 75.

121 *Ibid.*, p. 76.

122 *Ibid.*, p. 76. See also: DeMarco, *op. cit.*, pp. 15-17, 164; John T. Noonan, Jr., "Responding to Persons: Methods of Moral Argument in Debate over Abortion," *Theology Digest* 21 (1973), pp. 301-307; id., *A Private Choice....*, *op. cit.*, pp. 173-177.

123 John G. Milhaven, S.J., "The Abortion Debate: An Epistemological Interpretation," *Theological Studies* 31 (1970), pp. 112-117, 119.

124 *Ibid.*, pp. 117-121.

125 *Ibid.*, p. 120.

126 *Ibid.*, pp. 121-122.

127 *Ibid.*, p. 121.

128 *Ibid.*, p. 123. Springer states that the legal policy advocated by Milhaven is based on "sound reasoning"; "Notes on Moral Theology," *Theological Studies* 31 (1970), p. 495. Rudolph J. Gerber is less enthusiastic about the modern world view and the corresponding approach to abortion legislation. The secular criterion of humanity is utilitarian ("social involvement") and this understanding of man is carried forward into law. This results in a sociological jurisprudence which does not argue from "natural rights" but seeks to work out compromises between the conflicting social interests of individuals and groups in order to provide the greatest happiness for the greatest number; "Abortion: Two Opposing Legal Philosophies," *American Journal of Jurisprudence* 15 (1970), pp. 1-24; "Abortion: Parameters for Decision," *op. cit.*, pp. 561-584. See also: Ashley and O'Rourke, *op. cit.*, p. 240. Noonan describes the dynamics of American abortion law reform in less philosophical terms. Abortion on demand was brought about by a powerful *de facto* alliance of several ideological or professional groups, each working for liberalization for its own reasons: the American Law Institute, the medical profession, the American Civil Liberties Union, the Planned Parenthood Federation of America, population experts, feminist organizations, and

welfare administrators. In terms of public response the strongest supporters of liberalization were white upper-class males; *A Private Choice*...., *op. cit.*, pp. 33-46, 49-51.
[129] William E. May, "Abortion as Indicative of Personal and Social Identity," *Jurist* 33 (1973), pp. 203-206.
[130] Sebastian MacDonald, C.P., "The Meaning of Abortion," *American Ecclesiastical Review* 169 (1975), pp. 219-220, 292-293, 298-299.
[131] *Ibid.*, pp. 292-299, 303-314.
[132] Callahan, *Abortion: Law, Choice and Morality*, *op. cit.*, p. 285.
[133] *Ibid.*, p. 285. See also: Shaffer, *op. cit.*, pp. 100-102.
[134] MacDonald, *op. cit.*, pp. 292-299. See also: Leonard F.X. Mayhew, "Abortion: Two Sides and Some Complaints," *Ecumenist* 5, July-August 1967, p. 76.
[135] Drinan, "The Jurisprudential Options on Abortion," *op. cit.*, pp. 151-152. John M. Finnis states that the growing legal protection of the unborn child does not by itself establish that abortion on demand is substantially illegal because the law can confer legal personality on whatever it wishes and on whatever conditions it sees fit. However, it does not follow that the evolving legal personality of the fetus is without significance: these developments in law are an indication of a growing awareness that the distinction between viability and nonviability does not make sense; "Three Schemes of Regulation," in Noonan (ed.), *op. cit.*, pp. 199-200.
[136] Cf. notes 71 and 72 *supra*. See the critique of John R. Connery, S.J., "Callahan on Meaning of Abortion," *Linacre Quarterly* 37 (1970), p. 286.
[137] *Pastoral Constitution on the Church in the Modern World, "Gaudium et Spes,"* no. 51.
[138] *Declaration on Religious Liberty, "Dignitatis Humanae,"* no. 6.
[139] Drinan concedes this point; "Catholic Moral Teaching....," *op. cit.*, pp. 122-123.
[140] I accept Callahan's observation that the increase in the number of abortions under a permissive legal code cannot be attributed solely to the fact that the law has been liberalized. An important factor is the growing social acceptance of abortion which caused the law to be relaxed in the first place. However, Callahan does not deny that a permissive law has didactic significance and he further admits that under liberal statutes women will increasingly be pressured into abortions which they neither need nor want; *Abortion: Law, Choice and Morality*, *op. cit.*, pp. 501-502; "Abortion: Thinking and Experiencing," *op. cit.*, p. 296.
[141] James J. Diamond, "Humanizing the Abortion Debate," *America* 121 (1969), p. 39.
[142] "U.S. Bishops' New Pastoral Plan for Pro-Life Activities," in Daughters of St. Paul, *op. cit.*, pp. 283-284.
[143] *Ibid.*, p. 283.
[144] John Deedy, "U.S. Bishops on Abortion," *The Tablet* 235 (1981), pp. 1222-1223.

Chapter Ten

The American Catholic View on Abortion

In 1973, the year of *Roe* and *Doe*, Charles E. Curran presented a survey of contemporary Catholic thinking on the morality of abortion and examined various new opinions which had been formulated in recent years. He came to the conclusion that on this issue a division had developed in the Church:

> These positions are not held by the majority of Catholic theologians but there is a sizeable and growing number of Catholic theologians who do disagree with some aspects of the officially proposed Catholic teaching that direct abortion from the time of conception is always wrong.[1]

My analysis of the American Catholic abortion debate shows, I think, that in the United States the trend observed by Curran has continued and that the disagreement of Catholic theologians has not restricted itself to the moral aspects of the issue but extends to the legal side of the question. Furthermore, it is evident that this dissent is significant in the sense that the number of Catholic authors who find themselves at variance with the official teaching of their Church is considerable. Of course it is not possible to gauge statistically the extent of this heterodoxy, but having examined the professional ethical literature as well as the more competent journalistic efforts, I feel the conclusion is warranted that the majority of American Catholic moralists do have reservations about the Church's declared stand on abortion.[2]

I pointed out previously that these authors do not regard themselves as "dissenters." Virtually all of them argue from what they consider to be "Catholic" principles; they offer their views as legitimate extrapolations of the traditional moral position. Moreover, one could well argue that on the whole the degree of their divergence is less than substantial. Fundamentally, they share the Church's concern for the value that is at stake — prenatal life. There is practically no support in the American Catholic Church for the "blob" or "tissue" theory, and the majority of those who advocate a less restrictive moral policy do not propose radical innovations: they allow the operation for very serious reasons only, and they tend to restrict it to the first weeks of pregnancy. Robert F. Drinan and Daniel Callahan, who are the most liberal of the Catholic reformists, present their conclusions as tentative, and they do not rule out the possibility of error or abuse. Drinan admits that he has misgivings about the possible social consequences of a relaxation of the statutes, and Callahan states that like any other solution his own moral position has its liabilities.³ Callahan pleads forcefully in favor of legal abortion on request but it is clear that he regards such codes merely as a lesser evil:

> It may be counted a social and technological advance that abortion is becoming legally possible and medically safe as a method of procreation control where other methods have failed. But it is at best an advance to be looked upon with ambivalence. A single and faint cheer only is in order. Any method which requires the taking of human life, even though that life be far more potential than actual, falls short of the human aspiration, in mankind's better moments, of dignifying and protecting life.⁴

I. Fetal Life: Biology and Epistemology

Any rational approach to the moral problem inherent in the practice of abortion concentrates on two fundamental questions. The first is concerned with the quality of unborn human life and asks when the life of man begins. The second examines situations of conflict between the fetus and other human values and seeks to compose a set of rules or guidelines that will lead to responsible solutions. The question regarding the time of hominization must be resolved first. Unless this has been answered, the other moral and legal aspects cannot be considered satisfactorily. We have seen that American Catholic moralists are divided on the issue of the beginning of human life. Their opinions can be classified into four different "schools."

The adherents of the first school, which includes the American hierarchy, could be called "conceptionists." They base their assessment of the quality of fetal life upon a straightforward acceptance of the biological realities and, to them, the biological message is clear. In the ontogeny of the human individual the process of fertilization is of paramount importance because the combination of the parental sex cells gives rise to human life that is of a new and higher order. Fertilization, therefore, has metaphysical meaning and it marks the beginning of *personal* human existence. From then on the personal entity develops in a continuous and non-saltatory fashion. There are no further biological shifts and thus no other ontological thresholds.

Germain G. Grisez is the most explicit representative of the second school of thought; it recognizes the relevance of the biological data but does not regard these as philosophically conclusive. From this perspective the judgement as to personhood is more than a mere empirical observation and requires the application of a metaphysical postulate. However, the biological evidence does warrant the conclusion that the prenatal organism *very likely* constitutes a human person and, *at least,* deserves the benefit of the doubt.

The conceptionist position has been challenged from two different angles. Some authors draw attention to biological phenomena such as twinning, chimeras, and natural fetal loss and suggest that a straightforward acceptance of these facts reduces the significance of fertilization. Others develop the line of argument of the second school and emphatically question the equation of biology and philosophy. For them personhood is a nonempirical concept, formed from "extrascientific values and conceptual systems."[5]

Accordingly, a third and a fourth school established themselves. The third school accepts the biology-philosophy position of the conceptionists but interprets the empirical evidence in a different manner, proposing to assign full human status to the conceptus only after it has reached a certain point of physiological development between fertilization and birth (individualization, implantation, or brain activity). The fourth school sponsors the theory of developing personhood. It recognizes that the potentiality of the fetus has significance but feels that the unborn child has not actualized enough of that potential to be considered a person. The exponents of this school are not agreed on the additional criteria that the unborn child must satisfy in order to become a full member of the brotherhood of man. Albert R. Di Ianni states that a "true human body" is a "necessary and sufficient feature" in the concept of personhood, and he points to a difference in kind between the very early and the later fetus. Daniel C. Maguire distinguishes between the beginning and the end of the "trajectory to personhood" during which the child is at first "largely potentiality" but later "something significantly more." Di Ianni further observes that it is impossible to locate the precise point at which the difference in kind occurs.[6] Callahan will only recognize the fetus as a person after it has achieved "actualized rationality, interaction with others, affectivity, culture-making," or "a developed capacity for reasoning, willing, desiring and relating to others."

When considering the official teaching of the Catholic Church I have, throughout this book, restricted my attention to the views of the American bishops. However, we have now reached a point where it is necessary to refer to the position that the supreme Magisterium of the Church adopts on abortion and, first of all, the quality of prenatal life. Over the past two decades the Church at this level of its authority has made three major statements on the morality of the termination of pregnancy. The *Pastoral Constitution on the Church in the Modern World* (1965) of the Second Vatican Council and the Encyclical *Humanae Vitae* (1968) of Pope Paul VI equally affirm that human life must be protected from its very beginning but neither document explicitly equates fertilization and personalization nor rules explicitly that interference with the fetus at the beginning of its development constitutes an act of abortion.[7] But the *Declaration on Procured Abortion,* which was published by the Vatican's Sacred Congregation for the Doctrine of the Faith in 1974, did address itself specifically to the question of the beginning of human life.

The *Declaration* wholeheartedly accepts the relevance of the empirical data of human procreation and states that, from the time of fertilization, the life of the fetus is neither that of the father nor that of the mother: phenotypically and genotypically fertilization marks the beginning of a new human life, the life of a new human being.[8] Yet the document is careful not to overstate the biological argument. Its philosophical interpretation of the empirical evidence is restrained and comprises a single line: "The least that can be said is that present science, in its most evolved state, does not give any substantial support to those who defend abortion."[9] The *Declaration* opts for an approach similar to that of Grisez as it recognizes that the judgement on the personhood of the conceptus and on the legitimacy of abortion does not pertain to biology but to philosophy and ethics.[10] Like Grisez, it recalls the traditional obligation to follow the morally safer course in moral dilemmas where there is doubt about the facts of the situation:

> From a moral point of view this is certain: even if a doubt existed concerning whether the fruit of conception is already a human person, it is objectively a grave sin to dare to risk murder. "The one who will be a man is already one."[11]

It follows, then, that the position of the American hierarchy on the beginning of human life is more pronounced than that of the Sacred Congregation. Although it shows where its sympathies lie, the *Declaration* clearly does not wish to canonize the conceptionist view and assert dogmatically that personalization coincides with fertilization. Its argument is less emphatic: assuming it is not certain that a human person exists from the time of conception, we are not in an area where such doubt could be acted upon, for to destroy a human life which could be a person is to be indifferent to the human person as such.[12]

We saw that the conceptionist school is strongly opposed to the introduction of "extrascientific values and conceptual systems" into the determination of personhood. It qualifies such criteria as artificial because they are not applied to postnatal human life. Moreover, their employment leads to definitions that are arbitrary and to moral attitudes that are inconsistent. This objection is to the point, as is evident from Callahan's evaluation of fetal life. Callahan questions the conceptionist approach because it lacks sensitivity to difficult situations: it is unable to do "nuanced justice" to the conflict of interests in certain distressed pregnancies. He also finds it naïve to ask people to stick simply to the biological facts as such data are not philosophically self-explanatory.[13] Having thus established the need for additional and non-empirical criteria he advocates a "teleological" definition of personhood which he composes in the following manner: "We begin our analysis with postnatal human beings and then work backwards into the gestational process, observing the adult-aimed, forward-moving stages of development."[14] Callahan, therefore, measures the achieved characteristics of the fetus against those of an adult. It is not surprising that the unborn child fails by far to meet that standard, and in many ways: "At no stage of its development does the conceptus fulfill the definition of a person, which implies a developed capacity for reasoning, willing, desiring and relating to others."[15] Callahan concludes that even the life of a very late fetus is not inviolable and may be taken for "good reasons."[16] It is not clear why his criteria could not be legitimately employed to justify infanticide —unless the fetus suddenly realizes a substantially higher level of rational activity while it is in transit from the mother's womb into the hands of the midwife.

This objection continues to deserve serious consideration on the part of the developing personhood school. Those who maintain that the conceptionist argument lacks philosophical sophistication, and that the degree of development achieved before birth is insufficient to constitute an inviolable human person, must accept the burden of showing that the difference between the status of the fetus and that of the newborn child is more than a matter of degree and time. It must become clear that these lives are of a different *order*. I believe the Catholic reformists have not established that there is such vital inequality. I believe they postpone the time of personalization without adequate justification and therefore are vulnerable to the charge that in their laudable concern for pregnant women in distress they tamper with the definition of what it means to be human. Moreover, it will always remain biologically and philosophically true that abortion terminates a human existence in the sense that the child which eventually would have lived and learned and played will never live and learn and play.[17]

II. The Solution of Conflict Situations

The second question essential to the problem of the morality of abortion concerns the solution of conflicts between the life of the fetus and other human values, such as the life of the mother, her physical or mental health, or social or economic "indications." The Church argues that the end does not justify the means, and this policy rules out the application of abortion as a remedy to any condition of distress, however serious it is. At the same time we saw that there is significant support among Catholic moralists for a more consequentialist analysis of the act of abortion. From this perspective the intervention would be permissible for a "proportionate reason."

The 1974 *Declaration* of the Sacred Congregation for the Doctrine of the Faith does not present an elaborate philosophical exposé of the traditional distinction between direct and indirect killing. It briefly recalls the condemnation of direct abortion by Pope Pius XII, "that is, abortion which is either an end or a means," and it leaves the ethical technicalities to the moralists. [18] The document makes the point that bodily life is man's most fundamental good because it is the pre-condition for all his other goods: without it man could pursue none of them. This does not mean that physical life is man's highest value because there are causes for which one would be allowed to expose oneself to the risk of losing one's life. But this fundamental good of man may never be used as a means that can be disposed of, not even in order to obtain a higher good. Man is not expendable and this implies that the direct killing of an innocent person is always prohibited. The *Declaration* emphasizes that the first right of the human person is his right to life. This right is natural to him in the sense that it is not bestowed on him by society. It exists prior to its being recognized and in justice it is entitled to this recognition: society must protect the right to life above all other rights of man. [19] The Sacred Congregation admits that many pregnancies are surrounded by distress, and it agrees that in a number of cases one feels inclined to sacrifice fetal life for the sake of other human values which, in these circumstances, would seem to deserve priority. [20] But no such value may be given precedence over human life:

> We do not deny these very great dificulties. It may be a serious question of health, sometimes of life or death, for the mother; it may be the burden represented by an additional child, especially if there are good reasons to fear that the child will be abnormal or retarded; it may be the importance attributed in different classes of society to considerations of honor or dishonor, or loss of social standing, and so forth. We proclaim only that none of these reasons can ever objectively confer the right to dispose of another's life, even when that life is only beginning. With regard to the

future unhappiness of the child, no one, not even the father or mother, can act as its substitute —even if it is still in the embryonic stage —to choose in the child's name, life or death. The child itself, when grown up, will never have the right to choose suicide; no more may his parents choose death for the child while it is not of an age to decide for itself. Life is too fundamental a value to be weighed against even very serious disadvantages.[21]

We saw that Curran wants to apply the permissibility of killing in self-defense to abortion dilemmas. He notes that the traditional "exception," allowing the taking of an assailant's life, comprises *formally* unjust aggression (the assailant is subjectively guilty) as well as *materially* unjust aggression (he is not subjectively guilty, e.g., because he is mentally incapacitated). The Church, however, does not allow the fetus to be treated as any kind of aggressor because it considers that the presence and self-development of unborn life does not constitute an attack. This position was confirmed by Pope Pius XI in his Encyclical *Casti Connubii* (1930).[22] Curran disagrees and he proposes in problematic pregnancies to admit the same possibility of defense against aggression as is recognized outside the womb.

Curran does not explain why the activity of some unborn children deserves to be defined as "aggression." All that a fetus (and any fetus) is doing is growing to maturity in order to see the light of day. The most it can be accused of (in an extreme case) is that its *continued presence* in the maternal womb poses a threat to the life of the mother. The question therefore is: If someone's *continued existence* endangers my life, is my killing him a legitimate act of self-defense? It would seem that the answer has to be negative: I am obliged not to take that person's life, even if the fulfillment of this obligation results in my own death. In any case, Curran makes no effort to demonstrate that the right to self-defense becomes operative when one is in danger of death through the nonaggressive continued presence of someone else.[23]

It is argued, of course, that the mother's body belongs to herself, not to the fetus, and that she can exercise her right of ownership when a pregnancy endangers her life. But we must remember that there is a distinction between the duty we have to *save* someone's life and our duty *not to take* a person's life. The first duty is much weaker than the second. I am not obliged to save someone's life regardless of the cost. Thus, if a test-tube fetus were to die unless it could be implanted in a maternal womb, no woman would be obliged to accept it. It does not follow, however, that the mother's right to privacy entails her right to an abortion. Abortion is the taking of human life, and the prohibition of taking innocent and nonaggressive human life is much more intense than our duty to save that life when it is in danger.[24]

We have seen that Curran's explication of unjust aggression leads him to adopt a proportionalist position on abortion and that from different premises other Catholic moralists have drawn similar conclusions. There clearly is a deficiency in these propositions. The proportionalist is prepared to force the fetus to give up its life for the sake of the life of someone else. But unless a person is guilty of a capital crime or engaged in a dangerous and unjust assault, it is immoral to deprive him of his right to life for the benefit of another person nor can he be held responsible for the other's death if he refuses to sacrifice himself. *A fortiori,* he need not sacrifice himself when lesser values than human life are involved.[25] The proportionalist argument must establish that these rules do not apply to the human conceptus and that a woman in a certain set of circumstances is entitled to kill her innocent and nonaggressive child. In my estimation the Catholic proportionalist school has not proven its case nor is it clear why the various commensurate reasons —life, physical or mental health, and extreme poverty—which would warrant the destruction of prenatal life would not also justify in analogous cases of conflict the extermination of postnatal human beings.[26]

Contemporary moralists have little doubt that the traditional "exceptions" to the moral prohibition of killing have often been applied too easily. They are generally agreed that the conditions under which capital punishment and killing in war become permissible must be rigidly delimited and the area of legitimate killing reduced to instances where the taking of life has become truly inescapable. Some moralists even insist that the classical theories on capital punishment and just warfare stand in need of a more radical re-examination. One would expect that in conflict situations involving the unborn a similar attitude of restraint would prevail—unless it has been satisfactorily demonstrated that there is a substantial difference between intrauterine and extrauterine human life.

III. Moral Principles and Pastoral Counselling

The official Catholic argument on abortion is often faulted for intellectual abstractness and insensitivity to the existential problems of women. It is true that the Church's verdict never goes against the child while sometimes the circumstances surrounding a pregnancy are so tragic that they arouse the compassion and understanding of the most detached of ethicists. Nevertheless, an objective statement of the facts and a disciplined and controlled comparison of the values that are at stake are indispensable elements of a responsible approach to any distressful situation. They help those who are involved as participants or spectators to avoid what Richard A. McCormick has called the "standard traps of utilitarian analysis."[27] Stanley Hauerwas who writes from a Methodist point of view rightly indicates that this danger is particularly acute in the abortion debate:

> What creates difficulty for most of us about abortion is the hard cases where the taking of life seems to be a tragic but necessary act. In respect to these kinds of problems, what must be avoided is the possible arbitrariness of our subjectivities. The human capacity to give "good" reasons for being able to ignore the existence of the other, even to killing him, should never be underestimated. The more serious and basic the moral issue the more we are forced to make clear and justify our inchoate moral feelings that are sufficient for less significant issues.[28]

But genuine moral reasoning may not restrict itself to facts and syllogisms, no matter how valid these are. We saw that Bernard Häring distinguishes between "the level of moral theology" and "the level of pastoral counselling," and that McCormick emphasizes the pastoral dimension of Christian ethics which practices the art of achieving the possible. Both authors draw attention to the traditional concept of invincible ignorance and criticize its onesidedly intellectual connotation. They point out that the inability to understand a particular moral imperative is often not of an intellectual nature but must be attributed to existential difficulties which make it impossible for the person to assimilate emotionally the obligation as his or her own.

It is not difficult to discern a wide variety of factors which can seriously affect the pregnant woman's moral vision. First of all, there can be no doubt that fetal life (whatever its human status) is *sui generis*. It is invisible, an important psychological factor, as was explained by James M. Humber in the previous chapter. Its survival depends on the mother and on her alone, and certainly so in the earlier stages of pregnancy. Thus it is quite possible that her appreciation of its existence and of its value is limited and that she has a less intense emotional relationship with her unborn child than with her "living" offspring. Secondly, many women have been influenced by contemporary social attitudes toward fetal life and the termination of pregnancy, and have been exposed to the "subtle escalating pressures against childbearing."[29] They may have been contaminated by the superficial happiness-ethic of a "highly pragmatic, technologically sophisticated, and thoroughly pampered culture," and consequently may perceive pregnancy and childbirth primarily in terms of inconvenience and hardship.[30] Perhaps they have been persuaded that "no unwanted child should be born." Many women may honestly think that the traditional moral prohibition of abortion is erroneous or at least exaggerated. Thirdly, a pregnant woman may be the victim of social structures which are indifferent to her plight or which by their toleration of prejudice, poverty, injustice, or oppression are the cause of or are contributors to her distress. Fourthly, there may be circumstances of a special kind which form an obstacle to the personal assimilation of the moral imperative. It is completely understandable that a woman who has been raped, or who will have to care for a seriously handicapped child, or whose physical or emotional resources will be severely taxed by an addition to an already numerous family, fails to appreciate the difference between "unjust aggression" and "continuation of presence." Finally, there is a certain limitation inherent in the pregnancy situation itself. If the care of one or more of her "living" children becomes an insupportable burden for the mother, her problem could be solved by accommodating them in a children's home or by having them adopted. But if pregnancy or the prospect of childbirth has a similar effect on the mother-to-be there can be no such compromise. The choice is strictly "either—or."

If the counsellor therefore perceives that the woman is genuinely unable to cope with the moral demand and that further insistence will do more harm than good, he must accept the limitations of her moral insights and strengths and, in the words of McCormick, recognize the difference between "the good that ought to be and the good that cannot be as yet."[31] He will not exert undue pressure and dictate to her what she *must* do regardless of her condition and capacities. Without condoning her *decision* he will not judge the *woman* in the light of scientifically elaborated moral principles and rules but in the perspective of "the mystery of God's grace as it enters into the lives of individuals, with their strengths and capabilities, but also so often with their frailty and their lack of genuine freedom."[32]

As Hauerwas has observed, this is not a simple picture that provides a clear set of guidelines on how the issue should be handled,[33] and if the counsellor fails to persuade the woman, he may well feel that he has fallen short in his obligation to protect human life. But moral-pastoral counselling may not restrict its concern to ethical imperatives: it must be equally solicitous about the woman's personal conscience and do justice not only to the command but also to the possibility. This was the position of Alphonsus Liguori:

> The second opinion, the common and true one, however, maintains that, if the penitent labors under invincible ignorance (be it of human or divine law), and no worthwhile result is to be expected—in fact a prudent judgement indicates that admonition would do more harm than good—

then the confessor can omit it and is bound to do so, leaving the penitent undisturbed in his good faith.[34]

Alphonsus explains that one should be more intent on preventing the committing of a formal sin than of a material sin since God reckons only the formal sin as an offense.[35] It is often not sufficiently appreciated that the ethical interest of the Church goes beyond the objective moral order. The Church recognizes the importance of the subjective and it is entirely its tradition, confirmed by Vatican II, that an erroneous decision in a moral dilemma does not automatically indicate a bad conscience. Even when the option affects so fundamental a value as the inviolability of the human person, an erroneous but sincere conscience retains its proper human dignity and commands respect.[36] It remains true that an abortion contemplated in good faith is in its objective significance a violation at a fundamental level of the reverence due to human life and, therefore, the counsellor must seek to improve the mother's moral situation by "expanding her perspectives and maximizing her strengths" (McCormick). This does imply that he inculcates the moral norm but he will do this with the traditional pastoral prudence "that knows when and how to enlighten, and when and how to leave in good faith."[37] In their 1975 *Pastoral Plan for Pro-Life Activities* the American bishops emphasize the duty that the Church has to witness to the moral truth about abortion but, if my interpretation of the following passage is correct, they admit that in certain cases there may be question of a genuine inability to live up to the moral demand:

> Accurate information regarding the nature of an act and freedom from coercion are necessary in order to make responsible moral decisions. Choosing what is morally good also requires motivation. The Church has a unique responsibility to transmit the teaching of Christ and to provide moral principles consistent with that teaching. In regard to abortion, the Church should provide accurate information regarding the nature of the act, its effects and far-reaching consequences, and should show that abortion is a violation of God's laws of charity and justice. *In many instances*, the decision to do what is in conformity with God's law will be the ultimate determinant of the moral choice.[38]

Needless to say, there is discussion within the Church on the traditional differentiation between moral theology, as being primarily concerned with moral principles, and pastoral theology, as concentrating on individual persons and situations.[39] The English moralist John Mahoney discerns in contemporary Catholic moral theology a "command-possibility tension," and it is in this context that he locates the various theologies of compromise which have also surfaced in the American Catholic debate on abortion, such as "evaluative knowledge" (John F. Dedek), "situated freedom"

(William E. May), and a "theology of compromise" (Curran). Mahoney writes:

> (W)hat I think much of modern Roman Catholic moral theology is trying to achieve is the systematic incorporation of this pastoral art and ministry into the structure of scientific moral theology, a synthesis of command and possibility, the uniting of moral theology and pastoral theology into one theology of Christian moral behavior, which will take account not only of the conclusions of reason but also of the complexities of living, and which will make room for the compassion and the understanding, as well as for the demands, of the Gospel. Theologies of limited response, of situated freedom, of compromise, of the lesser evil, of the sin-filled situation, of the best in the circumstances —each of these, and others, I see as an attempt to resolve the command-possibility tension as it is actually experienced to a greater or lesser extent in the private and social lives of most human beings.[40]

Finally, the construction of a coherent ethical system that realistically provides for the mystery of human liberty and the reality of sin is a project that could well be carried out on an ecumenical basis. May states that in developing such an ethic he would find inspiration in John Macquarrie's views on conscience, sin, and grace.[41] McCormick also sees possibilities for an ecumenical synthesis of command and possibility:

> When some segments of the Protestant community say that every human choice stands in need of forgiveness, they are saying something unfamiliar to Catholic *moral* tradition (especially the manualist moral tradition) but not to Catholic *pastoral* practice. If [the Protestant] would speak more of the good that ought to be, and his Catholic counterpart would speak (as well as he can) more of what cannot yet be and why, the twain could easily mate into a position identifiable as catholic, because human and compassionate, yet evangelically uncompromising and radical.[42]

IV. Fetal Life and Human Law

The views of American Catholic moralists on the juridical-ethical aspects of the abortion problem can again be classified into four different schools.

The followers of the first school, which includes the American hierarchy, acknowledge the difference between morality and law but observe that the inviolability of unborn life is a moral imperative of a special kind because the issue touches upon the nature of the State and the very purpose of human law. The State's essential function is the protection by law of the human rights of its citizens; hence, it has the irremissible duty to safeguard their most fundamental right, the right to life. The authors establish by a philosophical argument (Grisez's "presumed fetal option") or on biological grounds that the fetus is a "legal person," and they conclude that the State has no choice but to extend the benefits of its laws to the unborn. Some supporters of this school are willing to consider a limited degree of abortion liberalization if this will forestall a complete relaxation of the statutes.

The second school puts greater emphasis on the distinction between law and morality and attaches less significance to the special character of the moral norm protecting unborn human life. Its followers regard the Catholic teaching on the morality of abortion as basically valid but point out that this position is unacceptable to many who do not belong to the Catholic fold. The Church has no right to insist that its moral beliefs be imposed by law on a pluralistic and democratic State and Catholics should be prepared to enter into a dialogue with other groups in the community. This dialogue will concentrate on the social consequences of abortion liberalization, and such discussions will eventually lead to "the best legal solution."

The adherents of the third school affirm that fetal life deserves the protection of the law, and they draw attention to the didactic or prophetic function of restrictive statutes. At the same time they admit that in a modern pluralistic society the possibilities of law enactment are limited and that the area of abortion is particularly problematic as far as law enforcement is concerned. Prophecy should therefore be combined with prudence, and this means that a Catholic could give his support to a moderately restrictive law. The fourth school defends the woman's right to control her fertility and accentuates the practical difficulties inherent in restrictive abortion codes. It rejects the traditional statutes, because they were unenforced and unenforceable and therefore harmful to the community, as well as moderate laws, because they do not produce the good effects that abortion reform seeks to realize. The interests of contemporary American society are best served by a legal policy of abortion on demand coupled with a set of supplementary legal measures and social provisions so as to offset any negative consequences liberalization might have.

It comes as no surprise that the *Declaration* of the Sacred Congregation for the Doctrine of the Faith clearly associates itself with the views of the first school. In its section on "Morality and Law," the document first summarizes the ideological and pragmatic considerations which have also been presented by American Catholic moralists in support of relaxation or complete liberalization:

In these days a vast body of opinion petitions the liberalization of [pro-
cured abortion]. There already exists a fairly general tendency which
seeks to limit, as far as possible, all restrictive legislation, especially
when it seems to touch upon private life. The argument of pluralism is
also used. Although many citizens, in particular the Catholic faithful,
condemn abortion, many others hold that it is licit, at least as a lesser evil.
Why force them to follow an opinion which is not theirs, especially in a
country where they are in the majority? In addition it is apparent that,
where they still exist, the laws condemning abortion appear difficult to
apply. The crime has become too common for it to be punished every
time, and the public authorities often find that it is wiser to close their eyes
to it. But the preservation of a law which is not applied is always to the
detriment of authority and of all the other laws. It must be added that
clandestine abortion puts women, who resign themselves to it and have
recourse to it, in the most serious dangers for future pregnancies and also
in many cases for their lives. Even if the legislator continues to regard
abortion as an evil, may he not propose to restrict its damage?[43]

In spite of these difficulties the Sacred Congregation affirms that
prophecy should prevail over pragmatism and that the restrictive laws must
be maintained. A repeal will be interpreted by many as an authorization of a
hitherto forbidden practice because they will conclude that the lawgiver
who continues to punish murder no longer considers abortion a crime
against life. This is a situation which may not be allowed to develop
because the natural moral law imposes upon the State the duty to preserve
each person's rights and to give special protection to the weakest. It follows, then, that a Christian cannot support the abortion reform movement
or vote for a permissive law.[44]

I pointed out previously that the authors who favor moderate or complete
liberalization have generally glossed over the question of the legal personhood of the fetus. Yet this remains the fundamental legal problem, and
granted the validity of the *moral* position of the Church, one must admit
that its case for a restrictive *legal* policy is a formidable one because it is
difficult to see how the Catholic moral view could permit a different legal
solution. Someone who is convinced that abortion is equivalent to murder
will not readily entertain the proposition that restrictive laws must be
repealed because they interfere with the doctor-patient relationship or with
the woman's right to control her fertility. He will also disregard the objection that his view is a mere private moral belief which he has no right to
impose by law on those who see the termination of pregnancy in a different
light. He will make the obvious point that even in a secular and democratic
society there are limits to the legal freedom which citizens can claim in the
name of privacy, moral pluralism, or liberty of conscience. In a pluralistic

society the lawgiver will on occasion decide not to enact certain laws in deference to the views of those convinced that the disputed action is not immoral, but there are laws which, because of their very content, must be passed anyway. If the prohibited activity relates to the fundamental rights of others, such as the right to life, then the necessity of law enactment and law enforcement prevails over the right of individual citizens to follow their conscience.[45] In these instances it is incorrect to say that the legislator attempts to enforce a sectarian moral norm: he simply tries to safeguard civil rights.

Furthermore, someone who regards abortion as murder will find it hard to accept the argument that restrictive laws force pregnant women in distress to have recourse to clandestine practitioners and that this results in their physical and mental injury, even death. From his point of view liberalization on these grounds would imply that the law withdraws its protection from some innocent citizens (the unborn) in favor of others (the mothers and the illegal operators) who are prepared to take the lives of these defenseless persons.[46] He will also have problems with the assertion that the traditional laws discriminate against the poor because the lower-income groups will find it much more difficult than the middle and upper classes to get a safe, illegal abortion. As Baruch A. Brody has observed, this is the equivalent of suggesting that, since there is inequality about who gets away with crime, we should allow everyone to get away with it.[47] Brody sees an obvious alternative:

> The obvious alternative to be pursued, even if it is difficult to achieve, is the abolishment of this inequality by no one's getting away with it. Even if this can never be achieved, however, this argument will not do: no man can claim an equal right to do something if that thing is a thing, like the taking of an innocent human life, which no man has a right to do.[48]

But maintenance of the traditional statutes does not preclude a legal arrangement for conditions of extreme hardship. The *Declaration* of the Sacred Congregation does stress the didactic and corrective function of legislation, and it insists that the law cannot declare to be right what is wrong. However, the document also admits that the lawgiver is not obliged to attach a penalty to every transgression.[49] As Augustine Regan has pointed out, human law can abstain from punishment and, applied to abortion, this means that the law can and should recognize one or two well-defined exceptions and thus provide for pregnancies where there is question of exceptional distress. In Regan's view this provision may not be formulated as a positive authorization to terminate these pregnancies, because the law does not have the power to dispose of unborn human life, but it should take the form of an exemption from penal sanctions.[50] I have noted Grisez's suggestion which is to extrapolate the concept of legally justifiable homicide into a legal indication permitting abortion in cases where otherwise both mother and child would die, and also to accommodate pregnancies resulting from rape. In a similar vein James J. Diamond argued that the law could permit an abortion in "life-threatening situations" including circumstances which are "so humanly devastating to the mother that reasonable people, committed legally and philosophically to guarding all life, cannot see daylight between 'devastation' and the actual death of the mother."[51] Diamond stipulates, however, that these abortion decisions be subject to the approval of a court of law since the fetus, like any other citizen, is entitled to "due process." Furthermore, the jurisprudence which will develop on this issue must be the object of our untiring vigilance.[52]

The practice of abortion affects the legal rights not only of the unborn but also of the medical profession. The *Declaration* states that no one may collaborate in the application of a law that makes abortion freely available.[53] Moreover, the conscientious refusal of doctors and other medical personnel to perform abortions or to assist in the operation must be respected:

> It is, for instance, inadmissible that doctors or nurses should find themselves obliged to cooperate closely in abortions and have to choose between the Christian law and their professional situation.[54]

We have seen that a similar conviction has been expressed in the course of the American Catholic debate and, given the liberationist emphasis on freedom and self-determination, it is difficult to see how even the most permissive abortion code could fail to incorporate a clause protecting the rights of hospitals and the medical profession in this area.[55]

V. The Task of the Church

We saw that the bishops and some of the authors oppose relaxation of the laws not merely on moral and philosophical-juridical grounds but also for pragmatic reasons. They look upon a liberal statute as a threat to the social fabric as they foresee a profound psychological impact on the community that will lead to a general erosion of respect for human life and to other moral and social calamities.

I have already pointed out that on this issue we must guard against oversimplifications. It is true that under a liberal code there is likely to be an increase in the number of abortions and that legal permission will be widely interpreted as legal approval; it does not necessarily follow that this new permissiveness will affect postnatal human beings. If popular opinion were to regard abortion as the killing of an innocent person, then the repeal of a restrictive code might well modify society's reluctance to terminate other forms of defenseless human life. But on abortion many people take a middle position. They do not recognize the fetus as a full human being but neither will they have it treated as waste matter, and they definitely evaluate the termination of its existence in the light of the dignity of human life. At the same time they credit the intervention for the remedy it provides to conditions of serious maternal or parental distress. The fetus, therefore, has a special status but abortion is deemed permissible in certain cases and up to a certain point of gestation.[56]

Under these circumstances it remains to be seen how far relaxation of the statutes will affect the attitude of the community towards human life outside the womb. Liberalization of abortion does not unduly complicate the distinction between prenatal and postnatal human beings. Moreover, it will be very difficult to find hard evidence that permissive abortion statutes have an adverse effect on society's observance of moral standards in other areas. In this context it is relevant to note that many fervent supporters of abortion on request with equal conviction defend human life on such issues as capital punishment and social justice. From a sociological point of view it will not do to lump together various symptoms of society's alleged moral decay and attribute these collectively to a liberal abortion ethos.[57] It is interesting to observe that the "slippery slope" argument is absent in the *Declaration* of the Sacred Congregation and does not figure in any other major statement by the Church's supreme Magisterium.[58]

When I analysed the juridical-ethical position that opposes any relaxation of the statutes, I registered the critique offered by some adherents of this school regarding the rationale underlying the new abortion ethos. To some the liberationist ideology was basically a cult of technology and perfection, while others depicted the reformists as sacrificing the unborn on the altar of convenience and permissiveness. It must be stressed that any rhetorical overkill is wholly alien to the pronouncements that have emanated from the central Magisterium of the Church. The Second Vatican Council denounced abortion as an "unspeakable crime"; yet it never held up to scorn women who have had their pregnancy terminated or even activists who seek to have abortion made legal.[59] A similar restraint is reflected in the declarations by the Popes. The Magisterium has no wish to brand the liberationists as a bunch of hedonists whose nefarious pursuits must be obstructed at all costs but proffers the argument that there is a strong tendency in the modern world to gloss over that fundamental human value which is life. Pope Paul VI made this point in a message to the World Health Organization on the occasion of the twenty-fifth anniversary of its foundation:

> At a moment when the outbreak of violence on so many points of the globe, on the one hand, and on the other hand the giddy whirl in which modern society is so often caught up and which dims true values, seem to undervalue life, all life, from its origin to its decline, it is our most fervent wish on this twenty-fifth anniversary, that the World Health Organization to which the International Community has entrusted the preservation and promotion of men's health, should maintain on all occasions the primacy of life and keep for mankind the complete contribution of an authentic deontology in regard to it.[60]

All sides to the American Catholic abortion debate are agreed that the Church's witness to the value of human life must be comprehensive and consistent. It may not restrict itself to fetuses alone but must embrace all forms of human life and come to man's rescue wherever and whenever his life, individually or collectively, is endangered or his dignity violated. It is precisely in this wider context that the Second Vatican Council locates the phenomenon of abortion:

> (W)hatever is opposed to life itself, such as any type of murder, genocide, abortion, euthanasia or willful self-destruction; whatever violates the integrity of the human person, such as mutilation, torments inflicted on body or mind, attempts to coerce the will itself; whatever insults human dignity, such as subhuman living conditions, arbitrary imprisonment, deportation, slavery, prostitution, the selling of women and children; as well as disgraceful working conditions, where men are treated as mere tools for profit, rather than as free and responsible persons; all these things and others of their like are infamies indeed.[61]

Nor may the Church express its commitment to fetal life in a verbal manner only. Sebastian MacDonald makes this point very strongly. He believes that Christians should protect the unborn by achieving as much good as possible rather than by proclaiming as much truth as possible.[62] It may come as a surprise that this reliance on welfare programs rather than on homilies is entirely in harmony with the mind of the Church. The *Declaration* states that it is *above all* necessary to combat the causes of abortion[63] and urges legislators to establish a definite social policy in this regard:

> (I)t is the task of the law to pursue a reform of society and of conditions of life in all milieux, starting with the most deprived, so that always and everywhere it may be possible to give every child coming into this world a welcome worthy of a person. Help for families and for unmarried mothers, assured grants for children, a statute for illegitimate children

and reasonable arrangements for adoption —a whole positive policy must be put into force so that there will always be a concrete, honorable and possible alternative to abortion.[64]

This emphasis on social justice loses none of its validity once the law has been liberalized. Under a permissive statute there is always a danger that the community will dodge its social and economic obligations towards families by making abortion available as an alternative solution to the problems of pregnancy and parenthood. A liberal law offers an easy and inexpensive way out and, especially in times of economic recession, the civil authorities might be tempted to adopt a policy that encourages abortion in order to reduce the costs of their welfare programs.[65] Much can be said about the inconsistency of the Church's witness on other issues affecting human life without faulting its resistance to the employment of abortion as a substitute for social and economic assistance.

There can be little doubt that there is at least *some* causal connection between present-day sexual permissiveness and the increase in the demand for abortion. It is generally accepted in the American Catholic Church that the faithful and the community at large must be educated toward greater responsibility in sexual relationships. Gregory Baum observed that this will inevitably involve a critique of the consumeristic attitudes toward sexuality which have developed in the contemporary world. Similarly, the *Declaration* makes the point that there is more to sex than orgasm, defining genuine sexual freedom as "the mastery progressively acquired by reason and by authentic love over instinctive impulse, without diminishing pleasure but keeping it in its proper place."[66] All sides to the debate further agree that the Church must address itself to the problem of nonidentification with unborn human life. It is difficult for people to associate themselves closely with the invisible prenatal organism, especially in the early stages of its development. Therefore the Church must help publicize the biological facts of prenatal man and the medical facts of the abortion procedure. It should do so with insistence but also with dignity, avoiding the rhetorical and pictorial overkill so characteristic of the abortion controversy.

Some authors believe that these social and educational initiatives do not exhaust the responsibility of the Church in this area. MacDonald and Callahan argued in the previous chapter that the abortion problem is basically a problem of conception control. In their analysis a decision to abort is in the majority of cases related to a failure to prevent conception which occurred either because the couple did not attempt to avoid pregnancy or because the method used was not effective. Abortion then becomes a supplementary or corrective means of birth control and as the fetus exerts a limited emotional appeal the unique anti-life character of the intervention is easily overlooked. This suggests that the solution of the abortion problem depends to a large extent on the improvements that are achieved in the field of contraception. The Church, however, does not accept contraception as a solution to the abortion problem or any other problem. In his 1968 Encyclical Letter *Humanae Vitae* Pope Paul VI ruled out all artificial means of birth control. Although on this issue he and his successors have had to face considerable opposition within their fold as well as outside the Church, they have not seen fit to reverse or modify their position.[67] The present Pope, John Paul II, has emphatically upheld the teaching of *Humanae Vitae* as the norm which guides the sexual expression of love in all marriages. In his Apostolic Exhortation *Familiaris Consortio* on the role of the Christian family in the modern world, the Pope rejects the use of contraception as a manipulation and degradation of the sexual relationship between man and woman, and as unworthy of the human person. In order to be authentically human the act of sexual intercourse must be an expression of a total and mutual self-giving in love, and therefore be open to the transmission of life. Contraception vitiates sexual intercourse on both counts. The Pope recognizes the need of family planning, not only for the sake of individual couples but also in view of the population problem that exists in many parts of the world. However, fertility control must be achieved by the use of natural methods which preserve the physical and psychological integrity of intercourse and thereby its human authenticity and moral licitness. The Pope further enjoins the public authorities to do everything possible to ensure that families receive all the assistance they need. The Church also must renew its commitment to the pastoral care of the family and make every effort to improve the quality of married life, at a spiritual as well as at a human level.[68] We have seen that some of the dissent arising from *Humanae Vitae* has surfaced in the American Catholic abortion debate. A number of authors, including some of those who support the official teaching on the inviolability of unborn life, have urged the Church to adopt a less negative policy toward contraception in order to help reduce the incidence of fetal death.[69]

VI. *Authority and Dissent*

The developments that have occurred in Catholic attitudes toward abortion raise the question of the authority of the Church on moral issues and of the extent to which its followers are bound to conform in word and deed to official doctrine. In its *Dogmatic Constitution on the Church* the Second

Vatican Council affirmed that the faithful have a special obligation to submit their intellect and will to the teaching authority of the Roman Pontiff. A Catholic must respectfully acknowledge the Magisterium of the Pope and give sincere assent to decisions made by him, even when he does not speak "ex cathedra," i.e., "infallibly" from the fullness of his apostolic authority. Not in all cases, however, do the Popes wish to elicit the same degree of assent. The intensity of their appeal can be gauged from the nature of the declaration in question, or from the frequency with which they propose the doctrine, or by the manner in which they formulate it. [70]

The formula employed by the 1974 *Declaration* leaves no doubt that on the question of abortion the Sacred Congregation for the Docrine of the Faith expects nothing less than definite assent to the official teaching. The document draws attention to the tradition of the Church which has consistently held that abortion, including interventions during the first days of pregnancy, is objectively a grave fault. It notes that in recent years the Roman Pontiffs have repeatedly confirmed the traditional doctrine and that Pope Paul VI has not hesitated to qualify the mind of the Church on this point as unchangeable. This position of the Popes has received emphatic support from many episcopal conferences as well as from individual bishops speaking on their own behalf. The Sacred Congregation further recalls that it has been entrusted with the task of defending and promoting faith and morals in the universal Church and states that it intends to do more than merely choose sides in an ethical dispute. With the authority proper to the Holy See it wishes to transmit to the faithful a constant teaching of the Magisterium and therefore its pronouncements impose a grave obligation upon their conscience. [71]

The gist of this firm and unvarying teaching of the Church is that the moral prohibition to kill directly innocent human life extends to unborn human life. It is in this manner that Pope Pius XII set out the traditional teaching. Paul VI confirmed this position as the "unchanged and unchangeable doctrine" of the Church. He explicitly endorsed the formulation of his predecessor:

> "Abortion and infanticide"—the Council emphasized—"are unspeakable crimes." The theological reason was clearly specified.... by Pius XII: "Every human being, even the infant in its mother's womb, has the right to life *immediately* from God, not from the parents or any human society or authority. Therefore there is no man, no human authority, no science, no medical, eugenic, social, economic or moral 'indication', which can show or give a valid juridical title for a *direct* deliberate disposing of an innocent human life—which is to say, a disposition that aims at its destruction either as an end in itself or as the means of attaining another end that is, perhaps, in no way unlawful in itself." [72]

It must be stressed that such statements do not preclude further research and discussion. One could consider, for example, the question of hominization. The Magisterium does not wish to assert categorically that personalization coincides with conception, although the Church clearly inclines toward the view that human growth is biologically and ontologically continuous from conception until adulthood. But some authors believe that implantation, like conception, constitutes a biological shift which has metaphysical meaning. We saw that they point to a number of events which take place in the third week of pregnancy and which suggest that there is a significant difference between the vital activity of the unimplanted entity and that of the implanted blastocyst. During the implantation process the fetus abandons its self-consumptive mode of sustenance and establishes a functional dependence on the maternal metabolic system. At the same time the hominal organizer terminates the pluripotentiality of the cells and initiates their organized differentiation into specific organ systems. At this point twinning and recombination are no longer possible, and there is a significant reduction in the incidence of fetal loss.[73] One could conclude that after implantation there is human life of a new and higher order. I noted the opinions of Häring and Diamond who regard the period between fertilization and the completion of implantation as a "gray" or "intervital" area and distinguish between acts that are anti-fertilizational, anti-implantational, and abortional. It may well be that their analysis and interpretation of the biological events are deficient and that they exaggerate the difference which implantation makes to the quality of fetal life, but they do not formally contradict the authentic teaching of the Magisterium on abortion.[74]

Similarly, it seems legitimate to ask if the Church's prohibition of direct abortion should not be refined in order to provide a solution for those cases, now medically rare, when, if nothing is done, both mother and fetus will die. Brody and Häring are convinced that the termination of these pregnancies is justified for the simple reason that there is something to gain and nothing to lose. They argue that the unborn child is not really deprived of its right to life because it will not survive in any case.[75] Callahan puts it much more strongly: to let the woman die is not only an abdication of human responsibility but also a definite moral evil, and a greater moral evil if there are others, like a husband and children, who depend on her.[76] The Magisterium has made it clear that the life of the fetus may not be sacrificed even to save the life of the mother,[77] but one wonders if this prohibition should remain in force when the unborn child is already irrevocably condemned to death.[78] In any case, even where the teaching of the Church seems established and irreformable, Vatican II has granted theologians and moralists "a lawful freedom of inquiry, of thought, and of expression,"[79] and we may take it that this implies a permission to investigate whether and to what extent the official doctrine is really beyond all dispute.[80] The Council added that the freedom of expression of theologians should be tempered by humility.[81] It must have been of the same mind as Häring who observes that a doubt expressed by some theologians is not sufficient to invalidate the official teaching of the Church.[82]

VII. American Catholicism and the Abortion Issue

As I mentioned in the first chapter, it has been alleged that the Christian attitude towards abortion derives largely from an anti-sexual bias or a pro-natalist ideology. (It would be helpful if the critics made up their mind: is it really possible to be anti-sexual and pro-natalist at the same time?) Admittedly, my investigation has been limited in scope because it has restricted itself to the hierarchical pronouncements and the moral reflections of only a small section of the Christian community. Moreover, it has been concerned with expressed material content rather than with sub-conscious, semiconscious, or disguised motivations. With these reservations in mind, however, I must state that my research has yielded little evidence that would substantiate those charges.

We have seen that the contemporary sexual ethos does figure in the American Catholic debate on abortion. Some authors believe that the abortion reform movement is basically inspired by an unwillingness to accept sexual moral codes, while others fear that reform of the law will establish a vicious circle by encouraging promiscuity, especially among the young. Others again deplore the consumerism that has contaminated sexual behavior and stress the need for greater responsibility in sexual relationships. Whether or not these observations and exhortations are valid, it is abundantly clear that in the overall debate they do not constitute the principal theme or even a major theme. Nor have I found any evidence of a jealous and vindictive attitude on the part of theologians who, in the words of Roy U. Schenk, suffer under the burden of compulsory celibacy and who demand that the price for pleasure be paid.[83] In the debate on the morality and legality of abortion the overriding concern of the Church is not with sex but with the right to life. The Church is unwilling to deprive one human being of its most fundamental right for the sake of another's less fundamental rights.[84] Its steadfast defense of the unborn is part of a comprehensive commitment to the welfare of man which is genuine, even if in practice it manifests inconsistencies.[85] The best analysis I have seen of the Catholic

position on abortion is that of Roger Wertheimer which combines accuracy
with simplicity:

> In the Church's view. . . the fetus is as much a human life as is the parent;
> they share the same moral status. Either can be a source of abiding
> anguish and hardship for the other—and sometimes there may be no
> escape. In this, our world, some people get stuck with the care of others,
> and sometimes there may be no way of getting unstuck, at least no just
> and decent way. Taking the other person's life is not such a way.[86]

There are other misconceptions which deserve to be laid to rest. Those
who resist the liberationist design are often accused by supporters of the
reform movement of attempting to impose a denominational ideology on
the whole community. The manuals did present the Catholic case against
abortion in the terminology of a sectarian theology but my research has also
revealed, I think, that the American Catholic Church has remedied this
defect. The Church has gone to great lengths to reformulate its view on the
moral as well as on the legal aspect of the question, and it has done this in
concepts and terms derived from biology, medicine, ethics, legal philosophy, and other secular disciplines. These sciences are "neutral" because
they are the common property and the joint concern of everyone in society.
One may disagree with the Church's moral and legal conclusions but it is no
longer valid to dismiss these as sectarian. Moreover, those who regard the
Church's pronouncements on the legality of abortion as an unwarranted
interference by religion in the affairs of the secular State should logically
challenge the right of the Church to speak on *any* social issue, including
capital punishment, nuclear disarmament, and racial discrimination.[87]
There is, in addition, the proposition that abortion decisions are medical
decisions and are the preserve of the medical profession. A pregnancy
cannot be terminated without the application of medical technology but, as
Thomas S. Szasz has noted, "this makes abortion no more a medical
problem than the use of the electric chair makes capital punishment a
problem of electrical engineering."[88]

The practice of abortion poses intricate moral and legal questions. The
Catholic view on the values that are at stake in this issue, and on the
priorities that must be established among these values, is more complex
and diverse than is often appreciated. I hope that this book will help to
clarify the various positions which Catholics adopt in this debate. If it
realizes this objective, it will bring the solution of the abortion problem a
little nearer, and I will consider my efforts amply rewarded.

NOTES

1 Charles E. Curran, "Abortion: Law and Morality in Contemporary Catholic Theology," *Jurist* 33 (1973), p. 183.

2 In other parts of the world also there has been growing diversity on abortion among Catholic moralists, and there has been a parallel development in Catholic medical circles and among the ordinary faithful. See: Charles E. Curran, *Transition and Tradition in Moral Theology* (Notre Dame, Ind.: University of Notre Dame Press, 1979), pp. 225-226; Malcolm Potts *et al., Abortion* (London: Cambridge University Press, 1977), pp. 357-361; James Hitchcock, *Catholicism and Modernity: Confrontation or Capitulation?* (New York: Seabury Press, 1979), pp. 164-175. Judith Blake examines public opinion in the U.S. in the years following the 1973 Supreme Court decisions and concludes that, while there has been a decline in disapproval of elective abortion, public support of the new statutes is less overwhelming than is often assumed; "The Abortion Decisions: Judicial Review and Public Opinion," in Edward Manier *et al.* (eds.), *Abortion: New Directions for Policy Studies* (Notre Dame, Ind.: University of Notre Dame Press, 1977), pp. 51-82. David F. Kelly describes the evolution of Catholic medical ethics in North America and indicates that in recent years there have been significant developments in Catholic moral methodology which have affected two distinctive characteristics of the traditional moral approach—the physicalist evaluation of human acts and the authority of the Magisterium of the Church; *The Emergence of Roman Catholic Medical Ethics in North America: A Historical-Methodological-Bibliographical Study* (New York: Edwin Mellen, 1979), pp. 402-448. See also: Curran, *ibid.,* pp. 201-204.

3 Robert F. Drinan, S.J., "The Jurisprudential Options on Abortion," *Theological Studies* 31 (1970), pp. 167-168; Daniel Callahan, *Abortion: Law, Choice and Morality* (New York: Macmillan, 1970), pp. 19-20.

4 Callahan, *op. cit.,* p. 506. He expresses concern about the formation of an abortion habit under a permissive legal code adding that such a habit is not easy to break by means of contraceptive methods of birth control; *ibid.,* p. 502.

5 *Ibid.,* p. 353.

6 Albert R. Di Ianni, S.M., "Is the Fetus a Person?" *American Ecclesiastical Review* 168 (1974), pp. 324-325. See also: Joseph F. Donceel, S.J., "Immediate Animation and Delayed Hominization," *Theological Studies* 31 (1970), pp. 100-101.

7 "Pastoral Constitution on the Church in the Modern World (nos. 27 and 51)," in Daughters of St. Paul (eds.), *Yes to Life* (Boston: St. Paul Editions, 1977), pp. 36-38; "Encyclical Letter 'Of Human Life' (no. 14)," *ibid.,* pp. 38-39. See also: John XXIII, "Encyclical Letter 'Christianity and Social Progress,' May 15, 1961 (nos. 196-199)," *ibid.,* pp. 35-36. In Bernard Häring's analysis the Vatican Council deliberately refrained from a decision with regard to what constitutes the conception of a human being; "New Dimensions of Responsible Parenthood," *Theological Studies* 37 (1976), p. 127. Augustine Regan, C.SS.R., believes that the condemnation of abortion in *Humanae Vitae* was meant to include attacks on the fertilized ovum before nidation; "Abortion—The Moral Aspect," *Studia Moralia* 10 (1972), p. 150. Pope John Paul II confirmed the traditional prohibition of abortion during his visit to the United States in October 1979; *Acta Apostolicae Sedis* 71 (1979), pp. 1225, 1270-1274.

8 Sacred Congregation for the Doctrine of the Faith, "Declaration on Procured Abortion," in Daughters of St. Paul, *op. cit.,* p. 73 (nos. 12 and 13).

⁹ *Ibid.*, p. 73 (no. 13). The official Latin text has "Hoc saltem dici potest..." which is more accurately translated as "This at least can be said..." See: *Acta Apostolicae Sedis* 66 (1974), p. 738.

¹⁰ Sacred Congretation, *op. cit.*, p. 73 (no. 13).

¹¹ *Ibid.*, p. 73 (no. 13). The quotation is from Tertullian, *Apologeticum* IX, 8.

¹² Another exponent of this school of thought is Gary M. Atkinson who argues that appeals to a particular definition of the term "person" to justify a position on abortion involve a judgement regarding the criteria of personhood. But the question of these criteria is as difficult to resolve as the abortion problem itself and, indeed, may be taken as a restatement of the abortion issue. At the same time it is only on the basis of a distinction between persons and nonpersons that differences in moral status can be ascribed. Therefore, in spite of the fact that the question of who is and who is not a person seems practically insoluble, the attention devoted to it is not misplaced. In Atkinson's perspective abortion can be said to have been justified by moral argument only if a satisfactory definition of personhood has been formulated; "Persons in the Whole Sense," *American Journal of Jurisprudence* 22 (1977), pp. 86-117. See also: Richard Stith, "The World as Reality, as Resource, and as Pretense," *American Journal of Jurisprudence* 20 (1975), pp. 146-147; Andrew C. Varga, *The Main Issues in Bioethics* (New York: Paulist Press, 1980), pp. 40-45. The Sacred Congregation emphasizes that the inviolability of fetal life is not established by the infusion of the spiritual soul. Even if animation occurs at some point after conception, in the early stages of pregnancy we are still dealing with a human life preparing itself for the reception of its soul by which its human identity will be completed. Moreover, it suffices that the presence of the soul is probable (and at no stage of gestation can one prove the contrary), in order to accept that the taking of life involves the risk of killing a human being who is already in possession of his soul; *op. cit.*, p. 81, footnote 19.

¹³ Callahan, *op. cit.*, pp. 351-353, 396; *id.*, "Abortion: Some Ethical Issues," in David F. Walbert and J. Douglas Butler (eds.), *Abortion, Society, and the Law* (Cleveland: Case Western Reserve University, 1973), p. 94. Gabriel Pastrana, O.P., feels that Callahan's approach to the empirical data deprives the biological evidence of its relevance and meaning; "Personhood and the Beginning of Human Life," *Thomist* 41 (1977), pp. 262-264. But at a later stage of the debate even John T. Noonan, Jr., admitted that the judgement on personhood involves, in part, a moral decision; *A Private Choice: Abortion in America in the Seventies* (New York: The Free Press, 1979), p. 161. See also: John O'Connor, "On Humanity and Abortion," *Natural Law Forum* 13 (1968), pp. 130-133; Di Ianni, *op. cit.*, pp. 310-312; Vern R. Walker, "Presumptive Personhood," *Linacre Quarterly* 45 (1978), pp. 179-186; Robert E. Joyce, "Personhood and the Conception Event," *New Scholasticism* 52 (1978), p. 99. Outside the Catholic camp the most elegant exponent of this position is Roger Wertheimer, "Understanding the Abortion Argument," *Philosophy and Public Affairs* 1 (1971), pp. 67-95; *id.*, "Philosophy on Humanity," in Manier *et al.* (eds.), *op. cit.*, pp. 117-136. James M. Humber admits that moral decisions cannot be made on the mere basis of a survey of the facts. But whether or not a being is properly classified as a human person is not a moral conclusion but a matter of fact. The moral judgement is made when one decides that it is morally wrong (or morally justifiable) to kill a human person; "The Case Against Abortion," *Thomist* 39 (1975), pp. 83-84. John Finnis argues that conception constitutes the "perfectly clear-cut beginning" of personhood; "The Rights and Wrongs of Abortion: A Reply to Judith Thomson," *Philosophy and Public Affairs* 2 (1973), pp.

144-145. William E. May presents a definition of personhood on the basis of human rationality and indicates how this criterion applies to the unborn; "What Makes a Human Being to Be a Being of Moral Worth?" *Thomist* 40 (1976), pp. 416-443. The criteria of Robert Barry, O.P., include individuality, self-development and rationality, and he concludes that it is not proper to deny personhood to the developing stages of human life on the plea that their capacities are not fully actualized; "Personhood: The Conditions for Identification and Description," *Linacre Quarterly* 45 (1978), pp. 64-81.

¹⁴ Callahan, *Abortion: Law, Choice and Morality, op. cit.,* p. 354.

¹⁵ *Ibid.,* p. 497.

¹⁶ *Ibid.,* pp. 500-501. A more extensive and incisive critique of Callahan's position is offered by Paul Ramsey in his "Abortion: A Review Article," *Thomist* 37 (1973), pp. 176-188.

¹⁷ Garth L. Hallett, S.J., "The Plain Meaning of Abortion," *America* 124 (1971), p. 633. In addition to the four schools of thought which I have identified, there are other approaches to the evaluation of fetal life but these enjoy no support among American Catholic moralists. Callahan refers to these as the "social consequences school," while Curran distinguishes between the "relational school" and the "conferred rights school." See: Callahan, *Abortion: Law, Choice and Morality, op. cit.,* pp. 390-394, 400-401; Curran, *Transition and Tradition in Moral Theology, op. cit.,* pp. 213-215, 217-219.

¹⁸ Sacred Congregation for the Doctrine of the Faith, *op. cit.,* pp. 71, 80 (no. 7 and footnote 3). For a clear explanation of the traditional distinction between direct and indirect killing, see: Augustine Regan, C.SS.R., *Thou Shalt Not Kill* (Theology Today Series, No. 38; Dublin: Mercier Press, 1979), pp. 37-54.

¹⁹ Sacred Congregation, *op. cit.,* pp. 71-74 (nos. 8-14).

²⁰ *Ibid.,* p. 74 (no. 14).

²¹ *Ibid.,* p. 74 (no. 14). See also: David Granfield, *The Abortion Decision* (revised ed.; Garden City, N.Y.: Doubleday Image Books, 1971), pp. 120-126; Donald DeMarco, *Abortion in Perspective: The Rose Palace or the Fiery Dragon?* (Cincinnati: Hiltz and Hayes, 1974), pp. 19-20; Benedict M. Ashley, O.P., and Kevin D. O'Rourke, O.P., *Health Care Ethics: A Theological Analysis* (St. Louis: Catholic Hospital Association, 1978), pp. 239-242. Given the premise that a human fetus is a human being, Wertheimer admits that "the entire conservative position unfolds with a simple, relentless logic, every principle of which would be endorsed by any sensible liberal"; "Understanding the Abortion Argument," *op. cit.,* p. 70. Mary Anne Warren who, like Wertheimer, writes from a non-Catholic perspective makes the same point but less emphatically. She concludes that if the fetus does have a full-fledged right to life, it is not possible to prove that abortion is morally permissible; "On the Moral and Legal Status of Abortion," in Richard A. Wasserstrom (ed.), *Today's Moral Problems* (New York: Macmillan, 1979), pp. 39-42. Barry affirms the right to life of the fetus on theological and philosophical grounds; *op. cit.,* pp. 78-80. But Philip J. Rossi, S.J., feels that the debate on personhood, rights, and choice has reached an impasse, and he suggests a different approach to the solution of the abortion problem. We should concentrate on improving the clarity of our thinking about the nature of what is good for human persons and about the conduct which effectively serves that good; " 'Rights' Are Not Enough: Prospects for a New Approach to the Morality of Abortion," *Linacre Quarterly* 46 (1979), pp. 109-117.

[22] Pius XI, "Encyclical Letter 'Christian Marriage'," in Daughters of St. Paul, *op. cit.*, p. 27. See also: Regan, "Abortion—The Moral Aspect," *op. cit.*, pp. 206-209.

[23] Baruch A. Brody, "Thomson on Abortion," *Philosophy and Public Affairs* 1 (1972), pp. 336-338; *id.*, "Abortion and the Sanctity of Human Life," *American Philosophical Quarterly* 10 (1973), pp. 133-135; Richard A. McCormick, S.J., "Notes on Moral Theology: The Abortion Dossier," *Theological Studies* 35 (1974), pp. 343-344. Brody writes from a non-Catholic viewpoint and argues from the *supposition* that the fetus is a human person. In his opinion this cannot be conclusively established; "Abortion and the Sanctity of Human Life," *op. cit.*, p. 133. Curran's view on the "aggression" of the unborn child was presented in Chapter V. At a later stage of the debate he no longer considered the fetus an unjust aggressor but adopted the analysis of McCormick who attributes the traditional permissibility of killing in self-defense to a proportionalist calculus. This approach could serve as a model for the solution of conflict situations involving unborn life; *Themes in Fundamental Moral Theology* (Notre Dame, Ind.: University of Notre Dame Press, 1977), pp. 71-72.

[24] Brody, "Thomson on Abortion," *op. cit.*, pp. 338-339. Judith Jarvis Thomson and Susan Teft Nicholson question this argument because it does not pay sufficient attention to the existence of a bodily life-support relationship between the woman and her unborn child. Thomson concludes that even if the fetus is a human person, the mother's ownership of her body tips the scales in her favor when the pregnancy is seriously distressed. She presents the hypothetical case of a famous violinist who has a fatal kidney ailment and who will not survive unless for a period of nine months his circulatory system can be plugged into that of another person so that it can use the other's kidneys. The Society of Music Lovers has discovered that you alone have the right blood type to help. They therefore kidnap you and anaesthetize you, and when you wake up you find that your circulatory system serves as a lifeline for the violinist. The musician himself is not guilty because he has been in coma throughout. Do you have the right to disconnect him even though you will bring about his death? Thomson's answer is affirmative and she sees an analogy with the case of a pregnancy due to rape where the mother has not given the unborn child permission to use her body for food and shelter. She concludes to the permissiblity of abortion in some cases; "A Defense of Abortion," *Philosophy and Public Affairs* 1 (1971), pp. 47-66. Arguing in a similar vein Nicholson emphasizes that the termination of pregnancy should be defined as a withdrawal of maternal assistance rather than as an act of killing. The question of whether or not a raped woman may permissibly abort is then a question of the extent to which one is obliged to make one's body available for sustaining another human being's life. Similarly, therapeutic abortions performed to save the life of the mother must be distinguished from acts of killing which do not consist in a termination of support in order to save the supporting person. Nicholson also believes that the Catholic position on the licitness of withholding extraordinary measures of life-support entails the recognition of a fetal indication for abortion in cases where this would be in the interest of the *fetus itself*; *Abortion and the Roman Catholic Church* (JRE Studies in Religious Ethics 2; Knoxville, Tennessee: Religious Ethics, Inc., 1978), pp. 49-95. See also: Mary B. Mahowald, "Abortion: Towards Continuing the Dialogue," *Cross Currents* 29 (1979), pp. 330-335; Curran, *Transition and Tradition in Moral Theology, op. cit.*, p. 223. McCormick feels that "a woman has a right to her own body" is the conclusion of an often unexamined argument but he admits that Nicholson asks some legitimate questions; "Abortion: Rules for Debate," *America* 139 (1978), p. 27; *id.*, "Abortion: A

Changing Morality and Policy?'' *Hospital Progress* 60, February 1979, p. 40. Other Catholic authors have pointed out that the case of the violinist is extreme and unusual, and they have questioned its analogy to a pregnancy due to rape, primarily because the violinist is an unjust aggressor. See: Atkinson, *op. cit.*, pp. 100-103; Finnis, *op. cit.*, p. 143; John R. Connery, S.J., "Abortion and the Duty to Preserve Life," *Theological Studies* 40 (1979), pp. 323-333.

25 Brody, "Abortion and the Sanctity of Human Life," *op. cit.*, p. 135.

26 McCormick confirms his proportionalist position; "Abortion: Rules for Debate," *op. cit.*, p. 29; *id.*, "Abortion: A Changing Morality and Policy?" *op. cit.*, pp. 38-40. See also: Timothy E. O'Connell, *Principles for a Catholic Morality* (New York: Seabury Press, 1976), pp. 167-169.

27 McCormick, "Notes on Moral Theology: The Abortion Dossier," *op. cit.*, p. 343.

28 Stanley Hauerwas, "Abortion: The Agent's Perspective," *American Ecclesiastical Review* 167 (1973), pp. 108-109. See also: McCormick, "Notes on Moral Theology: The Abortion Dossier," *op. cit.*, p. 356; *id.*, "Abortion: A Changing Morality and Policy?" *op. cit.*, p. 42; Di Ianni, *op. cit.*, pp. 317-318.

29 McCormick, "Notes on Moral Theology: The Abortion Dossier," *op. cit.*, p. 355.

30 *Ibid.*, pp. 355-356.

31 *Ibid.*, p. 341.

32 John Mahoney, S.J., "Ecumenical Witness on Moral Issues," *The Month* 10 (1977), p. 14. See also: Gerard J. McCarron, O.S.F.S., "Abortion and the Priest-Counselor," *Journal of Religion and Health* 15 (1976), pp. 282-283. McCormick observes that papal and episcopal statements on abortion generally manifest a great compassion for women in difficult circumstances and an unwillingness to judge personal guilt; "Notes on Moral Theology: The Abortion Dossier," *op. cit.*, p. 330. For a compassionate yet critical analysis of a number of abortion histories, see: James T. Burtchaell, C.S.C., *Rachel Weeping and Other Essays on Abortion* (Kansas City: Andrews and McMeel, 1982), pp. 1-60.

33 Hauerwas, *op. cit.*, p. 119.

34 St. Alphonsus Liguori, *Theologia Moralis,* Lib. VI, Tract. IV, Cap. II, n. 610. Cf. Leonardus Gaudé (ed.), *Opera Moralia Sancti Alphonsi Mariae de Ligorio* (Rome: Typis Polyglottis Vaticanis, 1905-1912), vol. III, p. 634. See also: Bernard Häring, "A Theological Evaluation," in John T. Noonan, Jr. (ed.), *The Morality of Abortion: Legal and Historical Perspectives* (Cambridge, Mass.: Harvard University Press, 1970), p. 140.

35 St. Alphonsus Liguori, *Praxis Confessarii,* Cap. I, n. 8. Cf. Gaudé, *op. cit.*, vol. IV, pp. 530 – 531. See also: Häring, "A Theological Evaluation," *op. cit.*, p. 141.

36 George M. Regan, C.M., *New Trends in Moral Theology: A Survey of Fundamental Moral Themes* (New York: Newman Press, 1971), pp. 159-162; Augustine Regan, "Abortion—The Moral Aspect," *op. cit.*, pp. 130-131, 210-211; McCormick, "Abortion: Rules for Debate," *op. cit.*, pp. 27, 30; O'Connell, *op. cit.*, pp. 91-93. Cf. Vatican II, *Pastoral Constitution on the Church in the Modern World, "Gaudium et Spes,"* no. 16.

37 Augustine Regan, "Abortion—The Moral Aspect," *op. cit.*, p. 211. See also: Ashley and O'Rourke, *op. cit.*, p. 239.

38 "U.S. Bishops' New Pastoral Plan for Pro-Life Activities, November 20, 1975," in Daughters of St. Paul, *op. cit.*, p. 281; emphasis supplied. At the 26th World Assembly of the World Health Organization the representative of the Holy See denounced the

modern trend toward abortion liberalization but added: "In making these reflections, I am limiting myself to positive law and have no intention of judging human dramas which are at the basis of individual decisions, the judge of which is, for believers, God, and for all, in any case, personal conscience illuminated by an upright moral law"; "Address of Holy See Representative to WHO, June 1973," *ibid.*, p. 63. The bishops of Connecticut emphasize that a Catholic must form his conscience in the light of the authentic teaching of the Church; "Your Conscience and Abortion—September, 1974," *ibid.*, p. 269. See also: DeMarco, *op. cit.*, p. 38

[39] James McManus, C.SS.R., Sean O'Riordan, C.SS.R., and Henry Stratton, "The 'Declaration on Certain Questions concerning Sexual Ethics': A Discussion," *Clergy Review* 61 (1976), p. 223; George M. Regan, *op. cit.*, pp. 161-162.

[40] Mahoney, *op. cit.*, p. 14. See also: Mahowald, *op. cit.*, pp. 332-333.

[41] William E. May, "Abortion as Indicative of Personal and Social Identity," *Jurist* 33 (1973), p. 216, footnote 50. The reference is to John Macquarrie's *Three Issues in Ethics* (New York: Harper and Row, 1970).

[42] McCormick, "Notes on Moral Theology: The Abortion Dossier," *op. cit.*, pp. 341-342. The American bishops state that ecumenical consultation is an important aspect of their pastoral strategy on abortion; "U.S. Bishops' New Pastoral Plan for Pro-Life Activities," *op. cit.*, p. 278. See also: National Council of Churches, "Guidelines for Ecumenical Debate on Abortion and Homosexuality," *Origins* 8 (1978-1979), pp. 517-519.

[43] Sacred Congregation, *op. cit.*, p. 76 (no. 19).

[44] *Ibid.*, pp. 76-77 (nos. 20-22). For an identical view on the function of law with regard to unborn life, see: Pius XI, *op. cit.*, pp. 26-28; Paul VI, "To the Catholic Jurists—December 9, 1972," in Daughters of St. Paul, *op. cit.*, pp. 42-44; Gordon C. Zahn, "A Religious Pacifist Looks at Abortion," *Commonweal* 94 (1971), p. 280; Noonan, *A Private Choice: Abortion in America in the Seventies, op. cit.*, pp. 13-19. Others question the argument that legalization of abortion on request merely puts the law in a position of neutrality on the issue of fetal life. See: Germain G. Grisez, *Abortion: The Myths, the Realities, and the Arguments* (New York: Corpus Books, 1970), pp. 454-455; Rudolph J. Gerber, "Abortion: Parameters for Decision," *International Philosophical Quarterly* 11 (1971), p. 578; Brody, "Abortion and the Law," *Journal of Philosophy* 68 (1971), pp. 367-368. See also: Callahan, "Abortion: Some Ethical Issues," *op. cit.*, p. 93.

[45] Brody, "Abortion and the Law," *op. cit.*, pp. 359-361; Robert M. Byrn, "Abortion-on-Demand: Whose Morality?" *Notre Dame Lawyer* 46 (1970), pp. 34-36; Wertheimer, "Understanding the Abortion Argument," *op. cit.*, pp. 71-72. Louisell and Noonan have discussed the feasibility aspect of restrictive abortion statutes and have argued that failure to enforce a law does not necessarily imply that this law should be repealed. They point to other laws which are frequently violated, without prosecution being initiated or without prosecution having success, such as laws against perjury and larceny, and they observe that no one pleads for their abrogation. This observation is correct but their argument is not entirely satisfactory because there is an important difference between laws against perjury and theft, and laws against abortion. The former enjoy wide public support even if they are frequently violated; no right-minded person has yet asked for their repeal. Restrictive abortion codes no longer have general public support, as is evident from the often acrimonious debates in countries which have so far retained them. Moreover, at the present time abortion involves a clinical intervention and as such it is a possible, if difficult, object of criminal investigation and

prosecution. But advances in the field of post-conceptive fertility control, such as the development of an abortifacient pill, might well remove the clinical aspects of early abortions. This would further diminish the law's ability to restrict the practice. See: David W. Louisell and John T. Noonan, Jr., "Constitutional Balance," in Noonan (ed.), *The Morality of Abortion: Legal and Historical Perspectives, op. cit.,* pp. 243-244. See also: John M. Finnis, "Three Schemes of Regulation," *ibid.,* pp. 179-180; Grisez, *op. cit.,* pp. 447-448; Brody, "Abortion and the Law," *op. cit.,* pp. 365-366.

[46] Brody, "Abortion and the Law," *op. cit.,* pp. 366-367.

[47] *Ibid.,* p. 367.

[48] *Ibid.,* p. 367.

[49] Sacred Congregation, *op. cit.,* p. 77 (no. 21). See also: Catholic Archbishops of Great Britain, "Abortion and the Right to Life," *Tablet* 234 (1980), pp. 93-94 (nos. 23-25).

[50] Augustine Regan, C.SS.R., "Abortion Laws and Fetal Right to Life," *Studia Moralia* 11 (1973), pp. 302-307. McCormick cites a 1973 statement by the Catholic and the Evangelical bishops of Germany which permits the lawmaker to identify those conflict situations where termination of pregnancy will not be punished; "Abortion: A Changing Morality and Policy?" *op. cit.,* p. 37. The American bishops do not seem to share this view. In March 1974 Cardinal Humberto Medeiros stated before the Sub-Committee on Constitutional Amendments of the Senate Committee on the Judiciary: "As for an amendment which would generally prohibit abortion but permit it in certain exceptional circumstances, such as when a woman's life is considered to be threatened, the Catholic Conference does not endorse such an approach in principle and could not conscientiously support it"; "Testimony," in National Conference of Catholic Bishops, United States Catholic Conference, *Documentation on the Right to Life and Abortion* (Washington, D.C.: Publications Office USCC, 1974), p. 42.

[51] James J. Diamond, "Pro-Life Amendments and Due Process," *America* 130 (1974), p. 28. McCormick thinks the law should permit an abortion when the life of the mother is at stake; when there is a grave threat to her physical health and to the length of her life; when the pregnancy is due to rape or incest; when fetal deformity is of such magnitude that life-supporting efforts would not be considered obligatory after birth; "Abortion: A Changing Morality and Policy?" *op. cit.,* p. 41. Donald A. Giannella proposes to distinguish between the first trimester and the later stages of pregnancy; "The Difficult Quest for a Truly Humane Abortion Law," *Villanova Law Review* 13 (1968), pp. 288-289.

[52] Diamond, *op. cit.,* p. 29. Giannella admits that an "intermediate valuation" of the fetus is very difficult to justify in theory and precarious to maintain in practice; *op. cit.,* pp. 277-278. See also: Gary M. Atkinson, "The Morality of Abortion," *International Philosophical Quarterly* 14 (1974), pp. 353-354.

[53] Sacred Congregation, *op. cit.,* p. 77 (no. 22).

[54] *Ibid.,* p. 77 (no. 22).

[55] The bishops of Connecticut emphasize the rights of medical personnel in this regard; *op. cit.,* pp. 268, 269, 271-273. See also: Editorial, "The Bishops' Plan for Pro-Life Activities," *America* 133 (1975), p. 454. In Noonan's analysis, the liberationists ride roughshod over the conscientious objections of persons and institutes; *A Private Choice: Abortion in America in the Seventies, op. cit.,* pp. 64, 83-89, 191.

[56] Norman St. John-Stevas, "Abortion, Catholics, and the Law," *Catholic World* 206 (1968), p. 151.

[57] Callahan, *Abortion: Law, Choice and Morality, op. cit.,* pp. 6-7, 474-475; *id.,* "Abor-

tion: Some Ethical Issues," *op. cit.*, pp. 93-94; Hauerwas, *op. cit.*, pp. 110-111; D. Gerber, "Abortion: The Uptake Argument," *Ethics* 83 (1972), pp. 82-83. The Sacred Congregation notes the contemporary wave of unqualified protests against the death penalty and war in all its forms; *op. cit.*, pp. 67-68 (no. 1).

[58] The argument occurs in one minor document only. See: "Address of Holy See Representative to WHO," *op. cit.*, p. 62.

[59] "Pastoral Constitution on the Church in the Modern World," *op. cit.*, p. 37 (no. 51).

[60] "Pope's Message for the 25th Anniversary of the World Health Organization—May, 1973," in Daughters of St. Paul, *op. cit.*, p. 46. See also: Bishops of Texas, "Open Letter on Abortion—April, 1971," *ibid.*, pp. 245-246. The bishops of Illinois recognize the good faith of their opponents on abortion; "Statement on Abortion—March 20, 1969," *ibid.*, pp. 205-206. See also: McCormick, "Abortion: Rules for Debate," *op. cit.*, p. 27; Margaret A. Farley, "Liberation, Abortion and Responsibility," *Reflection*, May 1974, pp. 9-10; Giannella, *op. cit.*, pp. 290-291.

[61] "Pastoral Constitution on the Church in the Modern World," *op. cit.*, pp. 36-37 (no. 27).

[62] Sebastian MacDonald, C.P., "The Meaning of Abortion," *American Ecclesiastical Review* 169 (1975), p. 314.

[63] Sacred Congregation, *op. cit.*, p. 79 (no. 26).

[64] *Ibid.*, p. 78 (no. 23). See also: Editorial, "The New Abortion Debate," *Commonweal* 104 (1977), pp. 451-452; McCormick, "Abortion: Rules for Debate," *op. cit.*, pp. 26-27. McCormick also mentions that the statements on abortion issued by the various Catholic hierarchies put more emphasis on the need for social reform than on any other aspect of the defense of unborn life; "Notes on Moral Theology: The Abortion Dossier," *op. cit.*, p. 330. For practical suggestions in this regard, see: *The New Technologies of Birth and Death: Medical, Legal and Moral Dimensions. Proceedings of the Workshop for Bishops of the United States and Canada, Dallas, January 28-31, 1980* (St. Louis: Pope John XXIII Medical-Moral Research and Education Center, 1980), pp. 80-97, 104-107.

[65] Bishops of Texas, *op. cit.*, pp. 247-250; Callahan, "Abortion: Some Ethical Issues," *op. cit.*, p. 97; Ashley and O'Rourke, *op. cit.*, p. 240; Noonan, *A Private Choice: Abortion in America in the Seventies, op. cit.*, pp. 64-67, 190.

[66] Sacred Congregation, *op. cit.*, p. 75 (no. 16). See also: McCormick, "Abortion: A Changing Morality and Policy?" *op. cit.*, p. 42. Noonan discusses the validity of the argument that permissive abortion laws confirm the irresponsible attitude men have in their relationship to women and their offspring; *A Private Choice: Abortion in America in the Seventies, op. cit.*, pp. 49-50.

[67] Paul VI, "Encyclical Letter 'Of Human Life'," *op. cit.*, pp. 38-39 (no. 14).

[68] John Paul II, *Familiaris Consortio*, nos. 31-32, 34-35, 45, 65. See especially the charter of family rights outlined in no. 46. Cf. *Acta Apostolicae Sedis* 74 (1982), pp. 117-120, 123-126, 136-139, 158-159. The Pope confirmed the traditional ban on contraception during his visit to the United States in October 1979; *Acta Apostolicae Sedis* 71 (1979), p. 1224. Cf. also: Francis X. Murphy, C.SS.R., "Catholic Perspectives on Population Issues II," *Population Bulletin*, vol. 35, no. 6 (Washington, D.C.: Population Reference Bureau, Inc., 1981), pp. 26-39.

[69] Granfield, *op. cit.*, pp. 210-211; Denis E. Hurley, O.M.I., "Population Control and the Catholic Conscience: Responsibility of the Magisterium," *Theological Studies* 35 (1974), pp. 159-163; John L. Thomas, S.J., "Family, Sex, and Marriage in a Contraceptive Culture," *Theological Studies* 35 (1974), pp. 134-153; MacDonald, *op. cit.*, pp. 309-315.

[70] *Dogmatic Constitution on the Church, "Lumen Gentium,"* no. 25.

[71] Sacred Congregation, *op. cit.,* pp. 68-71 (nos. 3-7). John Connery, S.J., confirms that the Christian tradition has always revealed a firm antiabortion attitude and that its condemnation of abortion was never in any way affected by theories regarding the time of fetal animation; *Abortion: The Development of the Roman Catholic Perspective* (Chicago: Loyola University Press, 1977), pp. 304-305. McCormick discovers a "total unanimity" in the contemporary teaching of the Pope and the bishops on the right to life from conception; "Notes on Moral Theology: The Abortion Dossier," *op. cit.,* p. 329. Ashley and O'Rourke regard the various pronouncements of the Magisterium not as definitive and infallible but as having "very great weight" because of their decisiveness and unanimity. Furthermore, the issues involved in the problem have been thoroughly discussed over a long period and the advance of medical knowledge has tended to support the Church's position; *op. cit.,* pp. 235-236. See also: Bishops of Illinois, *op. cit.,* pp. 202-203; Bishops of Texas, *op. cit.,* p. 243.

[72] Paul VI, "To the Catholic Jurists," *op. cit.,* p. 42, footnote deleted. Cf. Pius XII, "Allocution to Midwives—October 29, 1951," in Daughters of St. Paul, *op. cit.,* pp. 28-29.

[73] Cf. McCormick, "Abortion: Rules for Debate," *op. cit.,* p. 28.

[74] Cf. Regan, "Abortion Laws and Fetal Right to Life," *op. cit.,* pp. 304-305, footnote 79. It must be noted that the recognition of an "intervital" stage in fetal development would not automatically justify the use of IUDs and morning-after pills. The implication would rather be that the mode of operation of these "abortifacients" is contraceptive and not abortive.

[75] Brody, "Thomson on Abortion," *op. cit.,* p. 340; Häring, "A Theological Evaluation," *op. cit.,* p. 137.

[76] Callahan, *Abortion: Law, Choice and Morality, op. cit.,* p. 425.

[77] Pius XI, *op. cit.,* p. 27; Pius XII, "Allocution to Midwives," *op. cit.,* p. 29; Sacred Congregation, *op. cit.,* p. 74 (no. 14); Catholic Archbishops of Great Britain, *op. cit.,* pp. 93-94 (nos. 23-24). Connery is in agreement with the Magisterium on this point and argues that a position which prefers the taking of one life to the "natural" death of two people seems to come close to a kind of act-utilitarianism; "Callahan on Meaning of Abortion," *Linacre Quarterly* 37 (1970), p. 285. The American bishops have never pronounced themselves on this issue.

[78] McCormick cites a statement by the Catholic bishop of Augsburg and one by the Belgian hierarchy permitting abortion to save the life of the mother; "Abortion: Rules for Debate," *op. cit.,* p. 29; *id.,* "Abortion: A Changing Morality and Policy?" *op. cit.,* p. 40. See also: Regan, "Abortion Laws and Fetal Right to Life," *op. cit.,* pp. 304-305, footnote 79.

[79] *Pastoral Constitution on the Church in the Modern World, "Gaudium et Spes,"* no. 62.

[80] McCormick, "Abortion: Rules for Debate," *op. cit.,* p. 29; *id.,* "Abortion: A Changing Morality and Policy?" *op. cit.,* p. 38; Regan, "Abortion Laws and Fetal Right to Life," *op. cit.,* pp. 304-305, footnote 79. The Sacred Congregation states that it does not wish to pronounce on all aspects of the abortion issue and that it leaves a number of questions to the research and discussions of theologians; *op. cit.,* p. 80, footnote 3.

[81] *"Gaudium et Spes,"* no. 62.

[82] Häring, "A Theological Evaluation," *op. cit.,* p. 133. Other Catholic moralists, however, put more emphasis on the possibility and legitimacy of theological dissent. Curran thinks that the teaching of the hierarchical Magisterium on specific moral matters cannot claim a certitude that excludes the possibility of error. Sometimes the individual

Catholic, aware of all the risks, can rightly dissent from such teaching in theory and practice; *Themes in Fundamental Moral Theology, op. cit.,* pp. 111-118, 225-226. See also: Regan, *New Trends in Moral Theology: A Survey of Fundamental Moral Themes, op. cit.,* pp. 13, 136-142; Daniel Maguire, *Moral Absolutes and the Magisterium* (Washington: Corpus Papers, 1970); George J. Dyer (ed.), *An American Catholic Catechism* (New York: Seabury Press, 1975), p. 233.

[83] Roy U. Schenk, "Let's Think About Abortion," *Catholic World* 207, April 1968, p. 17.

[84] Ashley and O'Rourke, *op. cit.,* p. 242.

[85] Nicholson surveys twenty centuries of Christian thought in ten pages and comes to the conclusion that the Church's condemnation of abortion is partly attributable to its inadequate views on human sexuality and marriage; *op. cit.,* pp. 3-13. See also: Farley, *op. cit.,* p. 11. Connery questions the validity of Nicholson's analysis and also shows that the Church's defense of the fetus is not inspired by its emphasis on the necessity of baptism; "Abortion and the Duty to Preserve Life," *op. cit.,* p. 318, footnote 2; *id., Abortion: The Development of the Roman Catholic Perspective, op. cit.,* p. 310. See also: Grisez, *op. cit.,* p. 437; Noonan, *A Private Choice: Abortion in America in the Seventies, op. cit.,* pp. 53-54.

[86] Wertheimer, "Understanding the Abortion Argument," *op. cit.,* p. 72. See also: Burtchaell, *op. cit.,* pp. 321-323; Granfield, *op. cit.,* pp. 137-138.

[87] Callahan, "Abortion: Some Ethical Issues," *op. cit.,* p. 92; Giannella, *op. cit.,* pp. 291-301; Noonan, *A Private Choice: Abortion in America in the Seventies, op. cit.,* p. 54-63; Editorial, "Abortion, Religion and Political Life," *Commonweal* 106 (1979), pp. 35-38; Richard A. McCormick, S.J., "Notes on Moral Theology 1977: The Church in Dispute," *Theological Studies* 39 (1978), p. 123; Thomas L. Shaffer, "Abortion, the Law and Human Life," *Valparaiso University Law Review* 2 (1967), pp. 104-105. Episcopal statements on abortion generally note that their teaching is not specifically Catholic. See: McCormick, "Notes on Moral Theology: The Abortion Dossier," *op. cit.,* p. 330.

[88] Cited by Callahan, "Abortion: Some Ethical Issues," *op. cit.,* p. 96. Noonan discusses the validity of the argument that restrictive abortion laws were invented by men when women and their offspring were regarded as male property not to be disposed of without male consent; *A Private Choice: Abortion in America in the Seventies, op. cit.,* pp. 47-51. See also: Callahan, *ibid.,* pp. 97-99; Grisez, *op. cit.,* pp. 450-451.

BIBLIOGRAPHY

Included in this bibliography are all the books and articles which have been cited or consulted. Editorials are listed separately at the end.

Alexander, A., and Fiedler, M., Sr. "The Equal Rights Amendment." *America* 142 (1980), pp. 314-318.

Allen, William P. "Case in Focus." *Pastoral Life* 21, October 1972, pp. 36-40.

American Law Institute. *Model Penal Code: Proposed Official Draft.* Philadelphia: American Law Institute, 1962.

Ashford, T. "Countdown to an Abortion." *America* 136 (1977), pp. 128-130.

Ashley, Benedict M., O.P., and O'Rourke, Kevin D., O.P. *Health Care Ethics: A Theological Analysis.* St. Louis: Catholic Hospital Association, 1978.

Atkinson, Gary M. "The Morality of Abortion." *International Philosophical Quarterly* 14 (1974), pp. 347-362.

_____. "Persons in the Whole Sense." *American Journal of Jurisprudence* 22 (1977), pp. 86-117.

Atkinson, Gary M., and Moraczewski, Albert S., O.P. (eds.). *Genetic Counseling, the Church and the Law: A Report of the Task Force on Genetic Diagnosis and Counseling.* St. Louis: Pope John XXIII Medical-Moral Research and Education Center, 1980.

Ayd, Frank J., Jr. "Liberal Abortion Laws: A Psychiatrist's View." *American Ecclesiastical Review* 158 (1968), pp. 73-91.

_____. "Liberal Abortion Laws." *America* 120 (1969), pp. 130-132.

Bandman, Elsie L., and Bandman, Bertram (eds.). *Bioethics and Human Rights: A Reader for Health Professionals,.* Boston: Little, Brown and Co., 1978.

Barkley, Roy R. "The Attitude toward Abortion in Middle English Writings: A Note on the History of Ideas." *International Catholic Review: Communio* 9 (1982), pp. 176-183.

Barry, Robert, O.P. "Personhood: The Conditions of Identification and Description." *Linacre Quarterly* 45 (1978), pp. 64-81.

Baum, Gregory, O.S.A. "Abortion: An Ecumenical Dilemma." *Commonweal* 99 (1973), pp. 231-235.

Beauchamp, Tom L., and Childress, James F. *Principles of Biomedical Ethics.* New York: Oxford University Press, 1979.

Beauchamp, Tom L., and Walters, LeRoy (eds.). *Contemporary Issues in Bioethics.* Belmont, Cal.: Wadsworth, 1978.

Belgum, David. *When It's Your Turn to Decide.* Minneapolis: Augsburg, 1978.

Bennett, Owen, O.F.M. Conv. "Some Additional Arguments Against Abortion." *Homiletic and Pastoral Review* 73, January 1973, pp. 50-53.

Berger, Betty, O.S.F. "Private Hospital May Refuse to Perform Abortion." *Saint Louis University Law Journal* 18 (1974), pp. 440-460.

Berger, Patrick F., and Berger, Carol A. "The Credibility Gap that Kills." *America* 131 (1974), pp. 47-49.

_____. "The Edelin Decision." *Commonweal* 102 (1975), pp. 76-78.

Bernard, A. "The Born and the Unborn Alike: Deterioration of the American Family." *America* 136 (1977), pp. 270-272.

Bernardin, Archbishop Joseph L. "Abortion: Questions and Answers from a Catholic

Perspective." *L'Osservatore Romano: Weekly Edition in English*, November 4, 1976, pp. 9, 12.

_____. "Human Rights: Do We Practice What We Preach?" *Origins* 7 (1977), pp. 201-204.

Beusse, Robert B., and Shaw, Russell. "Maude's Abortion: Spontaneous or Induced?" *America* 129 (1973), pp. 324-326.

Bier, William C., S.J. (ed.). *Human Life: Problems of Birth, of Living, and of Dying.* Pastoral Psychology Series No. 9. New York: Fordham University Press, 1977.

Bishops of Maryland. "Statement on Abortion." *Catholic Mind* 66, March 1968, pp. 1-3.

Bishops of New Jersey. "Pastoral Letter on Abortion." *Catholic Mind* 66, June 1968, pp. 4-5.

Bittle, Celestine N., O.F.M.Cap. *Man and Morals: Ethics.* Milwaukee: Bruce, 1950.

Blake, Judith. "Abortion and Public Opinion: The 1960-1970 Decade." *Science* 171 (1971), pp. 540-549.

Bluford, Robert, Jr., and Petres, Robert E. *Unwanted Pregnancy.* New York: Harper and Row, 1973.

Blum, Virgil, S.J. "Politicizing the Catholic Community." *Hospital Progress* 56, September 1975, pp. 84-88.

Bouscaren, T. Lincoln. *Ethics of Ectopic Operations.* 2nd ed. Milwaukee: Bruce, 1944.

Boyle, Joseph M. "That the Fetus Should Be Considered a Legal Person." *American Journal of Jurisprudence* 24 (1979), pp. 59-71.

Brandmeyer, G. "Politics and Abortion." *Commonweal* 103 (1976), pp. 432-433.

Brennan, William C. "The Vanishing Protectors: Final Musings of an Unborn, Unwanted Child." *Social Justice Review* 66, November 1973, pp. 239-244.

Breslin, John B., S.J. "Birthright—Alternative to Abortion." *America* 125 (1971), pp. 116-119.

Broach, Claude U. (ed.). *Seminar on Abortion: The Proceedings of a Dialogue between Catholics and Baptists.* Charlotte, N.C.: Ecumenical Institute, 1975.

Broderick, Albert, O.P. "A Constitutional Lawyer Looks at the *Roe-Doe* Decisions." *Jurist* 33 (1973), pp. 123-133.

Brody, Baruch A. "Abortion and the Law." *Journal of Philosophy* 68 (1971), pp. 357-369.

_____. "Thomson on Abortion." *Philosophy and Public Affairs* 1 (1972), pp. 335-340.

_____. "Abortion and the Sanctity of Human Life." *American Philosophical Quarterly* 10 (1973), pp. 133-140.

_____. *Abortion and the Sanctity of Human Life: A Philosophical View.* Cambridge, Mass.: M.I.T. Press, 1975.

Brooke, C.P. "Legalized Abortion." *Catholic Mind* 70, May 1972, pp. 24-34.

Burtchaell, James T., C.S.C. "A Call and a Reply." *Christianity and Crisis* 37 (1977), pp. 270-271.

_____. (ed.). *Abortion Parley: Papers Delivered at the National Conference on Abortion Held at the University of Notre Dame in October 1979.* Kansas City: Andrews and McMeel, 1980.

_____. *Rachel Weeping and Other Essays on Abortion.* Kansas City: Andrews and McMeel, 1982.

Byrn, Robert M. "The Abortion Question: A Nonsectarian Approach." *Catholic Lawyer* 11 (1965), pp. 316-322.

_____. "Abortion in Perspective." *Duquesne University Law Review* 5 (1966), pp. 125-141.

_____. "Abortion: A Legal View." *Commonweal* 85 (1967), pp. 679-681.

_____. "Abortion: The Future in America." *America* 117 (1967), pp. 710-713.

_____. "Demythologizing Abortion Reform." *Catholic Lawyer* 14 (1968), pp. 180-189.

_____. "Abortion-on-Demand: Whose Morality?" *Notre Dame Lawyer* 46 (1970), pp. 5-40.

_____. "Goodbye to the Judaeo-Christian Era in Law." *America* 128 (1973), pp. 511-514.

_____. "*Wade* and *Bolton*: Fundamental Legal Errors and Dangerous Implications." *Catholic Lawyer* 19 (1973), pp. 243-250.

_____. "An American Tragedy: The Supreme Court on Abortion." *Fordham Law Review* 41 (1973), pp. 807-862.

_____. "The Abortion Amendments: Policy in the Light of Precedent." *Saint Louis University Law Journal* 18 (1974), pp. 380-406.

_____. "Confronting Objections to an Anti-Abortion Amendment." *America* 134 (1976), pp. 529-534.

_____. "The New Jurisprudence." *Journal of the American Medical Association* 236 (1976), pp. 359-360.

_____. "Judicial Imperialism: Forty Years of Supreme Court Decisions on Privacy and Abortion." *Hospital Progress* 58, November 1977, pp. 90-97.

Calderone, Mary Steichen (ed.). *Abortion in the United States: A Conference Sponsored by the Planned Parenthood Federation of America, Inc.* New York: Hoeber and Harper, 1958.

Callahan, Daniel. "The Sanctity of Life." *The Religious Situation: 1969.* Edited by Donald R. Cutler. Boston: Beacon Press, 1969, pp. 297-336.

_____. *Abortion: Law, Choice and Morality.* New York: Macmillan, 1970.

_____. "The New Setting of Abortion Decisions." *Ecumenist* 8 (1970), pp. 65-68.

_____. "Ethics and Population Limitation: What Ethical Norms Should Be Brought to Bear in Controlling Population Growth?" *Science* 175 (1972), pp. 487-494.

_____. "Abortion: Thinking and Experiencing." *Christianity and Crisis* 32 (1973), pp. 295-298.

_____. "Abortion and Medical Ethics." *Annals of the American Academy of Political and Social Science* 437, May 1978, pp. 116-127.

_____. "Abortion and Government Policy." *Family Planning Perspectives* 2, September/October 1979, pp. 275-279.

Cameron, Paul. "Abortion, Capital Punishment and the Judeo-Christian Ethic." *Linacre Quarterly* 48 (1982), pp. 316-332.

Canavan, Francis, S.J. "History Repeats Itself." *America* 114 (1966), pp. 738-742.

_____. "The Church's Right to Speak on Public Issues." *Catholic Mind* 65, April 1967, pp. 13-16.

_____. "The Theory of the Danforth Case." *Human Life Review* 2, Fall 1976, pp. 5-14.

Caron, Wilfred R. "New York Abortion Reform—A Critique." *Catholic Lawyer* 14 (1968), pp. 199-213.

Carr, Aidan M., O.F.M. Conv. "Questions Answered: Abortion and Vatican II's Declaration on Religious Liberty." *Homiletic and Pastoral Review* 67 (1966), pp. 73-75.

Castelli, J. "Anti-abortion, the Bishops and the Crusaders." *America* 134 (1976), pp. 442-444.

Catholic Archbishops of Great Britain. "Abortion and the Right to Life." *Tablet* 234 (1980), pp. 91-94.

Catholic Hospital Association. *Ethical and Religious Directives for Catholic Hospitals.*

2nd ed. St. Louis: Catholic Hospital Association, 1955.

———. *Ethical Issues in Nursing: A Proceedings*. St. Louis: Catholic Hospital Association, 1976.

Cavanagh, Denis. "Reforming the Abortion Laws: A Doctor Looks at the Case." *America* 122 (1970), pp. 406-411.

———. "Legalized Abortion: The Conscience Clause and Coercion." *Hospital Progress* 52, August 1971, pp. 86-90.

Cavnar, N. "Books on Abortion." *New Covenant* 10, July 1980, p. 31.

Chamberlain, Gary L. "The Abortion Debate is Revealing our Values." *New Catholic World* 215 (1972), pp. 206-208.

Coffey, Patrick J. "Toward a Sound Moral Policy on Abortion." *New Scholasticism* 47 (1973), pp. 105-112.

———. "When is Killing the Unborn a Homicidal Action?" *Linacre Quarterly* 43 (1976), pp. 85-93.

Cohen, Marshall, *et al.* (eds.). *The Rights and Wrongs of Abortion*. Princeton, N.J.: Princeton University Press, 1974.

The Commission on Population Growth and the American Future. *Population and the American Future*. New York: New American Library, 1972.

Conley, Patrick T., and McKenna, Robert J. "The Supreme Court on Abortion — A Dissenting Opinion." *Catholic Lawyer* 19 (1973), pp. 19-28.

Connell, Francis J., C.SS.R. *Morals in Politics and Professions: A Guide for Catholics in Public Life*. Westminster, Maryland: Newman Press, 1955.

Connery, John R., S.J. "Grisez on Abortion." *Theological Studies* 31 (1970), pp. 170-176.

———. "Callahan on Meaning of Abortion." *Linacre Quarterly* 37 (1970), pp. 280-287.

———. *Abortion: The Development of the Roman Catholic Perspective*. Chicago: Loyola University Press, 1977.

———. "Abortion: A Philosophical and Historical Analysis." *Hospital Progress* 58, April 1977, pp. 49-50.

———. "Abortion and the Duty to Preserve Life." *Theological Studies* 40 (1979), pp. 318-333.

Cooke, Robert E., *et al.* (eds.). *The Terrible Choice: The Abortion Dilemma. Based on the Proceedings of the International Conference on Abortion Sponsored by the Harvard Divinity School and the Joseph P. Kennedy Jr. Foundation*. New York: Bantam Books, 1968.

Cooke, Cardinal Terence. "The Impact of Abortion." *Origins* 10 (1980), pp. 283-285.

Coriden, James A. "Church Law and Abortion." *Jurist* 33 (1973), pp. 184-198.

Crawford, J. "Abortion Entitlement: Absolute or Qualified?" *Linacre Quarterly* 47 (1980), pp. 77-87.

Culliton, Joseph T. "Rahner on the Origin of the Soul: Some Implications regarding Abortion." *Thought* 53 (1978), pp. 203-214.

Curran, Charles E. *A New Look at Christian Morality*. Notre Dame, Ind.: Fides, 1968.

———. (ed.). *Absolutes in Moral Theology?* Washington, D.C.: Corpus Books, 1968.

———. *Medicine and Morals*. Washington, D.C.: Corpus Books, 1970.

———. *Catholic Moral Theology in Dialogue*. Notre Dame, Ind.: Fides, 1972.

———. "Abortion: Law and Morality in Contemporary Catholic Theology." *Jurist* 33 (1973), pp. 162-183.

———. *Politics, Medicine, and Christian Ethics: A Dialogue with Paul Ramsey*. Philadelphia: Fortress Press, 1973.

_____. *New Perspectives in Moral Theology.* Notre Dame, Ind.: Fides, 1974.

_____. "Commentary and Response." *Jurist* 35 (1975), pp. 77-80.

_____. *Ongoing Revision: Studies in Moral Theology.* Notre Dame, Ind.: Fides, 1975.

_____. *Themes in Fundamental Moral Theology.* Notre Dame, Ind.: University of Notre Dame Press, 1977.

_____. *Issues in Sexual and Medical Ethics.* Notre Dame, Ind.: University of Notre Dame Press, 1978.

_____. *Transition and Tradition in Moral Theology.* Notre Dame, Ind.: University of Notre Dame Press, 1979.

Curran, Charles E., and McCormick, Richard A., S.J. (eds.). *Moral Norms and Catholic Tradition.* Readings in Moral Theology No. 1. New York: Paulist Press, 1979.

Cutler, Donald R. (ed.). *Updating Life and Death: Essays in Ethics and Medicine.* Boston: Beacon Press, 1969.

Dailey, Thomas G. "The Catholic Position on Abortion." *Linacre Quarterly* 34 (1967), pp. 218-220.

Daughters of St. Paul (eds.). *Yes to Life.* Boston: St. Paul Editions, 1977.

Decker, Raymond G. "The Abortion Decision: Two Years Later: More Christian than its Critics." *Commonweal* 101 (1975), pp. 384-388.

Dedek, John F. "Abortion: A Theological Judgment." *Chicago Studies* 10 (1971), pp. 313-333.

_____. *Human Life: Some Moral Issues.* New York: Sheed and Ward, 1972.

_____. *Contemporary Medical Ethics.* New York: Sheed and Ward, 1975.

_____. *Titius and Bertha Ride Again: Contemporary Moral Cases.* New York: Sheed and Ward, no date.

Deedy, John. "The Church in the World: Catholics, Abortion, and the Supreme Court." *Theology Today* 30 (1973), pp. 279-286.

De George, Richard T. "Legal Enforcement, Moral Pluralism and Abortion." *Philosophy and Civil Law: Proceedings of the American Catholic Philosophical Association* 49 (1975), pp. 171-179.

Degnan, Daniel A., S.J. "Law, Morals and Abortion." *Commonweal* 100 (1974), pp. 305-308.

DeMarco, Donald. "Abortion: Legal and Philosophical Considerations." *American Ecclesiastical Review* 168 (1974), pp. 251-267.

_____. "The Foetus, his Humanity and his Rights." *Linacre Quarterly* 41 (1974), pp. 281-284.

_____. *Abortion in Perspective: The Rose Palace or the Fiery Dragon?* Cincinnati: Hiltz and Hayes, 1974.

_____. "The Abortion Movement: Retreat from Reality." *Homiletic and Pastoral Review* 80, January 1980, pp. 10-20.

_____. "The Child in the Silent Walk." *Linacre Quarterly* 48 (1981), p. 333-339.

Dendinger, Donald C., and Mathern, Timothy. "Abortion: Toward Developing a Policy in a Catholic Social Service Agency." *Social Thought* 6, Fall 1980, pp. 33-46.

Diamond, Eugene F. "The Physician and the Rights of the Unborn." *Linacre Quarterly* 34 (1967), pp. 174-181.

_____. "Who Speaks for the Fetus?" *Linacre Quarterly* 36 (1969), pp. 58-62.

_____. "The Humanity of the Unborn Child." *Catholic Lawyer* 17 (1971), pp. 174-180.

_____. "Contraception and Abortifacients." *Linacre Quarterly* 38 (1971), pp. 122-126.

_____. "The Morality of Crisis Pregnancy Counseling." *Linacre Quarterly* 41 (1974), pp. 168-173.

_____. "Do Medical Schools Discriminate Against Anti-Abortion Applicants?" *Linacre Quarterly* 43 (1976), pp. 29-35.

_____. "Redefining the Issues in Fetal Experimentation." *Journal of the American Medical Association* 236 (1976), pp. 281-283.

Diamond, James J. "Humanizing the Abortion Debate." *America* 121 (1969), pp. 36-39.

_____. "Pro-Life Amendments and Due Process." *America* 130 (1974), pp. 27-29.

_____. "The Troubled Anti-Abortion Camp." *America* 131 (1974), pp. 52-54.

_____. "Abortion, Animation, and Biological Hominization." *Theological Studies* 36 (1975), pp. 305-324.

Di Ianni, Albert R., S.M. "Is the Fetus a Person?" *American Ecclesiastical Review* 168 (1974), pp. 309-326.

Dillon, Valerie Vance. *In Defense of Life: A Handbook for Those Who Oppose the Destruction of the Unborn*. Toronto, N.J.: New Jersey Right to Life Committee, 1970.

Diocese of Rockville Center, New York. "Statement of the Diocese of Rockville Center, New York, June 1970." *Catholic Mind* 68, September 1970, p. 3.

Doherty, Dennis J. "The Morality of Abortion." *American Ecclesiastical Review* 169 (1975), pp. 37-47.

Doherty, Donald P. "Constitutional Law—Abortion Statute as Invasion of a Woman's Right of Privacy." *Saint Louis University Law Journal* 15 (1971), pp. 624-650.

Donceel, Joseph F., S.J. "Abortion: Mediate V. Immediate Animation." *Continuum* 5 (1967), pp. 167-171.

_____. "Immediate Animation and Delayed Hominization." *Theological Studies* 31 (1970), pp. 76-105.

_____. "Why is Abortion Wrong?" *America* 133 (1975), pp. 65-67.

Doyle, Eileen M. *Abortion: A Study in Human Values*. Revised ed. Rockville Centre, N.Y.: Committee for Life, 1974.

Drinan, Robert F., S.J. "Strategy on Abortion." *America* 116 (1967), pp. 177-179.

_____. "Abortion: Contemporary Protestant Thinking." *America* 117 (1967), pp. 713-715.

_____. "Catholic Moral Teaching and Abortion Laws in America." *The Catholic Theological Society of America: Proceedings of the Twenty-Third Annual Convention, Washington, D.C., June 17-20, 1968* 23 (1968), pp. 118-130.

_____. "The Jurisprudential Options on Abortion." *Theological Studies* 31 (1970), pp. 149-169.

_____. "The State of the Abortion Question." *Commonweal* 92 (1970), pp. 108-109.

_____. "The Abortion Decision." *Commonweal* 97 (1973), pp. 438-440.

_____. "Abortions on Medicaid? The Bartlett Amendment." *Commonweal* 102 (1975), pp. 102-103.

Dupré, Louis. "A New Approach to the Abortion Problem." *Theological Studies* 34 (1973), pp. 481-488.

Durbin, Thomas M. "The Catholic Hospital Faces Abortion." *American Ecclesiastical Review* 163 (1970), pp. 224-254.

Dyer, George J. (ed.). *An American Catholic Catechism*. New York: Seabury Press, 1975.

Edelstein, Robert, *et al*. "Moral Consistency and the Abortion Issue." *Commonweal* 100 (1974), pp. 59-61.

Ehrensing, Rudolph H. "The I.U.D.: How it Works: Is it Moral?" *National Catholic Reporter*, April 27, 1966, p. 6.

_____. "When is it Really Abortion?" *National Catholic Reporter*, May 25, 1966, p. 4.

Etzioni, Amitai, *Genetic Fix*. New York: Macmillan, 1973.

Facione, Peter A. "The Abortion Non-Debate." *Cross Currents* 23 (1973), pp. 349-353.

_____. "Callahan on Abortion." *American Ecclesiastical Review* 167 (1973), pp. 291-301.

Fagothey, Austin, S.J. *Right and Reason: Ethics in Theory and Practice*. 3rd ed. St. Louis: C.V. Mosby, 1963.

Farley, Leo O. "The Meaning of Life and Divine Transcendence." *The Catholic Theological Society of America: Proceedings of the Twenty-Third Annual Convention, Washington, D.C., June 17-20, 1968* 23 (1968), pp. 109-117.

Farley, Margaret A. "Liberation, Abortion and Responsibility." *Reflection* (Yale Divinity School), May 1974, pp. 9-13.

Fazziola, Peter J. "The Mystery of the Unborn." *The Bible Today*, No. 78, April 1975, pp. 388-390.

Feinberg, Joel (ed.). *The Problem of Abortion*. Belmont, Cal.: Wadsworth, 1973.

Finney, Patrick, and O'Brien, Patrick. *Moral Problems in Hospital Practice: A Practical Handbook*. St. Louis: Herder, 1956.

Finnis, John. "The Rights and Wrongs of Abortion: A Reply to Judith Thomson." *Philosophy and Public Affairs* 2 (1973), pp. 117-145.

Fitzgerald, James A. "Abortion on Demand." *Linacre Quarterly* 37 (1970), pp. 184-189.

_____. "Ramifications of Permissive Abortion." *Linacre Quarterly* 38 (1971), pp. 102-105.

Flaherty, Francis J. "Abortion, the Constitution, and the Human Life Statute." *Commonweal* 108 (1981), pp. 586-593.

Gaffney, Edward McGlynn. "Law and Theology: A Dialogue on the Abortion Decisions." *Jurist* 33 (1973), pp. 134-152.

Garrett, Thomas M., S.J. *Problems and Perspectives in Ethics*. New York: Sheed and Ward, 1968.

Garvey, John, and Morriss, Frank. *Abortion*. Chicago: Thomas More Press, 1979.

Geary, P. "Analysis of Recent Decisions involving Abortions." *Catholic Lawyer* 23 (1978), pp. 237-242.

Gerber, D. "Abortion: The Uptake Argument." *Ethics* 83 (1972), pp. 80-83.

Gerber, Rudolph J. "Abortion: Two Opposing Legal Philosophies." *American Journal of Jurisprudence* 15 (1970), pp. 1-24.

_____. "Abortion: Parameters for Decision." *International Philosophical Quarterly* 11 (1971), pp. 561-584.

Gest, John B. "Comment on Fr. Drinan's Article on Abortion Laws." *Catholic Lawyer* 14 (1968), pp. 326-328.

_____. "Proposed Abortion Laws 'Slaughter of the Innocents'." *Linacre Quarterly* 36 (1969), pp. 47-52.

Giannella, Donald A. "The Difficult Quest for a Truly Humane Abortion Law." *Villanova Law Review* 13 (1968), pp. 257-302.

Glenn, Gary D. "Abortion and Inalienable Rights in Classical Liberalism." *American Journal of Jurisprudence* 20 (1975), pp. 62-80.

Goldenberg, David. "The Right to Abortion: Expansion of the Right to Privacy through the Fourteenth Amendment." *Catholic Lawyer* 19 (1973), pp. 36-57.

Good, Frederick L., and Kelly, Otis F. *Marriage, Morals and Medical Ethics*. New York: P.J. Kenedy, 1951.

Gorman, Michael J. *Abortion and the Early Church*. Ramsey, N.J.: Paulist Press, 1982.

Granfield, David. "The Present Status of the Abortion Controversy." *American Ecclesiastical Review* 162 (1970), pp. 195-205.

_____. *The Abortion Decision*. Revised ed. Garden City, N.Y.: Doubleday Image Books, 1971.

_____. "The Legal Impact of the *Roe* and *Doe* Decisions." *Jurist* 33 (1973), pp. 113-122.

Grisez, Germain G. "Abortion and the Catholic Faith." *American Ecclesiastical Review* 159 (1968), pp. 96-115.

_____. "Toward a Consistent Natural-Law Ethics of Killing." *American Journal of Jurisprudence* 15 (1970), pp. 64-96.

_____. *Abortion: The Myths, the Realities, and the Arguments*. New York: Corpus Books, 1970.

Guttmacher, Alan F. (ed.). *The Case for Legalized Abortion Now*. Berkeley, Cal.: Diablo Press, 1967.

Hall, Robert E. (ed.). *Abortion in a Changing World: The Proceedings of an International Conference Convened in Hot Springs, Virginia, November 17-20, 1968, by the Association for the Study of Abortion*. Vols. I-II. New York: Columbia University Press, 1970.

Hallett, Garth L., S.J. "The Plain Meaning of Abortion." *America* 124 (1971), pp. 632-633.

Hammes, John A. *Human Destiny: Exploring Today's Value Systems*. Huntington, Ind.: Our Sunday Visitor, 1978.

Häring, Bernard, C.SS.R. *Medical Ethics*. Revised ed. Notre Dame, Ind.: Fides, 1975.

_____. "New Dimensions of Responsible Parenthood." *Theological Studies* 37 (1976), pp. 120-132.

Harrington, Paul V. "Abortion." *Linacre Quarterly* 32 (1965), pp. 339-345; 33 (1966), pp. 81-92, 153-167; 34 (1967), pp. 67-82, 158-173, 250-268, 311-333; 35 (1968), pp. 43-61, 126-143, 190-209, 264-280; 36 (1969), pp. 139-143, 174-196, 242-256; 37 (1970), pp. 117-134, 270-280; 38 (1971), pp. 55-61.

_____. "Human Life and Abortion." *Catholic Lawyer* 17 (1971), pp. 11-44.

Harrington, Timothy J. "Legalization of Abortion." *Homiletic and Pastoral Review* 69 (1969), pp. 685-690.

Harrison, Stanley M. "The Unwilling Dead." *Proceedings of the American Catholic Philosophical Association* 46 (1972), pp. 199-208.

Hauerwas, Stanley. "Abortion and Normative Ethics: A Critical Appraisal of Callahan and Grisez." *Cross Currents* 21 (1971), pp. 399-414.

_____. "Abortion: The Agent's Perspective." *American Ecclesiastical Review* 167 (1973), pp. 102-120.

Hayasaka, Yokochi, *et al.* "Japan's Twenty-Two Year Experience with a Liberal Abortion Law." *Linacre Quarterly* 38 (1971), pp. 33-44.

Hayes, Edward J., *et al. Moral Handbook of Nursing: A Compendium of Principles, Spiritual Aids, and Concise Answers regarding Catholic Personnel, Patients, and Problems*. New York: Macmillan, 1956.

Hayes, Thomas L. "Abortion: A Biological View." *Commonweal* 85 (1967), pp. 676-679.

Healy, Edwin F., S.J. *Moral Guidance: A Textbook in Principles of Conduct for Colleges and Universities*. Chicago: Loyola University Press, 1942.

_____. *Medical Ethics*. Chicago: Loyola University Press, 1956.

Healy, James, S.J. "Abortion: Some References and Questions." *Social Studies* 65 (1974), pp. 317-331.

Hellegers, Andre E. "A Look at Abortion." *National Catholic Reporter*, March 1, 1967, p. 4.

_____. "Abortion, the Law, and the Common Good." *Medical Opinion and Review*, May 1967, pp. 76-93.

_____. "Law and the Common Good." *Commonweal* 86 (1967), pp. 418-423.

_____. "Fetal Development." *Theological Studies* 31 (1970), pp. 3-9.

_____. "*Wade* and *Bolton*: Medical Critique." *Catholic Lawyer* 19 (1973), pp. 251-258.

_____. "The Beginnings of Personhood: Medical Considerations." *Perkins Journal* 27, Fall 1973, pp. 11-15.

_____. "Amazing Historical and Biological Errors in Abortion Decision." *Hospital Progress* 54, May 1973, pp. 16-17.

_____. *Abortion: A Help or Hindrance to Public Health? Testimony submitted before Congress April 25, 1974 in support of a human life amendment.* Washington, D.C.: National Committee for a Human Life Amendment, 1974.

Henle, Robert J., S.J. "Georgetown University Statement on Abortion." *Catholic Mind* 71, September 1973, pp. 9-10.

_____. "The 'Demystification' of Life." *Commonweal* 104 (1977), pp. 457-460.

Hennessy, Augustine P., C.P., *et al.* "The Debate on Legalized Abortion." *Sign* 46, June 1967, pp. 34-35.

Heyer, Robert (ed.). *Medical/Moral Problems.* New York: Paulist Press, 1976.

Higgins, G. "The Prolife Movement and the New Right." *America* 143 (1980), pp. 107-110.

Higgins, Thomas J., S.J. *Man as Man: The Science and Art of Ethics.* Milwaukee: Bruce, 1949.

Hilgers, Thomas W. "Human Reproduction: Three Issues for the Moral Theologian." *Theological Studies* 38 (1977), pp. 136-152.

_____. "An Evaluation of Intrauterine Devices." Reprint from *International Review of Natural Family Planning* 2 (1978), no pagination.

Hilgers, Thomas W., and Horan, Dennis J. (eds.). *Abortion and Social Justice.* New York: Sheed and Ward, 1972.

Hilgers, Thomas W., *et al.* (eds.). *New Perspectives on Human Abortion.* Frederick, Maryland: University Publications of America, 1981.

Hitchcock, James. *Catholicism and Modernity: Confrontation or Capitulation?* New York: Seabury Press, 1979.

Hogan, G. "Abortion and the Handicapped: Present Practice in the Light of History." *Social Thought* 6 (1980), pp. 37-46.

Hogan, Joseph E., C.M. "The Conscience of the Law." *Catholic Lawyer* 21 (1975), pp. 190-196.

Hollis, Harry (ed.). *A Matter of Life and Death: Christian Perspectives.* Nashville: Broadman Press, 1977.

Horan, Dennis J. "Abortion and the Conscience Clause: Current Status." *Catholic Lawyer* 20 (1974), pp. 289-302.

_____. "Viability, Values, and the Vast Cosmos." *Catholic Lawyer* 22 (1976), pp. 1-37.

Horan, Dennis J., and Gorby, John D. "Abortion and Human Rights." *Human Life Review* 2, Summer 1976, pp. 21-33.

Humber, James M. "The Case against Abortion." *Thomist* 39 (1975), pp. 65-84.

_____. "Abortion, Fetal Research, and the Law." *Social Theory and Practice* 4 (1977), pp. 127-147.

Humber, James M., and Almeder, Robert E. (eds.). *Biomedical Ethics and the Law.* New York: Pflaum Press, 1976.

Hurley, Denis E., O.M.I. "Population Control and the Catholic Conscience: Responsibility of the Magisterium." *Theological Studies* 35 (1974), pp. 154-163.

Hurley, Mark J. "The Value of Human Life: Challenge to a Brave New World." *Hospital Progress* 58, February 1977, pp. 70-73.

Huser, Roger J., O.F.M. *The Crime of Abortion in Canon Law: A Historical Synopsis and Commentary*. Canon Law Studies No. 162. Washington, D.C.: Catholic University of America Press, 1942.

Jacobs, William J. "Abortion: A Challenge to Catholic Health Care Personnel." *Pastoral Life* 22, September 1973, pp. 34-39.

_____. *The Pastor and the Patient: An Informal Guide to New Directions in Medical Ethics*. New York: Paulist Press, 1973.

Johnson, Harvey J. "Is Embryonic or Fetal Life Human Life?" *Social Justice Review* 60 (1968), pp. 420-421.

Johnson, John G. "The Dynamics of the Abortion Debate." *America* 146 (1982), pp. 106-109.

Joyce, Robert E. "Personhood and the Conception Event." *New Scholasticism* 52 (1978), pp. 97-109.

Joyce, Robert E., and Joyce, Mary Rosera. *Let Us Be Born: The Inhumanity of Abortion*. Chicago: Franciscan Herald Press, 1970.

Keane, Philip S., S.S. *Sexual Morality: A Catholic Perspective*. New York: Paulist Press, 1977.

Kearns, James A. "Case Comment." *Notre Dame Lawyer* 48 (1973), pp. 715-727.

Keefe, Donald J., S.J. "The Life and Death of the Law." *Hospital Progress* 53, March 1972, pp. 64-74.

Kelly, David F. *The Emergence of Roman Catholic Medical Ethics in North America: A Historical-Methodological-Bibliographical Study*. New York: Edwin Mellen, 1979.

Kelly, Gerald, S.J. *Medico-Moral Problems*. St. Louis: Catholic Hospital Association, 1958.

Kelly, James R. "Beyond the Stereotypes: Interviews with Right-to-Life Pioneers." *Commonweal* 108 (1981), pp. 654-659.

Kenealy, William J., S.J. "Law and Morals." *Catholic Lawyer* 9 (1963), pp. 200-210, 264.

Kennedy, Joseph P., et al. "Church-State: A Legal Survey—1966-68." *Notre Dame Lawyer* 43 (1968), pp. 684-780.

Kenny, John P., O.P. *Principles of Medical Ethics*. 2nd edition. Westminster, Maryland: Newman Press, 1962.

Kindregan, Charles P. *The Quality of Life: Reflections on the Moral Values of American Law*. Milwaukee: Bruce, 1969.

_____. *Abortion, the Law, and Defective Children: A Legal-Medical Study*. Washington: Corpus Books, 1969.

Klotz, John W. *A Christian View of Abortion*. St. Louis: Concordia Publishing House, 1973.

Kohl, Marvin. *The Morality of Killing: Sanctity of Life, Abortion and Euthanasia*. London: Peter Owen, 1974.

Krause, James E. "Is Abortion Absolutely Prohibited?" *Continuum* 6 (1968), pp. 436-440.

Labby, Daniel H. (ed.). *Life or Death: Ethics and Options*. Seattle: University of Washington Press, 1968.

Lader, Lawrence. *Abortion*. Indianapolis: Bobbs-Merrill, 1966.

_____. *Abortion II: Making the Revolution*. Boston: Beacon Press, 1973.

Lane, Thomas A. "Population and the Crisis of Culture." *Homiletic and Pastoral Review* 75, April 1975, pp. 61-65.

Lauth, Edward J., Jr. "Liberal Abortion Laws: The Antithesis of the Practice of Medicine." *Linacre Quarterly* 34 (1967), pp. 367-373.

Lavelle, Joseph P. "Is Abortion Good Medicine?" *Linacre Quarterly* 35 (1968), pp. 16-23.

Leadership Conference of Women Religious. "Choose Life: Promoting the Value and Quality of Life." *Origins* 7 (1977-1978), pp. 161-167.

Lebacqz, Karen A. "Prenatal Diagnosis and Selective Abortion." *Linacre Quarterly* 40 (1973), pp. 109-127.

Leiser, Burton M. *Liberty, Justice, and Morals: Contemporary Value Conflicts*. New York: Macmillan, 1973.

Liston, Mary F. "Abortion Decisions—Impact on Nursing Practice, Maternal and Child Care." *Jurist* 33 (1973), pp. 230-236.

Little, David. "Abortion: Law, Choice and Morality." *Commonweal* 93 (1970), pp. 72-75.

Loesch, Juli. "Abortion and an Attempt at Dialogue." *America* 140 (1979), pp. 234-236.

Los Angeles Catholic-Jewish Respect Life Committee. "Respect for Life: Jewish and Roman Catholic Reflections on Abortion and Related Issues—September 1977." *Catholic Mind* 76, February 1978, pp. 54-64.

Louisell, David W. "Abortion, the Practice of Medicine and the Due Process of Law." *University of California at Los Angeles Law Review* 16 (1969), pp. 233-254.

_____. "A Constitutional Amendment to Restrict Abortion." *Catholic Mind* 74, December 1976, pp. 25-31.

Louisell, David W., and Carroll, Charles. "The Father as Non-Parent." *Catholic World* 210 (1969), pp. 109-110.

Luce, Clare Boothe. "Two Books on Abortion and the Questions They Raise." *National Review* 23 (1971), pp. 27-33.

Lynch, John J., S.J. "Legalized Abortion: Commission Hears Ecumenical Discussion." *Linacre Quarterly* 35 (1968), pp. 38-41.

Lynch, Robert N. " 'Abortion' and 1976 Politics." *America* 134 (1976), pp. 177-178.

Lynch, William. "Comments on 'Medication to Prevent Pregnancy after Rape'." *Linacre Quarterly* 44 (1977), pp. 223-228.

McAllister, Joseph B. *Ethics: With Special Application to the Medical and Nursing Professions*. 2nd ed. Philadelphia: W.B. Saunders, 1955.

McCarron, Gerard J., O.S.F.S. "Abortion and the Priest-Counselor." *Journal of Religion and Health* 15 (1976), pp. 282-290.

McCarthy, Donald G. (ed.). *Beginnings of Personhood: Inquiries into Medical Ethics I*. Houston: Institute of Religion and Human Development, 1973.

_____. "Medication to Prevent Pregnancy after Rape." *Linacre Quarterly* 44 (1977), pp. 210-222.

McCarthy, Donald G., and Moraczewski, Albert S., O.P. (eds.). *An Ethical Evaluation of Fetal Experimentation: An Interdisciplinary Study*. St. Louis: Pope John XXIII Medical-Moral Research and Education Center, 1976.

McCarthy, John F. *In Defense of Human Life*. Houston: Lumen Christi Press, 1970.

McCormick, Richard A., S.J. "Abortion." *America* 112 (1965), pp. 877-881.

_____. "Conference Without Consensus." *America* 117 (1967), pp. 320-321.

_____. "Abortion: Aspects of the Moral Question." *America* 117 (1967), pp. 716-719.

_____. "Past Church Teaching on Abortion." *The Catholic Theological Society of*

America: Proceedings of the Twenty-Third Annual Convention, Washington, D.C., June 17-20, 1968 23 (1968), pp. 131-151.

_____. "Notes on Moral Theology." *Theological Studies* 32 (1971), pp. 66-122.

_____. *Ambiguity in Moral Choice: The 1973 Pere Marquette Theology Lecture*. Milwaukee: Marquette University Press, 1973.

_____. "Notes on Moral Theology." *Theological Studies* 34 (1973), pp. 53-102.

_____. "Notes on Moral Theology: The Abortion Dossier." *Theological Studies* 35 (1974), pp. 312-359.

_____. "Notes on Moral Theology." *Theological Studies* 36 (1975), pp. 77-129.

_____. "Notes on Moral Theology." *Theological Studies* 38 (1977), pp. 57-114.

_____. "Abortion: Rules for Debate." *America* 139 (1978), pp. 26-30.

_____. "Notes on Moral Theology." *Theological Studies* 39 (1978), pp. 76-138.

_____. "Abortion: A Changing Morality and Policy?" *Hospital Progress* 60, February 1979, pp. 36-44.

_____. *How Brave a New World? Dilemmas in Bioethics*. Garden City, N.Y.: Doubleday, 1981.

_____. "Notes on Moral Theology." *Theological Studies* 42 (1981). pp. 74-121.

McCormick, Richard A., S.J., and Ramsey, Paul (eds.). *Doing Evil to Achieve Good: Moral Choice in Conflict Situations*. Chicago: Loyola University Press, 1978.

MacDonald, Sebastian, C.P. "The Meaning of Abortion." *American Ecclesiastical Review* 169 (1975), pp. 219-236, 291-315.

McFadden, Charles J., O.S.A. *Medical Ethics*. 3rd edition. Philadelphia: F.A. Davis, 1953.

_____. *The Dignity of Life: Moral Values in a Changing Society*. Huntington, Ind.: Our Sunday Visitor, 1976.

_____. *Challenge to Morality: Life Issues-Moral Answers*. Huntington, Ind.: Our Sunday Visitor, 1978.

McHugh, John A., O.P., and Callan, Charles J., O.P. *Moral Theology: A Complete Course. Based on St. Thomas Aquinas and the Best Modern Authorities*. Revised and enlarged edition by Edward P. Farrell, O.P. Vols. I-II. New York City: Joseph F. Wagner, 1958.

McHugh, Msgr. James T. "Priests and the Abortion Question." *Dimension* 5 (1973), pp. 164-169.

_____. "Reaction to 'Choose Life' Text." *Origins* 7 (1977-1978), pp. 315-317.

McKernan, Martin F., Jr. "Recent Abortion Litigation." *Catholic Lawyer* 17 (1971), pp. 1-10.

_____. "Compelling Hospitals to Provide Abortion Services." *Catholic Lawyer* 20 (1974), pp. 317-327.

McManus, James, C.SS.R., O'Riordan, Sean, C.SS.R., and Stratton, Henry. "The 'Declaration on Certain Questions concerning Sexual Ethics': A Discussion." *Clergy Review* 61 (1976), pp. 231-237.

McNulty, James V. "The Therapeutic Abortion Law: A Fight for Life." *Linacre Quarterly* 33 (1966), pp. 340-343.

Mace, David R. *Abortion: The Agonizing Decision*. Nashville: Abingdon Press, 1972.

Maguire, Daniel C. *Moral Absolutes and the Magisterium*. Washington, D.C: Corpus Papers, 1970.

_____. *Death by Choice*. New York: Schocken Paperbacks, 1975.

_____. *The Moral Choice*. Garden City, N.Y.: Doubleday, 1978.

Mahoney, John, S.J. "Ecumenical Witness on Moral Issues." *Month* 10 (1977), pp. 12-14.

Mahowald, Mary B. "Abortion: Towards Continuing the Dialogue." *Cross Currents* 29 (1979), pp. 330-335.

Maledon, William J. "The Law and the Unborn Child: The Legal and Logical Inconsistencies." *Notre Dame Lawyer* 46 (1971), pp. 349-372.

Mangan, Joseph T., S.J. "The Wonder of Myself: Ethical-Theological Aspects of Direct Abortion." *Theological Studies* 31 (1970), pp. 125-148.

Manier, Edward, *et al.* (eds.). *Abortion: New Directions for Policy Studies*. Notre Dame, Ind.: University of Notre Dame Press, 1977.

Mappes, Thomas A., and Zembaty, Jane S. *Social Ethics: Morality and Social Policy*. New York: McGraw-Hill, 1977.

Marcin, Mary J. Regan, and Marcin, Raymond B. "The Physician's Decision-Making Role in Abortion Cases." *Jurist* 35 (1975), pp. 66-76.

Marshall, John. *Medicine and Morals*. Twentieth Century Encyclopedia of Catholicism. vol. 129. New York: Hawthorn Books, 1960.

Marshall, Bishop J., and Snelling, R. "Abortion and Catholic Public Officials." *Origins* 7 (1977-1978), pp. 136-138.

Marshener, William H. "Metaphysical Personhood and the I.U.D." *The Wanderer* 107 (1974), No. 40 (October 3), pp. 1, 6; No. 41 (October 10, pp. 7-8; No. 45 (November 11), pp. 7, 9.

Martin, Michael M. "Ethical Standards for Fetal Experimentation." *Fordham Law Review* 43 (1975), pp. 547-570.

Marx, Paul, O.S.B. *The Death Peddlers: War on the Unborn*. Collegeville, Minnesota: St. John's University Press, 1971.

May, William E. "Abortion as Indicative of Personal and Social Identity." *Jurist* 33 (1973), pp. 199-217.

_____. "The Morality of Abortion." *Linacre Quarterly* 41 (1974), pp. 66-78.

_____. *Becoming Human: An Invitation to Christian Ethics*. Dayton: Pflaum, 1975.

_____. "Ethics and Human Identity: The Challenge of the New Biology." *Horizons* 3 (1976), pp. 17-37.

_____. "What Makes a Human Being to Be a Being of Moral Worth?" *Thomist* 40 (1976), pp. 416-443.

_____. *Human Existence, Medicine and Ethics: Reflections on Human Life*. Chicago: Franciscan Herald Press, 1977.

_____. "The Moral Meaning of Human Acts." *Homiletic and Pastoral Review* 79, October 1978, pp. 10-21.

Mayhew, Leonard F.X. "Abortion: Two Sides and Some Complaints." *Ecumenist* 5, July-August 1967, pp. 75-77.

Medeiros, Archbishop Humberto S. *Homily on Abortion: Text of Homily Delivered on December 27, 1970*. Boston, Mass.: Daughters of St. Paul, 1971.

_____. "Abortion Legislation and the Right to Life." *Social Justice Review* 64, June 1971, pp. 84-86.

_____. "A Consistent Ethic of Life and the Law." *Catholic Mind* 70, May 1972, pp. 35-42.

Meehan, Francis X. "Social Justice and Abortion." *America* 138 (1978), pp. 478-481.

Meehan, Mary. "Catholic Liberals & Abortion." *Commonweal* 108 (1981), pp. 650-654.

Melvin, Edward J. *One Nation Under God*. Huntington, Ind.: Our Sunday Visitor, 1975.

Milhaven, John G., S.J. "Exit for Ethicists." *Commonweal* 91 (1969), pp. 135-140.
_____. "The Abortion Debate: An Epistemological Interpretation." *Theological Studies* 31 (1970), pp. 106-124.
_____. *Toward a New Catholic Morality*. Garden City, N.Y.: Doubleday Image Books, 1972.
Mohr, James C. *Abortion in America: The Origins and Evolution of National Policy: 1800-1900*. New York: Oxford University Press, 1978.
Monagle, John F. "The Ethics of Abortion." *Social Justice Review* 65 (1972), pp. 111-119.
The Monks of Solesmes (eds.). *The Human Body: Papal Teachings*. Boston: St. Paul Editions, 1960.
Moore, Elizabeth N. "Moral Sentiment in Judicial Opinions on Abortion." *Santa Clara Lawyer* 15 (1975), pp. 591-634.
Moore-Čavar, Emily C. *International Inventory of Information on Induced Abortion*. New York: International Institute for the Study of Human Reproduction, Columbia University, 1974.
Moriarty, Claire. "Women's Rights vs. Catholic Dogma." *International Socialist Review* 34, March 1973, pp. 8-11+.
Munson, Ronald. *Intervention and Reflection: Basic Issues in Medical Ethics*. Belmont, Cal.: Wadsworth, 1979.
Murphy, Alfred Camillus, O.P. "Abortion, Sterilization, Birth Control: A Medico-Moral Viewpoint." *Dominicana* 47 (1962), pp. 235-258.
Murphy, Francis X., C.SS.R. *Catholic Perspectives on Population Issues II*. Population Bulletin, vol. 35, No. 6. Washington, D.C.: Population Reference Bureau, 1981.
Murray, John Courtney, S.J. *We Hold These Truths: Catholic Reflections on the American Proposition*. New York: Sheed and Ward, 1960.
Murray, Michael V., S.J. *Problems in Ethics*. New York: Henry Holt, 1960.
Nardone, Roland M. "The Nexus of Biology and the Abortion Issue." *Jurist* 33 (1973), pp. 153-161.
National Association of Catholic Chaplains. "Statement on Abortion." *Catholic Mind* 69, February 1971, p. 4.
_____. (ed.). *Pastoral Care of the Sick: A Practical Guide for the Catholic Chaplain in Health Care Facilities*. Washington, D.C.: United States Catholic Conference, 1974.

NATIONAL CONFERENCE OF CATHOLIC BISHOPS:
National Conference of Catholic Bishops. *Human Life in Our Day: A Collective Pastoral Letter of the American Hierarchy Issued November 15, 1968*. Washington, D.C.: Publications Office United States Catholic Conference, 1968.
United States Catholic Conference, Department of Health Affairs. *Ethical and Religious Directives for Catholic Health Facilities*. Washington, D.C.: Publications Office United States Catholic Conference, 1971.
National Conference of Catholic Bishops, Committee on Population and Pro-Life Activities. *Respect Life Program 1973*. Washington, D.C.: United States Catholic Conference, 1973.
National Conference of Catholic Bishops, United States Catholic Conference. *Documentation on the Right to Life and Abortion*. Washington, D.C.: Publications Office United States Catholic Conference, 1974.
Family Life Division, United States Catholic Conference. *Respect Life! Respect Life Program: A Catholic Community Experience*. Washington, D.C.: United States Catholic Conference, 1974.

National Conference of Catholic Bishops. *To Live in Christ Jesus: A Pastoral Reflection on the Moral Life*. Washington, D.C.: United States Catholic Conference, 1976.

National Conference of Catholic Bishops, United States Catholic Conference. *Documentation on Abortion and the Right to Life II*. Washington, D.C.: Publications Office United States Catholic Conference, 1976.

Bishops' Committee for Pro-Life Activities, National Conference of Catholic Bishops. *Respect Life! The 1976 Respect Life Handbook*. Washington, D.C.: Respect Life Committee NCCB, 1976.

Committee for Pro-Life Activities, National Conference of Catholic Bishops. *Respect Life! Respect Life Program 1977-1978: A Catholic Community Experience*. Washington, D.C.: Bishops' Committee for Pro-Life Activities, 1977.

United States Catholic Conference. "Abortion: An Affirmative Public Good?" *Origins* 9 (1980), pp. 534-535.

Committee for Pro-Life Activities of the National Conference of Catholic Bishops, and Our Sunday Visitor. *Abortion, Attitudes, and the Law*. Washington, D.C.: Bishops' Committee for Pro-Life Activities, no date.

National Council of Churches. "Guidelines for Ecumenical Debate on Abortion and Homosexuality." *Origins* 8 (1978-1979), pp. 517-519.

National Federation of Priests' Councils. "A Letter on Approaches to the Abortion Issue." *Catholic Mind* 75, March 1977, pp. 9-10.

Neale, Ann, and Uddo, Basile J. "The Human Life Amendment: Two Views." *National Catholic Reporter*, April 24, 1981, pp. 10-11.

Neuhaus, Richard J. "The Dangerous Assumptions." *Commonweal* 86 (1967), pp. 408-413.

The New Technologies of Birth and Death: Medical, Legal and Moral Dimensions. Proceedings of the Workshop for Bishops of the United States and Canada, Dallas, January 28-31, 1980. St. Louis: Pope John XXIII Medical-Moral Research and Education Center, 1980.

Newman, Jay. "An Empirical Argument Against Abortion." *New Scholasticism* 51 (1977), pp. 384-395.

Nicholson, Susan Teft. *Abortion and the Roman Catholic Church*. Journal of Religious Ethics Studies in Religious Ethics 2. Knoxville, Tennessee: Religious Ethics, Inc., 1978.

Nielsen, Harry A. "Toward a Socratic View of Abortion." *American Journal of Jurisprudence* 18 (1973), pp. 105-113.

Nolan-Haley, Jacqueline M., and Hilgers, Thomas W. "Roe v. Wade: Some Definitional Considerations." *Human Life Review* 3, Winter 1977, pp. 55-62.

Noonan, John T., Jr. *Contraception: A History of Its Treatment by the Catholic Theologians and Canonists*. Cambridge, Mass.: The Belknap Press of Harvard University Press, 1965.

_____. "Abortion and the Catholic Church: A Summary History." *Natural Law Forum* 12 (1967), pp. 85-131.

_____. "Deciding Who Is Human." *Natural Law Forum* 13 (1968), pp. 134-140.

_____. "Amendment of the Abortion Law: Relevant Data and Judicial Opinion." *Catholic Lawyer* 15 (1969), pp. 124-135.

_____. "The Constitutionality of the Regulation of Abortion." *Hastings Law Journal* 21, November 1969, pp. 51-65.

_____. (ed.). *The Morality of Abortion: Legal and Historical Perspectives*. Cambridge, Mass.: Harvard University Press, 1970.

_____. "Responding to Persons: Methods of Moral Argument in Debate over Abortion." *Theology Digest* 21 (1973), pp. 291-307.

_____. "The Family and the Supreme Court." *Catholic University Law Review* (1973), pp. 255-274.

_____. "USA and Abortion." *Tablet* 230 (1976), pp. 494-496.

_____. "A Half-Step Forward: The Justices Retreat on Abortion:" *Human Life Review* 3, Fall 1977, pp. 11-18.

_____. "Abortion in the American Context." *Human Life Review* 3, Winter 1977, pp. 29-38.

_____. "The Dynamics of Anti-Abortionism." *Catholic Mind* 76, May 1978, pp. 7-13.

_____. "The American Consensus on Abortion." *Human Life Review* 4, Winter 1978, pp. 60-63.

_____. *A Private Choice: Abortion in America in the Seventies.* New York: Free Press, 1979.

_____. "The Abortion Power." *Human Life Review* 5, Spring 1979, pp. 16-27.

_____. "The Jargon of Hypocrisy." *New Covenant* 10, October 1980, pp. 12-16.

_____. "In the Human Life Bill." *Catholic Mind* 79, November 1981, pp. 52-64.

Novak, Michael. "Abortion is Not Enough." *Christian Century* 84 (1967), pp. 430-431.

O'Boyle, Cardinal. "Pastoral Letter on Abortion." *Catholic Mind* 69, March 1971, pp. 5-8.

O'Connell, Timothy E. "For American Catholics: End of an Illusion." *America* 128 (1973), pp. 514-517.

_____. *Principles for a Catholic Morality.* New York: Seabury Press, 1978.

O'Connell, William T. "The Silent Life: An Embryological Review." *Linacre Quarterly* 35 (1968), pp. 179-189.

O'Connor, John. "On Humanity and Abortion." *Natural Law Forum* 13 (1968), pp. 127-133.

O'Donnell, Thomas J., S.J. *Morals in Medicine.* 2nd ed. Westminster, Maryland: Newman Press, 1959.

_____. "Current Medical-Moral Comment." *Linacre Quarterly* 32 (1965), pp. 235-237.

_____. "Current Medical-Moral Comment." *Linacre Quarterly* 34 (1967), pp. 364-366.

_____. "Abortion, II (Moral Aspect)." *New Catholic Encyclopedia.* New York: McGraw-Hill, 1967. Vol. I, pp. 28-29.

_____. "Current Medical-Moral Comment: Contrasts." *Linacre Quarterly* 35 (1968), pp. 35-37.

_____. *Medicine and Christian Morality.* New York: Alba House, 1976.

Orloski, Richard J. "Abortion: Legal Questions and Legislative Alternatives." *America* 131 (1974), pp. 50-51.

O'Rourke, Kevin D., O.P. "Because the Lord Loved You." *Hospital Progress* 54, August 1973, pp. 73-77.

_____. "Rationale and Implications of Sanctity of Life Commitment." *Hospital Progress* 55, February 1974, pp. 57-59, 81.

_____. "The Right of Privacy: What Next?" *Hospital Progress* 56 (1975), pp. 59-63.

Osgniach, Augustine J., O.S.B. *The Christian State.* Milwaukee: Bruce, 1943.

Osofsky, Howard J., and Osofsky, Joy D. (eds.). *The Abortion Experience: Psychological and Medical Impact.* Hagerstown, Maryland: Medical Department Harper and Row, 1973.

Ostheimer, Nancy C., and Ostheimer, John M. (eds.). *Life or Death—Who Controls?* New York; Springer, 1976.

Ostling, Richard N. "The Changing Abortion Debate." *Theology Today* 34 (1977), pp. 161-166.

O'Sullivan, J. Vincent. "The Effects of Legalized Abortion in England." *Linacre Quarterly* 38 (1971), pp. 230-236.

Pable, Martin W. "Pastoral Counseling and Abortion." *Priest* 31, No. 10, 1975, pp. 15-16.

Paganelli, Vitale H. "A Review of the March, 1970, *Theological Studies*; Abortion Issue." *Linacre Quarterly* 37 (1970), pp. 206-210.

Pastrana, Gabriel, O.P. "Personhood and the Beginning of Human Life." *Thomist* 41 (1977), pp. 247-294.

Patterson, Margot. "Abortion: Can the Constitution Rule it Out?" *National Catholic Reporter,* April 24, 1981, pp. 9-10.

Perkins, Robert L. (ed.). *Abortion: Pro and Con.* Cambridge, Mass.: Schenkman Publishing Co., 1974.

Pleasants, Julian R. "A Morality of Consequences." *Commonweal* 86 (1967), pp. 413-416.

Pollard, Joseph K. *Medical, Moral, and Pastoral Issues Today.* Northport, N.Y.: Costello, 1980.

Potts, Malcolm, *et al. Abortion.* Cambridge: Cambridge University Press, 1977.

Powell, John, S.J. *Abortion: The Silent Holocaust.* Allen, Texas: Argus Communications, 1981.

Preston, W. "The Unborn Child." *Linacre Quarterly* 46 (1979), pp. 50-54.

Pretuso, R., and Miller, D. "The Experience of Abortion." *America* 140 (1979), pp. 510-512.

Proceedings of the Conference Held under the Auspices of the National Committee on Maternal Health, Inc., June 19th-20th, 1942: The Abortion Problem. Baltimore: Williams and Wilkins, 1944.

Quay, Eugene. "Justifiable Abortion: Medical and Legal Foundations." *Georgetown Law Journal* 49 (1960-1961), pp. 173-256, 395-538.

Quinn, A. James, and Griffin, James A. "The Rights of the Unborn." *Jurist* 31 (1971), pp. 577-613.

Quinn, Archbishop J. "Taking Up the Role of Prophets: Statement on the Fifth Anniversary of the U.S. Supreme Court's Jan. 22, 1973, Abortion Rulings." *Origins* 7 (1978), pp. 524-526.

Ramsey, Paul. "Abortion: A Review Article." *Thomist* 37 (1973), pp. 174-226.

Ransil, Bernard J. *Abortion.* Paramus, N.J.: Paulist Press Deus Books, 1969.

Ratner, Herbert. "A Doctor Talks About Abortion." *Catholic Mind* 64, May 1966, pp. 45-50.

_____. "Right to Life Homily." *Linacre Quarterly* 47 (1980), pp. 110-113.

Reed, Evelyn, and Moriarty, Claire. *Abortion and the Catholic Church: Two Feminists Defend Women's Rights.* New York: Pathfinder Press, 1973.

Reed, George E. "Supreme Court Rejects Spousal and Parental Rights in Abortion Decision." *Hospital Progress* 57, August 1976, p. 18+.

Regan, Augustine, C.SS.R. "Abortion—The Moral Aspect." *Studia Moralia* (Rome: Editiones Academiae Alfonsianae) 10 (1972), pp. 127-217.

_____. "Abortion Laws and Fetal Right to Life." *Studia Moralia* (Rome: Editiones Academiae Alfonsianae) 11 (1973), pp. 265-313.

_____. *Thou Shalt Not Kill.* Theology Today Series, No. 38. Dublin: Mercier, 1977.

Regan, George M., C.M. *New Trends in Moral Theology: A Survey of Fundamental Moral Themes.* New York: Newman Press, 1971.

Reich, Warren T., *et al.* "Catholic Hospital Ethics: The Report of the Commission on Ethical and Religious Directives for Catholic Hospitals Commissioned by the Board of Directors of the Catholic Theological Society of America." *Linacre Quarterly* 39 (1972), pp. 246-268.

Reich, Warren T. (ed.). *Encyclopedia of Bioethics.* Vols. I-IV. New York: Free Press, 1978.

Reidy, Maurice. *Foundations for a Medical Ethic: A Personal and Theological Exploration of the Ethical Issues in Medicine Today.* Ramsey, N.J.: Paulist Press, 1978.

Reinsdorf, Walter. "Occasional Homily: On Human Life." *Homiletic and Pastoral Review* 75, January 1975, pp. 65-68.

Reiser, Stanley Joel, *et al.* (eds.). *Ethics in Medicine: Historical Perspectives and Contemporary Concerns.* Cambridge, Mass.: M.I.T. Press, 1977.

Rice, Charles E. *The Vanishing Right to Live.* Garden City, N.Y.: Doubleday, 1969.

———. "The Dred Scott Case of the Twentieth Century." *Houston Law Review* 10 (1973), pp. 1059-1086.

———. *Beyond Abortion: The Theory and Practice of the Secular State.* Chicago: Franciscan Herald Press, 1979.

Riga, Peter J. "Byrn and Roe: The Threshold Question and Juridical Review." *Catholic Lawyer* 23 (1978), pp. 309-331.

Rigali, Norbert J., S.J. "Catholics and Liberalized Abortion Laws." *Catholic World* 213 (1971), pp. 283-285.

———. "Theologians and Abortion." *Priest* 30, June 1974, pp. 22-25.

Romanowski, Richard R. "Abortion—A Fetal Viewpoint." *Linacre Quarterly* 34 (1967), pp. 276-281.

Rosen, Harold (ed.). *Therapeutic Abortion.* New York: Julian Press, 1954. Reprinted as *Abortion in America: Medical, Psychiatric, Legal, Anthropological, and Religious Considerations.* Boston: Beacon Press, 1967.

Ross, E.J. *Basic Sociology.* Milwaukee: Bruce, 1953.

Rossi, Philip J., S.J. " 'Rights' Are Not Enough: Prospects for a New Approach to the Morality of Abortion." *Linacre Quarterly* 46 (1979), pp. 109-117.

Rousseau, Mary F. "Abortion and Intimacy." *America* 140 (1979), pp. 429-432.

Rudel, Harry W., *et al. Birth Control: Contraception and Abortion.* New York: Macmillan, 1973.

Ryan, Mary Perkins (ed.). *Toward Moral Maturity.* Paramus, N.J.: Paulist Press, 1968.

Ryle, Edward J. "Some Sociological and Psychological Reflections on the Abortion Decisions." *Jurist* 33 (1973), pp. 218-229.

Sacred Congregation for the Doctrine of the Faith. *Declaration on Procured Abortion.* Vatican City: Typis Polyglottis Vaticanis, 1974.

Saltman, Jules, and Zimering, Stanley. *Abortion Today.* Springfield, Ill.: C.C. Thomas, 1973.

Sarvis, Betty, and Rodman, Hyman. *The Abortion Controversy.* New York: Columbia University Press, 1973.

Scanlan, Alfred L. "Recent Developments in the Abortion Area." *Catholic Lawyer* 21 (1975), pp. 315-321.

Schall, James V., S.J. *Human Dignity and Human Numbers.* Staten Island, N.Y.: Alba House, 1971.

———. *Christianity and Life.* San Francisco: Ignatius Press, 1981.

Schenk, Roy U. "Let's Think About Abortion." *Catholic World,* 207, April 1968, pp. 15-17.

Schulte, Eugene J. "Tax-Supported Abortions: The Legal Issues." *Catholic Lawyer* 21 (1975), pp. 1-7.

_____. "Conscience Clause May Be Next Target of Proabortion Forces!" *Hospital Progress* 57, August 1976, p. 19+.

Schwager, Sister Virginia, S.P. "Legal and Ethical Problems in Catholic Health Facilities." *Linacre Quarterly* 19 (1973), pp. 259-265.

Segers, Mary C. "Abortion: The Last Resort." *America* 133 (1975), pp. 456-458.

_____. "Does the First Amendment Bar the Hyde Amendment?" *Christianity and Crisis* 39, No. 3 (5 March 1979), pp. 36-38.

_____. "Abortion Politics and Policy: Is There a Middle Ground?" *Christianity and Crisis* 40, No. 2 (18 February 1980), pp. 21-27.

Shaffer, Thomas L. "Abortion, the Law and Human Life." *Valparaiso University Law Review* 2 (1967), pp. 94-106.

Shaffer, Thomas L., *et al.* "Commentary." *Hospital Progress* 54, March 1973, pp. 84-96b.

Shannon, Thomas A. (ed.). *Bioethics: Basic Writings on the Key Ethical Questions that Surround the Major, Modern Biological Possibilities and Problems.* New York: Paulist Press, 1976.

Shannon, Thomas A., and DiGiacomo, James J. *An Introduction to Bioethics.* New York: Paulist Press, 1979.

Shaw, Russell. *Abortion and Public Policy.* Washington, D.C.: National Catholic Welfare Conference Family Life Bureau, 1966.

_____. *Abortion on Trial.* Dayton, Ohio: Pflaum Press, 1968.

Shehan, Cardinal Lawrence. "Pastoral Letter on Abortion." *Catholic Mind* 69, March 1971, pp. 8-11.

Sherain, Howard. "Beyond *Roe* and *Doe*: The Rights of the Father." *Notre Dame Lawyer* 50 (1975), pp. 483-495.

Simons, Francis. "The Catholic Church and the New Morality." *Cross Currents* 16 (1966), pp. 429-445.

Slesinsky, Robert. "Created in the Image of God: Man and Abortion." *Linacre Quarterly* 43 (1976), pp. 36-48.

Sloane, R. Bruce, and Horwitz, Diana Frank. *A General Guide to Abortion.* Chicago: Nelson-Hall, 1973.

Smith, David T. (ed.). *Abortion and the Law.* Cleveland: Case Western Reserve University, 1967.

Springer, Robert H., S.J. "Notes on Moral Theology." *Theological Studies* 28 (1967), pp. 308-335.

_____. "Notes on Moral Theology." *Theological Studies* 31 (1970), pp. 476-511.

_____. "Notes on Moral Theology." *Theological Studies* 32 (1971), pp. 465-488.

_____. "Marriage, the Family, and Sex — A Roman Catholic View." *Perspectives in Biology and Medicine* 19 (1976), pp. 187-197.

Steinfels, Peter. "The Search for an Alternative." *Commonweal* 108 (1981), pp. 660-664.

Stith, Richard. "A Secular Case Against Abortion on Demand." *Commonweal* 95 (1971), pp. 151-154.

_____. "The World as Reality, as Resource, and as Pretense." *American Journal of Jurisprudence* 20 (1975), pp. 141-153.

St. John-Stevas, Norman. *Life, Death and the Law: Law and Christian Morals in England and the United States.* Bloomington, Ind.: Indiana University Press, 1961.

_____. *The Right to Life*. New York: Holt, Rinehart and Winston, 1964.

_____. "Abortion Laws." *Commonweal* 85 (1966), pp. 163-166.

_____. "Abortion: The English Experience." *America* 117 (1967), pp. 707-709.

_____. "Abortion, Catholics, and the Law." *Catholic World* 206 (1968), pp. 149-152.

_____. "The Tragic Results of Abortion in England." *Linacre Quarterly* 39 (1972), pp. 30-38.

St. Thomas More Institute for Legal Research. "Further Comment on People v. Belous." *Catholic Lawyer* 16 (1970), pp. 92-97.

Sullivan, T. "The Right to Life and Self-Consciousness." *America* 139 (1978), pp. 222-224.

Tatalovich, Raymond, and Daynes, Byron W. "The Trauma of Abortion Politics." *Commonweal* 108 (1981), pp. 644-649.

Taussig, Frederick J. *Abortion, Spontaneous and Induced: Medical and Social Aspects*. St. Louis: C.V. Mosby, 1936.

Taylor, T. Raber. "A Lawyer Reviews Plan for Legalized Abortion." *Linacre Quarterly* 26 (1959), pp. 137-140.

Thomas, John L., S.J. "Family, Sex, and Marriage in a Contraceptive Culture." *Theological Studies* 35 (1974), pp. 134-153.

Thomas, Larry L. "Human Potentiality: Its Moral Relevance." *Personalist* 59 (1978), pp. 266-272.

Thomson, Judith Jarvis. "A Defense of Abortion." *Philosophy and Public Affairs* 1 (1971), pp. 47-66.

_____. "Rights and Death." *Philosophy and Public Affairs* 2 (1973), pp. 146-159.

Tietze, Christopher. *Induced Abortion: A World Review, 1981*. New York: Population Council, 1981.

Tinnelly, Joseph T., C.M. "Abortion and Penal Law." *Catholic Lawyer* 5 (1959), pp. 187-191.

Tobin, William J. "Ethical and Moral Considerations Concerning Abortion." *Homiletic and Pastoral Review* 67 (1967), pp. 1023-1031; 68 (1967), pp. 48-58.

Torrey, E. Fuller (ed.). *Ethical Issues in Medicine: The Role of the Physician in Today's Society*. Boston: Little, Brown and Co., 1968.

Trinkaus, Walter R., *et al*. "Abortion Legislation and the Establishment Clause." *Catholic Lawyer* 15 (1969), pp. 108-123.

Trinkaus, Walter R. "The Abortion Decision: Two Years Later: Dred Scott Revisited." *Commonweal* 101 (1975), pp. 384, 388-390.

Vaccari, Michael A. "Personhood Before Implantation." *International Review of Natural Family Planning* 1 (1977), pp. 215-228.

Van der Poel, Cornelius J., C.S.Sp. *The Search for Human Values*. New York: Paulist Press, 1971.

Varga, Andrew C. *The Main Issues in Bioethics*. New York: Paulist Press, 1980.

Vaughan, Richard P., S.J. "Psychotherapeutic Abortion." *America* 113 (1965), pp. 436-438.

_____. "Abortion and the Law." *Homiletic and Pastoral Review* 66 (1966), pp. 643-649.

Vaux, Kenneth (ed.). *Who Shall Live? Medicine—Technology—Ethics*. Philadelphia: Fortress Press, 1970.

Vaux, Kenneth. "The Giving and Taking of Life: New Power at Life's Thresholds." *Christian Century* 92 (1975), pp. 384-387.

Veatch, Robert M. (ed.). *Population Policy and Ethics: The American Experience*. New York: Irvington, 1977.

Verkamp, Bernard J. "Personhood, Abortion and the Law." *America* 146 (1982), pp. 46-48.

Wade, Francis C., S.J. "Potentiality in the Abortion Discussion." *Review of Metaphysics* 29 (1975), pp. 239-255.

Walbert, David F., and Butler, J. Douglas (eds.). *Abortion, Society, and the Law.* Cleveland: Press of Case Western Reserve University, 1973.

Walker, Vern R. "Presumptive Personhood." *Linacre Quarterly* 45 (1978), pp. 179-186.

Wasserstrom, Richard A. (ed.). *Today's Moral Problems.* 2nd edition. New York: Macmillan, 1979.

Wassmer, Thomas A., S.J. *Christian Ethics for Today.* Milwaukee: Bruce, 1969.

_____. "Contemporary Attitudes of the Roman Catholic Church toward Abortion." *Journal of Religion and Health* 7 (1968), pp. 311-323.

Weber, Paul J. "Perverse Observations on Abortion." *Catholic World* 212 (1970), pp. 74-77.

Welch, Jerome A. *Catholicism Today.* Fort Wayne, Ind.: Jewel Publications, 1977.

Wertheimer, Roger. "Understanding the Abortion Argument." *Philosophy and Public Affairs* 1 (1971), pp. 67-95.

Westley, R. "Abortion Debate: Finding a True Pro-Life Stance." *America* 134 (1976), pp. 489-492.

Whitehead, K.D. *Respectable Killing: The New Abortion Imperative.* New Rochelle, N.Y.: Catholics United for the Faith, 1972.

_____. *Agenda for the "Sexual Revolution."* Chicago: Franciscan Herald Press, 1981.

Williams, Bruce A., O.P. "The March of Dimes and Abortion." *Homiletic and Pastoral Review* 74, October 1973, pp. 48-58.

Williams, George Huntston. "Religious Residues and Presuppositions in the American Debate on Abortion." *Theological Studies* 31 (1970), pp. 10-75.

Williams, Glanville. *The Sanctity of Life and the Criminal Law.* New York: Alfred A. Knopf, 1957.

Willke, Dr. and Mrs. J.C. *Handbook on Abortion.* Revised ed. Cincinnati: Hiltz Publishing Co., 1973.

Witherspoon, Joseph Parker. "Impact of the Abortion Decisions upon the Father's Role." *Jurist* 35 (1975), pp. 32-65.

_____. "Representative Government, the Federal Judicial and Administrative Bureaucracy, and the Right to Life." *Texas Tech Law Review* 6 (1975), pp. 363-384.

_____. "The New Pro-Life Legislation: Patterns and Recommendations." *St. Mary's Law Journal* 7 (1976), pp. 637-697.

Wogaman, Philip J. (ed.). *The Population Crisis and Moral Responsibility.* Washington, D.C.: The Population Institute and Public Affairs Press, 1973.

Zahn, Gordon C. "A Religious Pacifist Looks at Abortion." *Commonweal* 94 (1971), pp. 279-282.

EDITORIALS:

"Abortion and the Law." *America* 104 (1961), p. 811.

"Note: The Current Trend to Liberalize Abortion Laws—An Analysis and Criticism." *Catholic Lawyer* 10 (1964), pp. 161-173.

"Morality and Policy." *America* 112 (1965), pp. 280, 351, 450, 520-521, 747.

"Abortion Law Reform." *America* 112 (1965), p. 703.

"Growing Consensus on Abortion." *America* 114 (1966), p. 219.

"Private Morality and Public Policy." *America* 114 (1966), p. 722.

"Abortion Laws." *Commonweal* 83 (1966), p. 685.

"Arguing Abortions." *Commonweal* 85 (1966), p. 312.

"Abortion and Mental Health." *America* 116 (1967), p. 239.

"On Imposing Catholic Views on Others." *America* 116 (1967), pp. 273-274.

"The Abortion Question: Life and Law in a Pluralistic Society." *America* 117 (1967), p. 706.

"Abortion and Pluralism." *Commonweal* 85 (1967), pp. 582-583.

"Abortion and Dialogue." *Commonweal* 85 (1967), pp. 667-668.

"Public Policy and Abortion Laws." *America* 120 (1969), pp. 239-240.

"Open Letter to American Doctors." *America* 122 (1970), pp. 490-491.

"The Abortion Debate." *Commonweal* 92 (1970), pp. 131-132.

"Abortion: The Catholic Presentation." *America* 124 (1971), p. 62.

"Abortion and the Church." *America* 128 (1973), pp. 110-111.

"Abortion and U.S. Protestants." *America* 128 (1973), pp. 156-157.

"Abortion: Deterrence, Facilitation, Resistance." *America* 128 (1973), pp. 506-507.

"The Abortion Decision." *Commonweal* 97 (1973), pp. 435-436.

"Abortion Decision: A Year Later." *America* 130 (1974), p. 22.

"The Bishops' Plan for Pro-Life Activities." *America* 133 (1975), pp. 454-455.

"Political Responsibility and Abortion." *America* 134 (1976), p. 173.

"Politics and Abortion." *Commonweal* 103 (1976), pp. 131-132.

"Another Double Standard: Call to Concern Campaign." *America* 137 (1977), p. 274.

"The New Abortion Debate." *Commonweal* 104 (1977), pp. 451-452.

"Do Catholics Have Constitutional Rights? Hyde Amendment Challenge." *Commonweal* 105 (1978), pp. 771-773.

"Abortion, Religion and Political Life." *Commonweal* 106 (1979), pp. 35-38.

"Abortion and the Constitution." *America* 143 (1980), p. 24.

"Church and State in Boston." *America* 143 (1980), p. 180.

"Edges of Life." *Commonweal* 107 (1980), p. 421.

"Notifying the Parents." *America* 144 (1981), pp. 289-290.

"Abortions for the Poor." *America* 145 (1981), p. 134.

"Federal Abortion." *America* 145 (1981), pp. 232-233.

"The Bishops and the Abortion Amendment." *America* 145 (1981), pp. 312-313.

"Triage in the Womb." *Commonweal* 108 (1981), p. 421.

"Parental Rights." *America* 146 (1982), pp. 143-144.